BROKEN ANGELS™

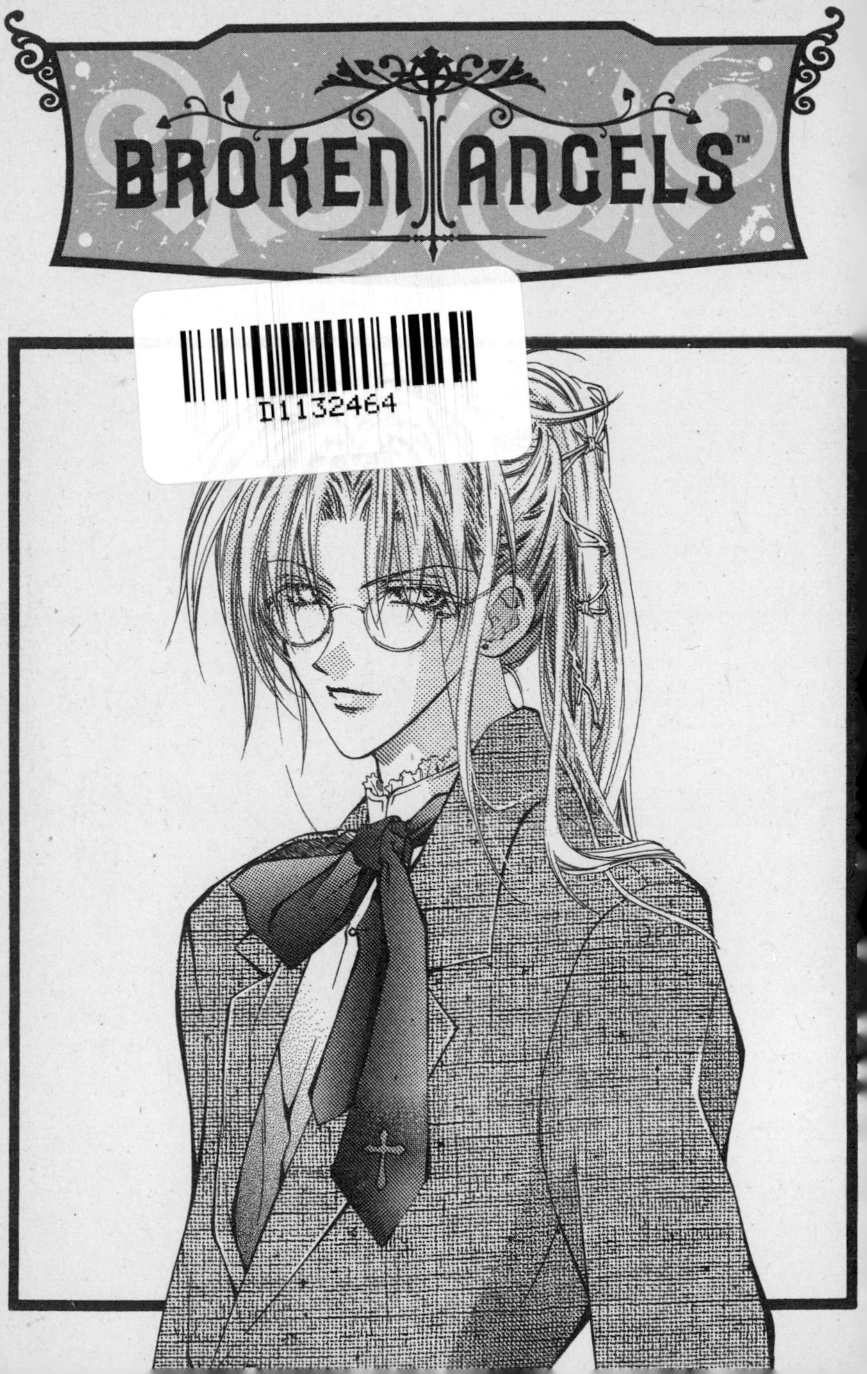

Broken Angels Vol. 2
Created by Setsuri Tsuzuki

Translation - Nayoung Aimee Kwon
English Adaptation - Jessica Cathryn Feinberg
Copy Editor - Hope Donovan
Retouch and Lettering - Bowen Park
Production Artist - Bowen Park
Cover Layout - James Lee

Editor - Tim Beedle
Digital Imaging Manager - Chris Buford
Managing Editor - Lindsey Johnston
VP of Production - Ron Klamert
Editor-in-Chief - Rob Tokar
Publisher - Mike Kiley
President and C.O.O. - John Parker
C.E.O. and C.C.O. - Stuart Levy

A  Manga

TOKYOPOP Inc.
5900 Wilshire Blvd. Suite 2000
Los Angeles, CA 90036

E-mail: info@TOKYOPOP.com
Come visit us online at www.TOKYOPOP.com

ISBN: 1-59816-160-1

First TOKYOPOP printing: June 2006
10 9 8 7 6 5 4 3 2 1
Printed in the USA

BROKEN ANGELS™

Volume 2

Created by
Setsuri Tsuzuki

HAMBURG // LONDON // LOS ANGELES // TOKYO

Meet the Cast

Things of great beauty are often fleeting and fragile.

FUJIWARA SUNAO
A HIGH SCHOOL FRESHMAN
CAPABLE OF CONTROLLING WATER.
HER CAREFREE ATTITUDE AND
INSISTENCE ON DRESSING LIKE A BOY
MAKE HER A DIFFICULT STUDENT, YET
SHE HAS A SOFT SPOT FOR THOSE
IN NEED.

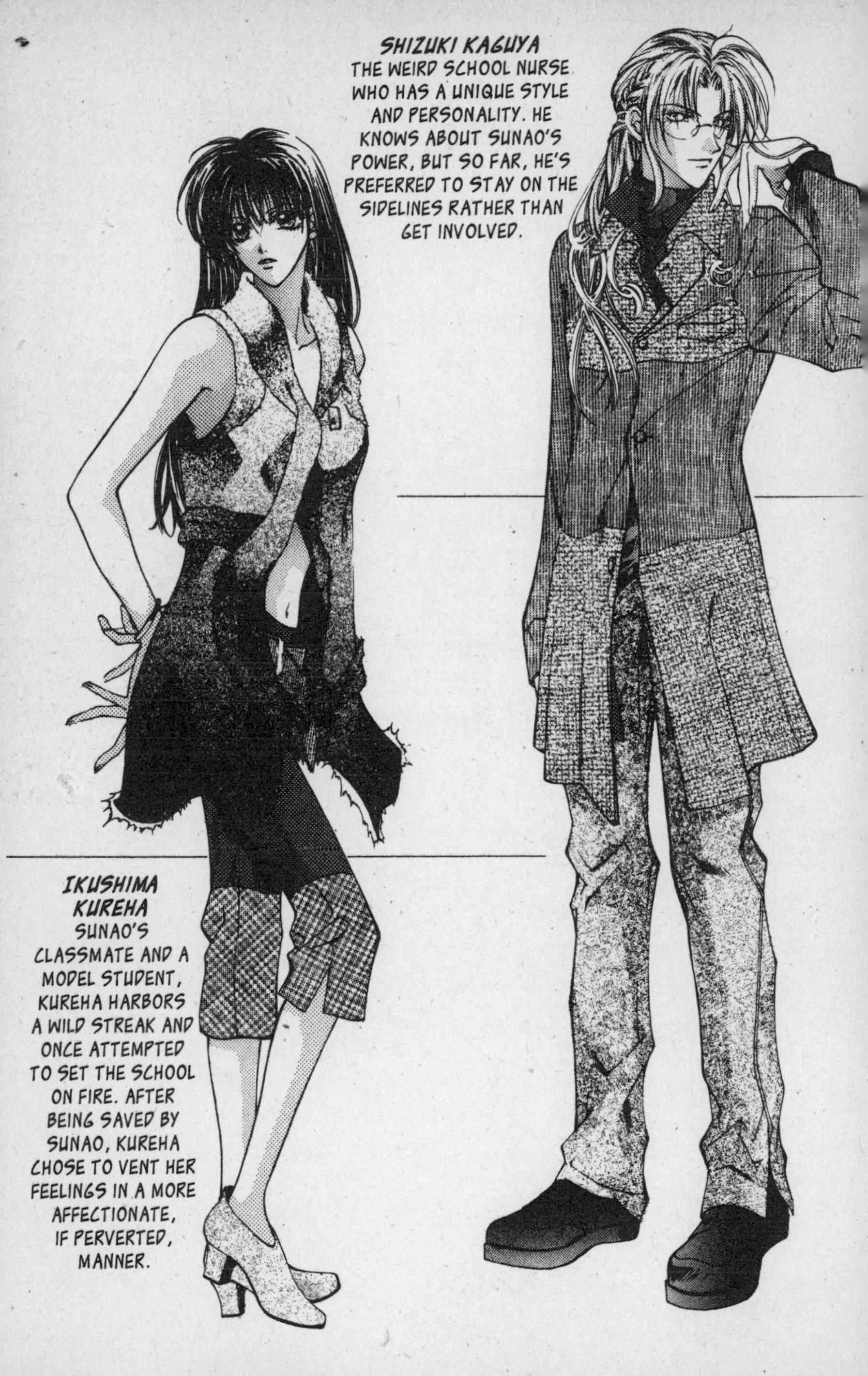
SHIZUKI KAGUYA
THE WEIRD SCHOOL NURSE WHO HAS A UNIQUE STYLE AND PERSONALITY. HE KNOWS ABOUT SUNAO'S POWER, BUT SO FAR, HE'S PREFERRED TO STAY ON THE SIDELINES RATHER THAN GET INVOLVED.
IKUSHIMA KUREHA
SUNAO'S CLASSMATE AND A MODEL STUDENT, KUREHA HARBORS A WILD STREAK AND ONCE ATTEMPTED TO SET THE SCHOOL ON FIRE. AFTER BEING SAVED BY SUNAO, KUREHA CHOSE TO VENT HER FEELINGS IN A MORE AFFECTIONATE, IF PERVERTED, MANNER.

Contents

Story So Far

Fujiwara Sunao isn't like ordinary teenagers. For starters, she's quiet and tomboyish, preferring to disguise herself as a boy rather than deal with the unwarranted attention of male high schoolers. She also possesses a remarkable power over water. It obeys her every whim with no regard to physics or natural law. However, perhaps Sunao's single most defining trait is her compassion. Despite her inherent shyness, she can't help lending a hand to people in need. Of course, she can't do this on her own.

Ikushima Kureha is the school's top student and class president, but all is not what it seems to be with this wild child. After Sunao showed her the importance of forging her own destiny, she chose to saddle her destiny alongside Sunao's, and now acts as Sunao's ally and de facto girlfriend. Shizuki Kaguya is the school's nurse. Despite his age and unusual personality, he's taken an interest in Sunao's affairs. Hokage Minai is Sunao's mysterious guardian. While he's not related to her, she lives with him and he treats her like a daughter or younger sibling. These three unique individuals have become Sunao's "family." Call them weirdos if you'd like, but it's a strange world, and if you're going to catch a freak, perhaps it's best if you're a bit of one yourself. When it comes to unexplained phenomena, if Sunao and her crew are on the case, it's as good as cracked.

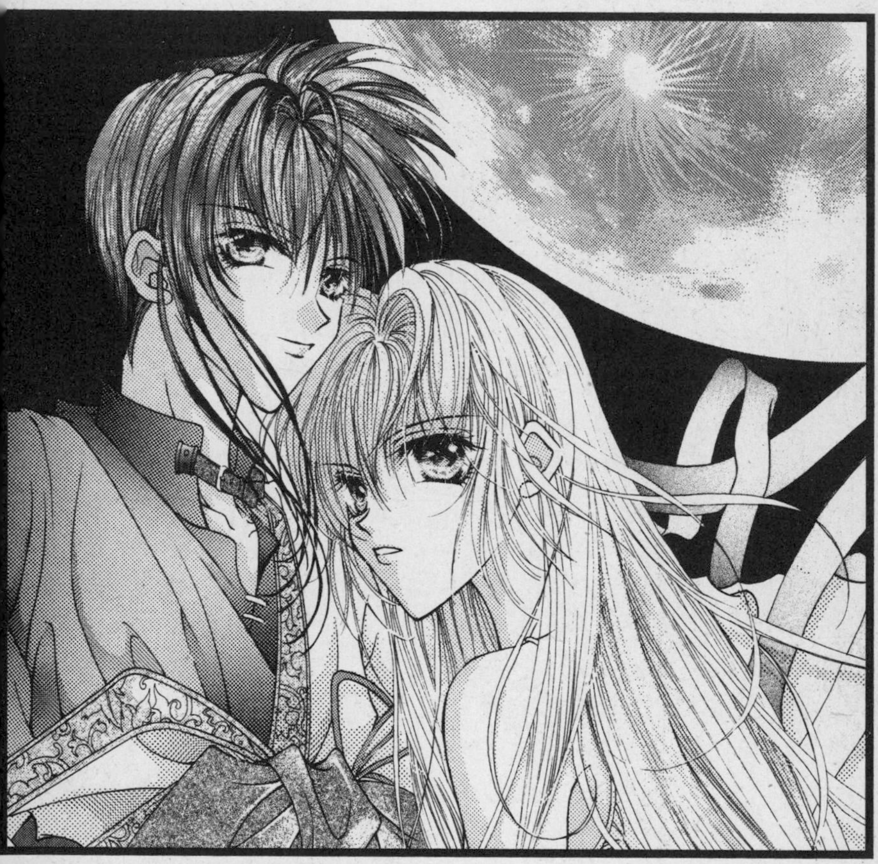

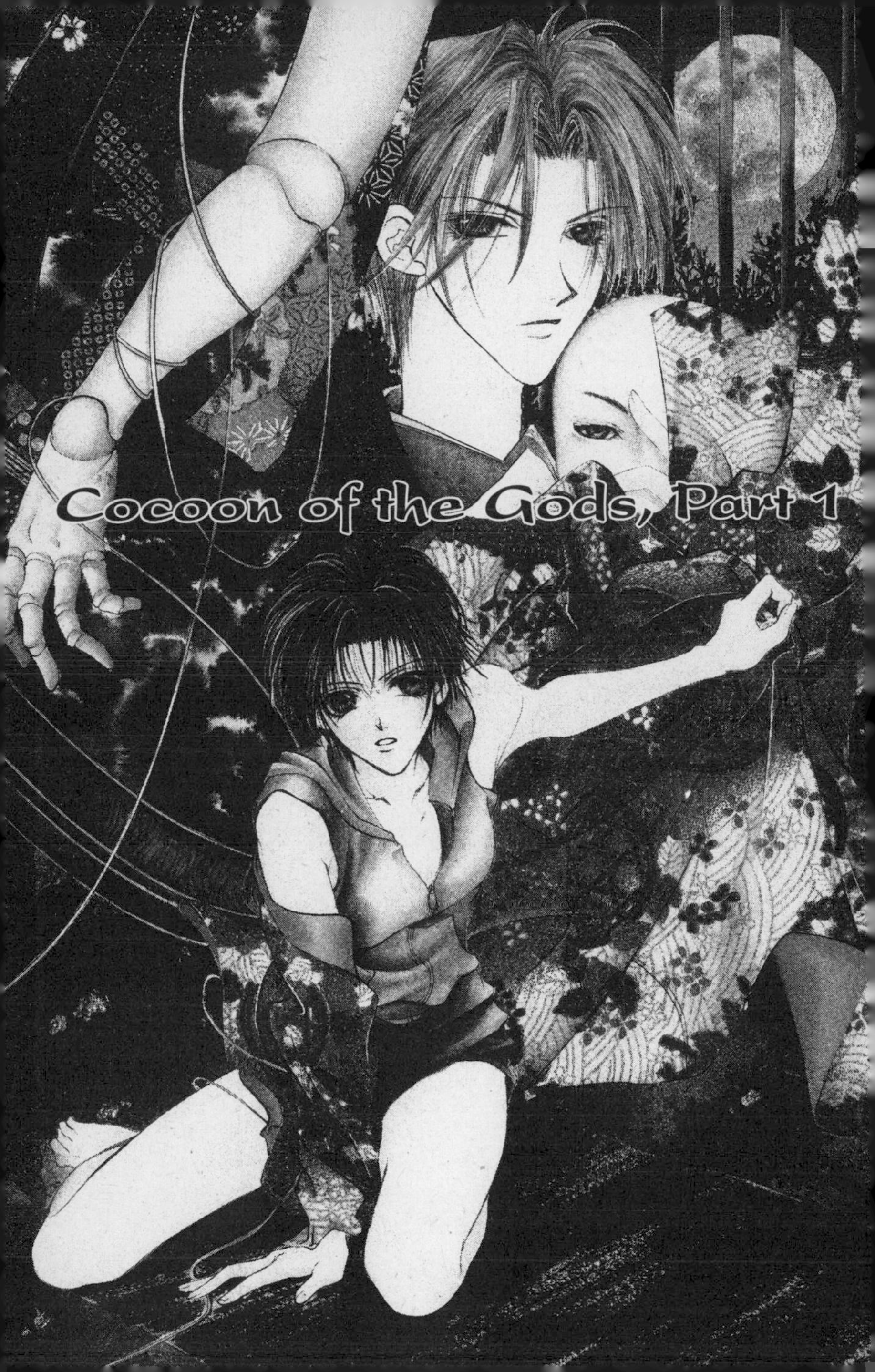
Cocoon of the Gods, Part 1

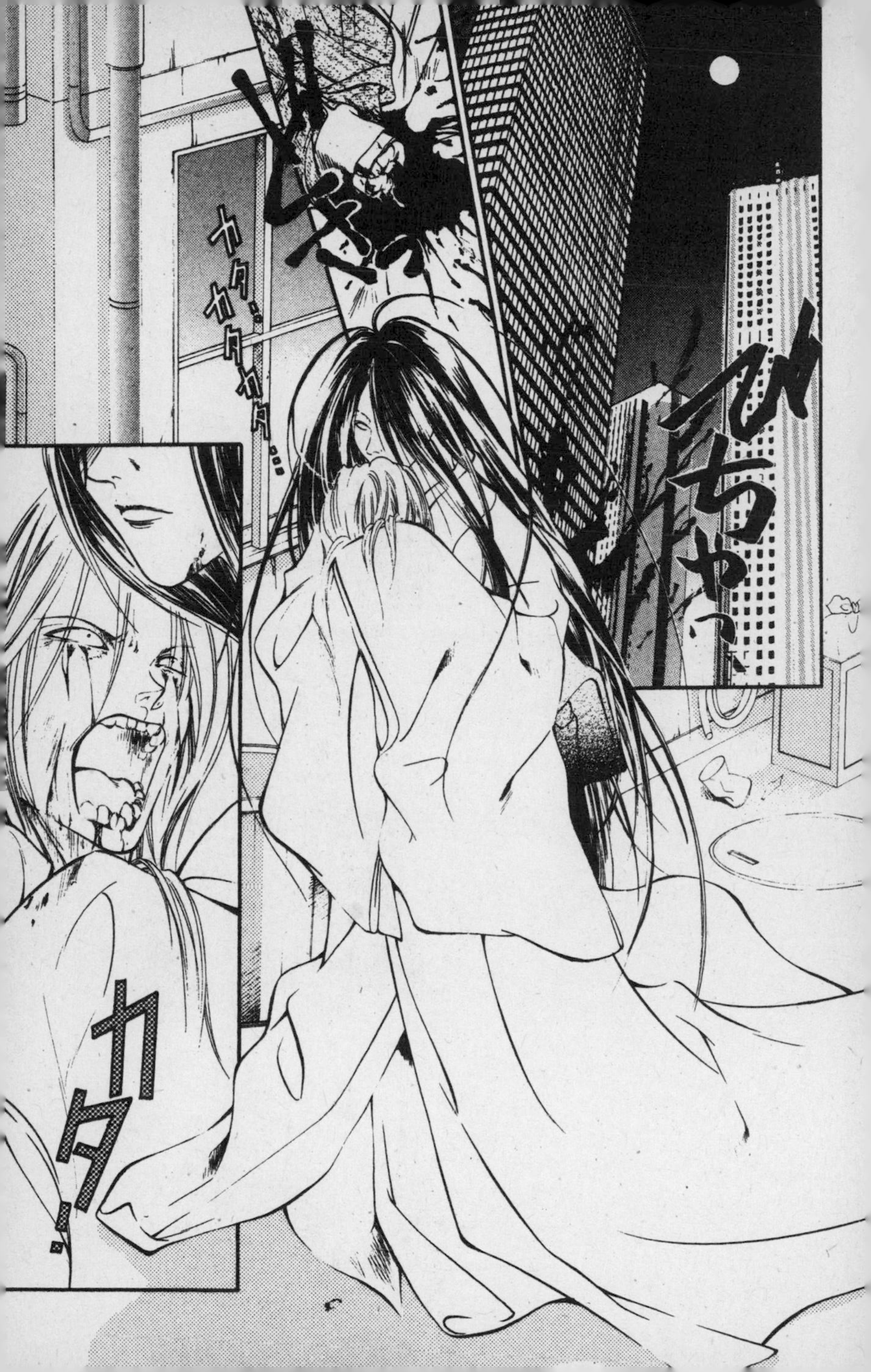
ぐさっ
びちゃっ
カタ…カタカタカタ…
カタ…

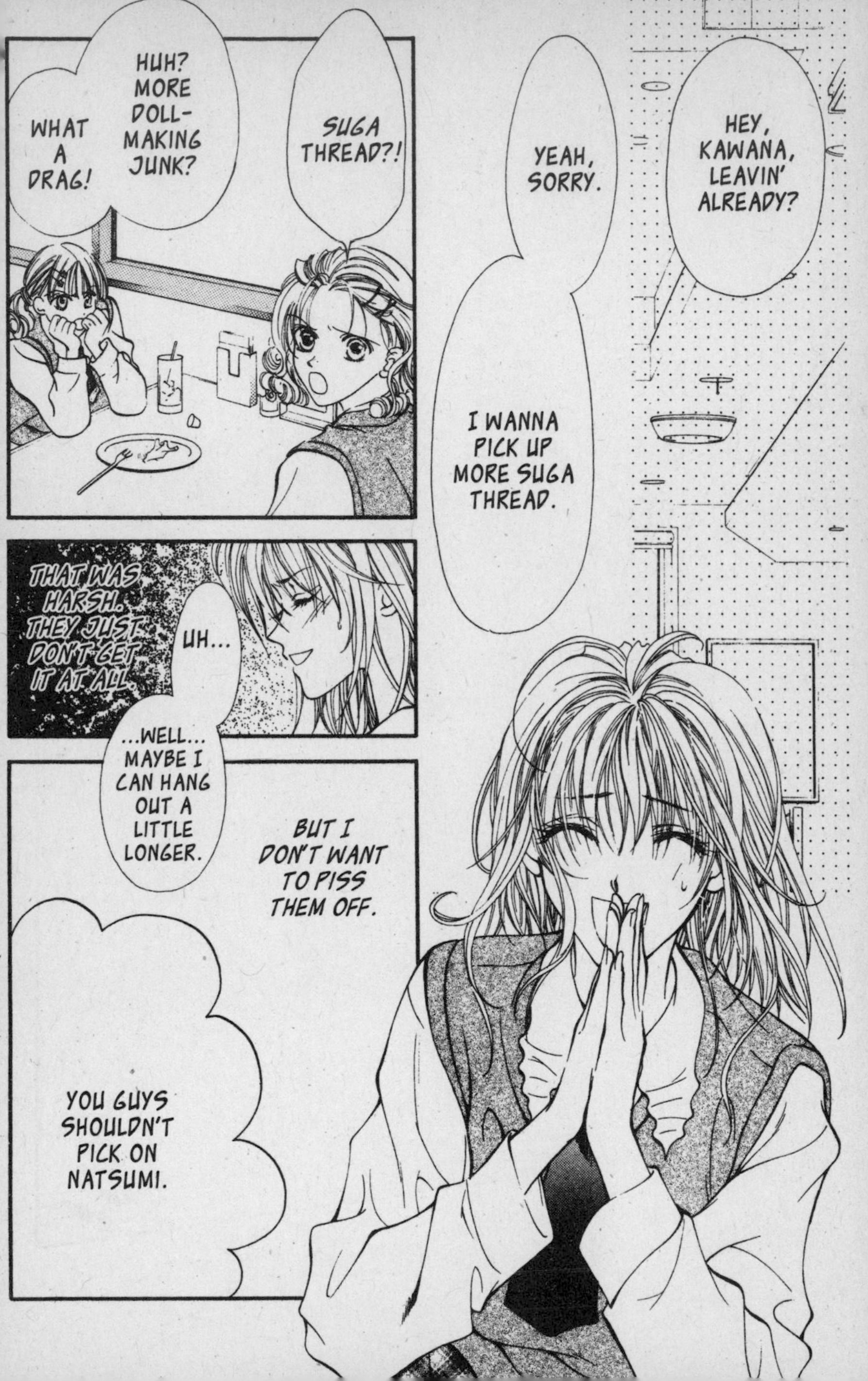
HEY, KAWANA, LEAVIN' ALREADY?
YEAH, SORRY.
I WANNA PICK UP MORE SUGA THREAD.
SUGA THREAD?!
HUH? MORE DOLL-MAKING JUNK?
WHAT A DRAG!
UH...
THAT WAS HARSH. THEY JUST DON'T GET IT AT ALL.
...WELL... MAYBE I CAN HANG OUT A LITTLE LONGER.
BUT I DON'T WANT TO PISS THEM OFF.
YOU GUYS SHOULDN'T PICK ON NATSUMI.

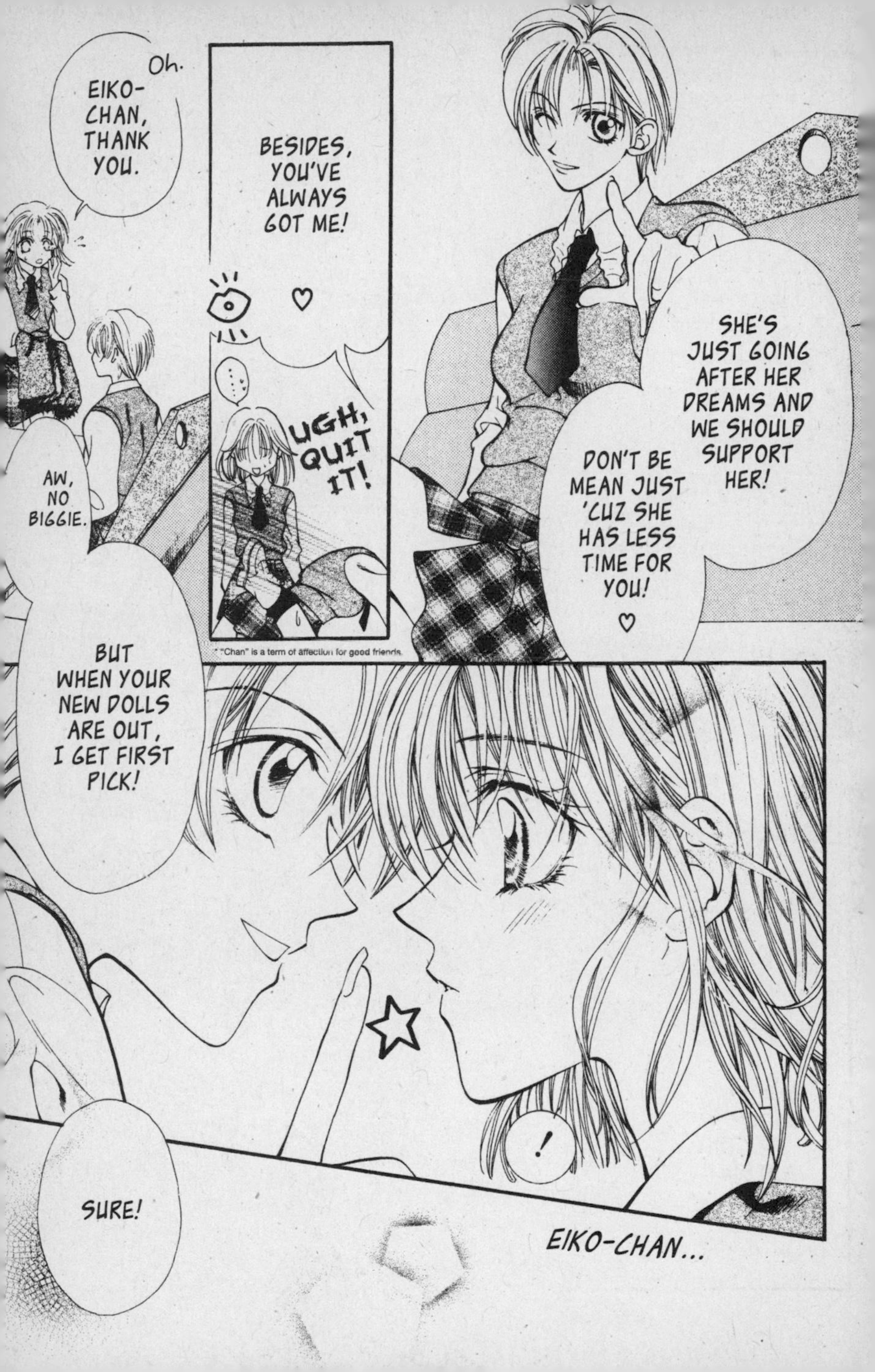
SHE'S JUST GOING AFTER HER DREAMS AND WE SHOULD SUPPORT HER!
DON'T BE MEAN JUST 'CUZ SHE HAS LESS TIME FOR YOU! ♡
BESIDES, YOU'VE ALWAYS GOT ME! ♡
UGH, QUIT IT!
...
Oh.
EIKO-CHAN, THANK YOU.
AW, NO BIGGIE.
BUT WHEN YOUR NEW DOLLS ARE OUT, I GET FIRST PICK!
!
EIKO-CHAN...
SURE!
* "Chan" is a term of affection for good friends.

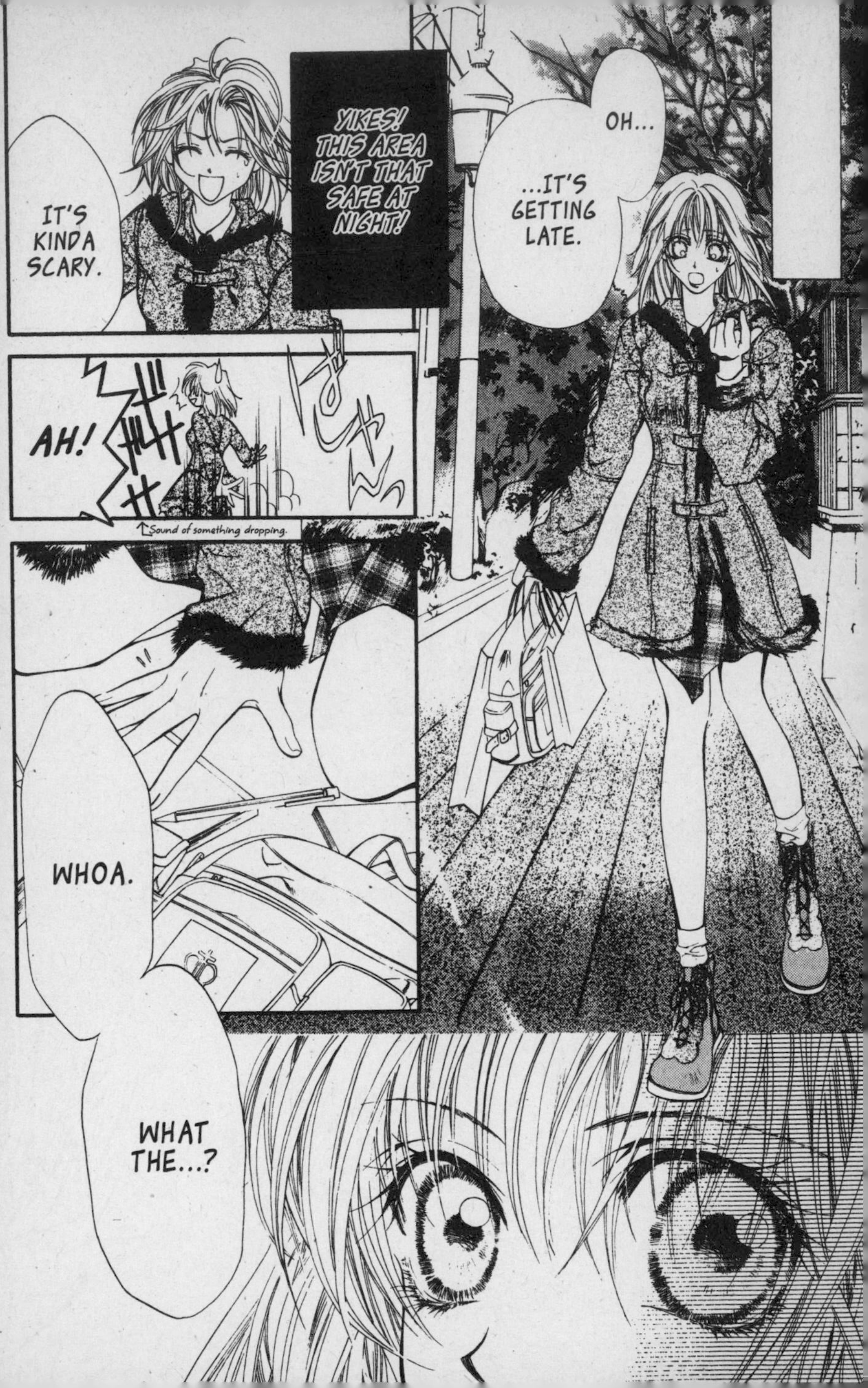
OH...
...IT'S GETTING LATE.
YIKES! THIS AREA ISN'T THAT SAFE AT NIGHT!
IT'S KINDA SCARY.
AH!
Sound of something dropping.
WHOA.
WHAT THE...?

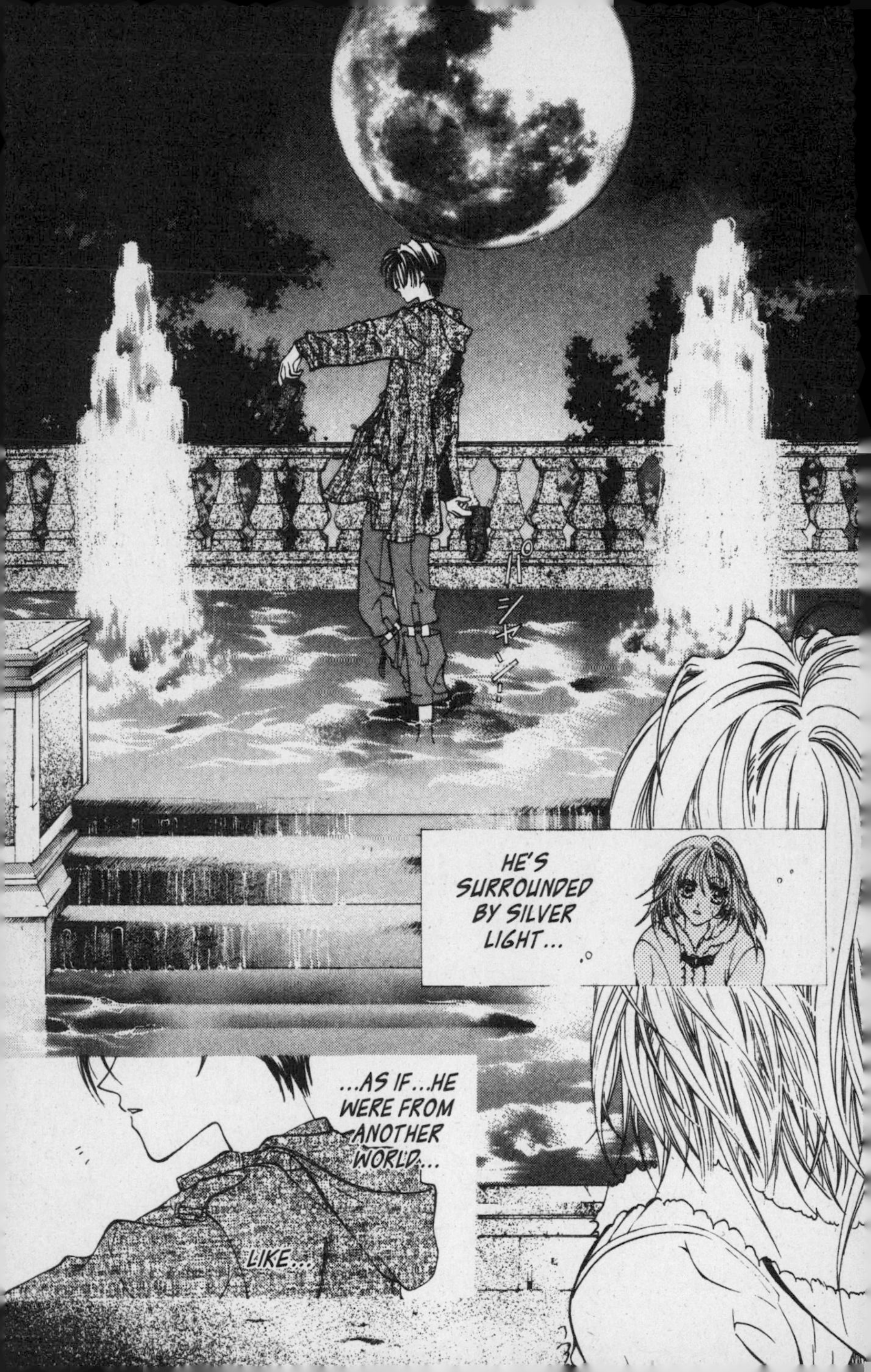
パシャーン
HE'S SURROUNDED BY SILVER LIGHT...
...AS IF...HE WERE FROM ANOTHER WORLD...
LIKE...

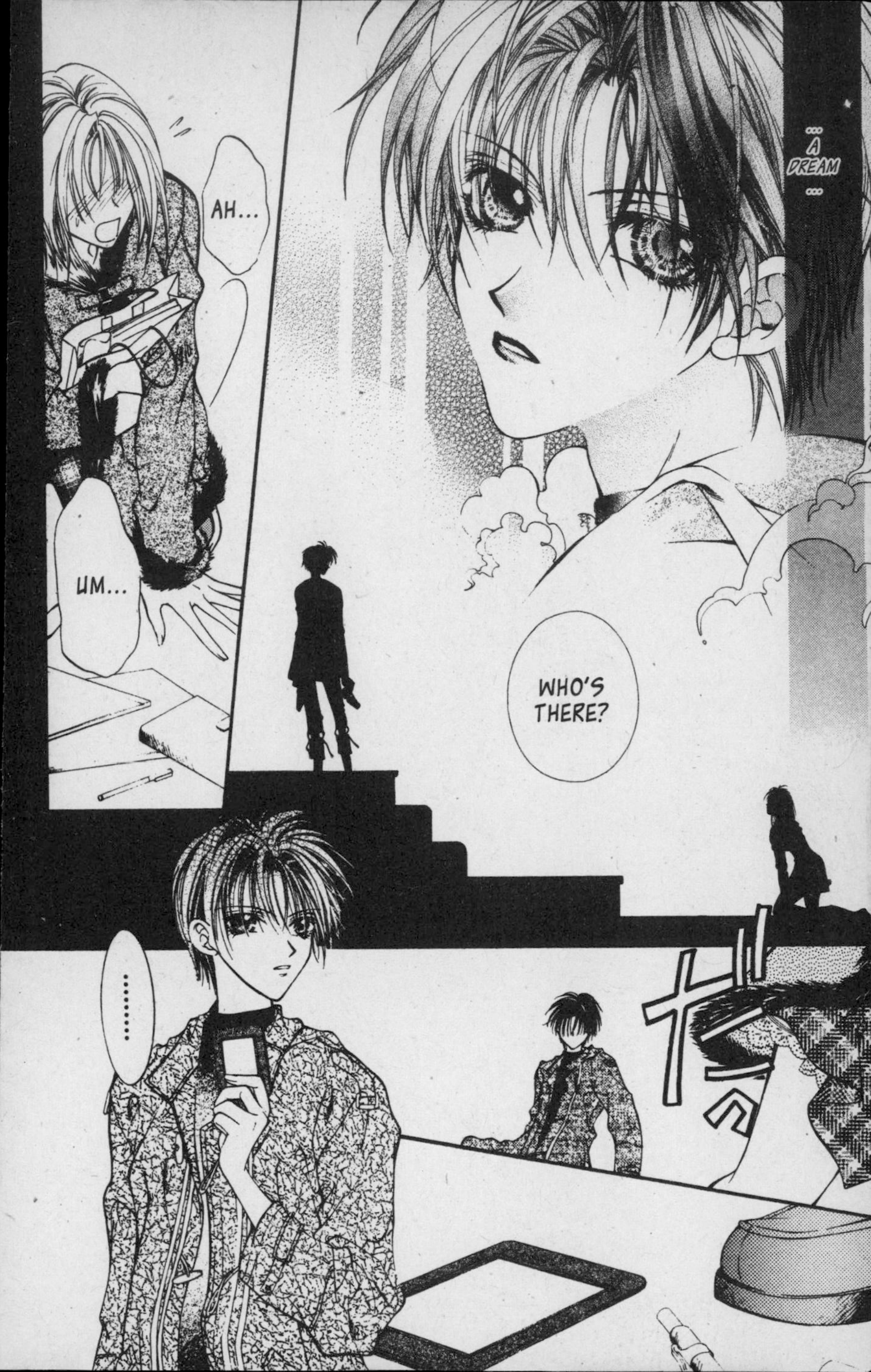
...A DREAM...
WHO'S THERE?
AH...
UM...
....

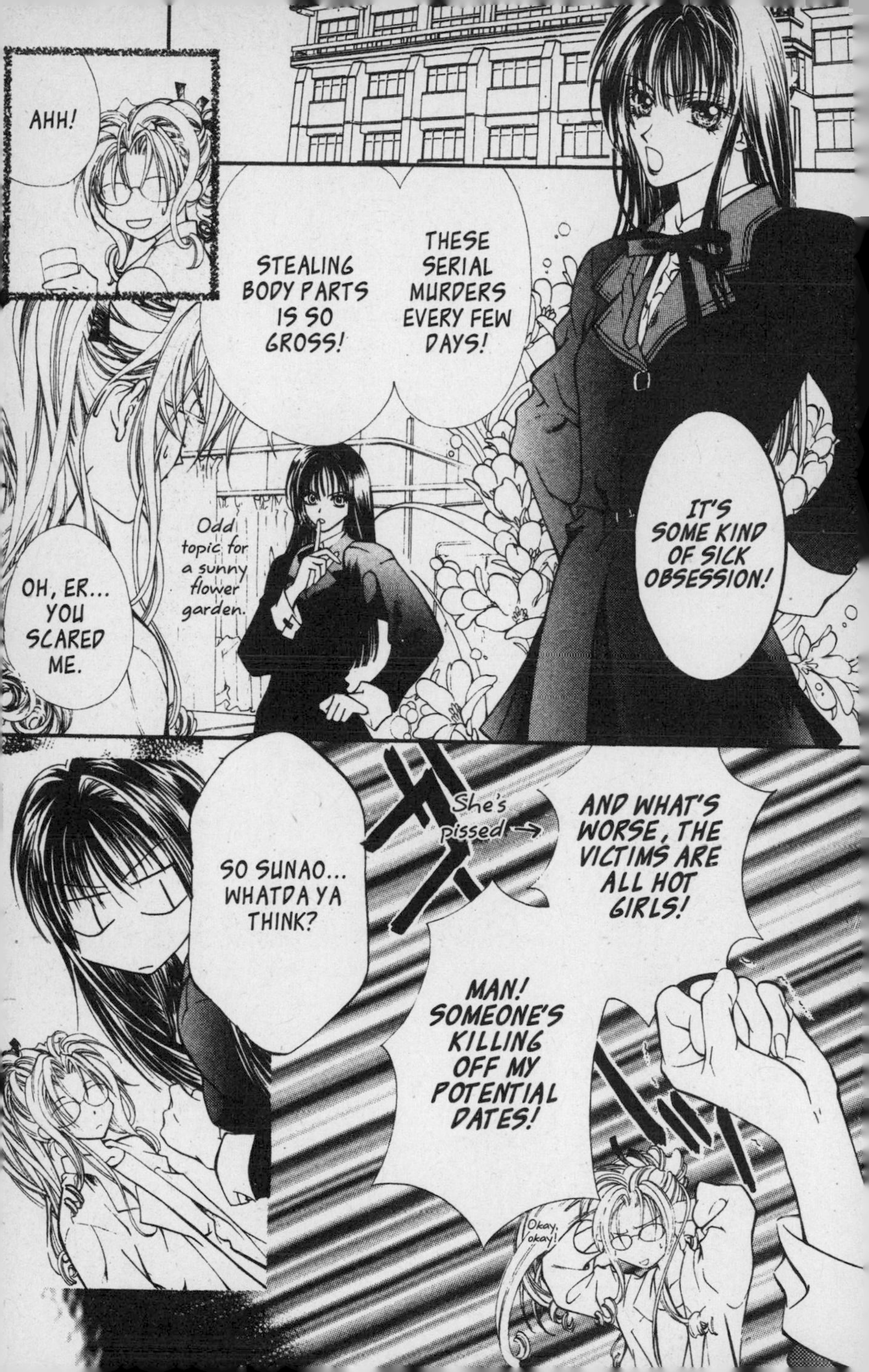
THESE SERIAL MURDERS EVERY FEW DAYS!
STEALING BODY PARTS IS SO GROSS!
IT'S SOME KIND OF SICK OBSESSION!
Odd topic for a sunny flower garden.
AHH!
OH, ER... YOU SCARED ME.
AND WHAT'S WORSE, THE VICTIMS ARE ALL HOT GIRLS!
She's pissed →
MAN! SOMEONE'S KILLING OFF MY POTENTIAL DATES!
Okay, okay!
SO SUNAO... WHATDA YA THINK?

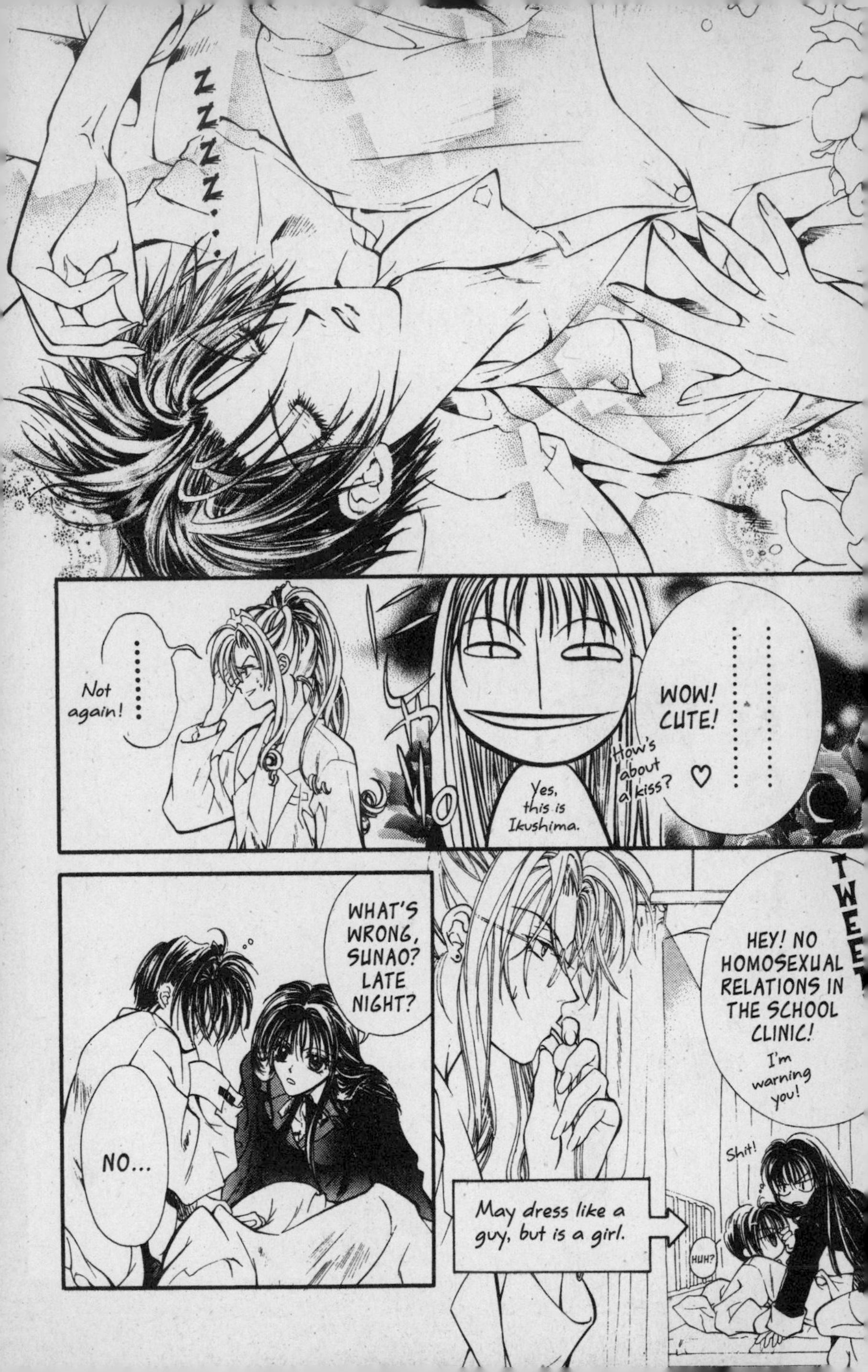

ZZZZ...
WOW! CUTE! ......
How's about a kiss? ♥
Yes, this is Ikushima.
Not again! ......
TWEET
HEY! NO HOMOSEXUAL RELATIONS IN THE SCHOOL CLINIC!
I'm warning you!
Shit!
HUH?
May dress like a guy, but is a girl.
WHAT'S WRONG, SUNAO? LATE NIGHT?
NO...

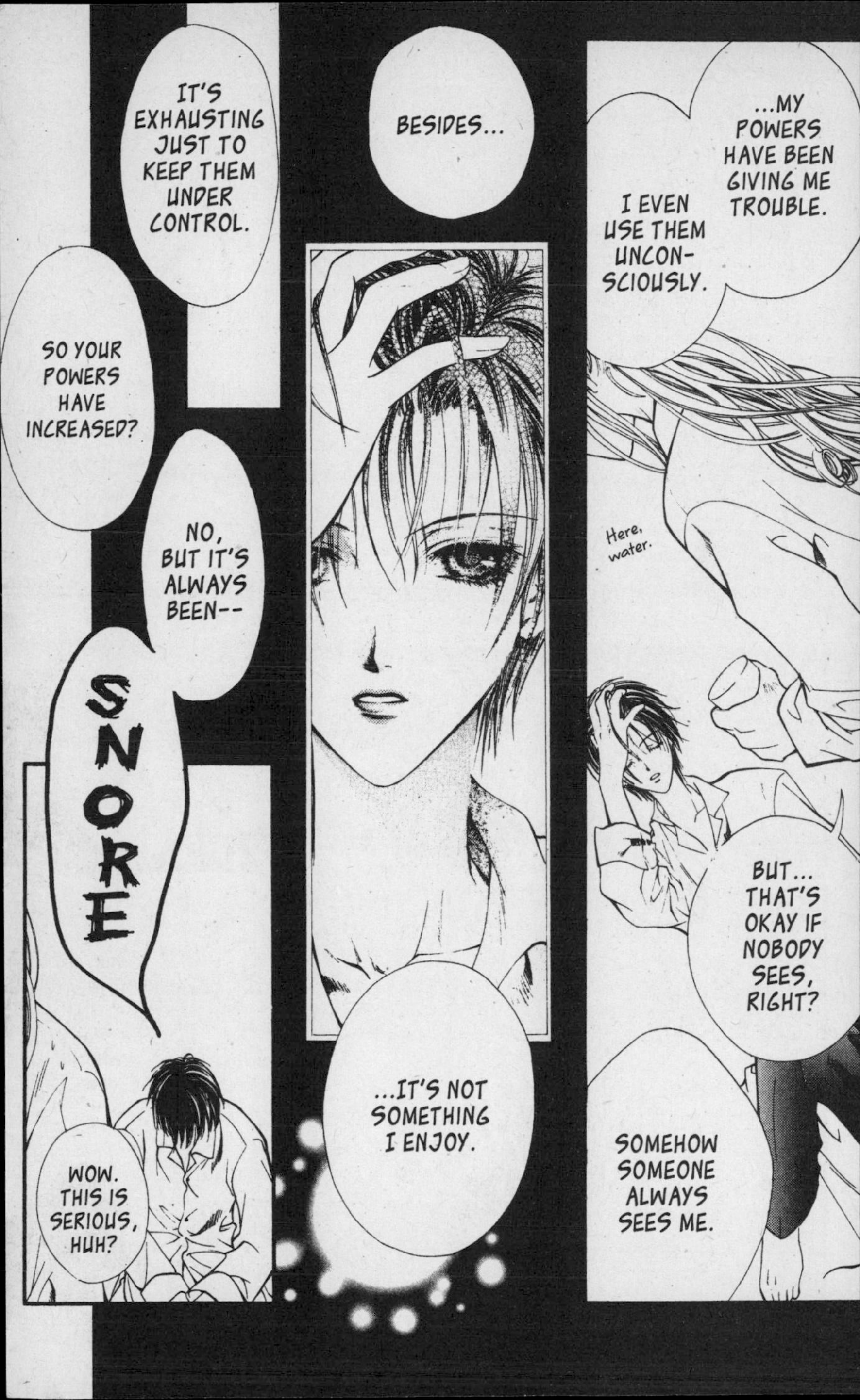
...MY POWERS HAVE BEEN GIVING ME TROUBLE.
I EVEN USE THEM UNCON-SCIOUSLY.
Here, water.
BUT... THAT'S OKAY IF NOBODY SEES, RIGHT?
SOMEHOW SOMEONE ALWAYS SEES ME.
BESIDES...
...IT'S NOT SOMETHING I ENJOY.
IT'S EXHAUSTING JUST TO KEEP THEM UNDER CONTROL.
SO YOUR POWERS HAVE INCREASED?
NO, BUT IT'S ALWAYS BEEN--
SNORE
WOW. THIS IS SERIOUS, HUH?

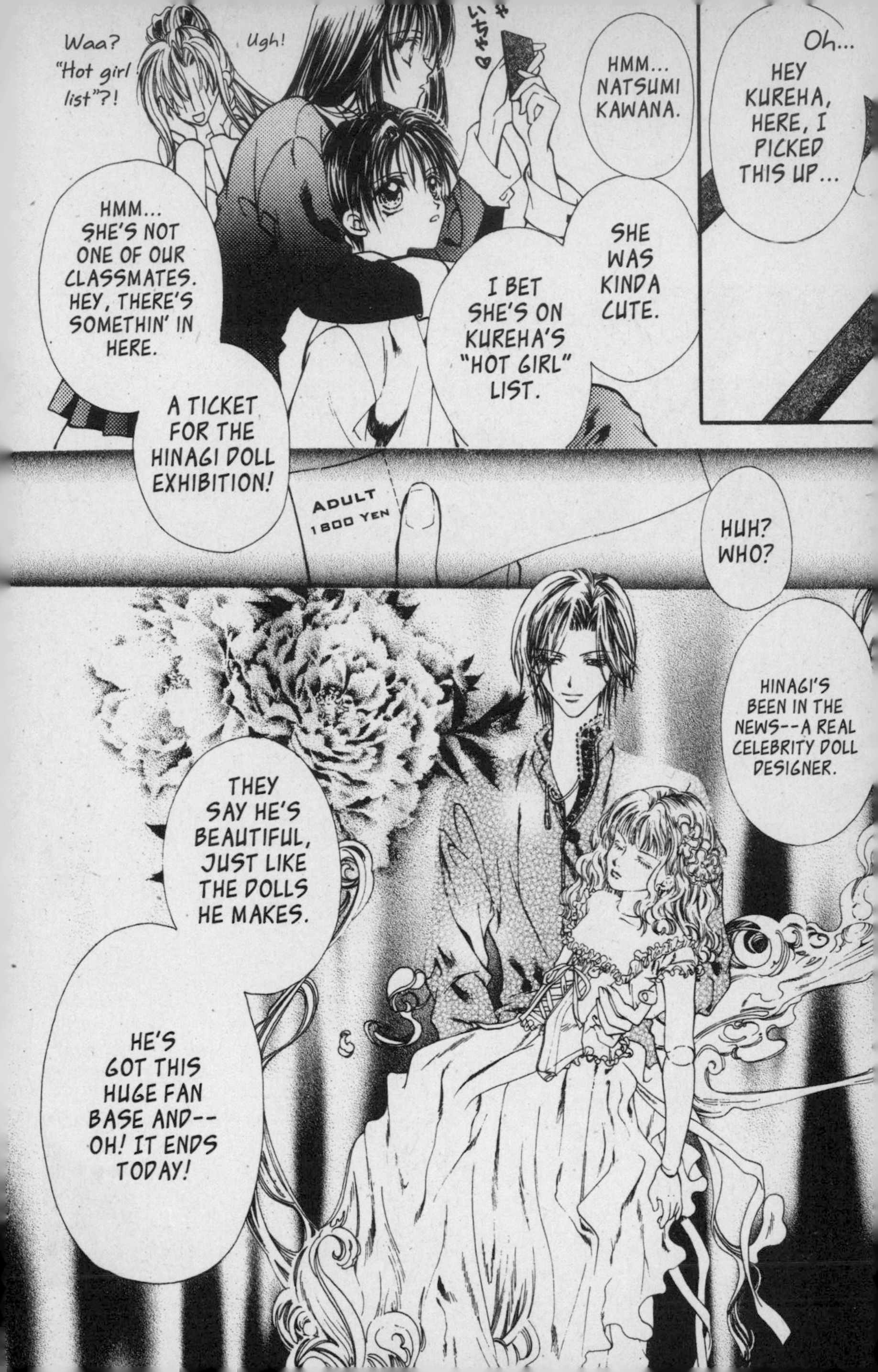
Oh... HEY KUREHA, HERE, I PICKED THIS UP...
HMM... NATSUMI KAWANA.
SHE WAS KINDA CUTE.
I BET SHE'S ON KUREHA'S "HOT GIRL" LIST.
Ugh!
Waa? "Hot girl list"?!
HMM... SHE'S NOT ONE OF OUR CLASSMATES. HEY, THERE'S SOMETHIN' IN HERE.
A TICKET FOR THE HINAGI DOLL EXHIBITION!
HUH? WHO?
ADULT 1800 YEN
HINAGI'S BEEN IN THE NEWS--A REAL CELEBRITY DOLL DESIGNER.
THEY SAY HE'S BEAUTIFUL, JUST LIKE THE DOLLS HE MAKES.
HE'S GOT THIS HUGE FAN BASE AND--OH! IT ENDS TODAY!

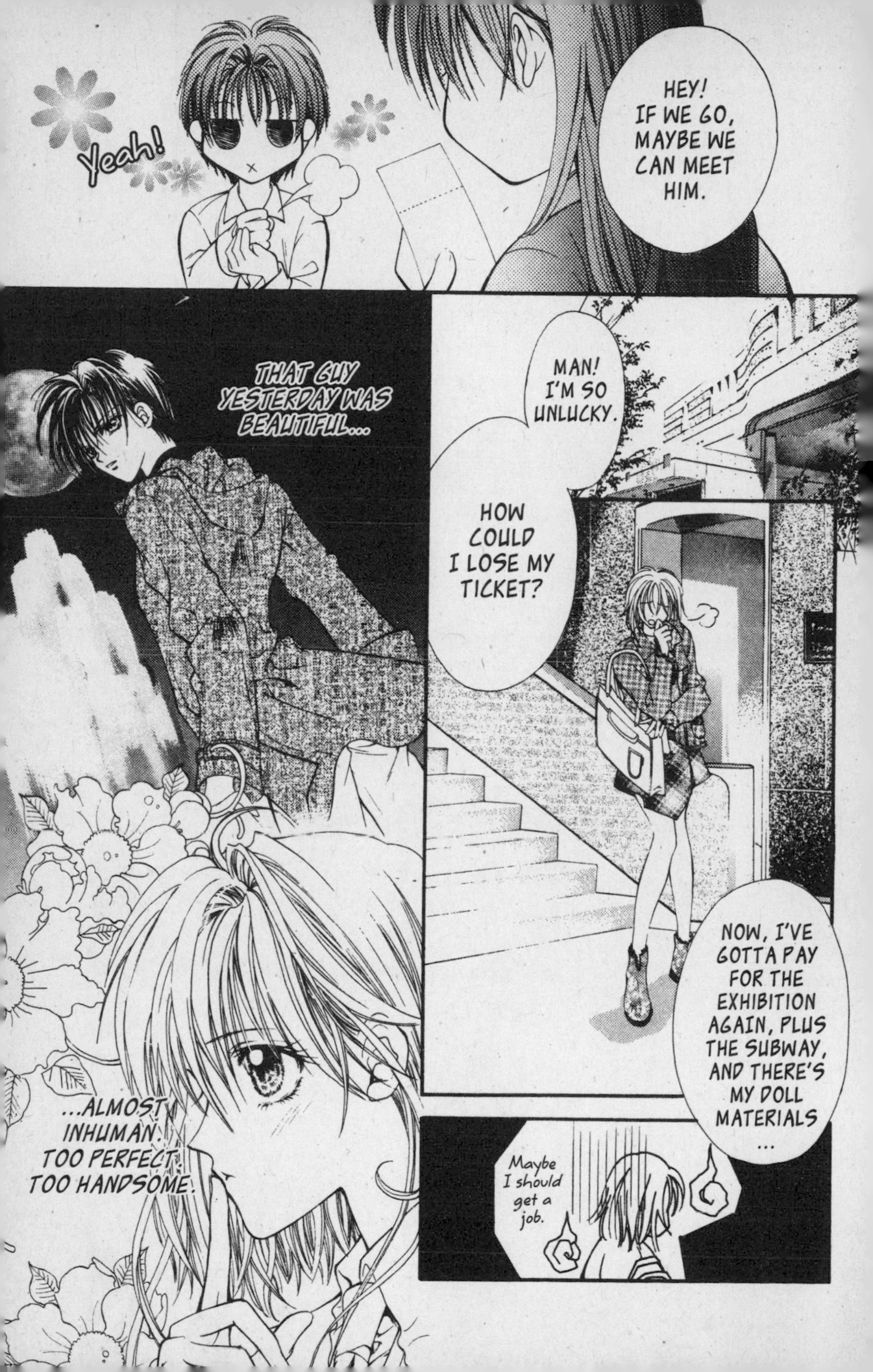
HEY! IF WE GO, MAYBE WE CAN MEET HIM.
Yeah!
MAN! I'M SO UNLUCKY.
HOW COULD I LOSE MY TICKET?
NOW, I'VE GOTTA PAY FOR THE EXHIBITION AGAIN, PLUS THE SUBWAY, AND THERE'S MY DOLL MATERIALS ...
Maybe I should get a job.
THAT GUY YESTERDAY WAS BEAUTIFUL...
...ALMOST INHUMAN. TOO PERFECT. TOO HANDSOME.

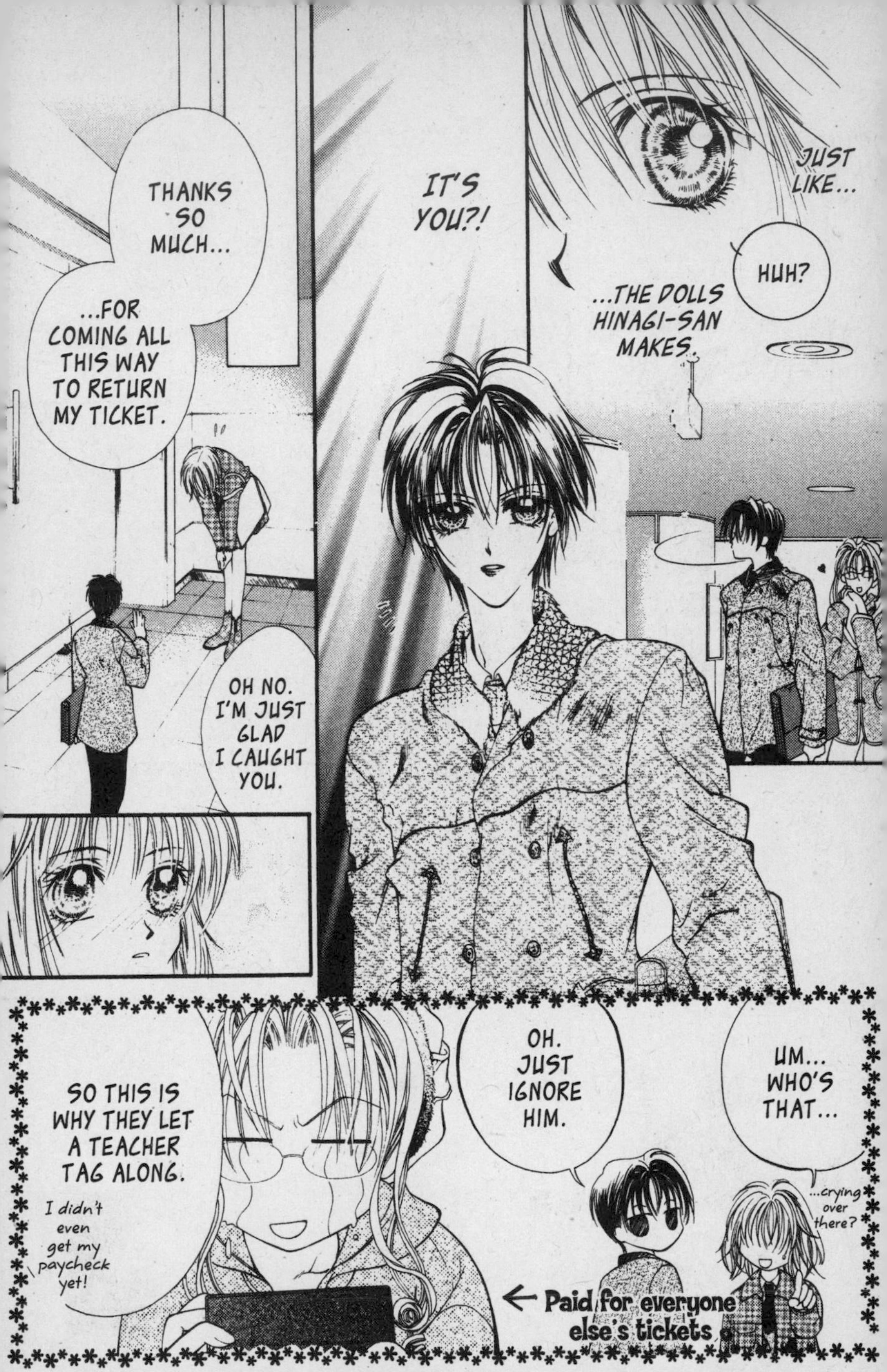
JUST LIKE...
HUH?
...THE DOLLS HINAGI-SAN MAKES.
IT'S YOU?!
THANKS SO MUCH...
...FOR COMING ALL THIS WAY TO RETURN MY TICKET.
OH NO. I'M JUST GLAD I CAUGHT YOU.
UM... WHO'S THAT...
...crying over there?
OH. JUST IGNORE HIM.
← Paid for everyone else's tickets
SO THIS IS WHY THEY LET A TEACHER TAG ALONG.
I didn't even get my paycheck yet!

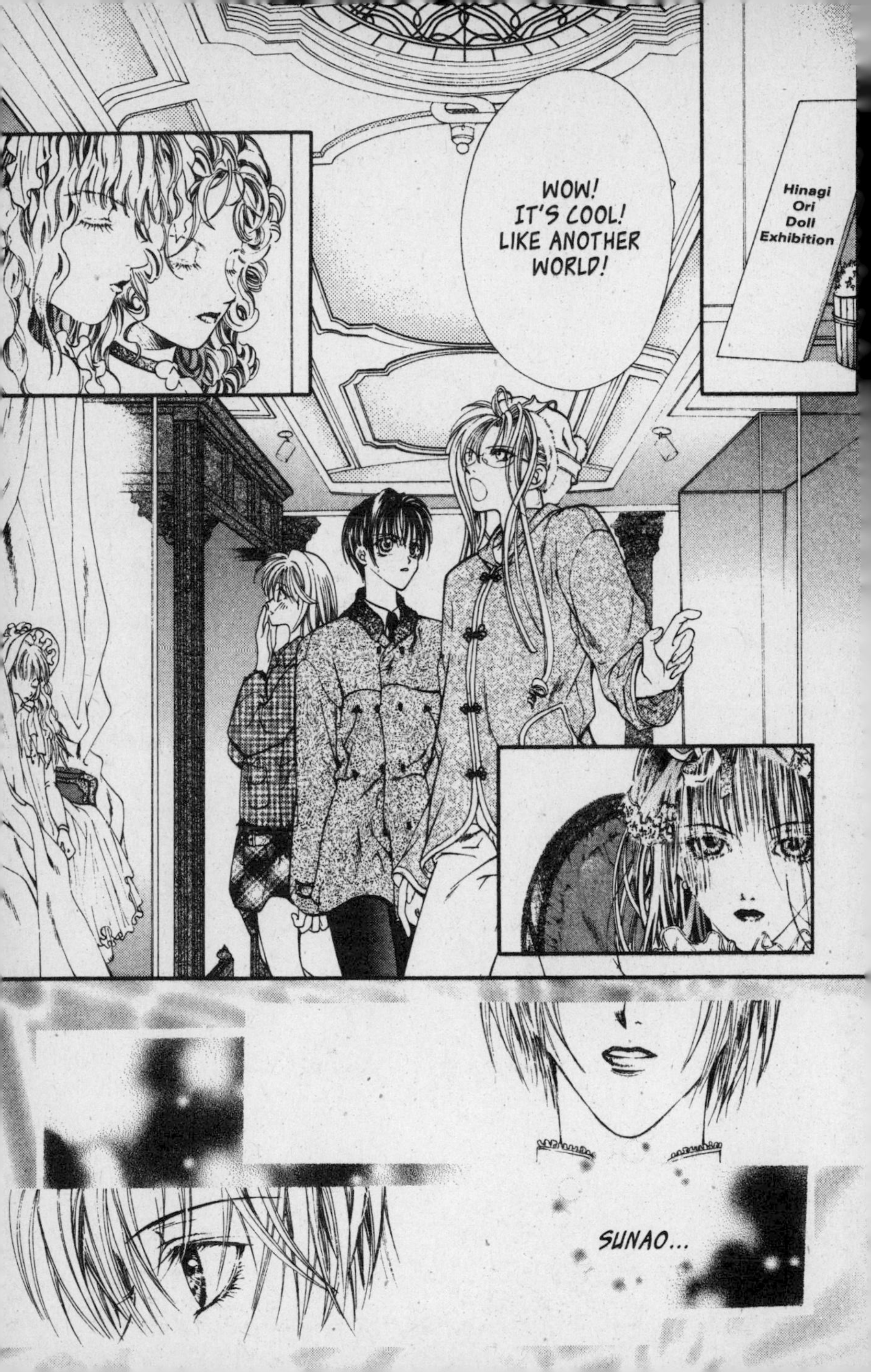
Hinagi Ori Doll Exhibition
WOW! IT'S COOL! LIKE ANOTHER WORLD!
SUNAO...

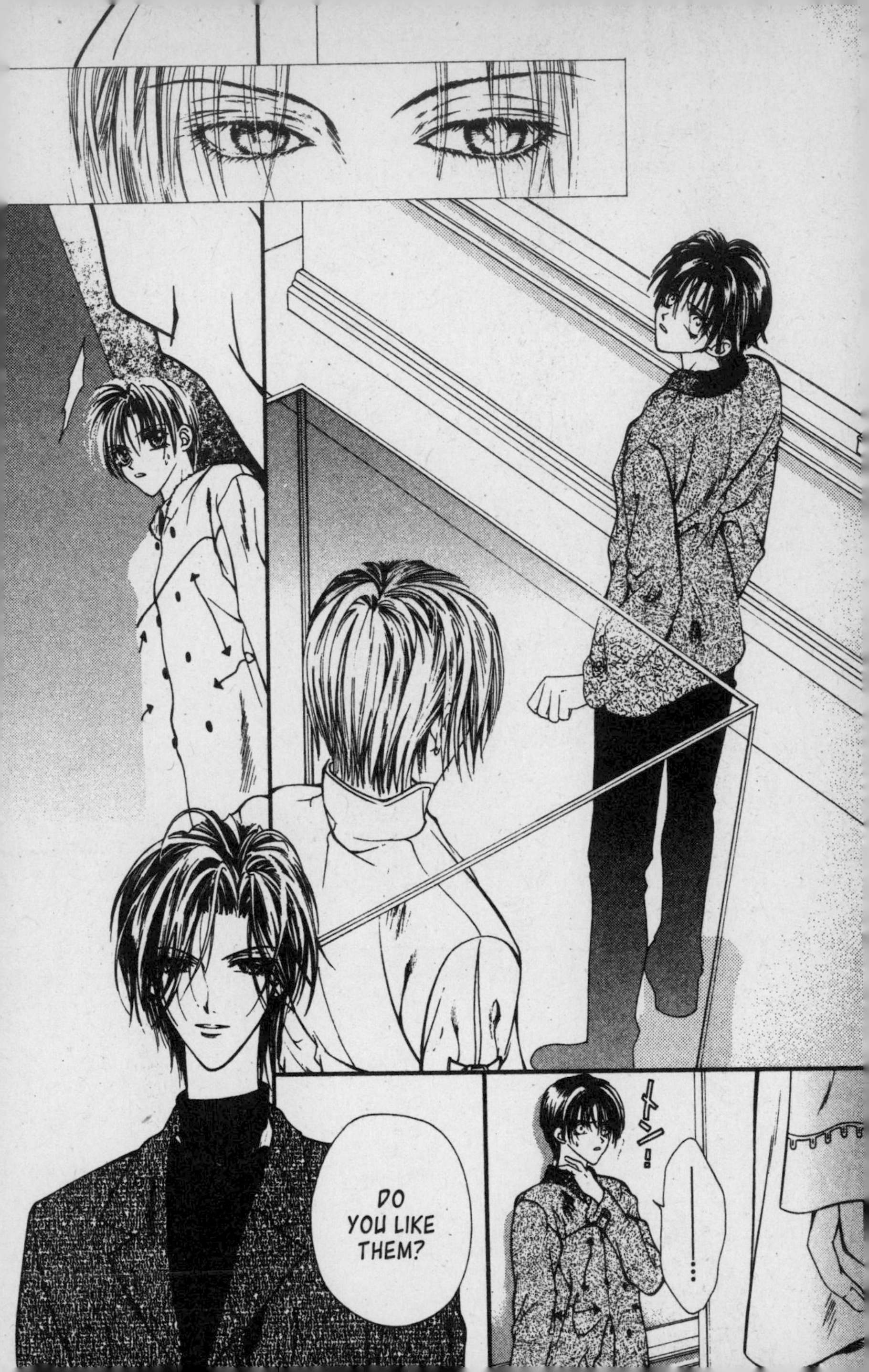
—...
DO YOU LIKE THEM?

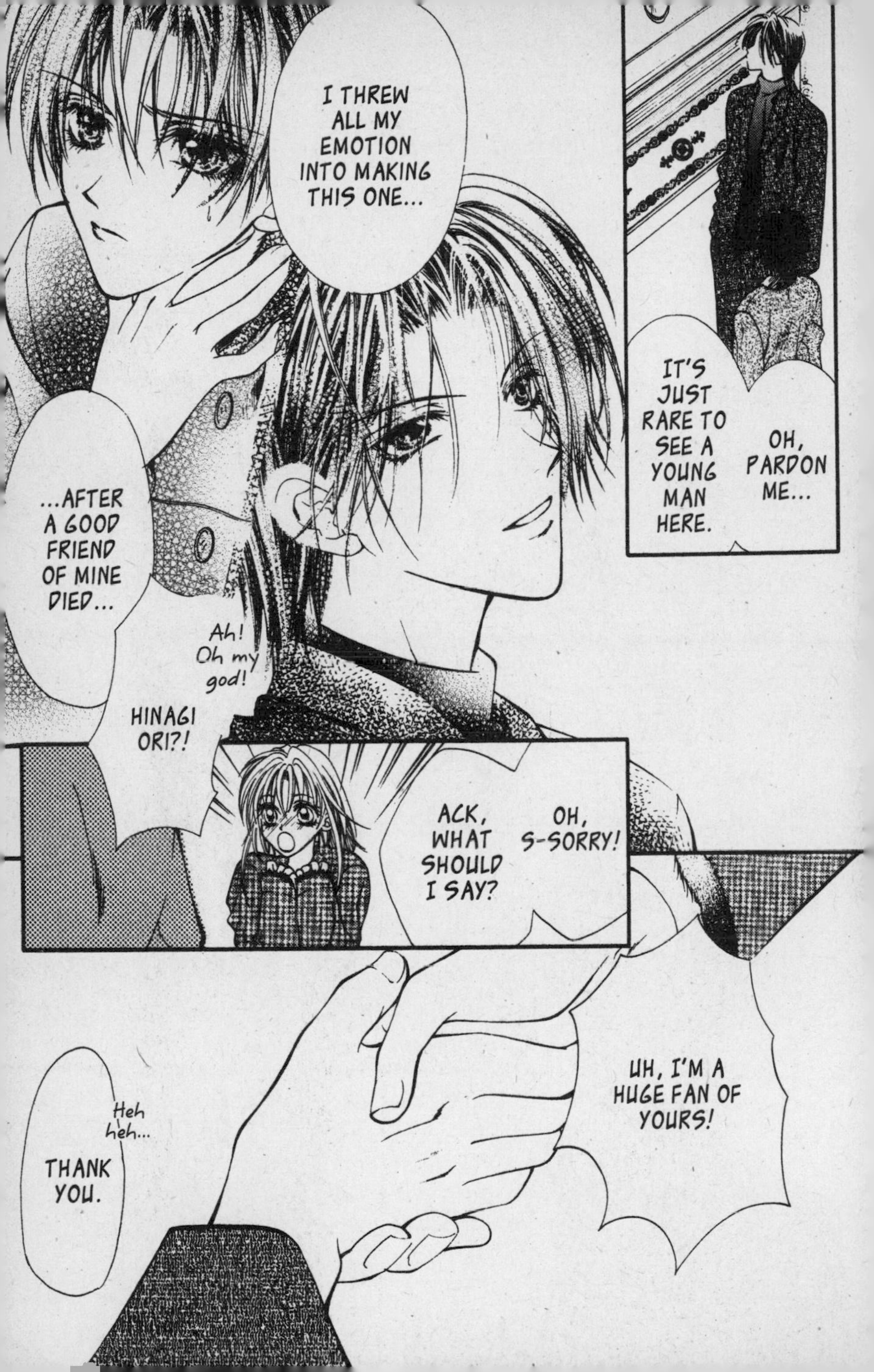
OH, PARDON ME...
IT'S JUST RARE TO SEE A YOUNG MAN HERE.
I THREW ALL MY EMOTION INTO MAKING THIS ONE...
...AFTER A GOOD FRIEND OF MINE DIED...
Ah! Oh my god!
HINAGI ORI?!
OH, S-SORRY!
ACK, WHAT SHOULD I SAY?
UH, I'M A HUGE FAN OF YOURS!
Heh heh...
THANK YOU.

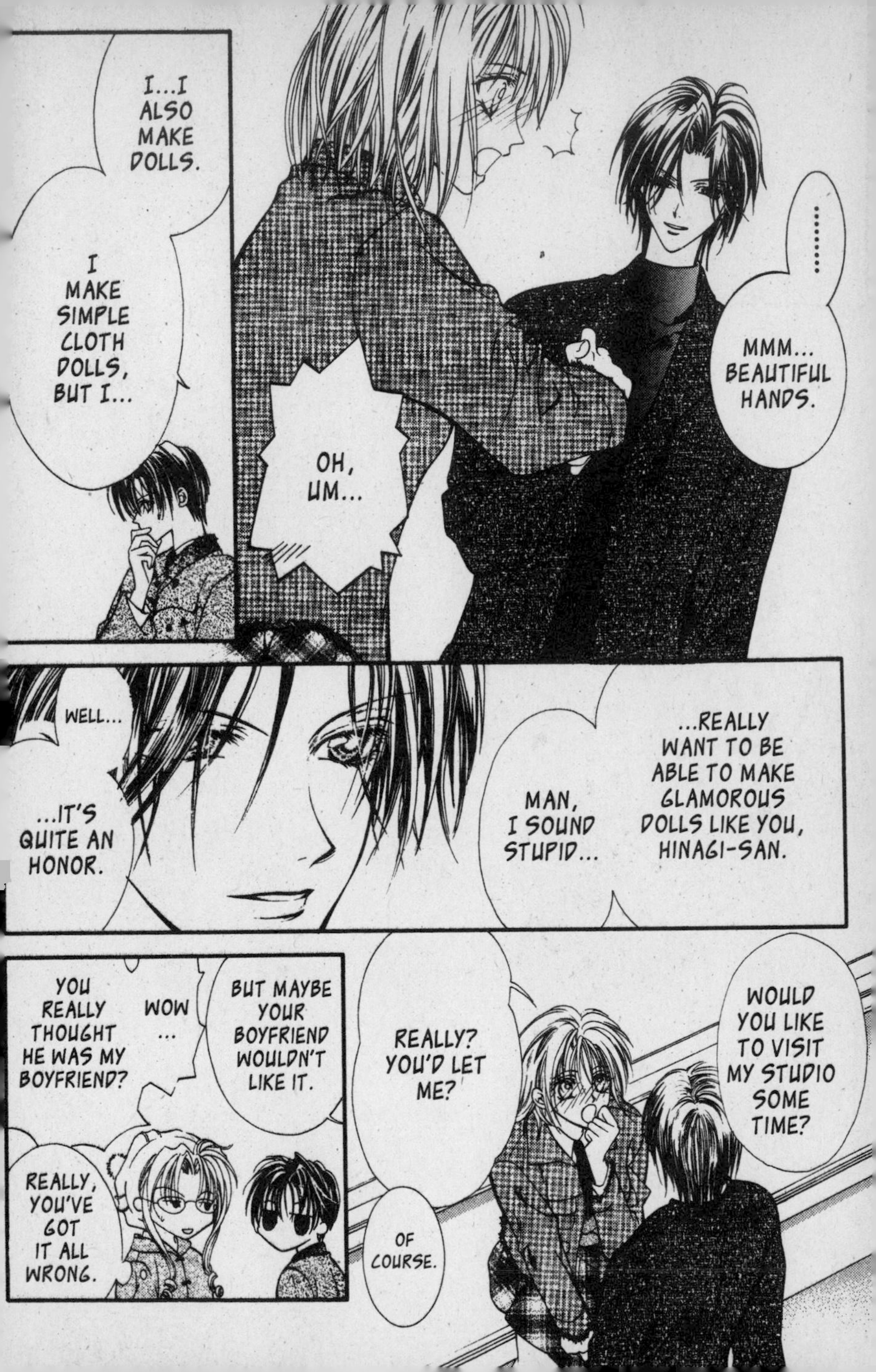
......
MMM... BEAUTIFUL HANDS.
OH, UM...
I...I ALSO MAKE DOLLS.
I MAKE SIMPLE CLOTH DOLLS, BUT I...
...REALLY WANT TO BE ABLE TO MAKE GLAMOROUS DOLLS LIKE YOU, HINAGI-SAN.
MAN, I SOUND STUPID...
WELL...
...IT'S QUITE AN HONOR.
WOULD YOU LIKE TO VISIT MY STUDIO SOME TIME?
REALLY? YOU'D LET ME?
OF COURSE.
BUT MAYBE YOUR BOYFRIEND WOULDN'T LIKE IT.
WOW ...
YOU REALLY THOUGHT HE WAS MY BOYFRIEND?
REALLY, YOU'VE GOT IT ALL WRONG.

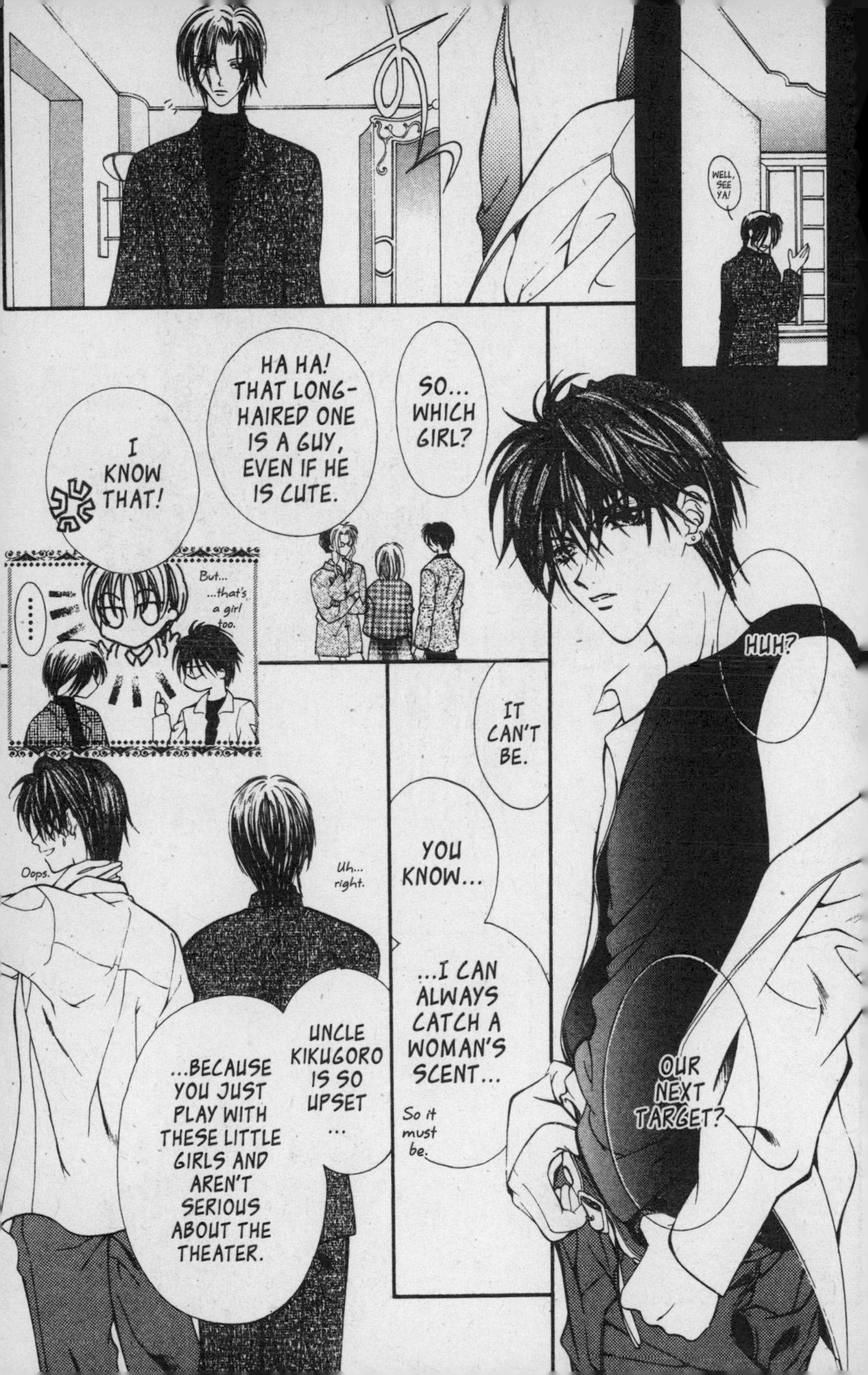
WELL, SEE YA!
HUH?
OUR NEXT TARGET?
SO... WHICH GIRL?
HA HA! THAT LONG-HAIRED ONE IS A GUY, EVEN IF HE IS CUTE.
I KNOW THAT!
......
But... ...that's a girl too.
IT CAN'T BE.
YOU KNOW...
...I CAN ALWAYS CATCH A WOMAN'S SCENT...
So it must be.
UNCLE KIKUGORO IS SO UPSET...
...BECAUSE YOU JUST PLAY WITH THESE LITTLE GIRLS AND AREN'T SERIOUS ABOUT THE THEATER.
Uh... right.
Oops.

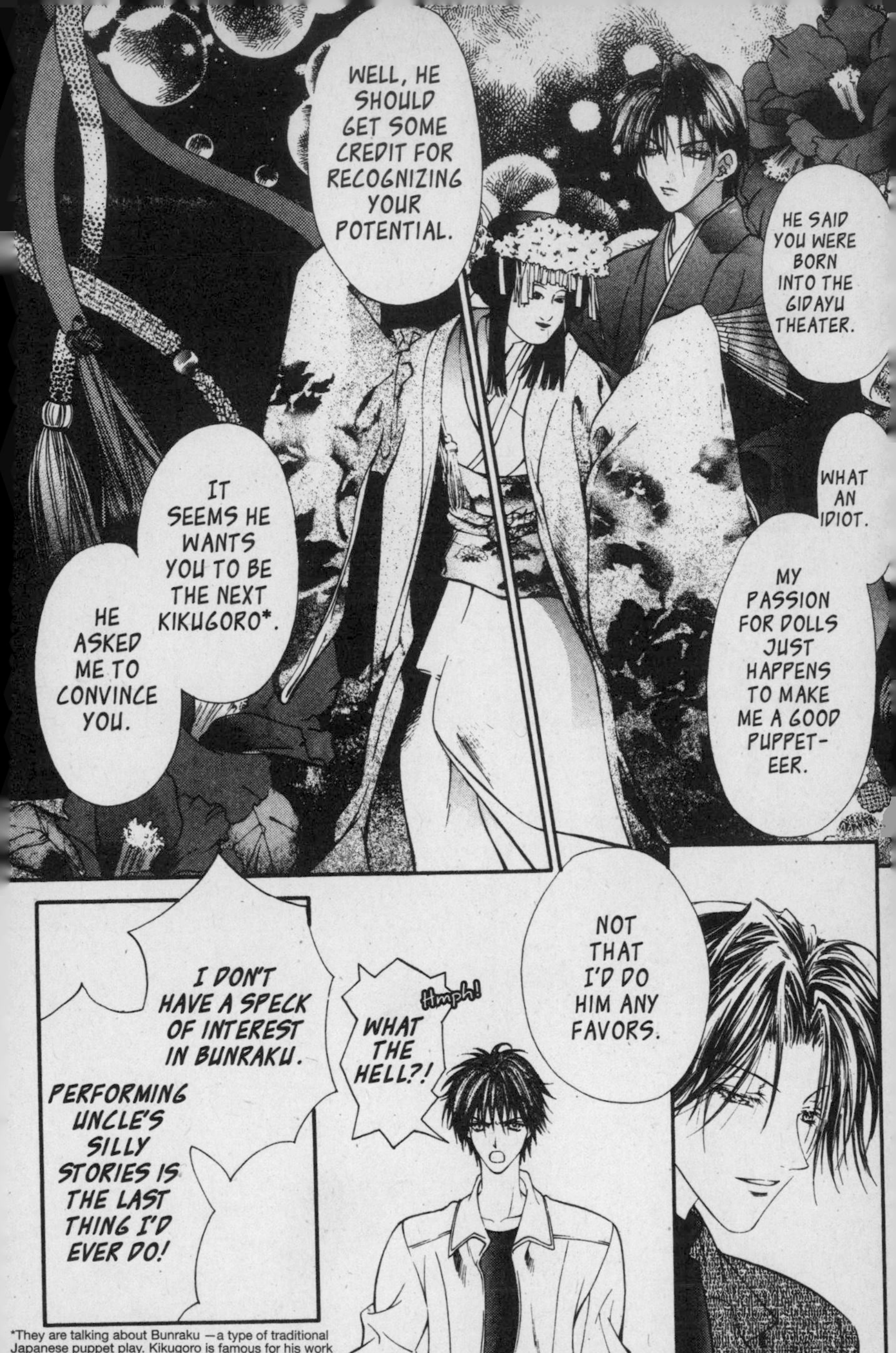
HE SAID YOU WERE BORN INTO THE GIDAYU THEATER.
WELL, HE SHOULD GET SOME CREDIT FOR RECOGNIZING YOUR POTENTIAL.
IT SEEMS HE WANTS YOU TO BE THE NEXT KIKUGORO*.
HE ASKED ME TO CONVINCE YOU.
WHAT AN IDIOT.
MY PASSION FOR DOLLS JUST HAPPENS TO MAKE ME A GOOD PUPPET-EER.
NOT THAT I'D DO HIM ANY FAVORS.
Hmph!
WHAT THE HELL?!
I DON'T HAVE A SPECK OF INTEREST IN BUNRAKU.
PERFORMING UNCLE'S SILLY STORIES IS THE LAST THING I'D EVER DO!

*They are talking about Bunraku —a type of traditional Japanese puppet play. Kikugoro is famous for his work in Japanese puppet theatre.

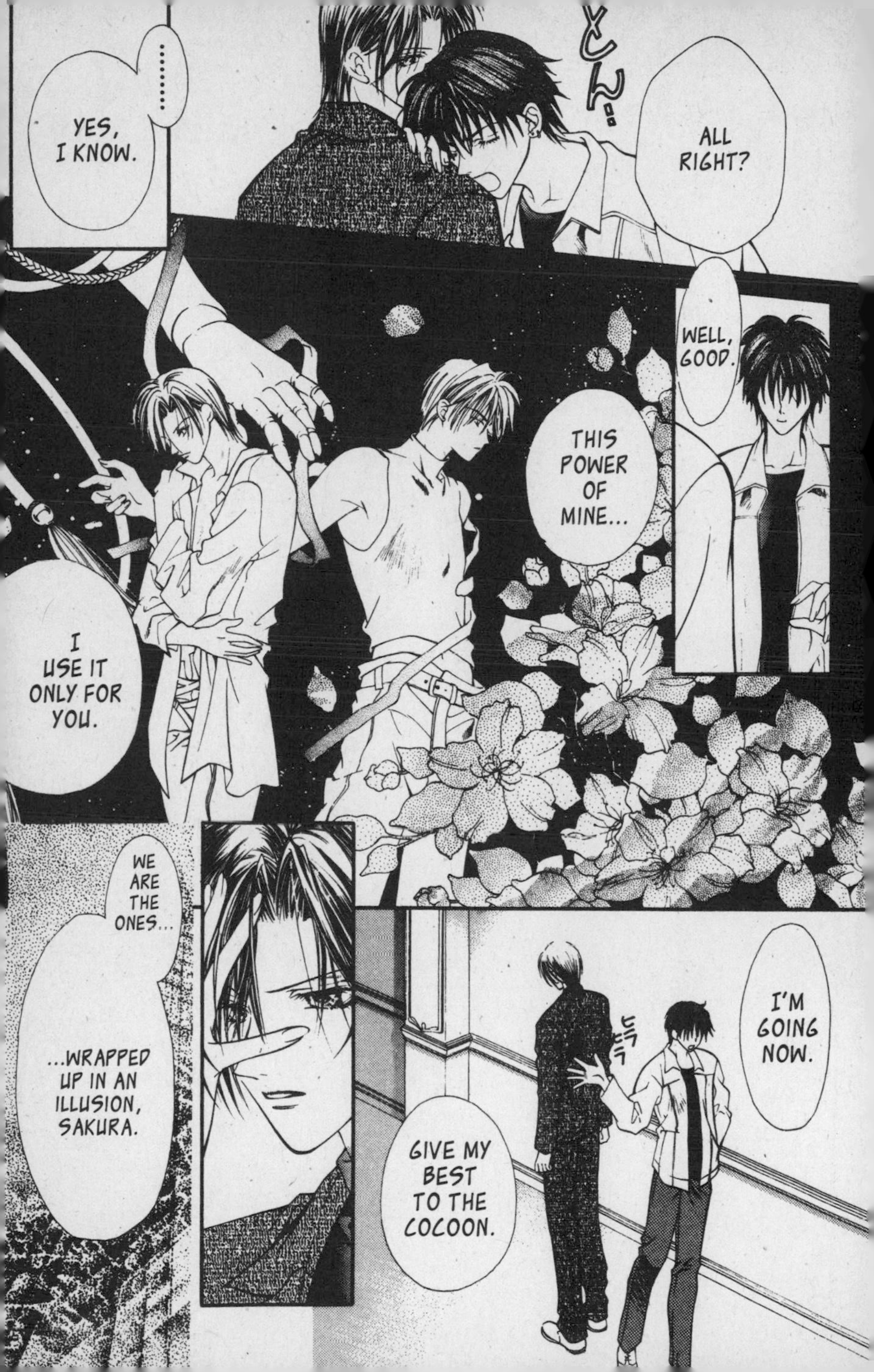
ALL RIGHT?
......
YES, I KNOW.
WELL, GOOD.
THIS POWER OF MINE...
I USE IT ONLY FOR YOU.
I'M GOING NOW.
GIVE MY BEST TO THE COCOON.
WE ARE THE ONES...
...WRAPPED UP IN AN ILLUSION, SAKURA.

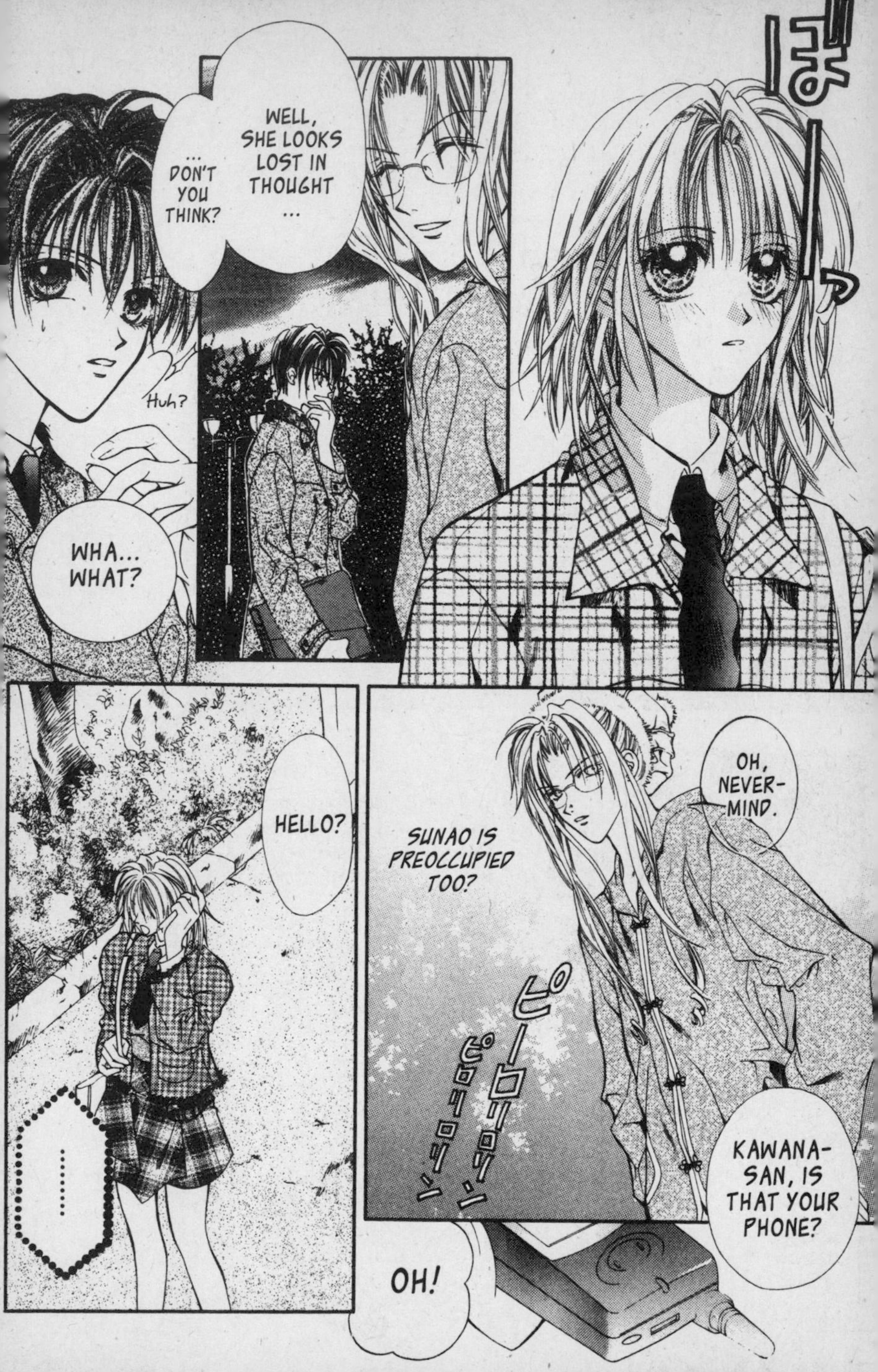
ぼーっ
WELL, SHE LOOKS LOST IN THOUGHT ...
... DON'T YOU THINK?
Huh?
WHA... WHAT?
OH, NEVER-MIND.
SUNAO IS PREOCCUPIED TOO?
KAWANA-SAN, IS THAT YOUR PHONE?
OH!
HELLO?
......

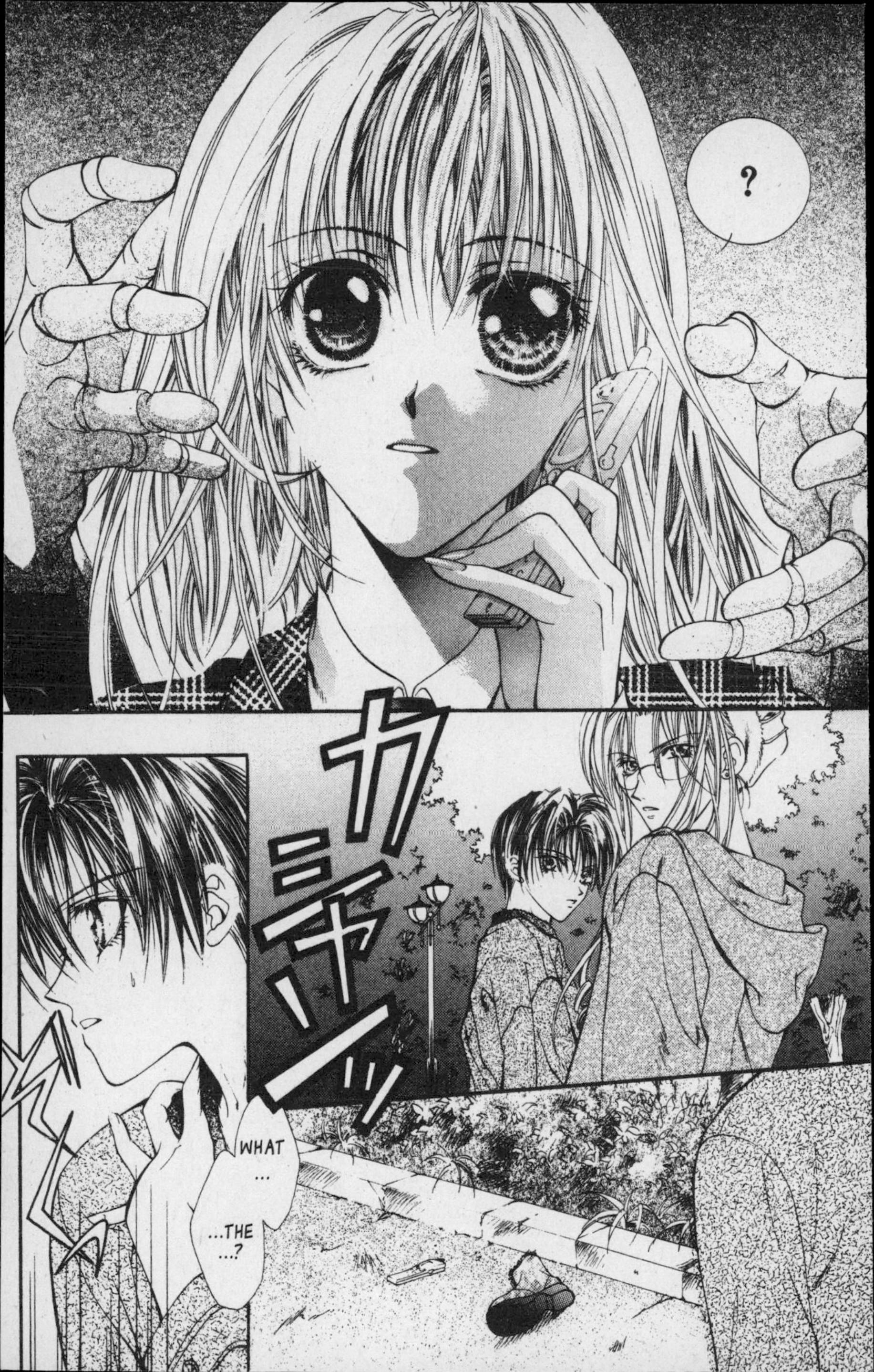
?
カシャンッ
WHAT ...
...THE ...?

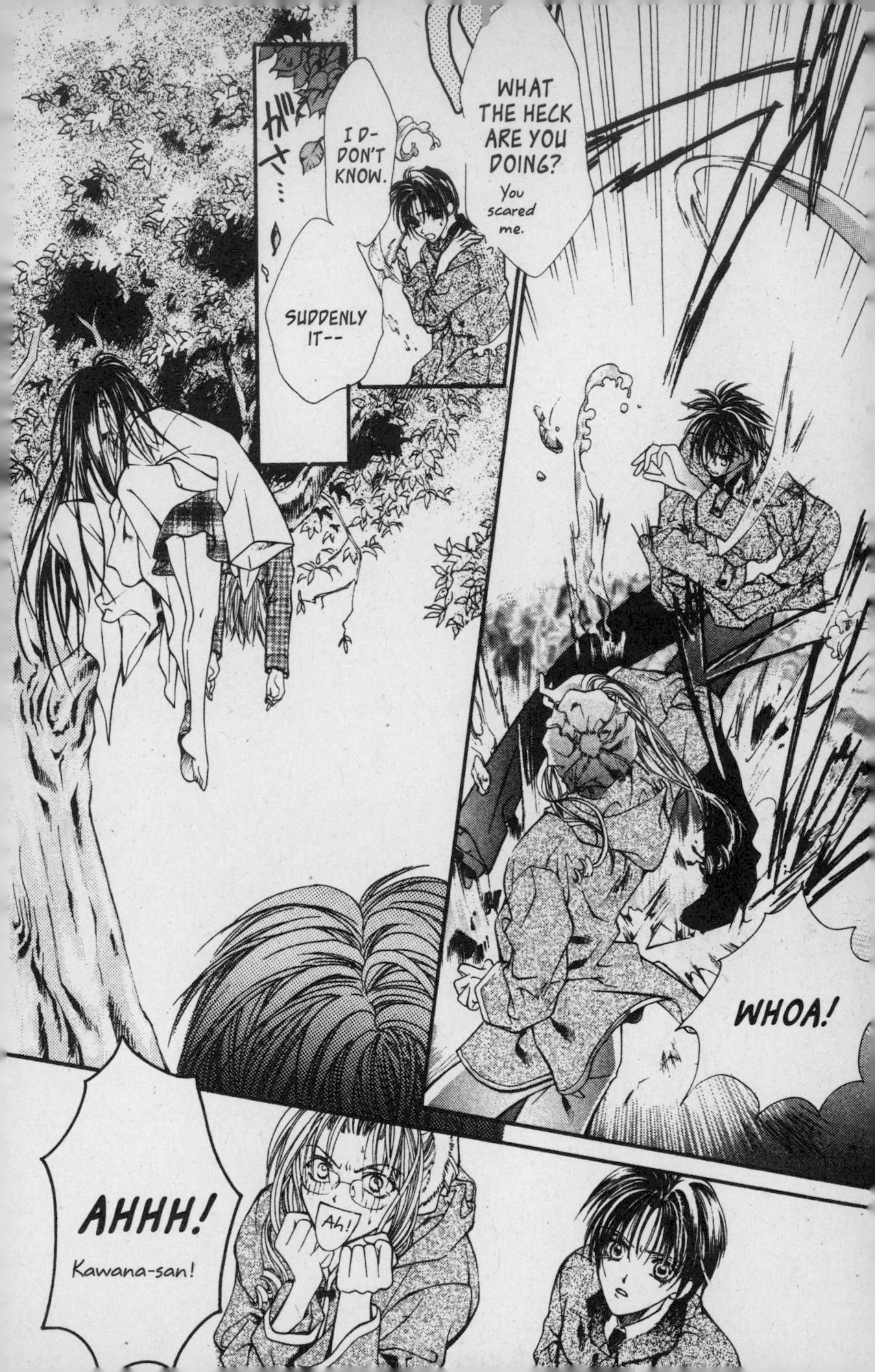
WHOA!
WHAT THE HECK ARE YOU DOING?
You scared me.
I D-DON'T KNOW.
SUDDENLY IT--
がさ…
Ah!
AHHH!
Kawana-san!

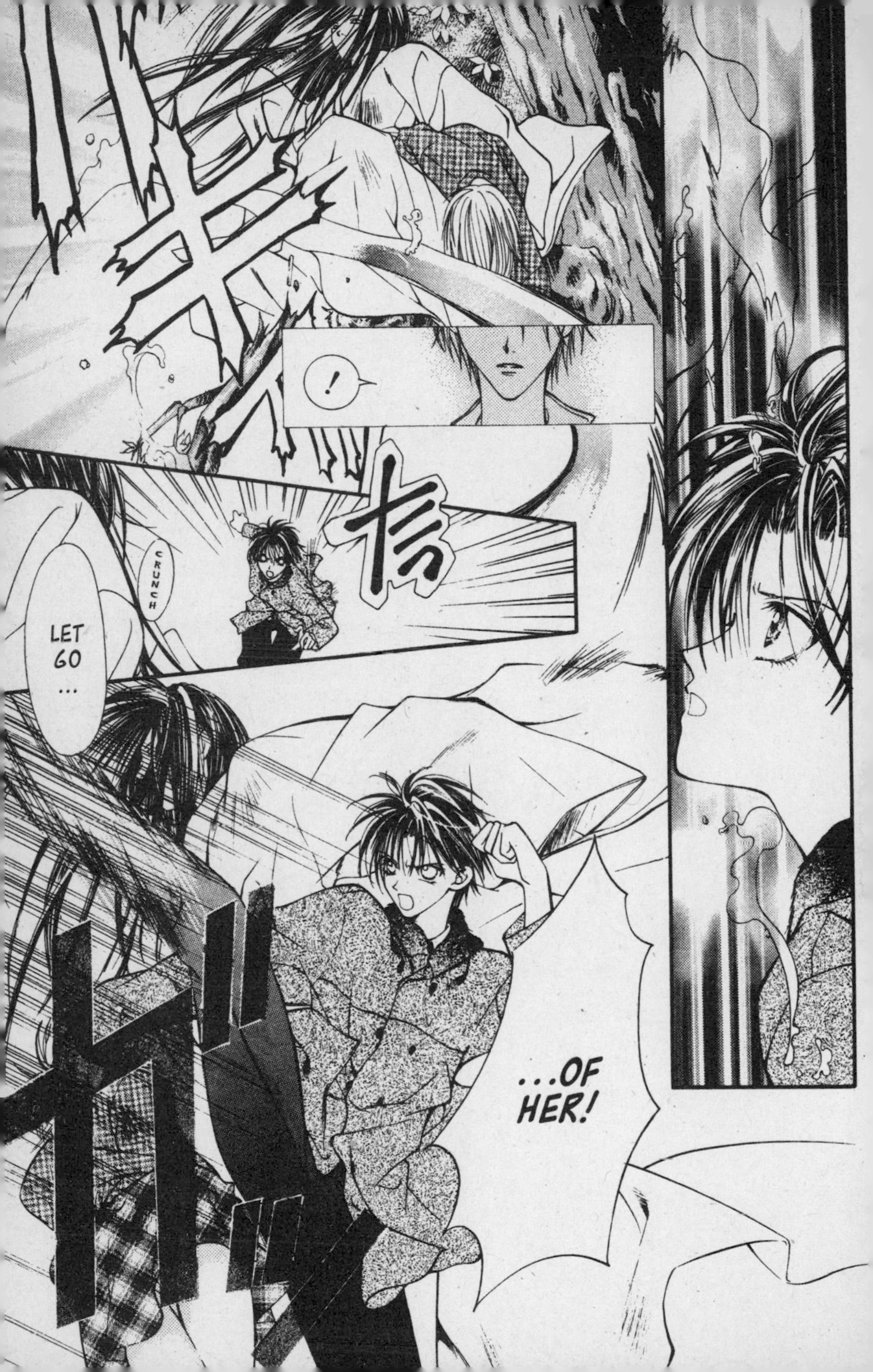
!
CRUNCH
LET GO ...
...OF HER!

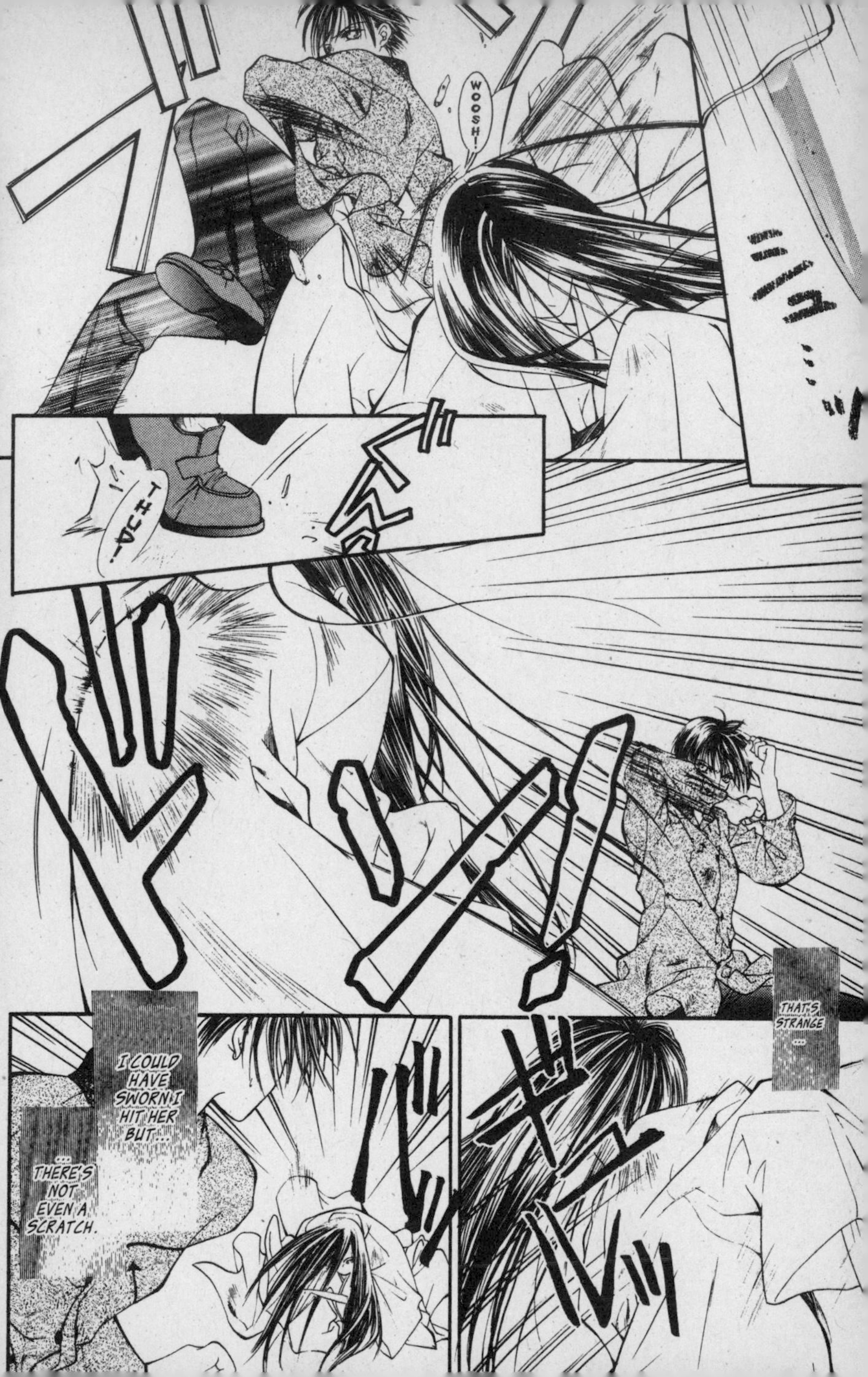
WOOSH!
THUD!
THAT'S STRANGE...
I COULD HAVE SWORN I HIT HER BUT...
...THERE'S NOT EVEN A SCRATCH.

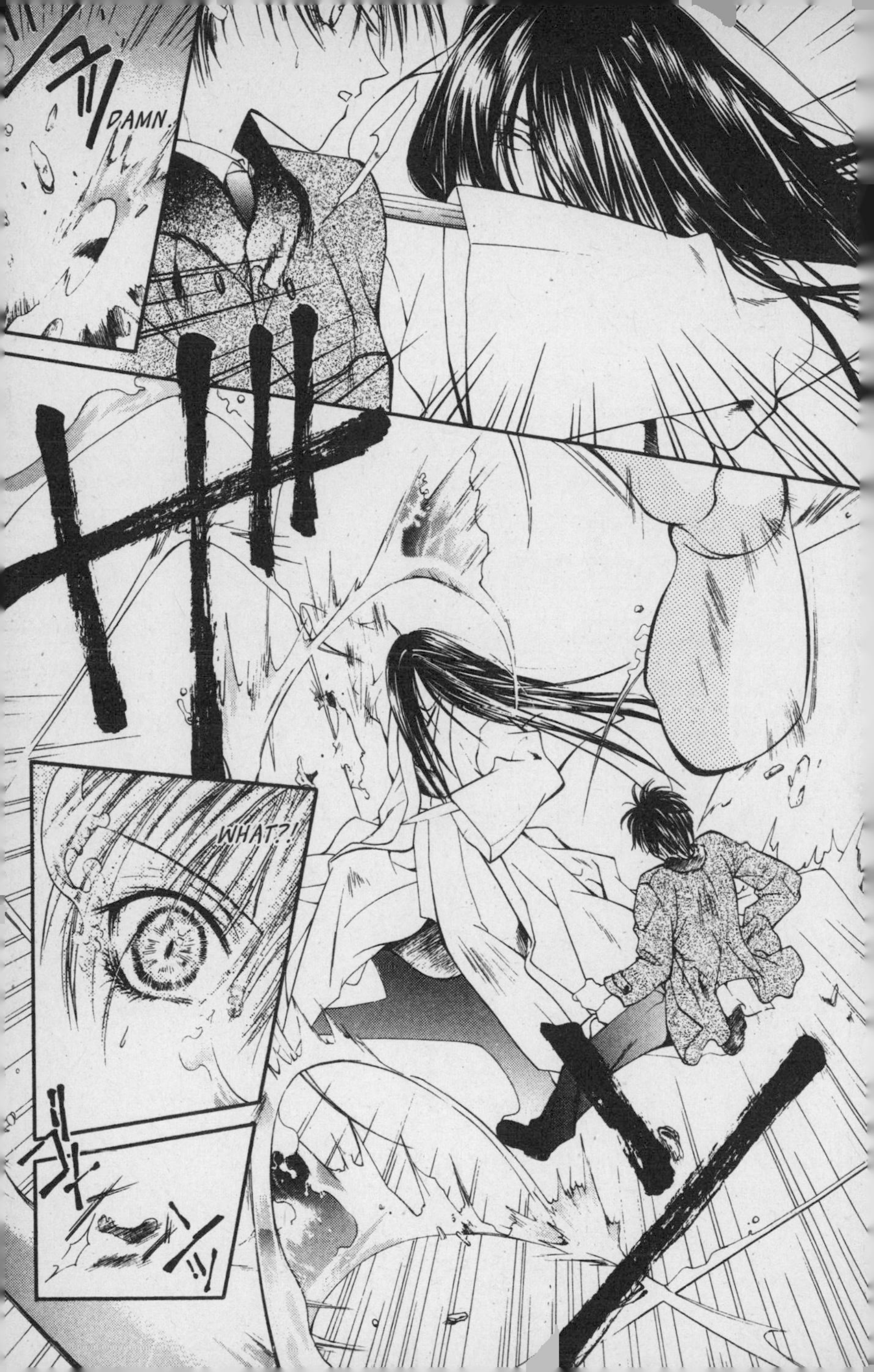
DAMN.
WHAT?!

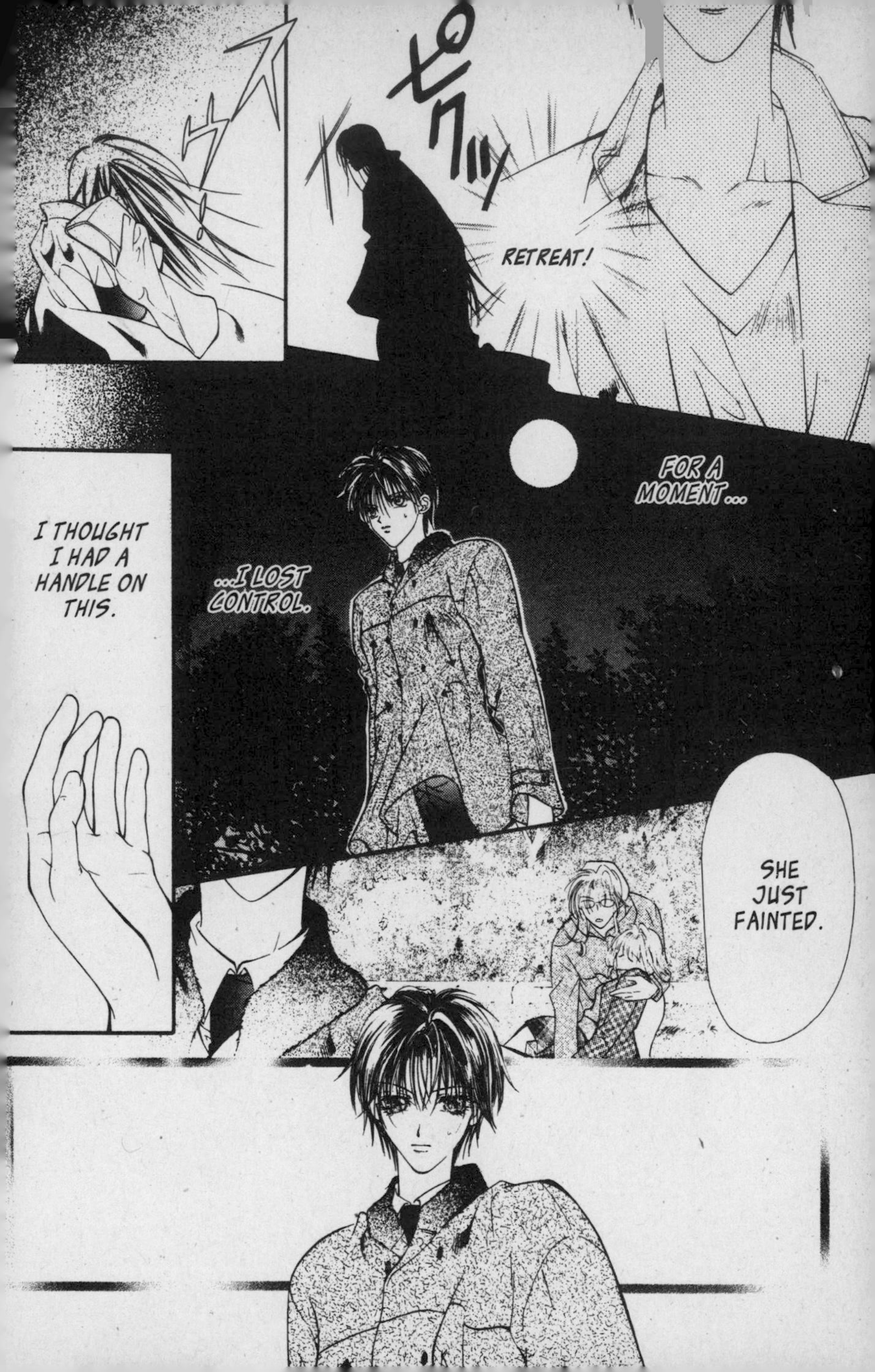
RETREAT!
ピクッ
FOR A MOMENT...
...I LOST CONTROL.
I THOUGHT I HAD A HANDLE ON THIS.
SHE JUST FAINTED.

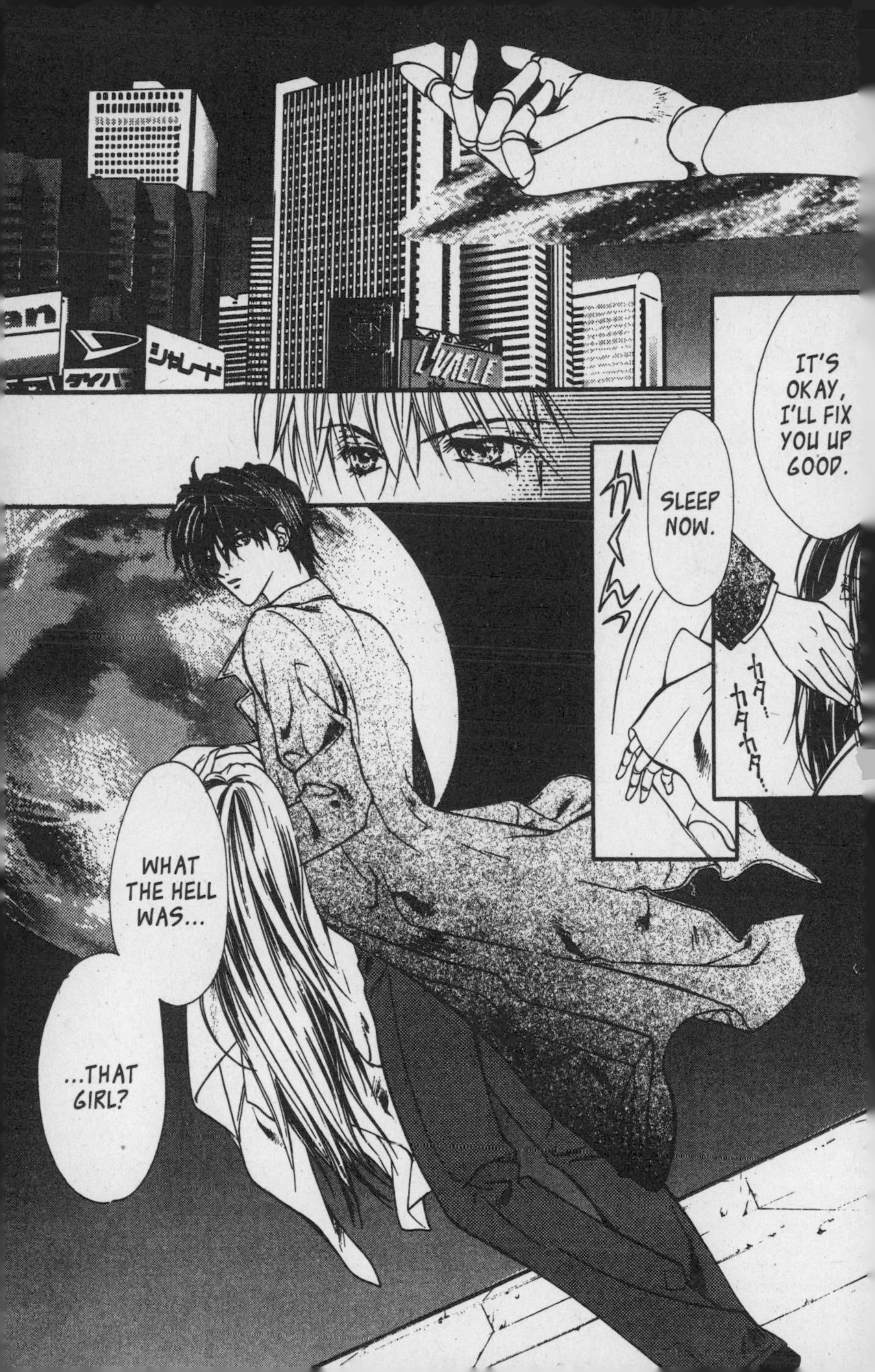
シャレード
IT'S OKAY, I'LL FIX YOU UP GOOD.
カタ…
カタカタ…
SLEEP NOW.
WHAT THE HELL WAS...
...THAT GIRL?

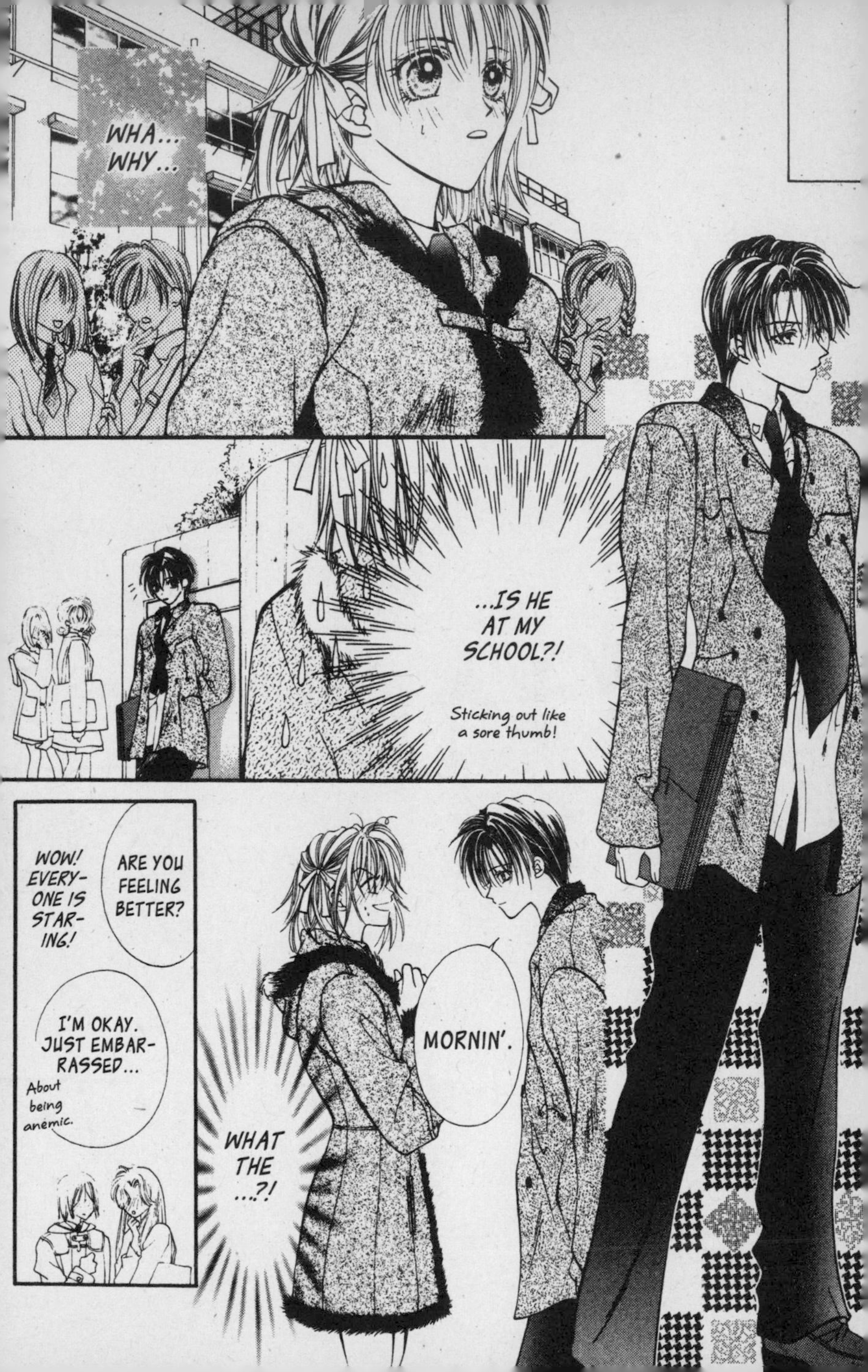
WHA... WHY...
...IS HE AT MY SCHOOL?!
Sticking out like a sore thumb!
MORNIN'.
WHAT THE ...?!
ARE YOU FEELING BETTER?
WOW! EVERY-ONE IS STAR-ING!
I'M OKAY. JUST EMBAR-RASSED...
About being anémic.

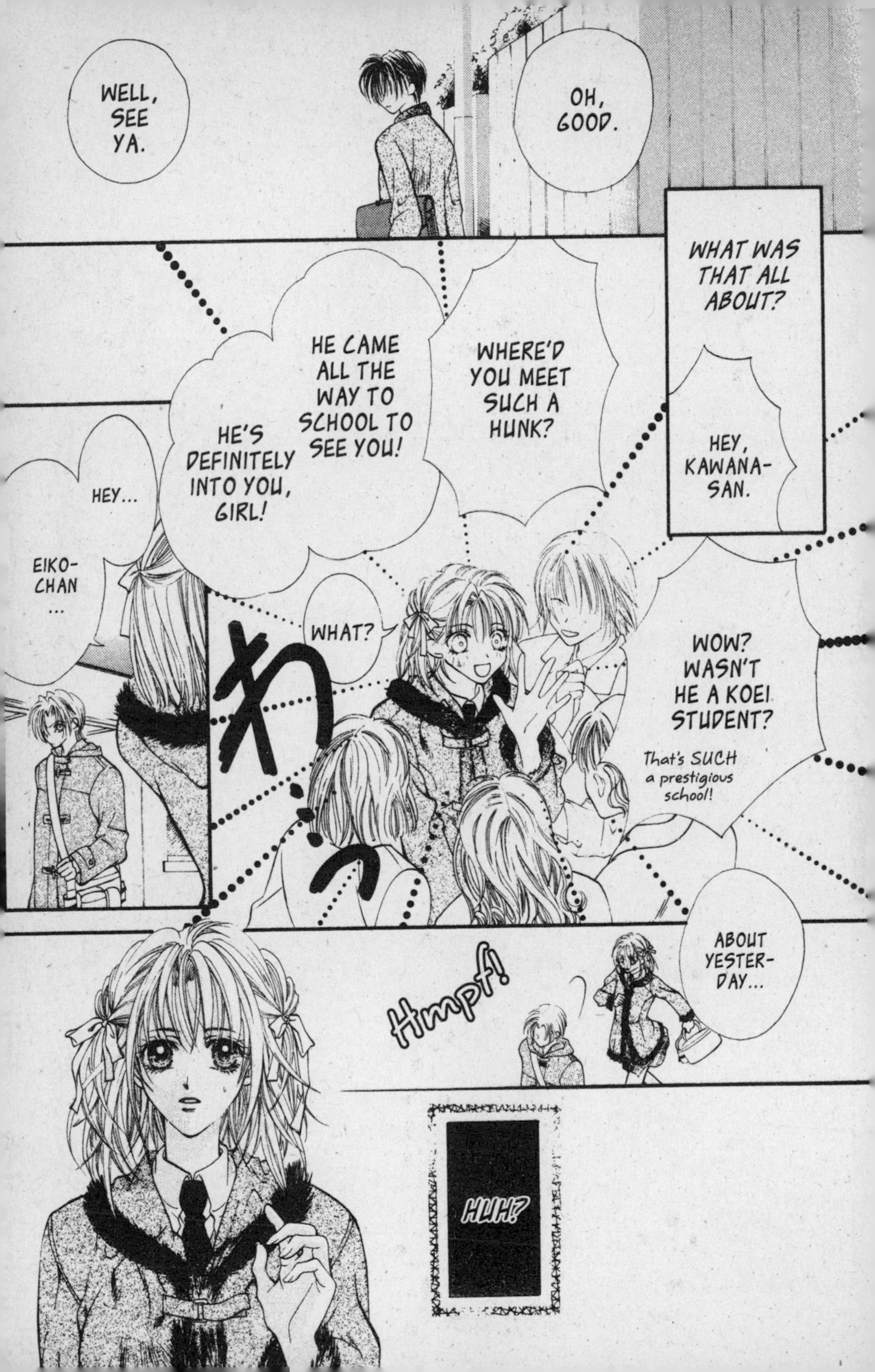
OH, GOOD.
WELL, SEE YA.
WHAT WAS THAT ALL ABOUT?
HEY, KAWANA-SAN.
WOW? WASN'T HE A KOEI STUDENT?
That's SUCH a prestigious school!
WHERE'D YOU MEET SUCH A HUNK?
HE CAME ALL THE WAY TO SCHOOL TO SEE YOU!
HE'S DEFINITELY INTO YOU, GIRL!
WHAT?
わっ
HEY...
EIKO-CHAN ...
ABOUT YESTER-DAY...
Hmpf!
HUH?

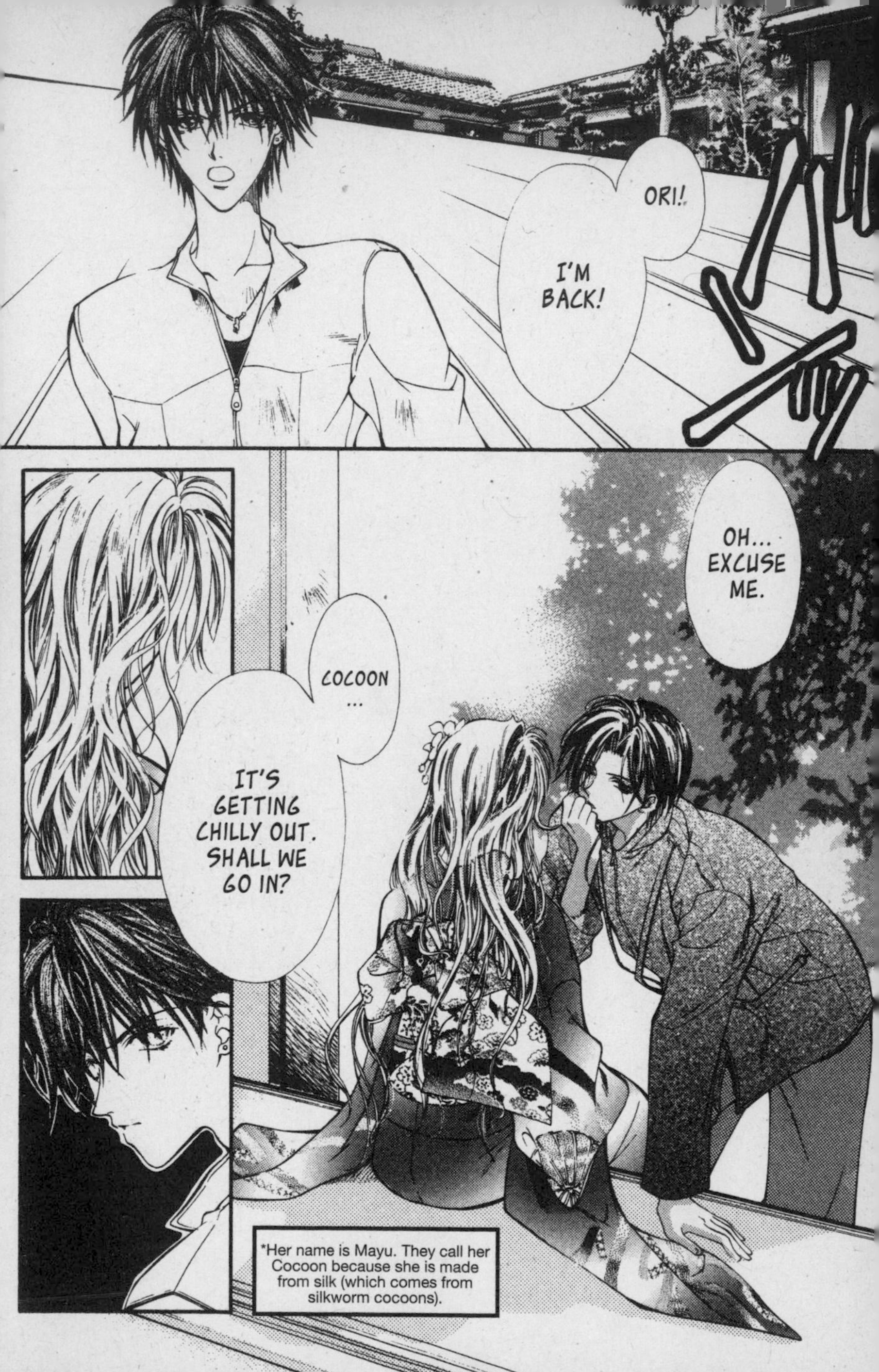
ORI!
I'M BACK!
OH... EXCUSE ME.
COCOON ...
IT'S GETTING CHILLY OUT. SHALL WE GO IN?
*Her name is Mayu. They call her Cocoon because she is made from silk (which comes from silkworm cocoons).

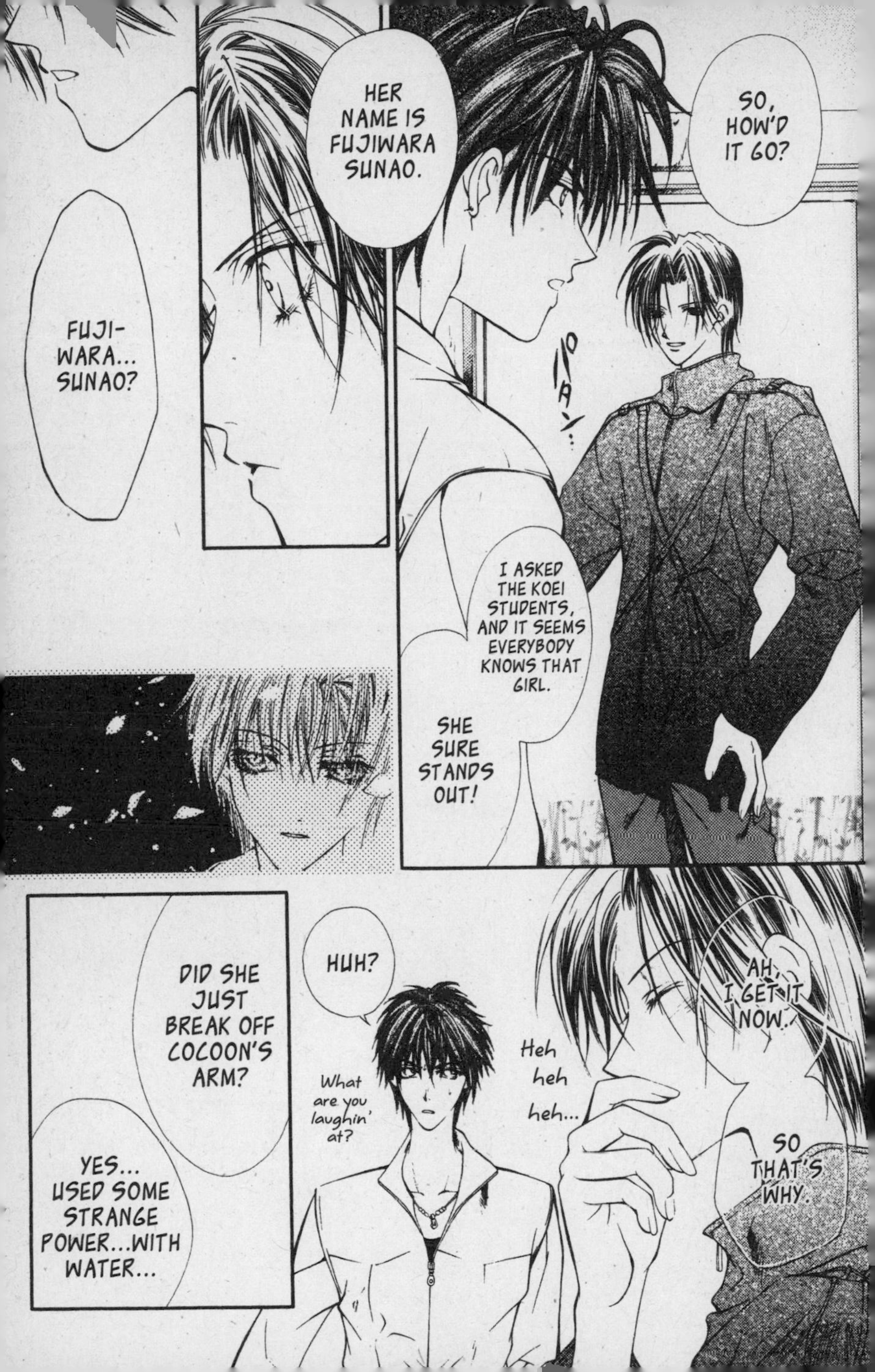
SO, HOW'D IT GO?
HER NAME IS FUJIWARA SUNAO.
I ASKED THE KOEI STUDENTS, AND IT SEEMS EVERYBODY KNOWS THAT GIRL.
SHE SURE STANDS OUT!
FUJI-WARA... SUNAO?
AH, I GET IT NOW.
SO THAT'S WHY.
Heh heh heh...
HUH?
What are you laughin' at?
DID SHE JUST BREAK OFF COCOON'S ARM?
YES... USED SOME STRANGE POWER...WITH WATER...

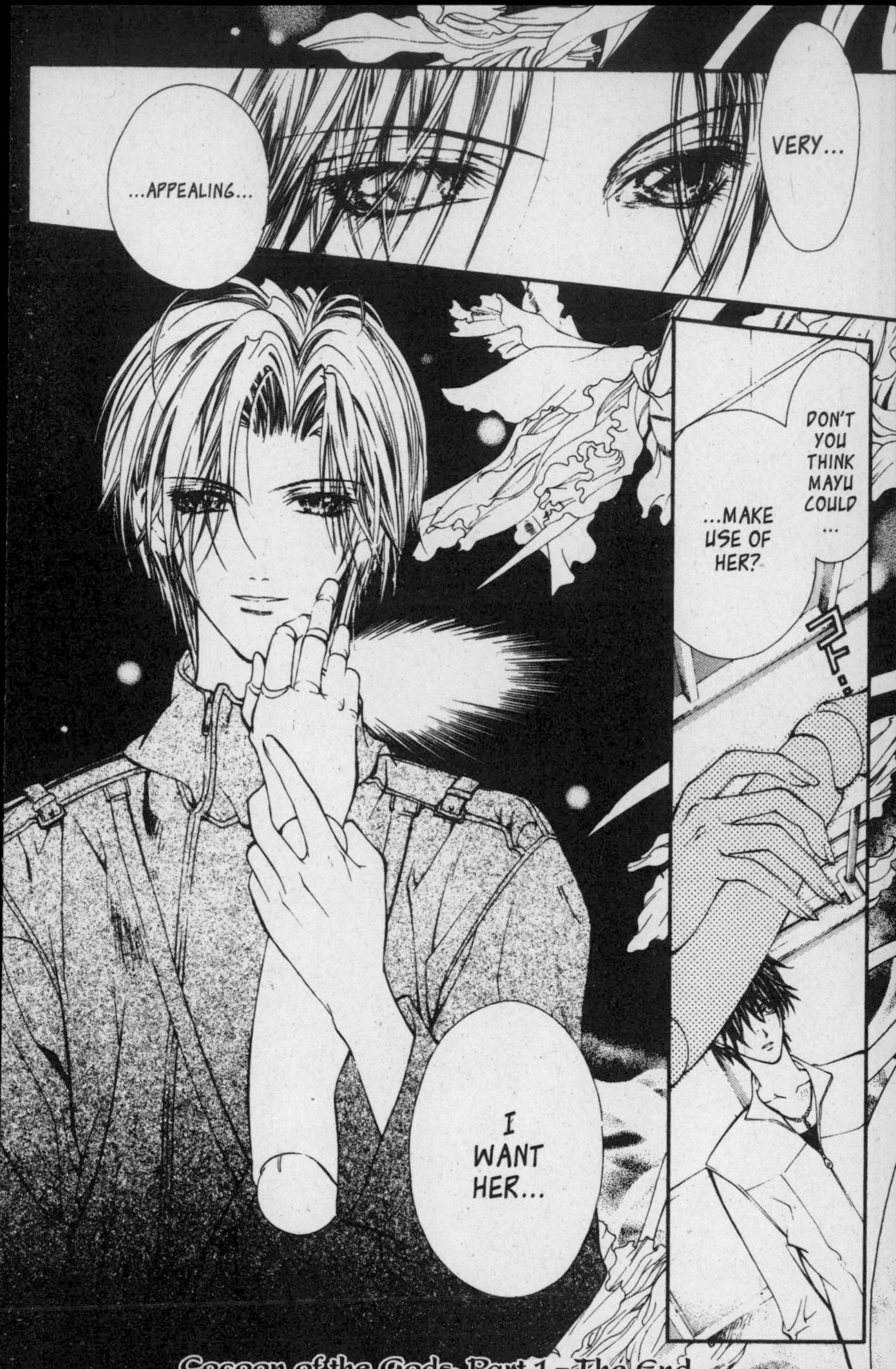
VERY...
...APPEALING...
DON'T YOU THINK MAYU COULD ...
...MAKE USE OF HER?
I WANT HER...

Cocoon of the Gods, Part 1 – The End

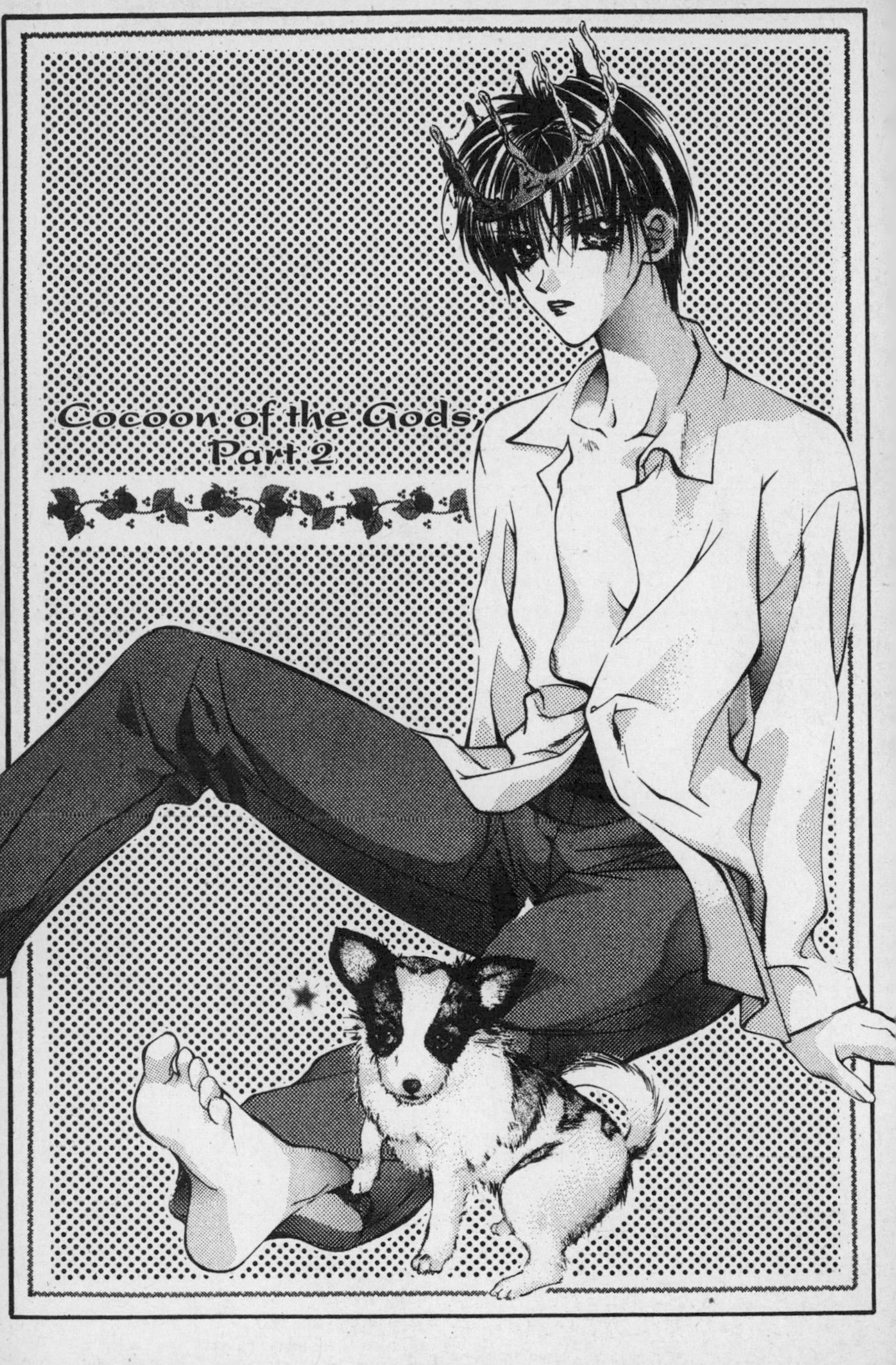
Cocoon of the Gods,
Part 2

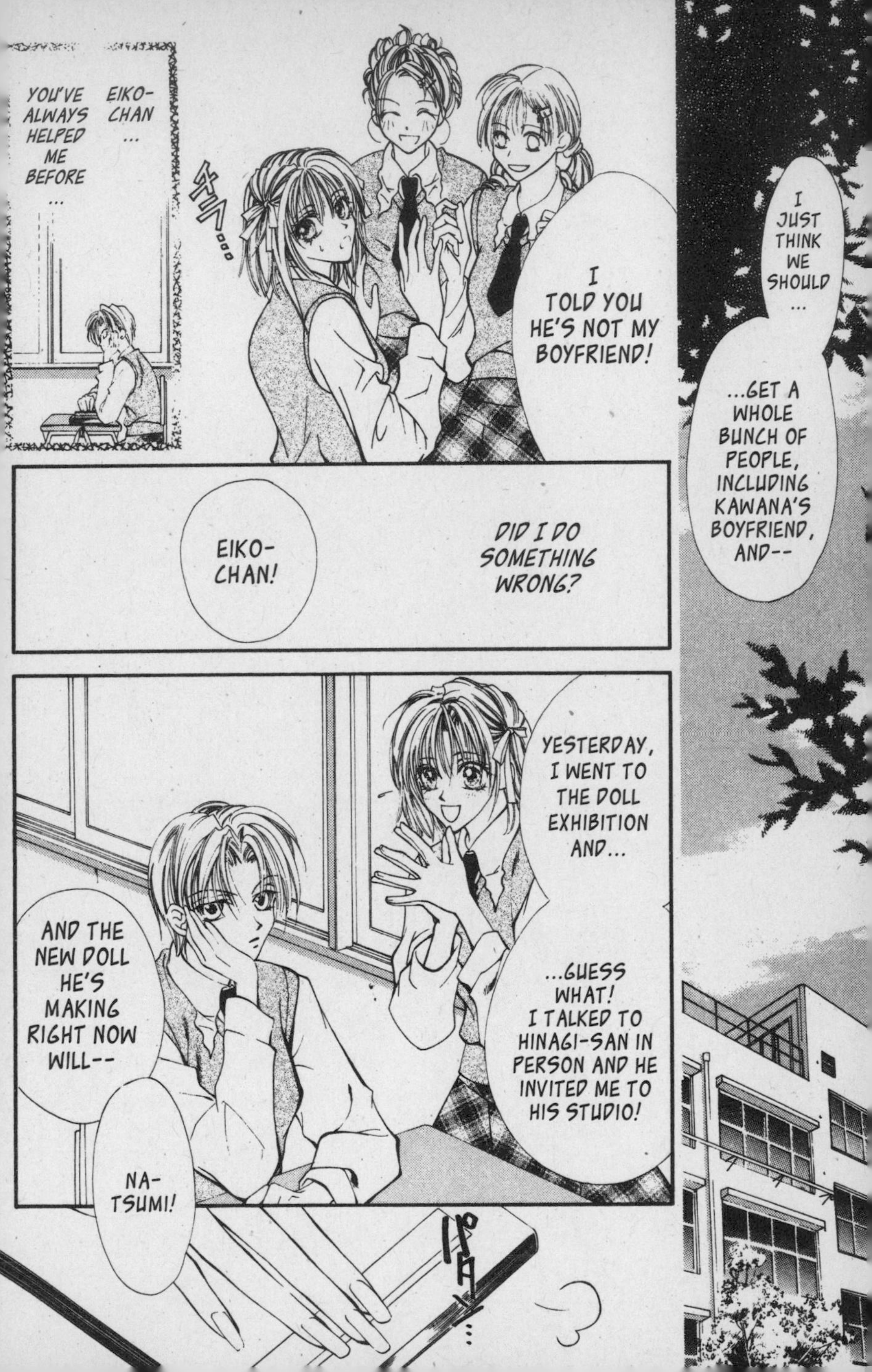
I JUST THINK WE SHOULD ...
...GET A WHOLE BUNCH OF PEOPLE, INCLUDING KAWANA'S BOYFRIEND, AND--
I TOLD YOU HE'S NOT MY BOYFRIEND!
EIKO-CHAN ...
YOU'VE ALWAYS HELPED ME BEFORE ...
DID I DO SOMETHING WRONG?
EIKO-CHAN!
YESTERDAY, I WENT TO THE DOLL EXHIBITION AND...
...GUESS WHAT! I TALKED TO HINAGI-SAN IN PERSON AND HE INVITED ME TO HIS STUDIO!
AND THE NEW DOLL HE'S MAKING RIGHT NOW WILL--
NA-TSUMI!

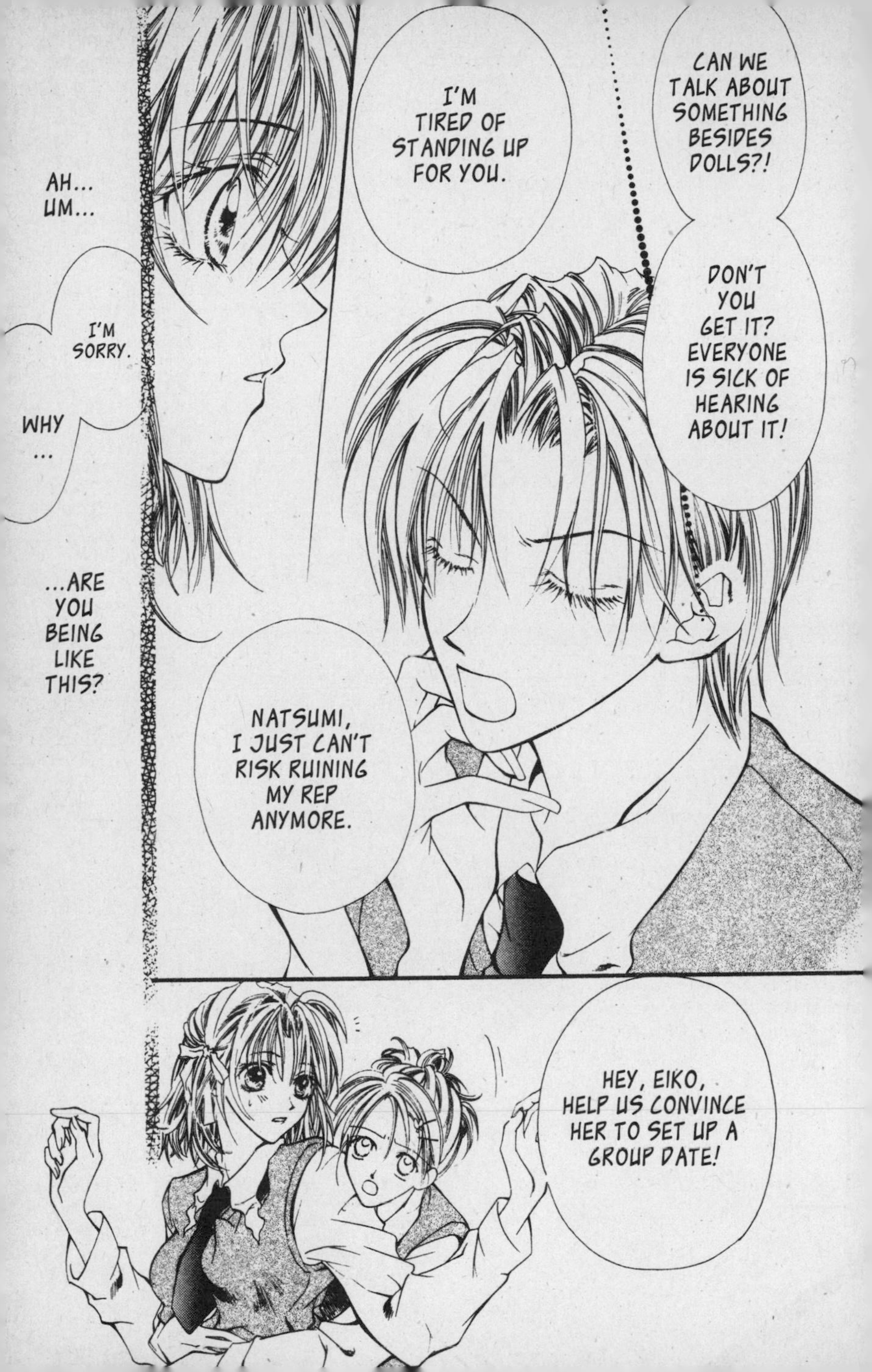
CAN WE TALK ABOUT SOMETHING BESIDES DOLLS?!
DON'T YOU GET IT? EVERYONE IS SICK OF HEARING ABOUT IT!
I'M TIRED OF STANDING UP FOR YOU.
NATSUMI, I JUST CAN'T RISK RUINING MY REP ANYMORE.
AH... UM...
I'M SORRY.
WHY ...
...ARE YOU BEING LIKE THIS?
HEY, EIKO, HELP US CONVINCE HER TO SET UP A GROUP DATE!

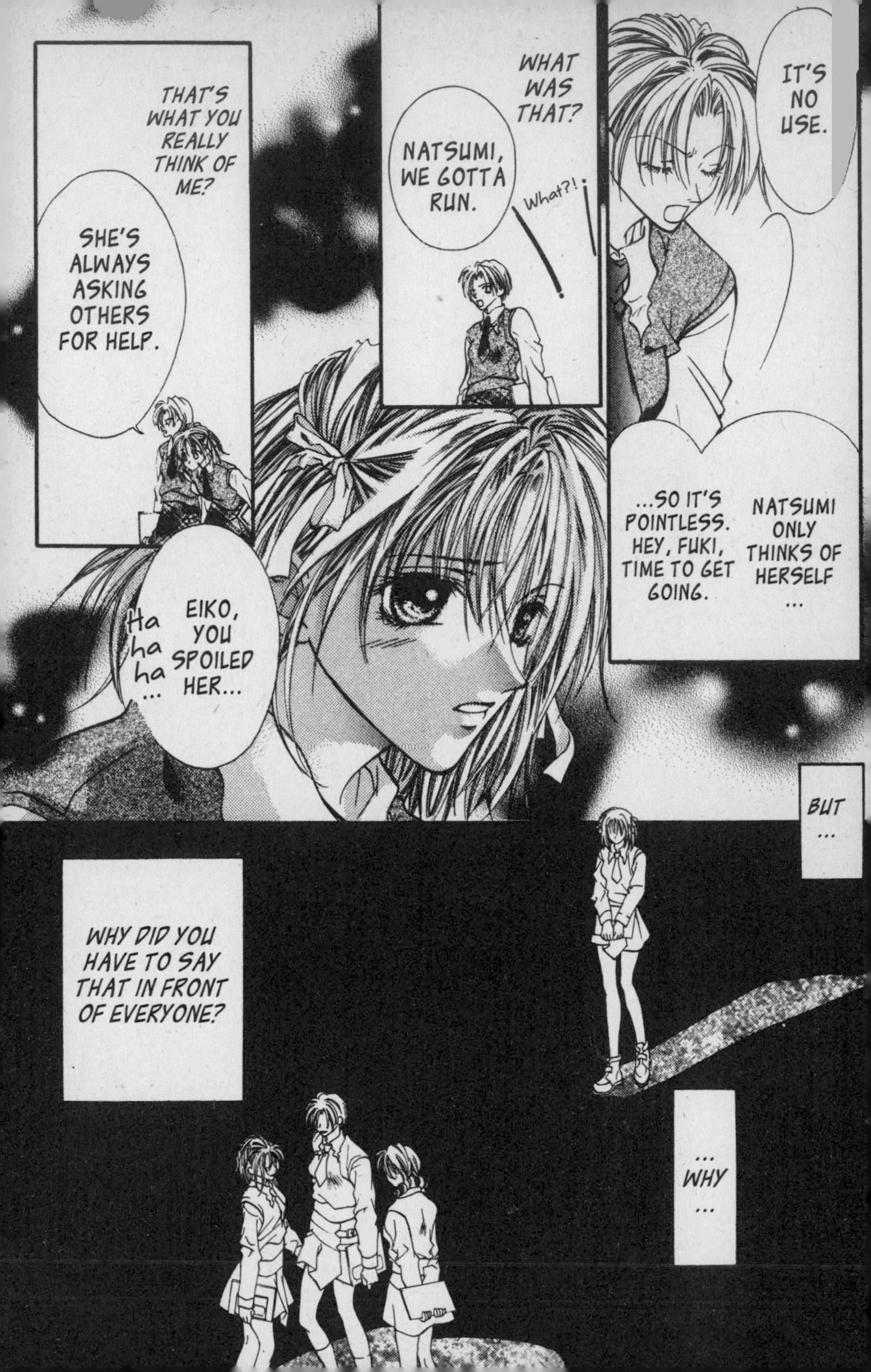
IT'S NO USE.
NATSUMI ONLY THINKS OF HERSELF ...
...SO IT'S POINTLESS. HEY, FUKI, TIME TO GET GOING.
WHAT WAS THAT?
NATSUMI, WE GOTTA RUN.
What?!
THAT'S WHAT YOU REALLY THINK OF ME?
SHE'S ALWAYS ASKING OTHERS FOR HELP.
EIKO, YOU SPOILED HER...
Ha ha ha ...
BUT ...
WHY DID YOU HAVE TO SAY THAT IN FRONT OF EVERYONE?
... WHY ...

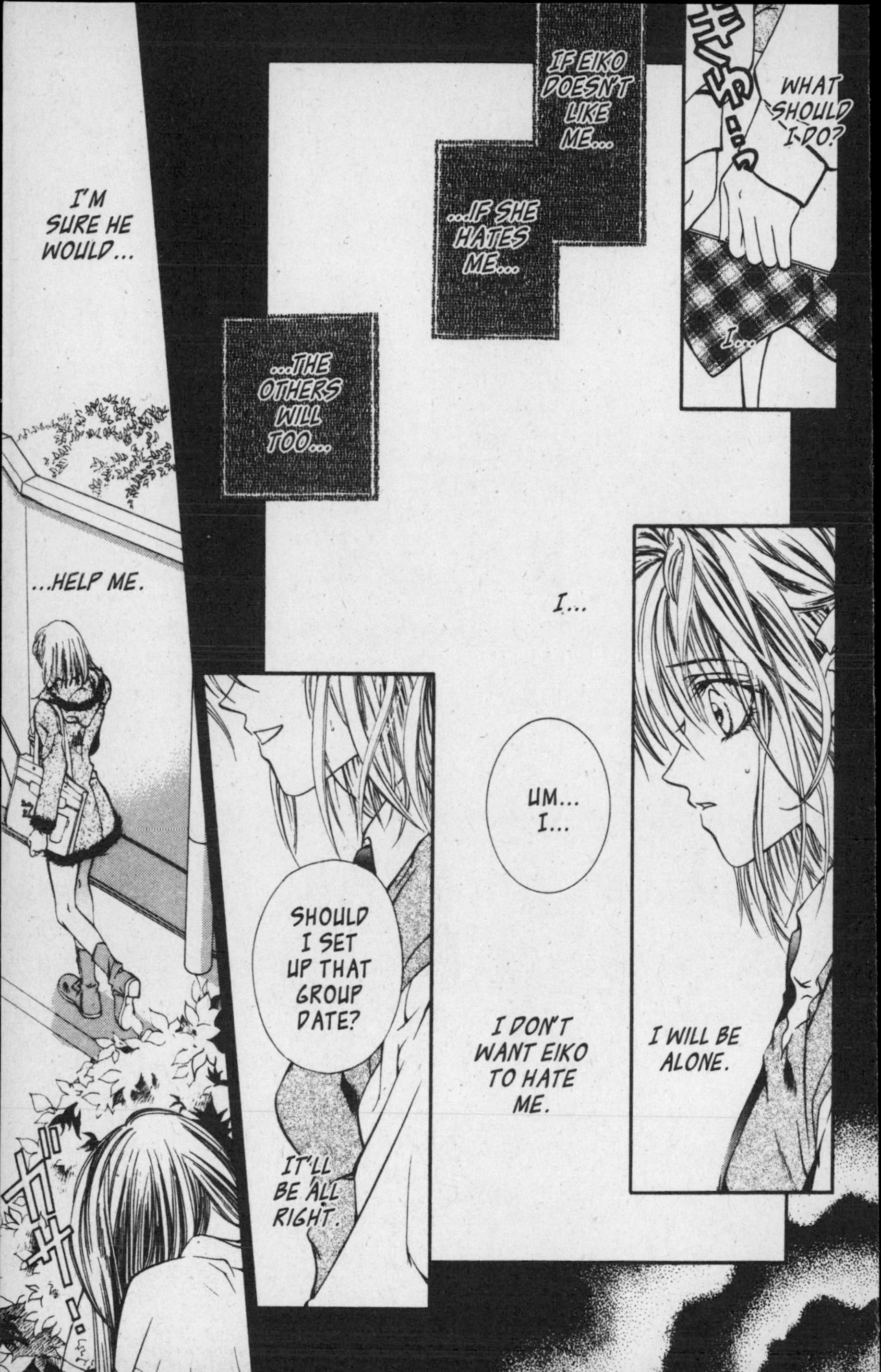
WHAT SHOULD I DO?
I...
IF EIKO DOESN'T LIKE ME...
...IF SHE HATES ME...
...THE OTHERS WILL TOO...
I'M SURE HE WOULD...
...HELP ME.
I...
I WILL BE ALONE.
UM... I...
I DON'T WANT EIKO TO HATE ME.
SHOULD I SET UP THAT GROUP DATE?
IT'LL BE ALL RIGHT.

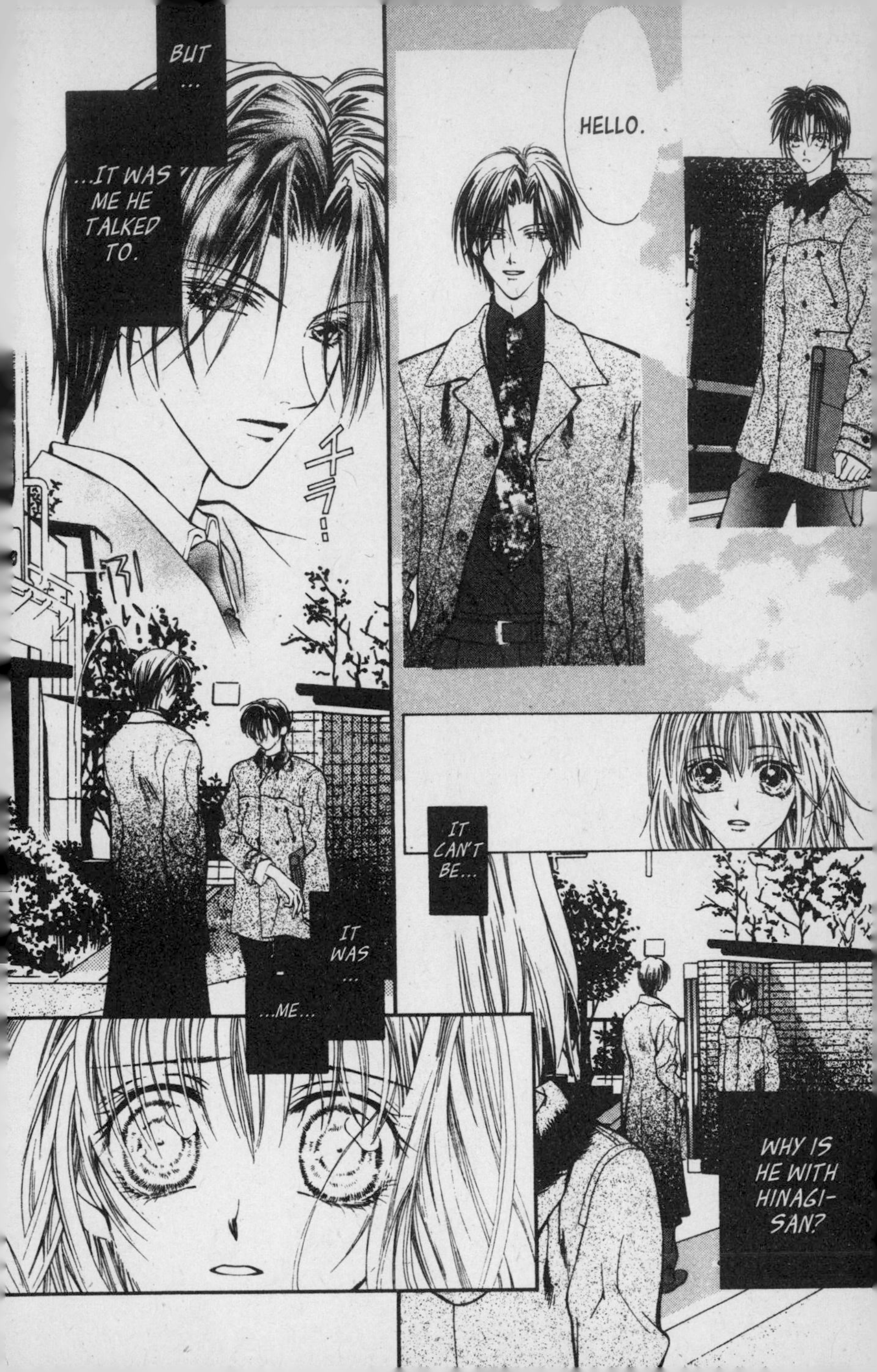
HELLO.
BUT...
...IT WAS ME HE TALKED TO.
チラ!!
IT CAN'T BE...
IT WAS...
...ME...
WHY IS HE WITH HINAGI-SAN?

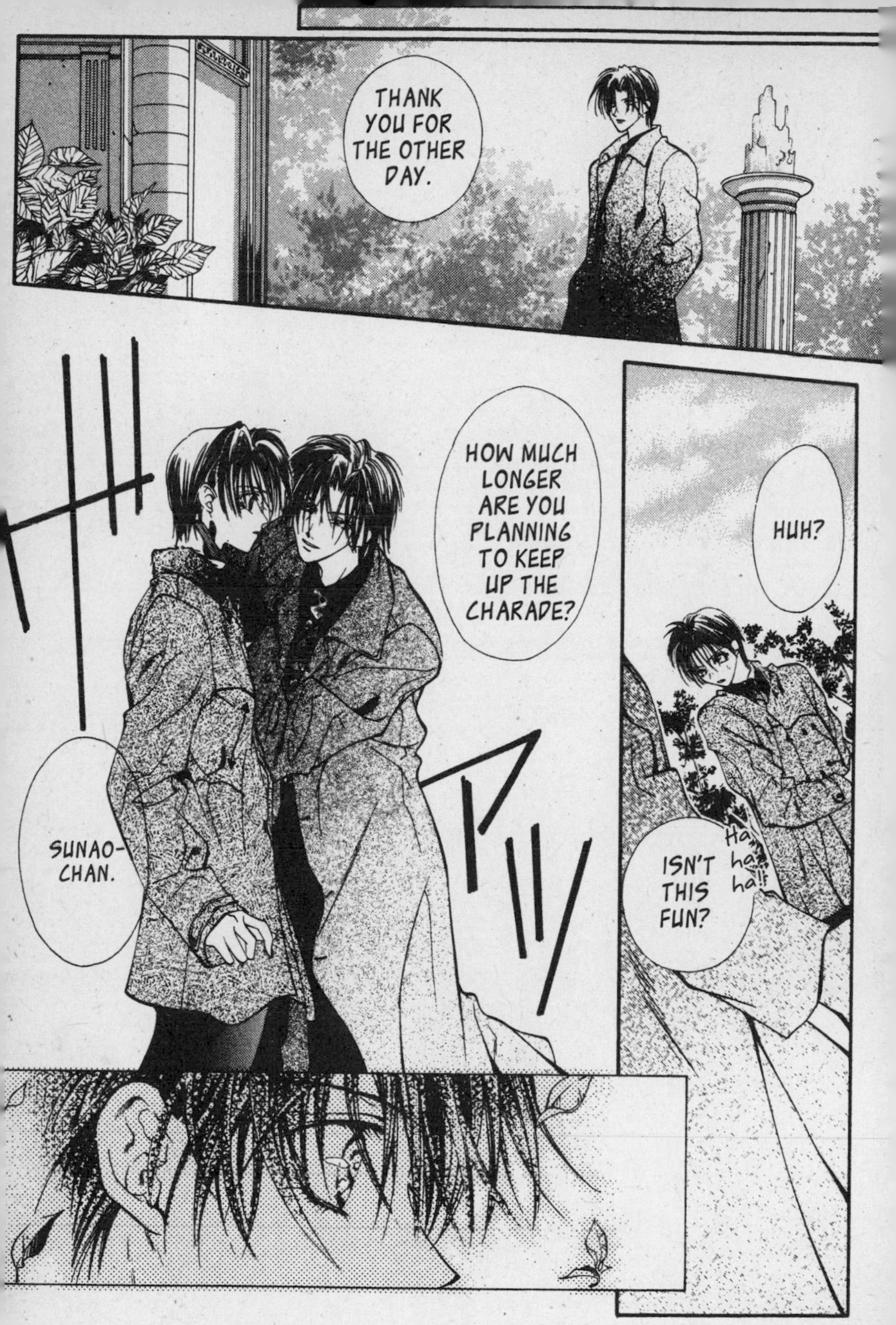
THANK YOU FOR THE OTHER DAY.
HUH?
ISN'T THIS FUN?
Ha ha ha!
HOW MUCH LONGER ARE YOU PLANNING TO KEEP UP THE CHARADE?
SUNAO-CHAN.

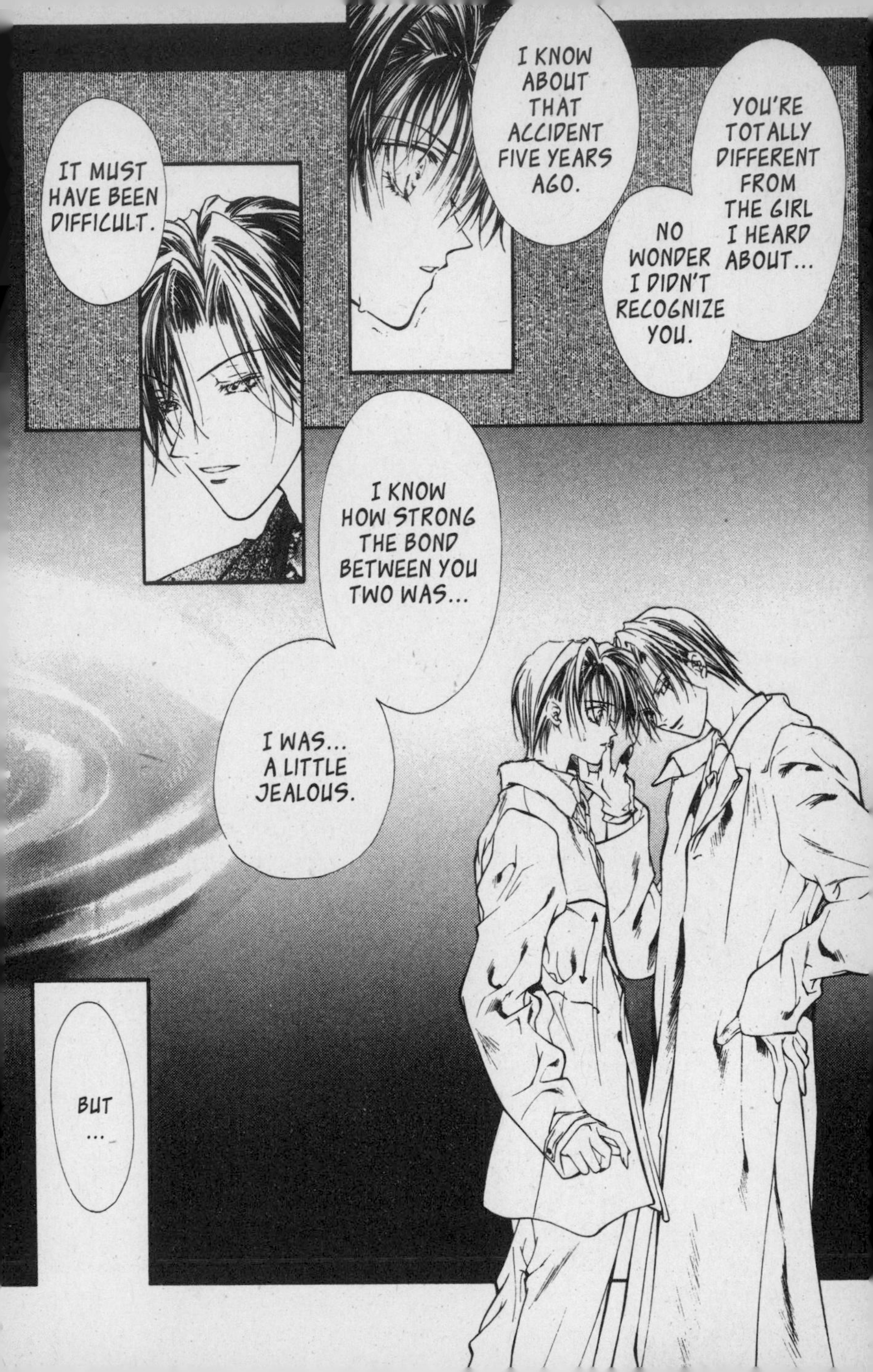
YOU'RE TOTALLY DIFFERENT FROM THE GIRL I HEARD ABOUT...
NO WONDER I DIDN'T RECOGNIZE YOU.
I KNOW ABOUT THAT ACCIDENT FIVE YEARS AGO.
IT MUST HAVE BEEN DIFFICULT.
I KNOW HOW STRONG THE BOND BETWEEN YOU TWO WAS...
I WAS... A LITTLE JEALOUS.
BUT ...

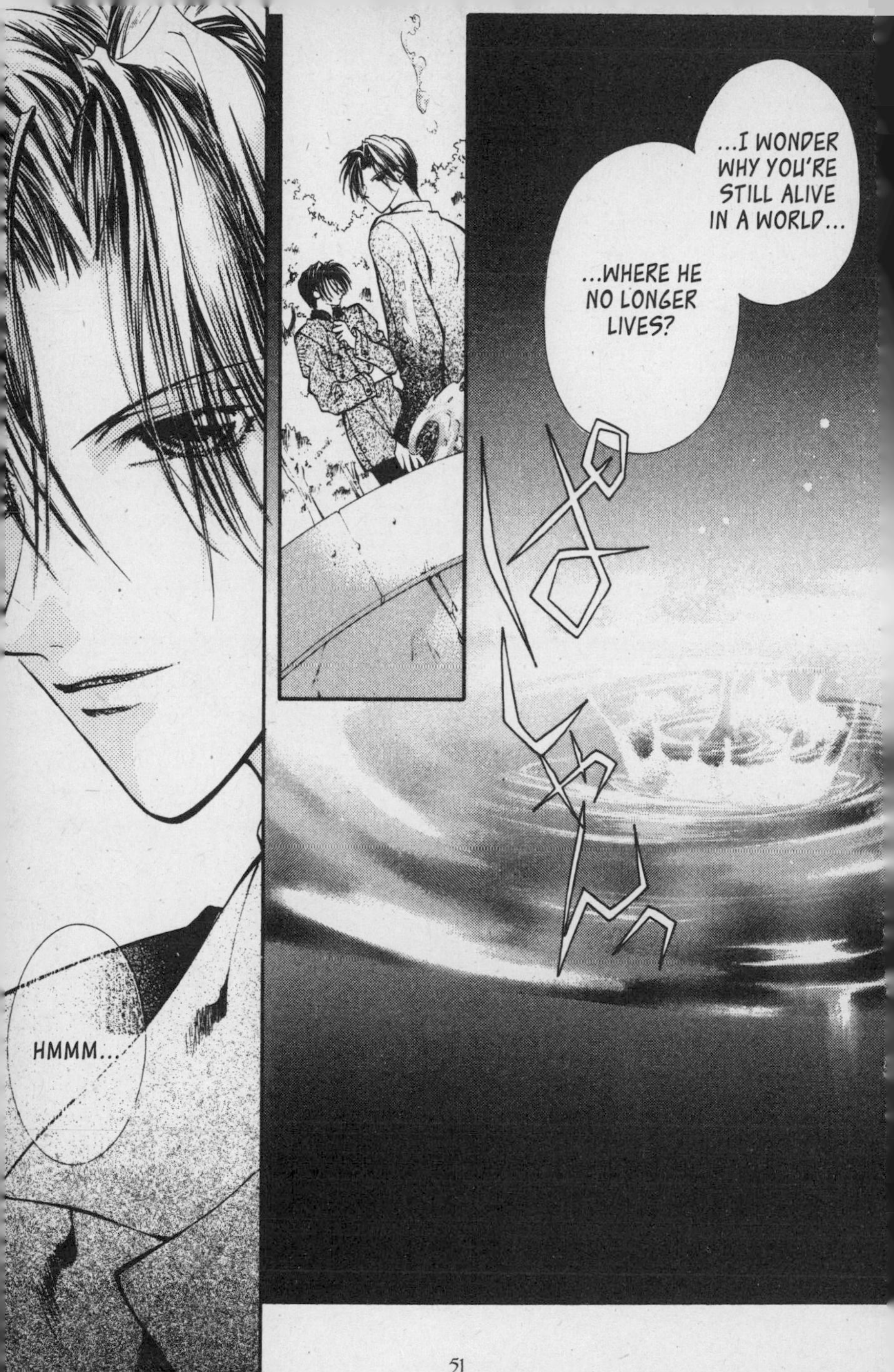
...I WONDER WHY YOU'RE STILL ALIVE IN A WORLD...
...WHERE HE NO LONGER LIVES?
HMMM...

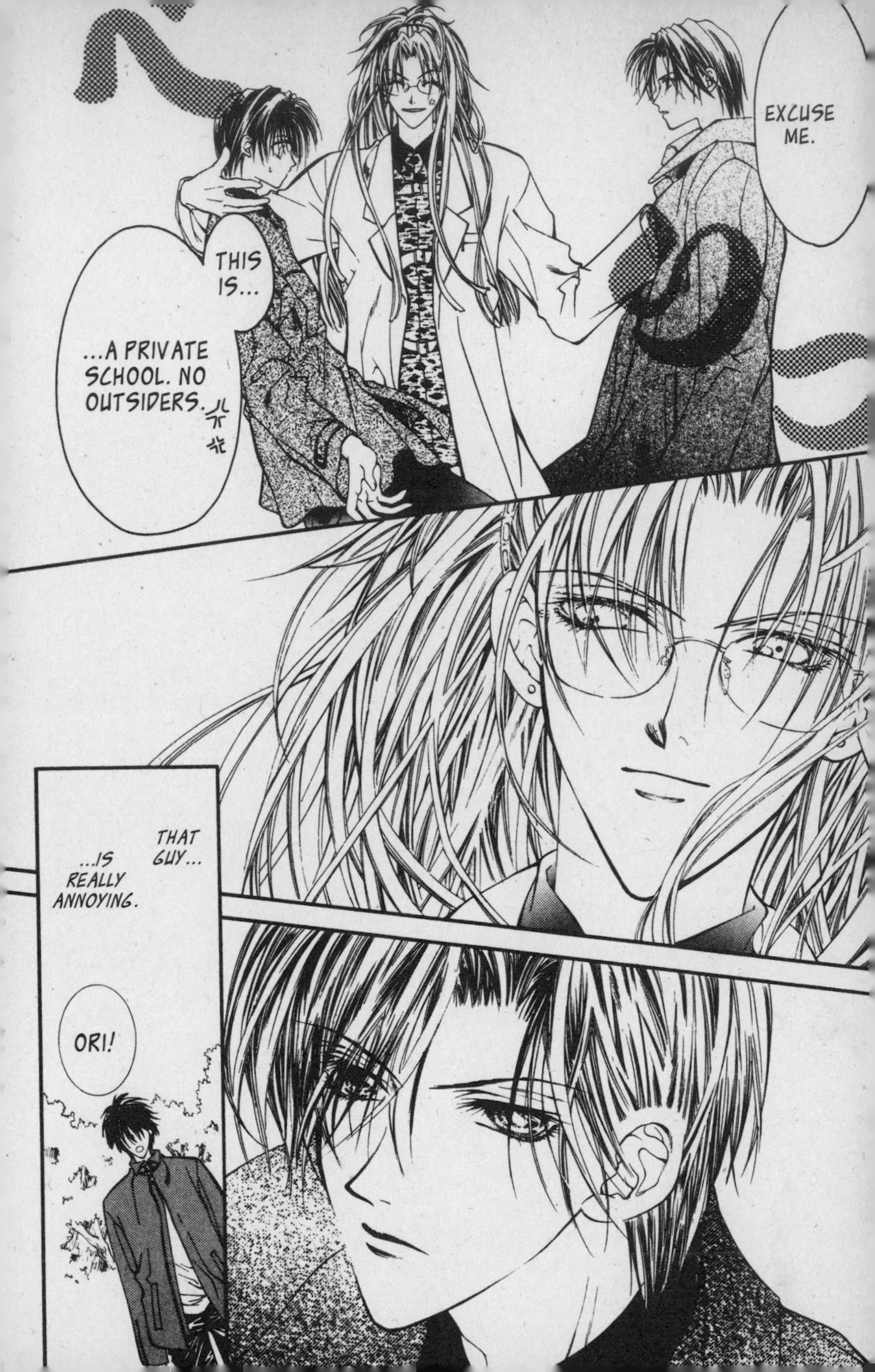
EXCUSE ME.
THIS IS...
...A PRIVATE SCHOOL. NO OUTSIDERS.
THAT GUY...
...IS REALLY ANNOYING.
ORI!

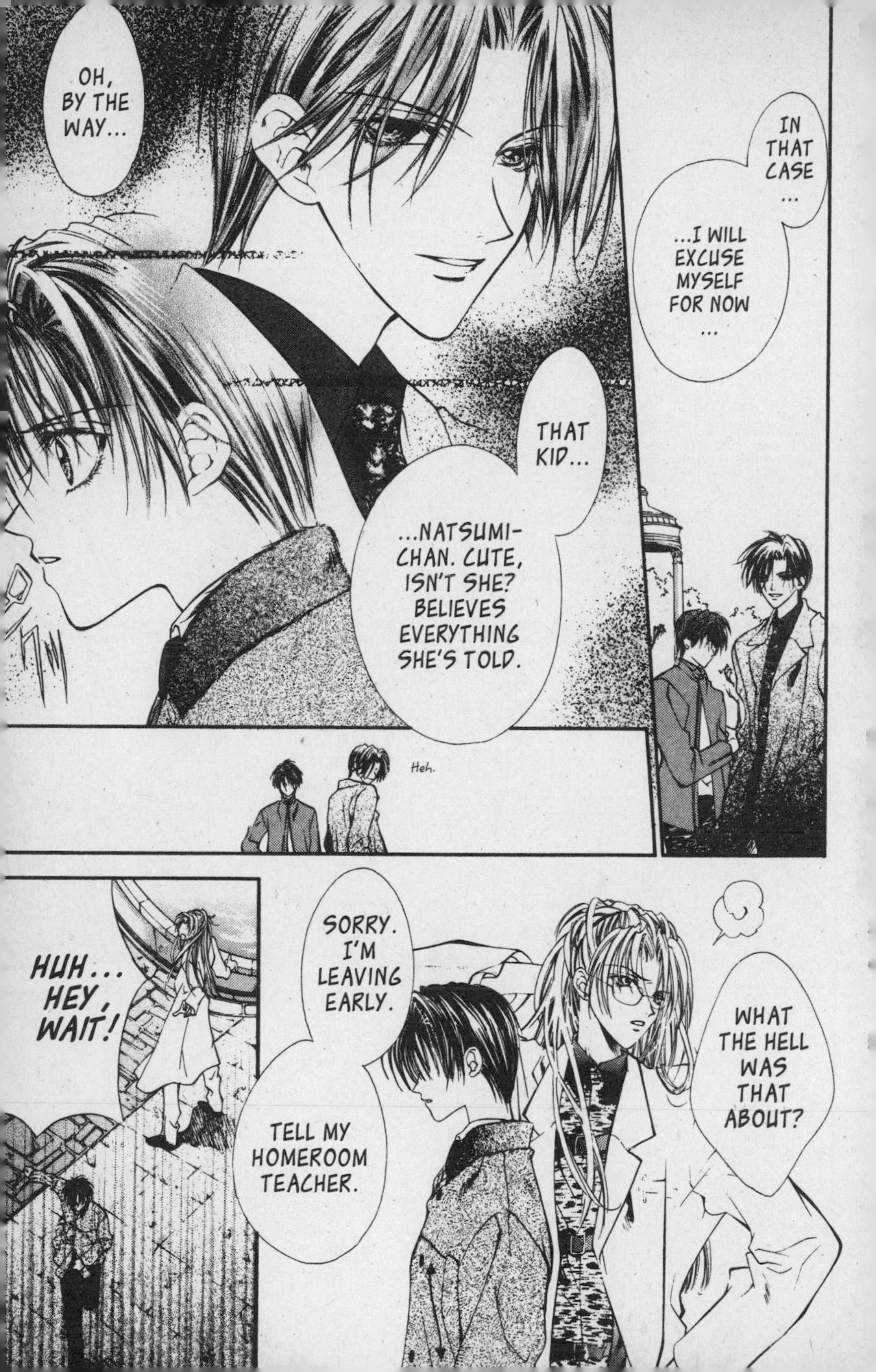

IN THAT CASE ...
...I WILL EXCUSE MYSELF FOR NOW ...
OH, BY THE WAY...
THAT KID...
...NATSUMI-CHAN. CUTE, ISN'T SHE? BELIEVES EVERYTHING SHE'S TOLD.
Heh.
WHAT THE HELL WAS THAT ABOUT?
SORRY. I'M LEAVING EARLY.
TELL MY HOMEROOM TEACHER.
HUH... HEY, WAIT!

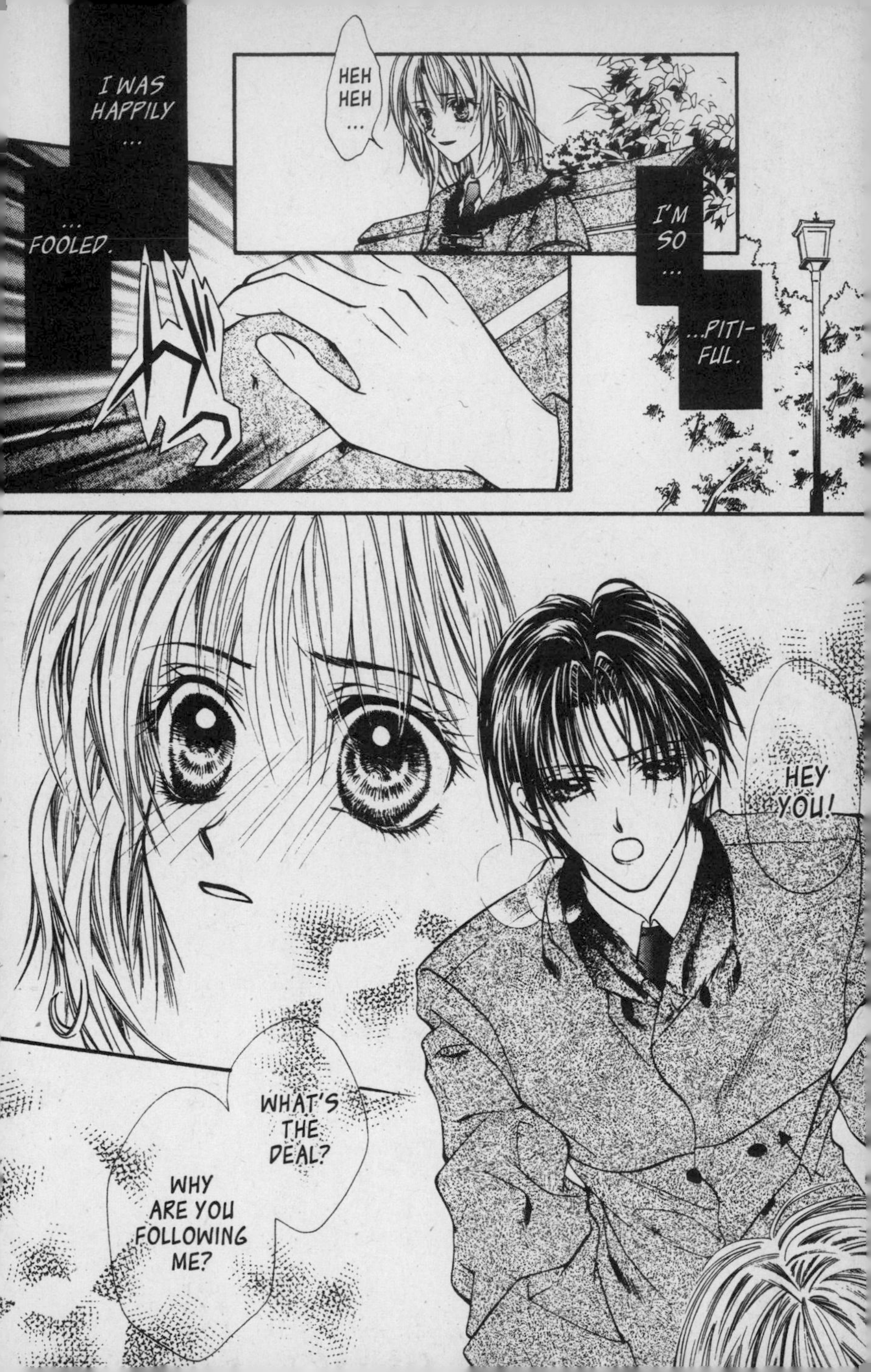
HEH HEH ...
I WAS HAPPILY ...
... FOOLED.
I'M SO ...
...PITI-FUL.
HEY YOU!
WHAT'S THE DEAL?
WHY ARE YOU FOLLOWING ME?

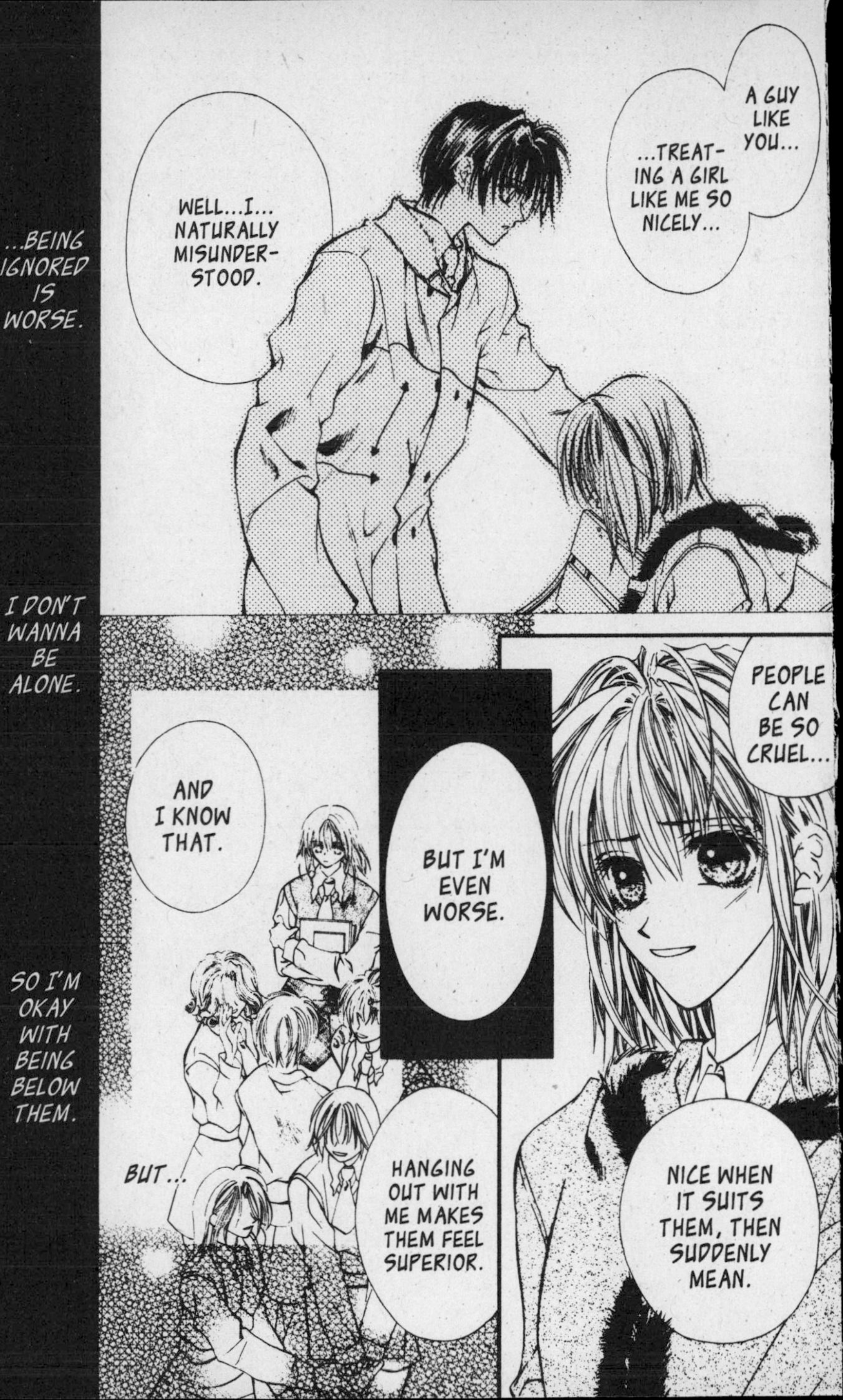
A GUY LIKE YOU...
...TREATING A GIRL LIKE ME SO NICELY...
WELL...I... NATURALLY MISUNDERSTOOD.
...BEING IGNORED IS WORSE.
PEOPLE CAN BE SO CRUEL...
NICE WHEN IT SUITS THEM, THEN SUDDENLY MEAN.
BUT I'M EVEN WORSE.
HANGING OUT WITH ME MAKES THEM FEEL SUPERIOR.
AND I KNOW THAT.
BUT...
I DON'T WANNA BE ALONE.
SO I'M OKAY WITH BEING BELOW THEM.

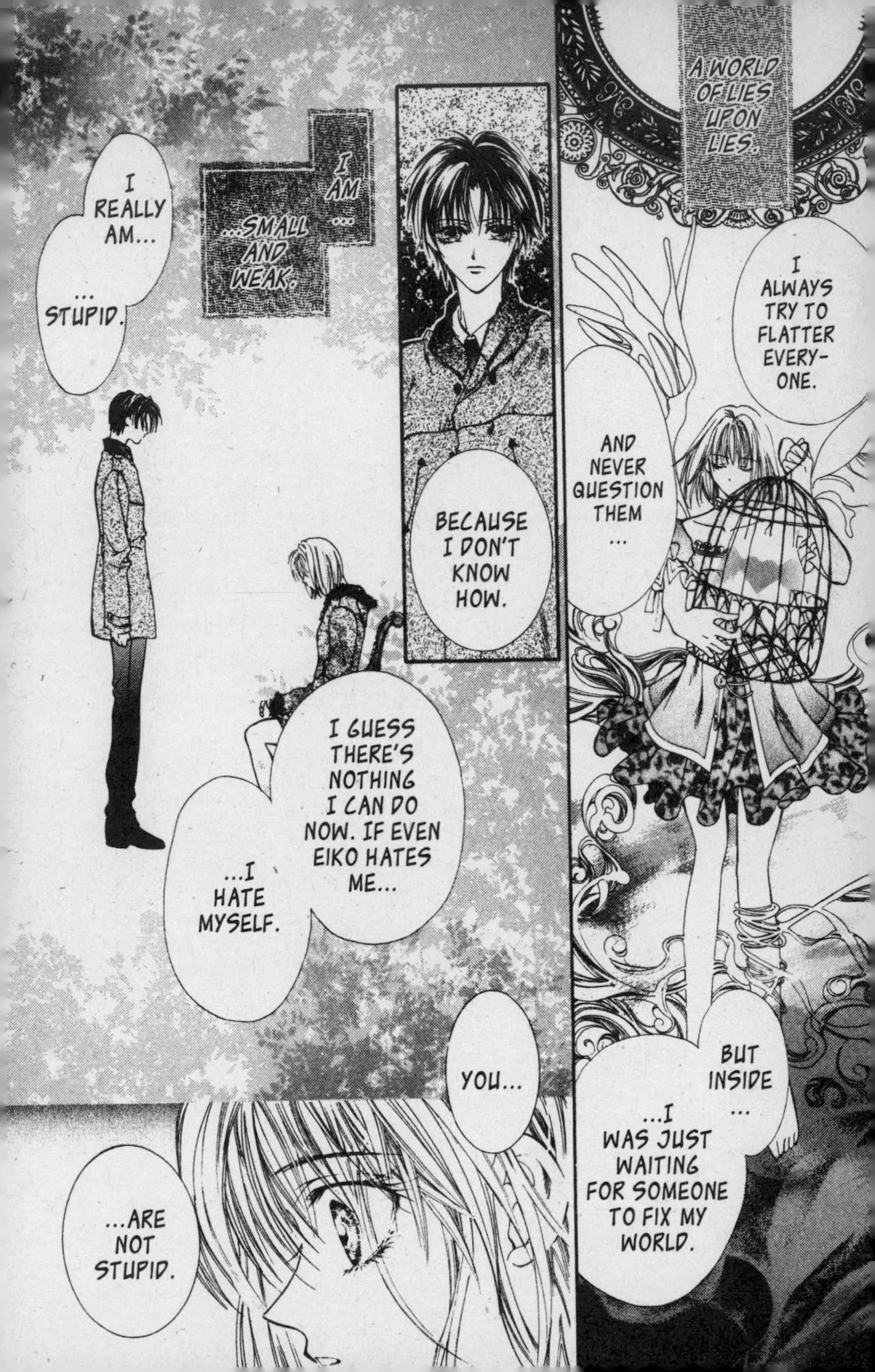
A WORLD OF LIES UPON LIES.
I ALWAYS TRY TO FLATTER EVERY-ONE.
AND NEVER QUESTION THEM...
BUT INSIDE...
...I WAS JUST WAITING FOR SOMEONE TO FIX MY WORLD.
BECAUSE I DON'T KNOW HOW.
I AM...
...SMALL AND WEAK.
I REALLY AM... ...STUPID.
I GUESS THERE'S NOTHING I CAN DO NOW. IF EVEN EIKO HATES ME...
...I HATE MYSELF.
YOU...
...ARE NOT STUPID.

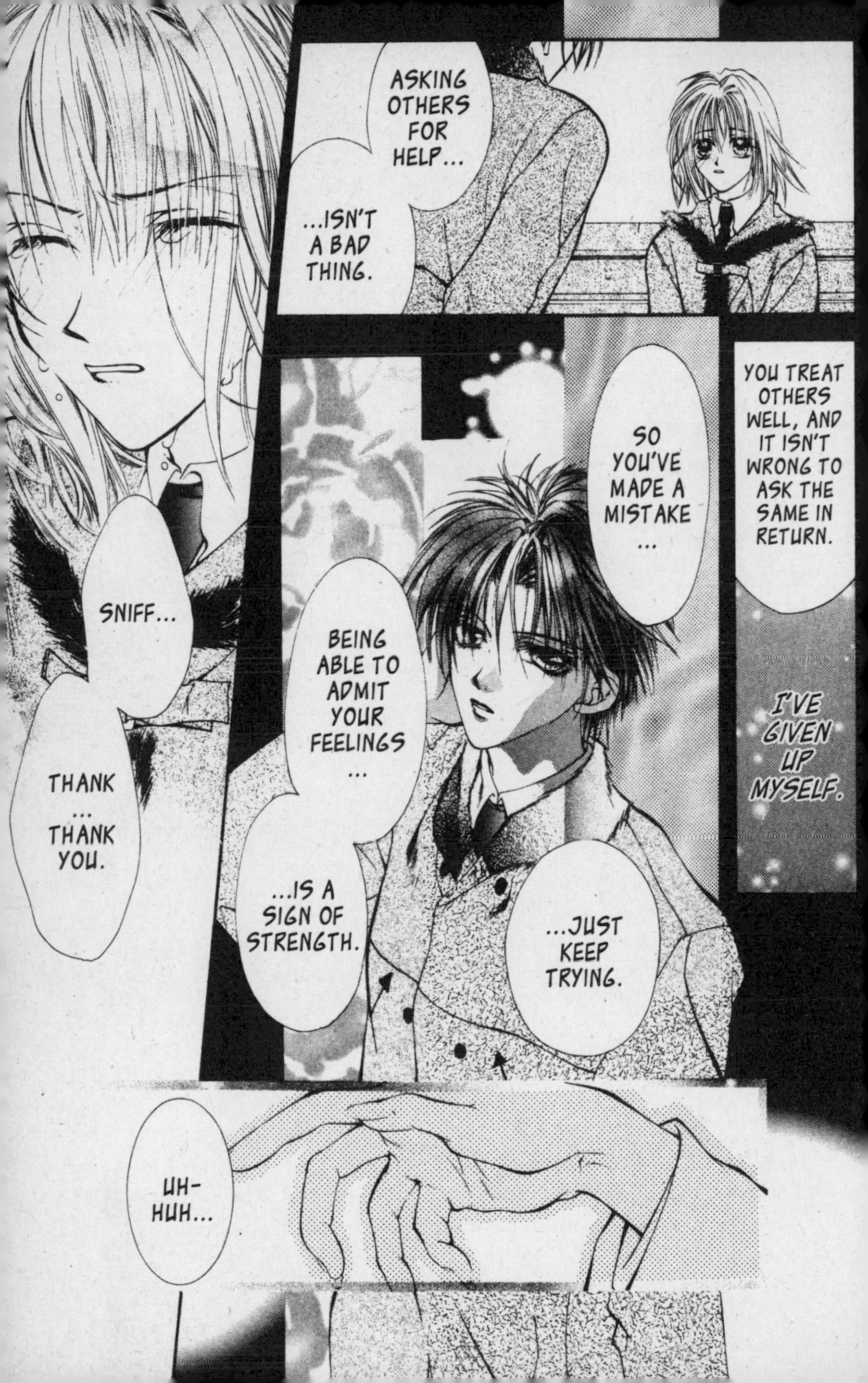
ASKING OTHERS FOR HELP...
...ISN'T A BAD THING.
YOU TREAT OTHERS WELL, AND IT ISN'T WRONG TO ASK THE SAME IN RETURN.
I'VE GIVEN UP MYSELF.
SO YOU'VE MADE A MISTAKE ...
...JUST KEEP TRYING.
BEING ABLE TO ADMIT YOUR FEELINGS ...
...IS A SIGN OF STRENGTH.
SNIFF...
THANK ... THANK YOU.
UH-HUH...

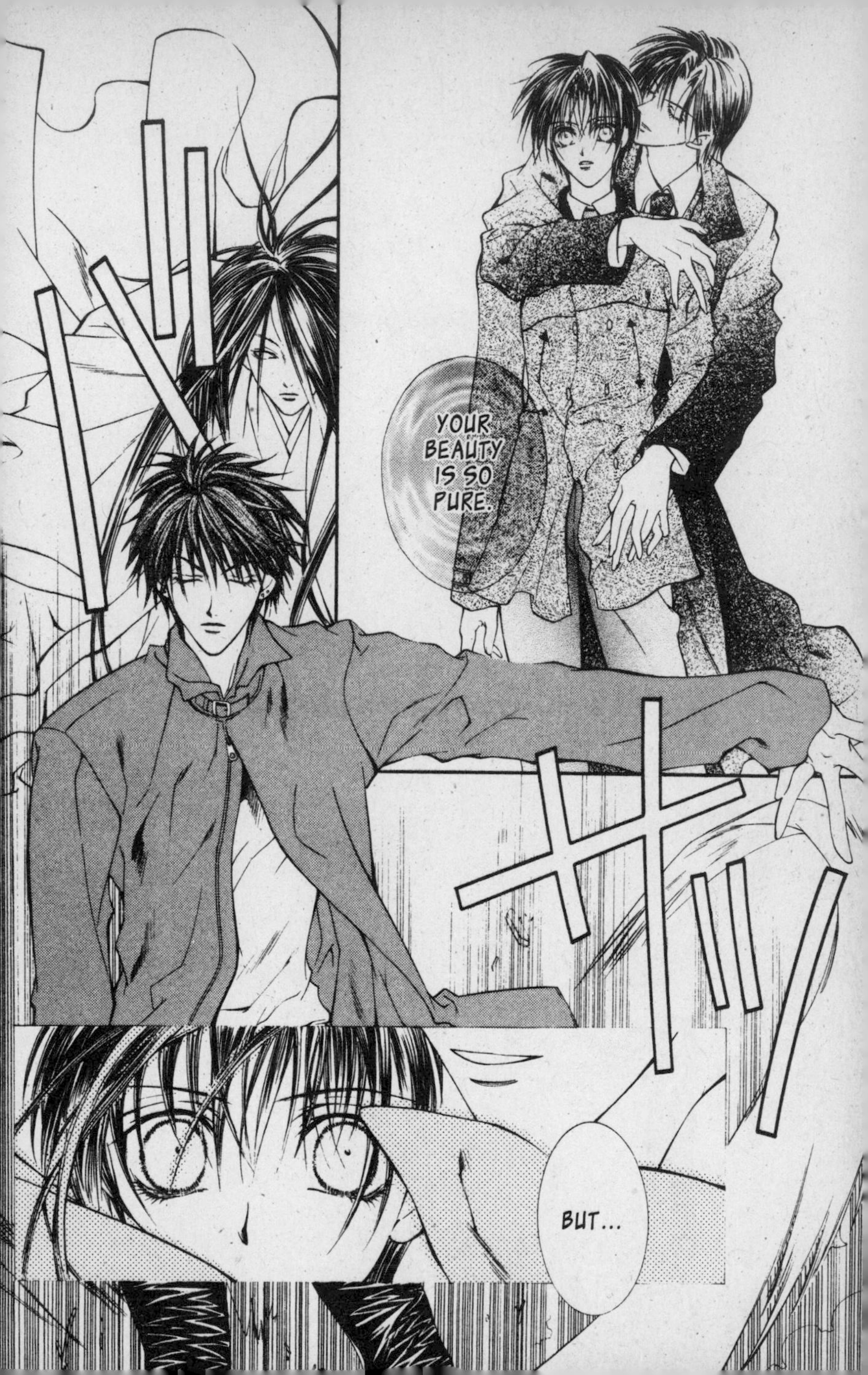
YOUR BEAUTY IS SO PURE.
BUT...

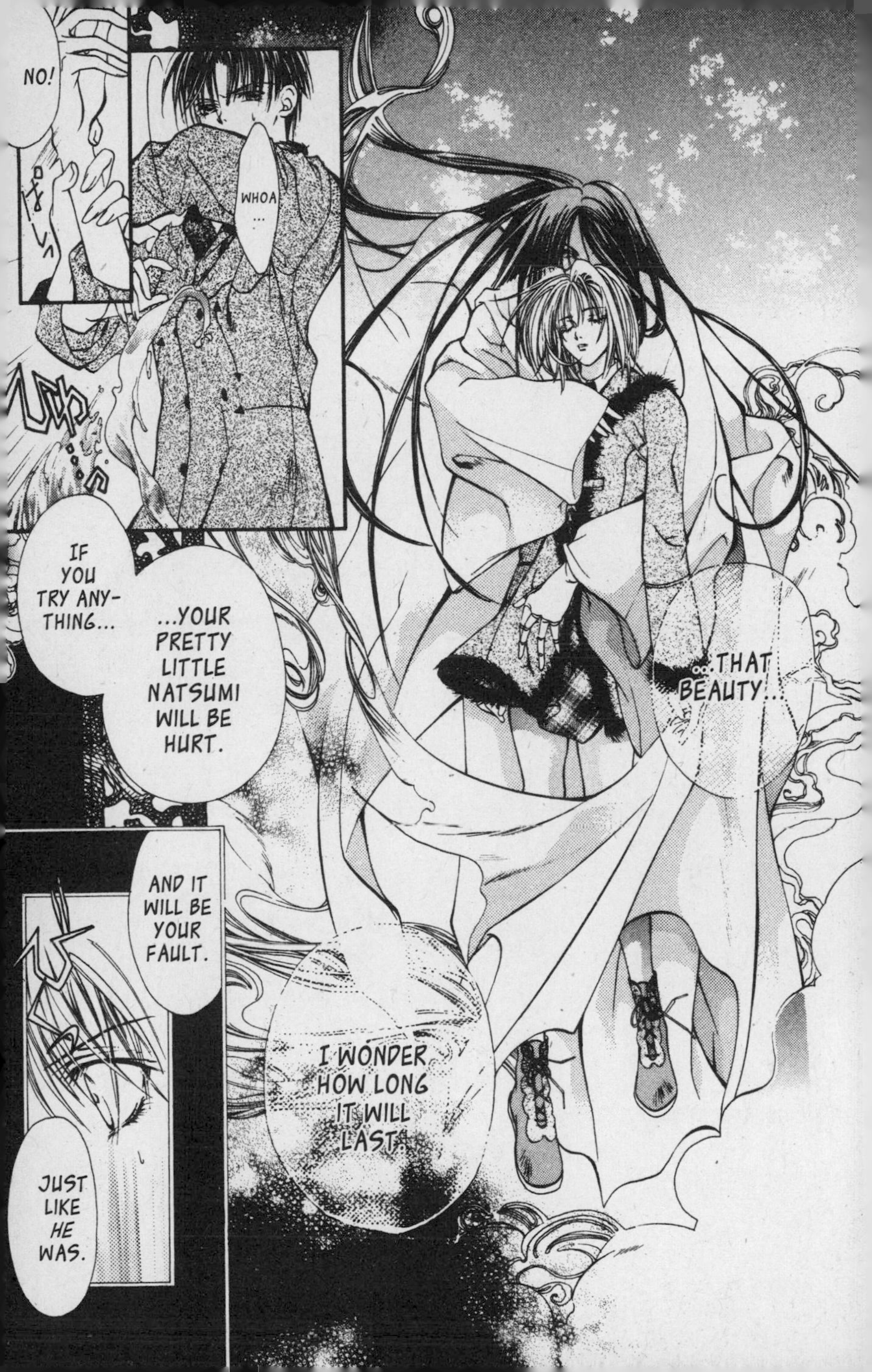
...THAT BEAUTY...
I WONDER HOW LONG IT WILL LAST.
WHOA...
NO!
IF YOU TRY ANY-THING...
...YOUR PRETTY LITTLE NATSUMI WILL BE HURT.
AND IT WILL BE YOUR FAULT.
JUST LIKE HE WAS.

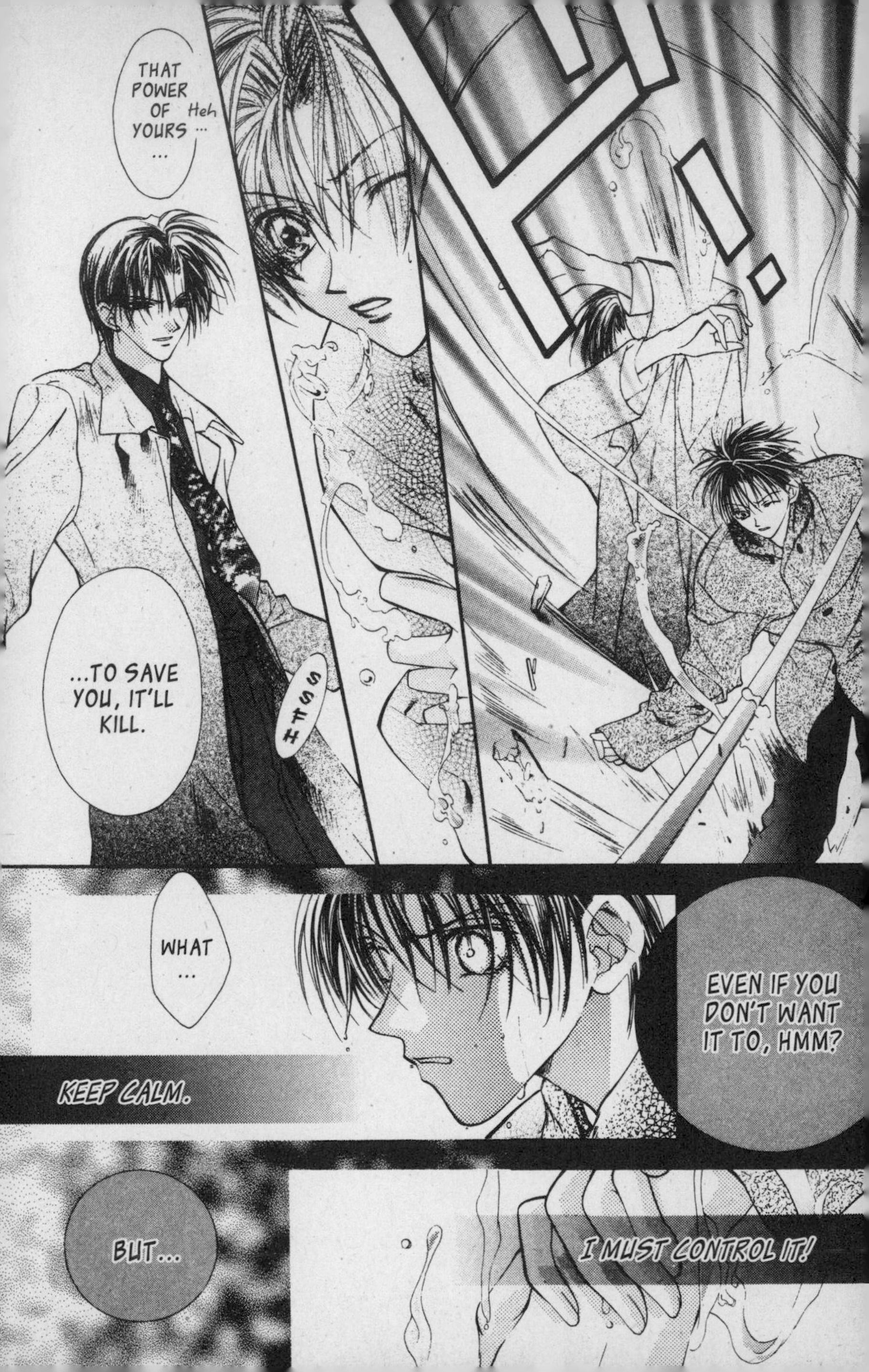
SSSH
THAT POWER OF YOURS ...
Heh ...
...TO SAVE YOU, IT'LL KILL.
EVEN IF YOU DON'T WANT IT TO, HMM?
WHAT ...
KEEP CALM.
I MUST CONTROL IT!
BUT...

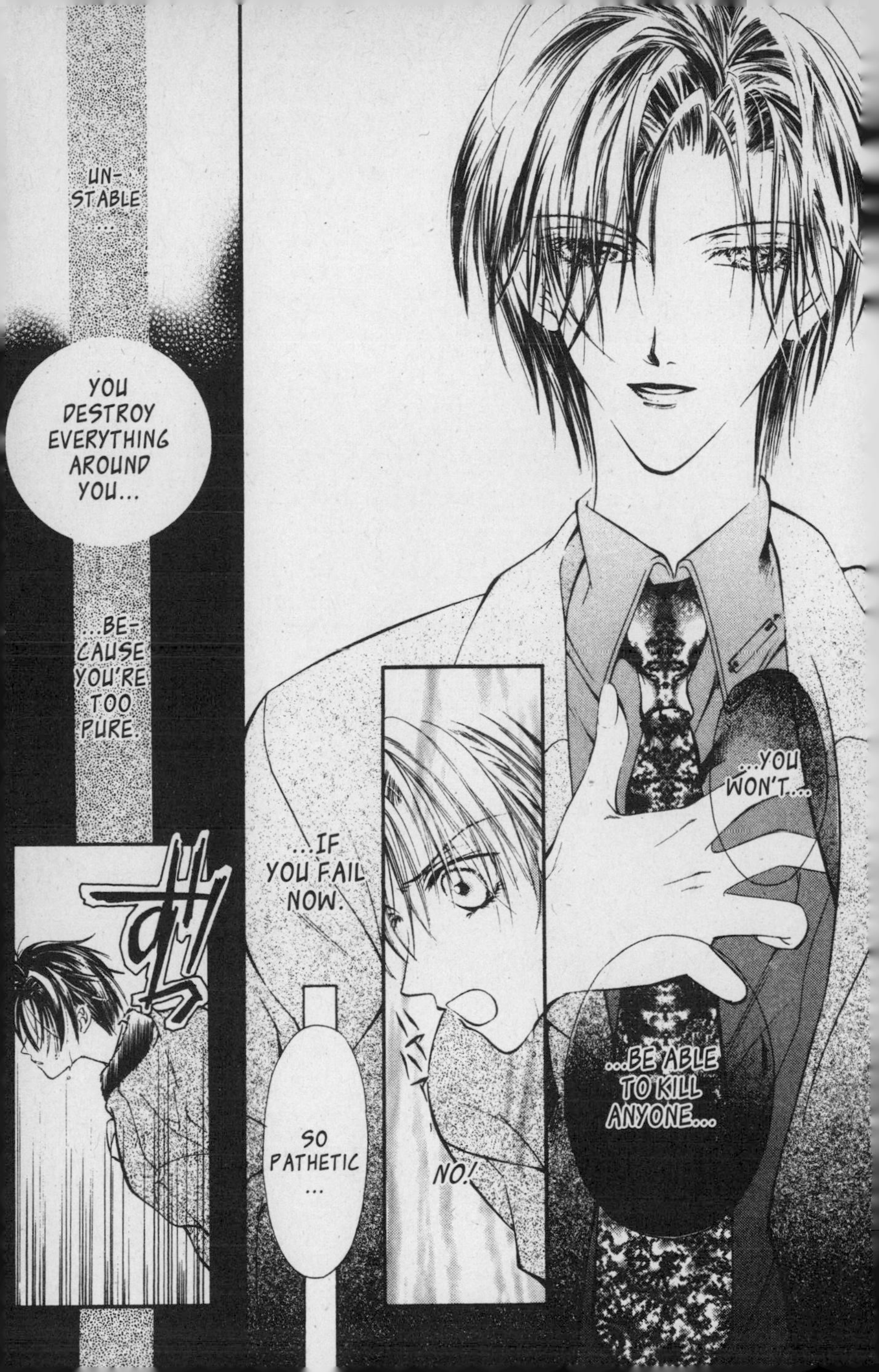
...YOU WON'T...
...BE ABLE TO KILL ANYONE...
...IF YOU FAIL NOW.
NO!
SO PATHETIC ...
UN-STABLE ...
YOU DESTROY EVERYTHING AROUND YOU...
...BE-CAUSE YOU'RE TOO PURE.

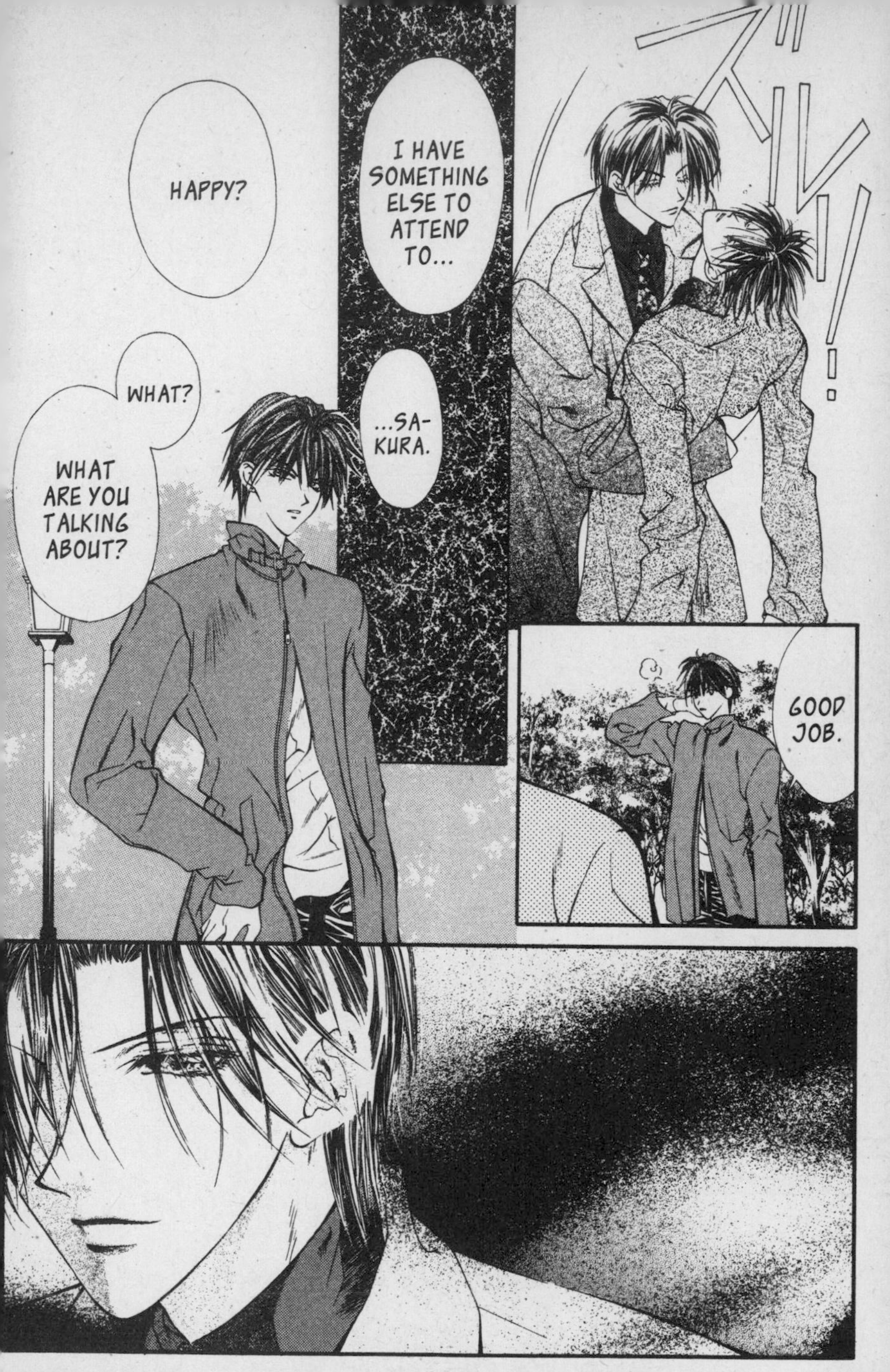
GOOD JOB.
I HAVE SOMETHING ELSE TO ATTEND TO...
...SA-KURA.
HAPPY?
WHAT?
WHAT ARE YOU TALKING ABOUT?

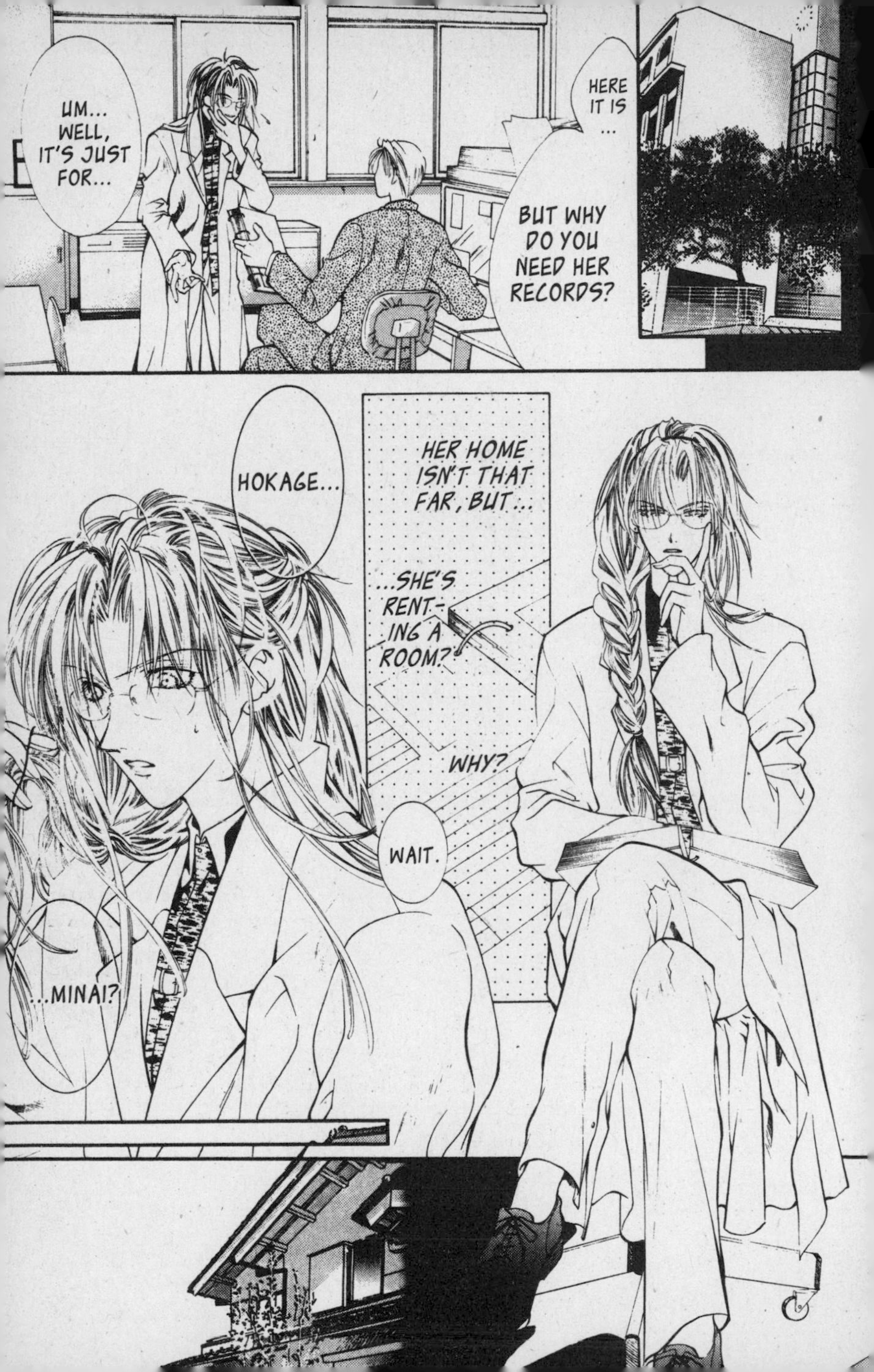
HERE IT IS ...
BUT WHY DO YOU NEED HER RECORDS?
UM... WELL, IT'S JUST FOR...
HER HOME ISN'T THAT FAR, BUT...
...SHE'S RENT-ING A ROOM?
WHY?
WAIT.
HOKAGE...
...MINAI?

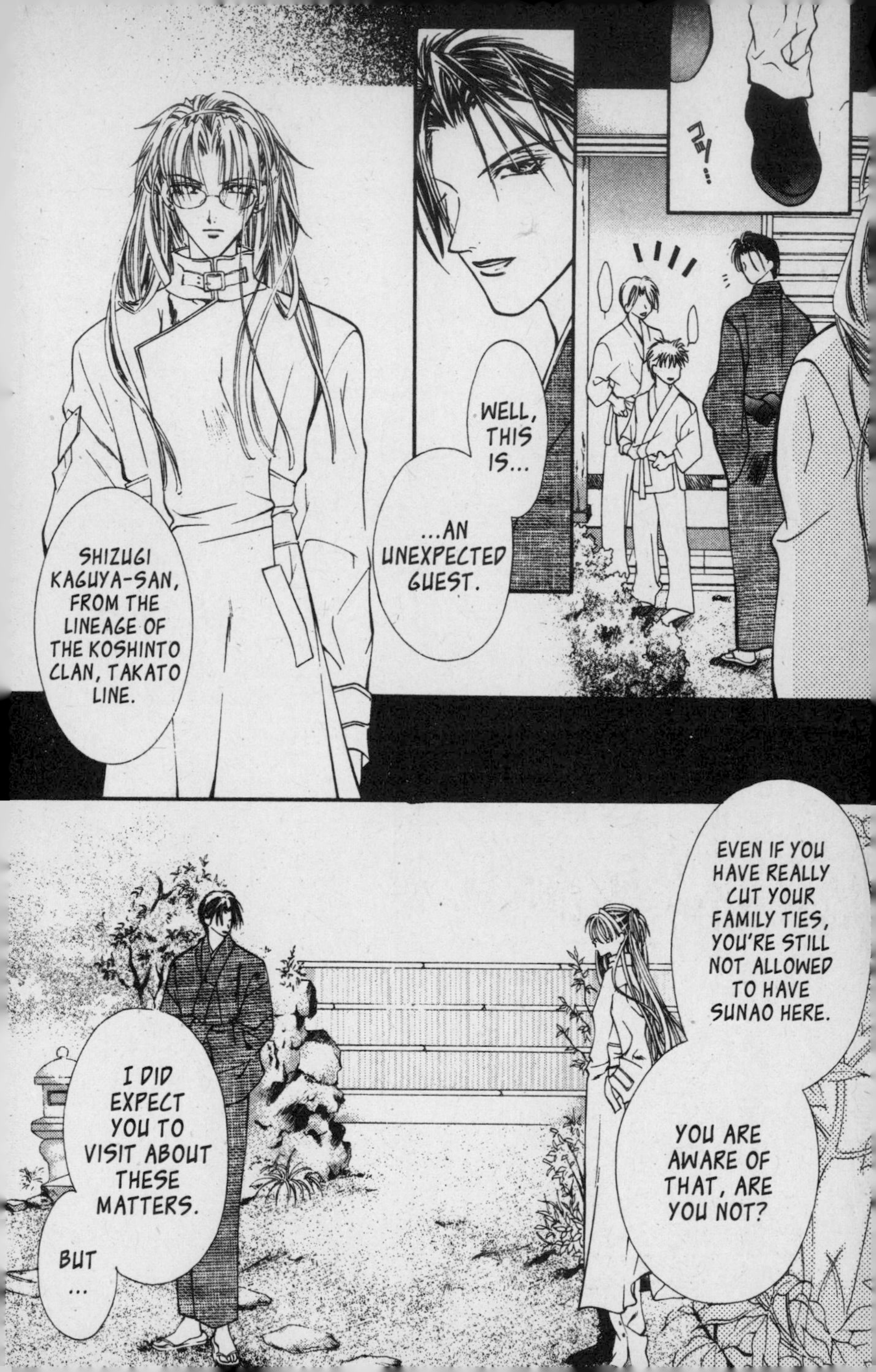
コツ…
WELL, THIS IS...
...AN UNEXPECTED GUEST.
SHIZUGI KAGUYA-SAN, FROM THE LINEAGE OF THE KOSHINTO CLAN, TAKATO LINE.
EVEN IF YOU HAVE REALLY CUT YOUR FAMILY TIES, YOU'RE STILL NOT ALLOWED TO HAVE SUNAO HERE.
YOU ARE AWARE OF THAT, ARE YOU NOT?
I DID EXPECT YOU TO VISIT ABOUT THESE MATTERS.
BUT ...

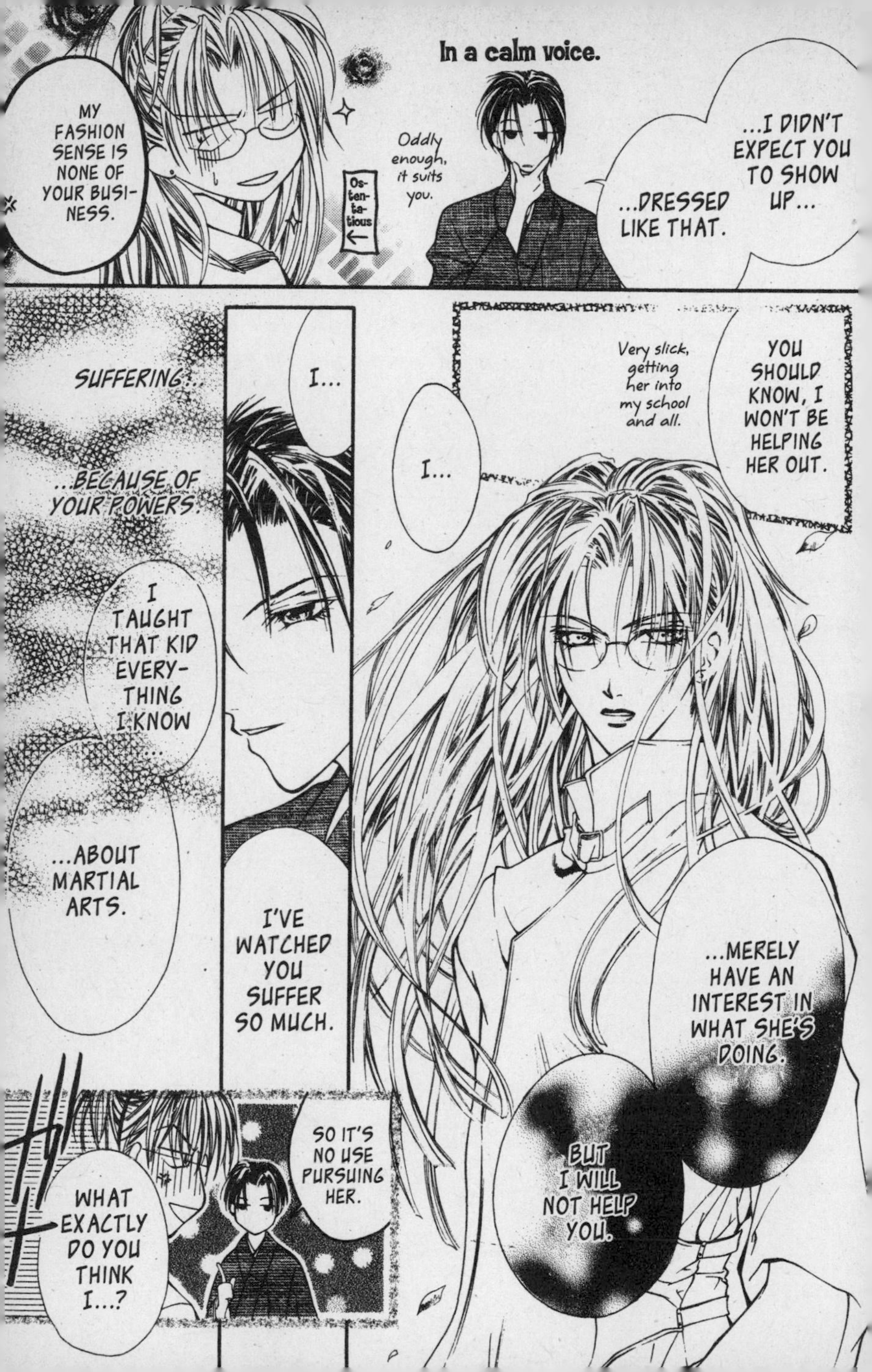
In a calm voice.
...I DIDN'T EXPECT YOU TO SHOW UP...
...DRESSED LIKE THAT.
Oddly enough, it suits you.
Os-ten-ta-tious ←
MY FASHION SENSE IS NONE OF YOUR BUSI-NESS.
YOU SHOULD KNOW, I WON'T BE HELPING HER OUT.
Very slick, getting her into my school and all.
I...
I...
...MERELY HAVE AN INTEREST IN WHAT SHE'S DOING.
BUT I WILL NOT HELP YOU.
I'VE WATCHED YOU SUFFER SO MUCH.
SUFFERING...
...BECAUSE OF YOUR POWERS.
I TAUGHT THAT KID EVERY-THING I KNOW...
...ABOUT MARTIAL ARTS.
SO IT'S NO USE PURSUING HER.
WHAT EXACTLY DO YOU THINK I...?

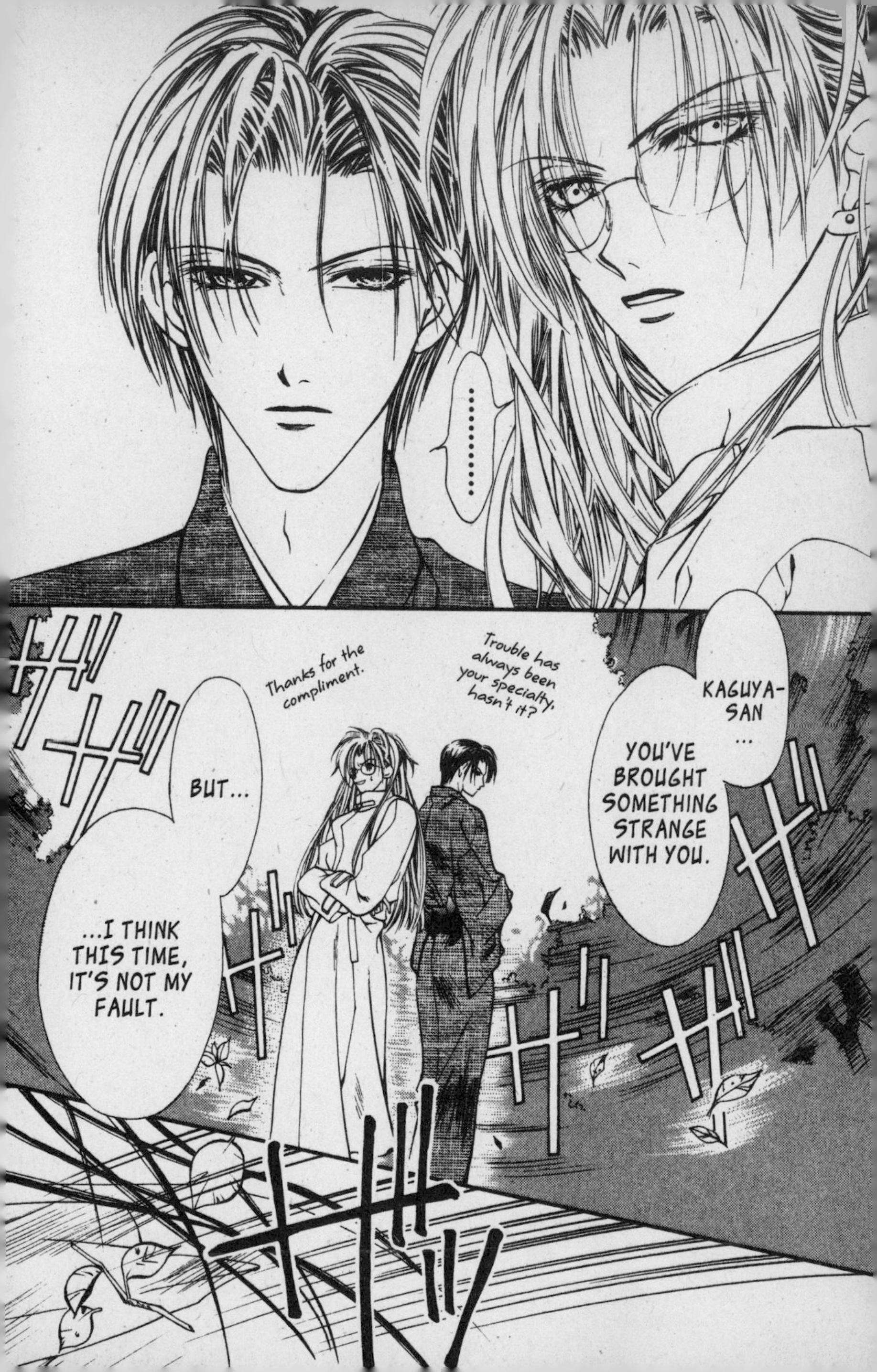
......
KAGUYA-SAN ...
YOU'VE BROUGHT SOMETHING STRANGE WITH YOU.
Trouble has always been your specialty, hasn't it?
Thanks for the compliment.
BUT...
...I THINK THIS TIME, IT'S NOT MY FAULT.

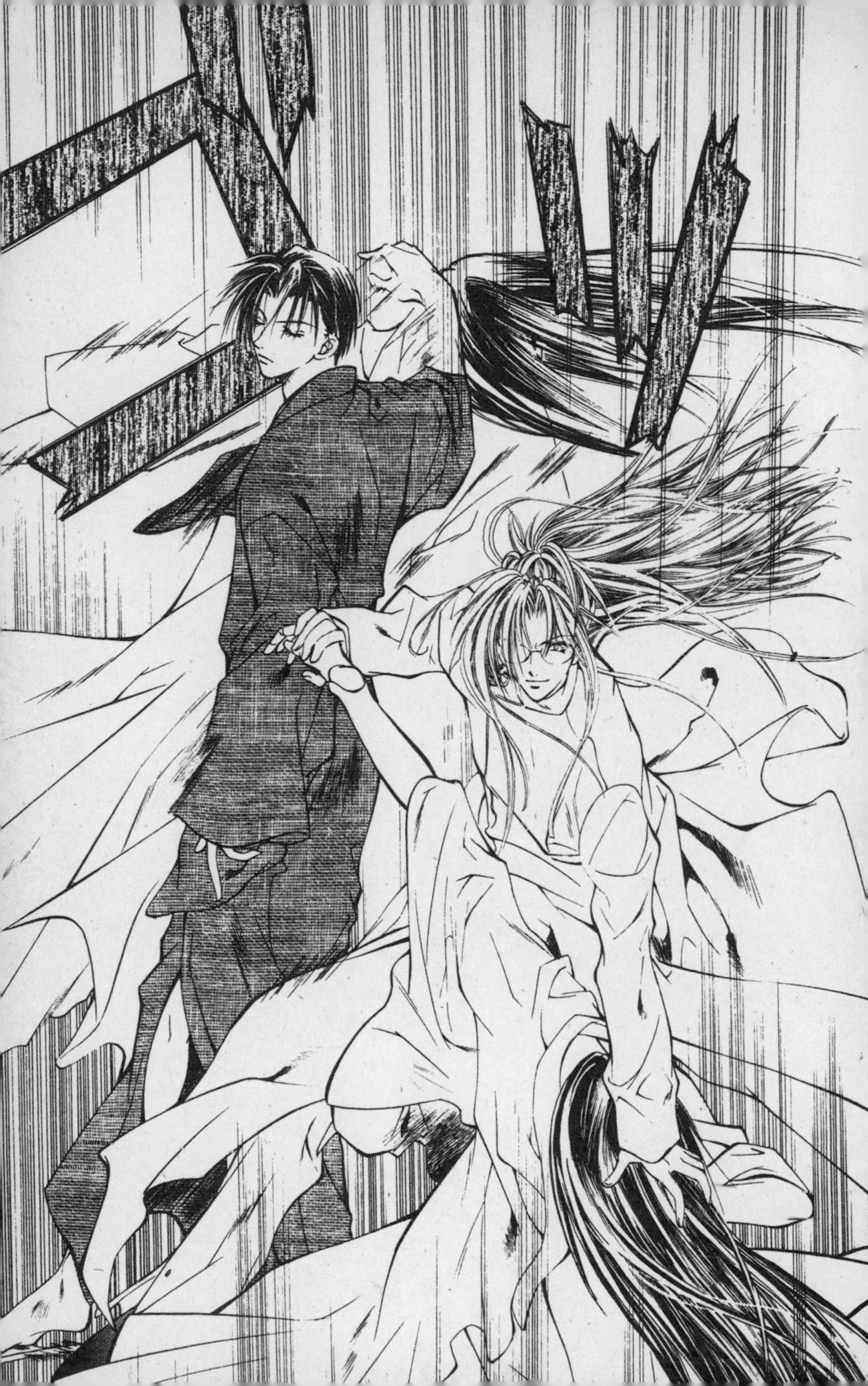

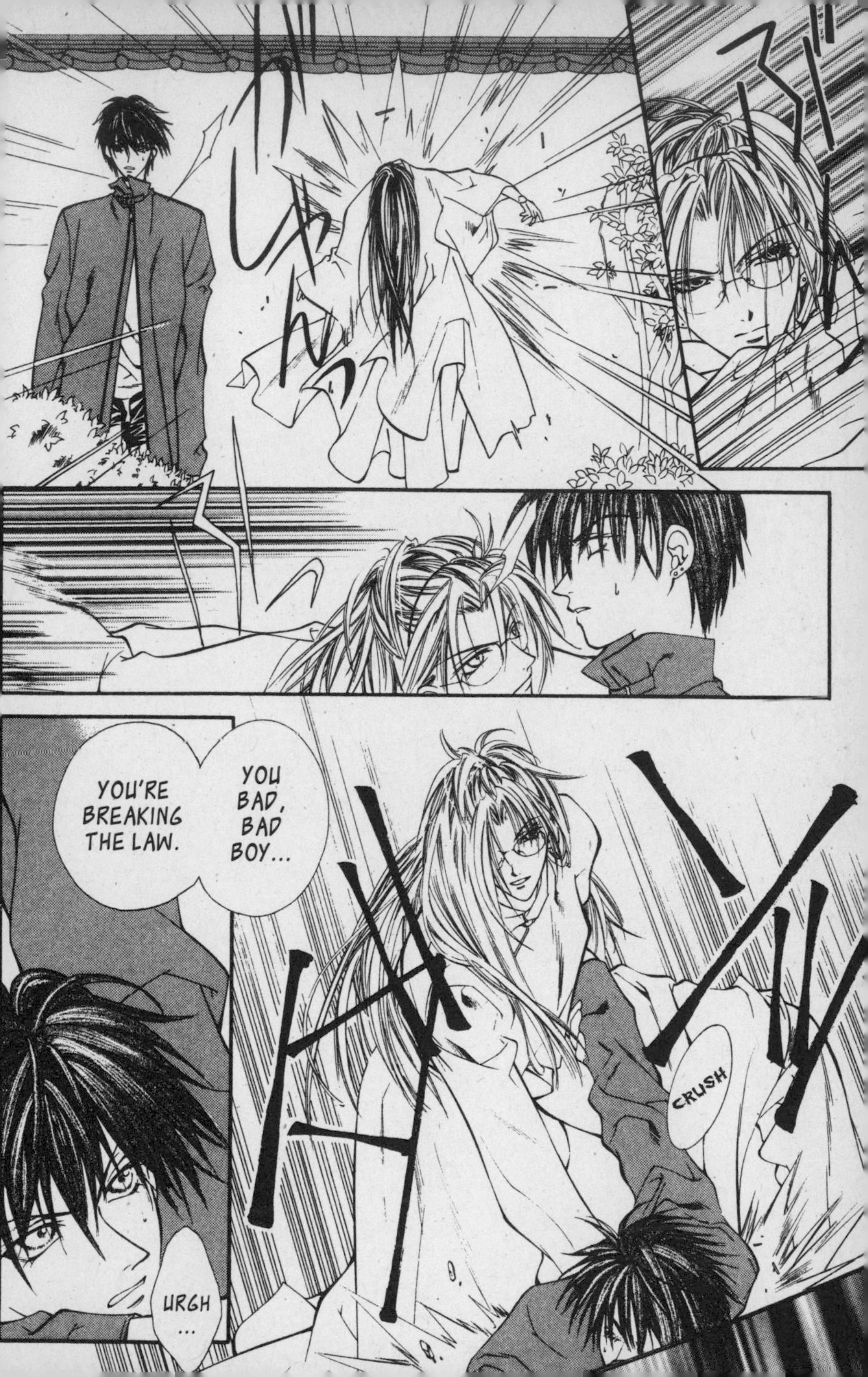
YOU BAD, BAD BOY...
YOU'RE BREAKING THE LAW.
CRUSH
URGH ...

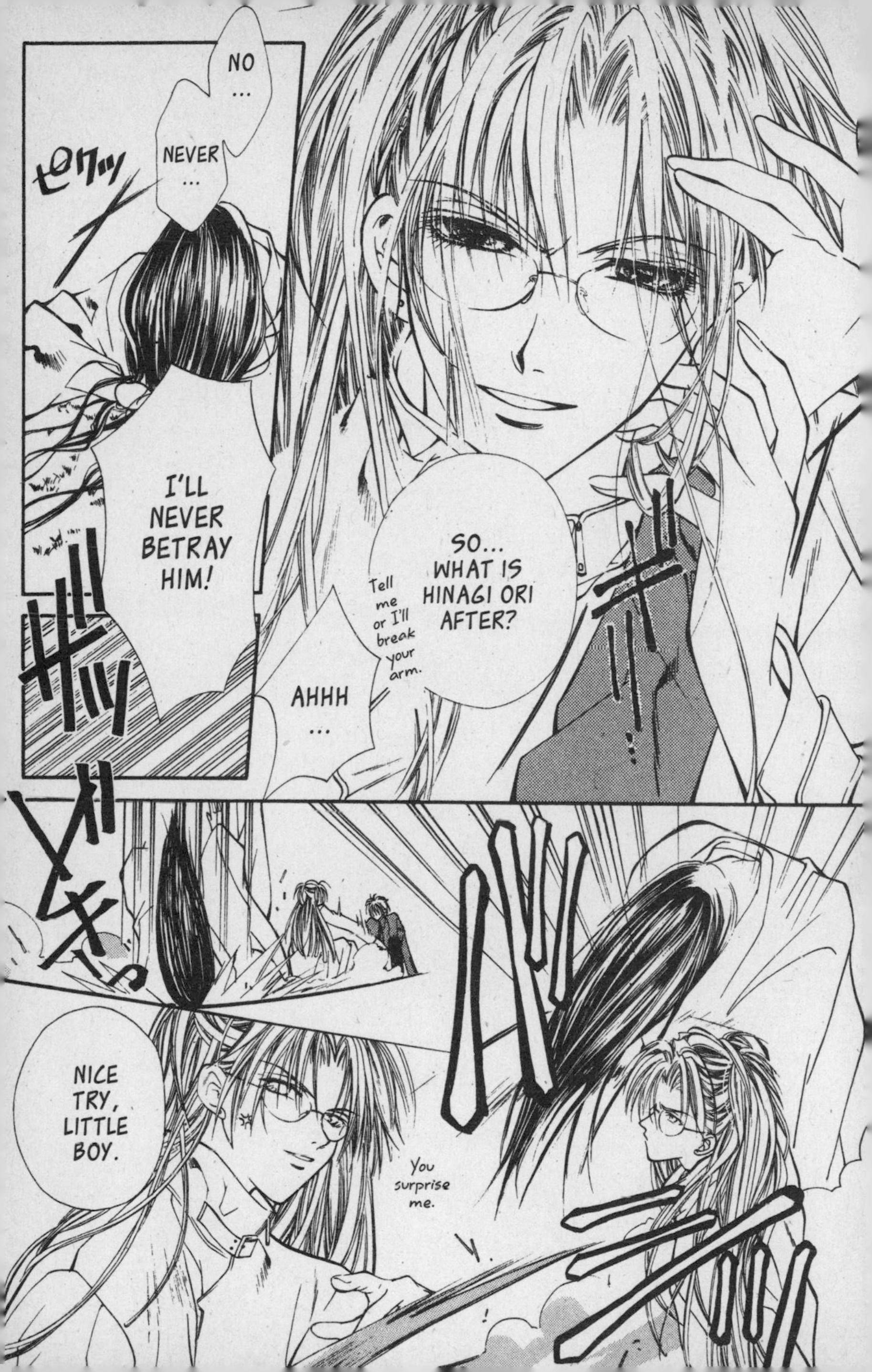
SO... WHAT IS HINAGI ORI AFTER?
Tell me or I'll break your arm.
AHHH ...
NO ...
NEVER ...
I'LL NEVER BETRAY HIM!
NICE TRY, LITTLE BOY.
You surprise me.

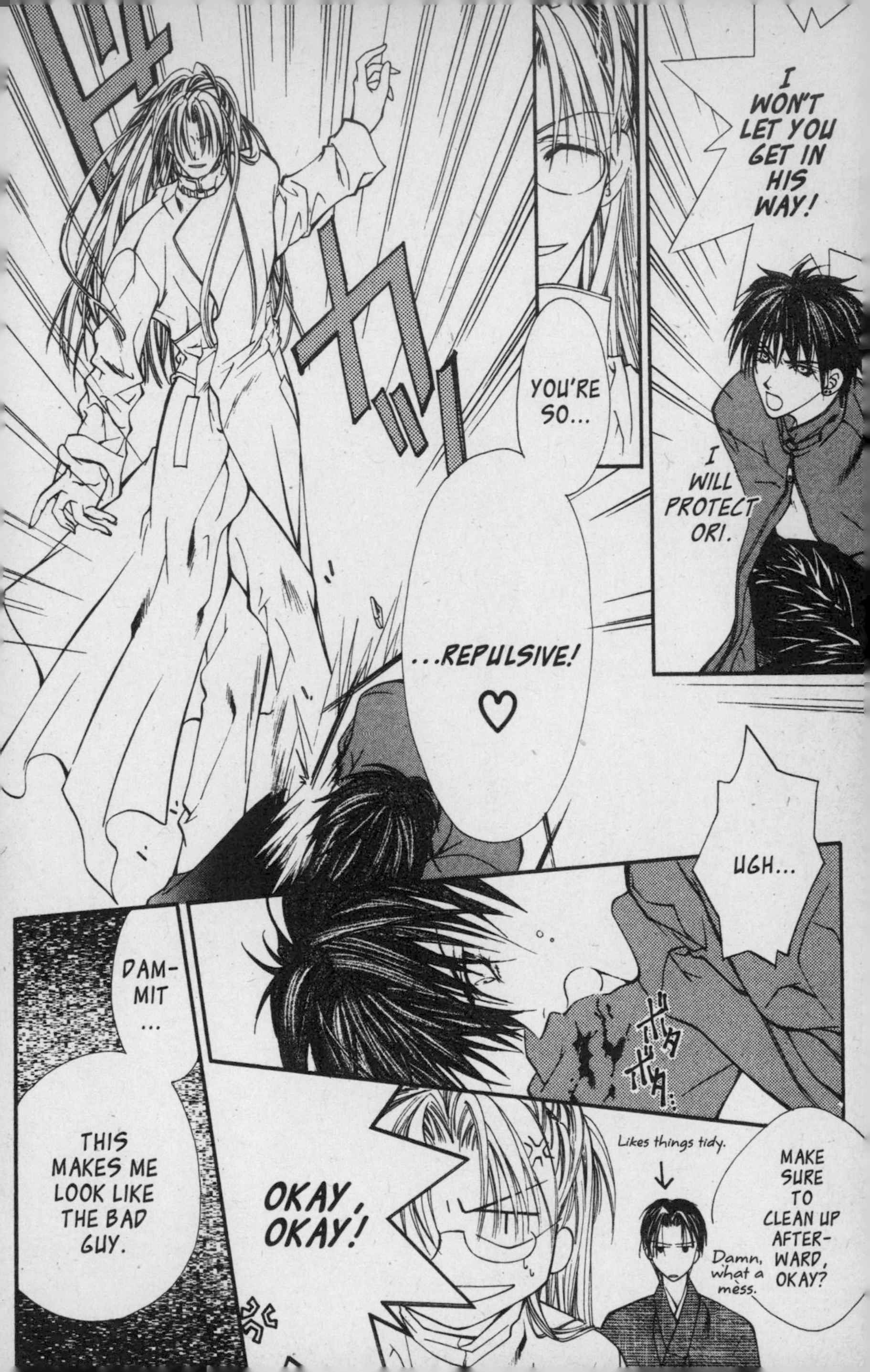
I WON'T LET YOU GET IN HIS WAY!
I WILL PROTECT ORI.
YOU'RE SO...
...REPULSIVE! ♡
UGH...
DAM-MIT...
Likes things tidy.
MAKE SURE TO CLEAN UP AFTER-WARD, OKAY?
Damn, what a mess.
OKAY, OKAY!
THIS MAKES ME LOOK LIKE THE BAD GUY.

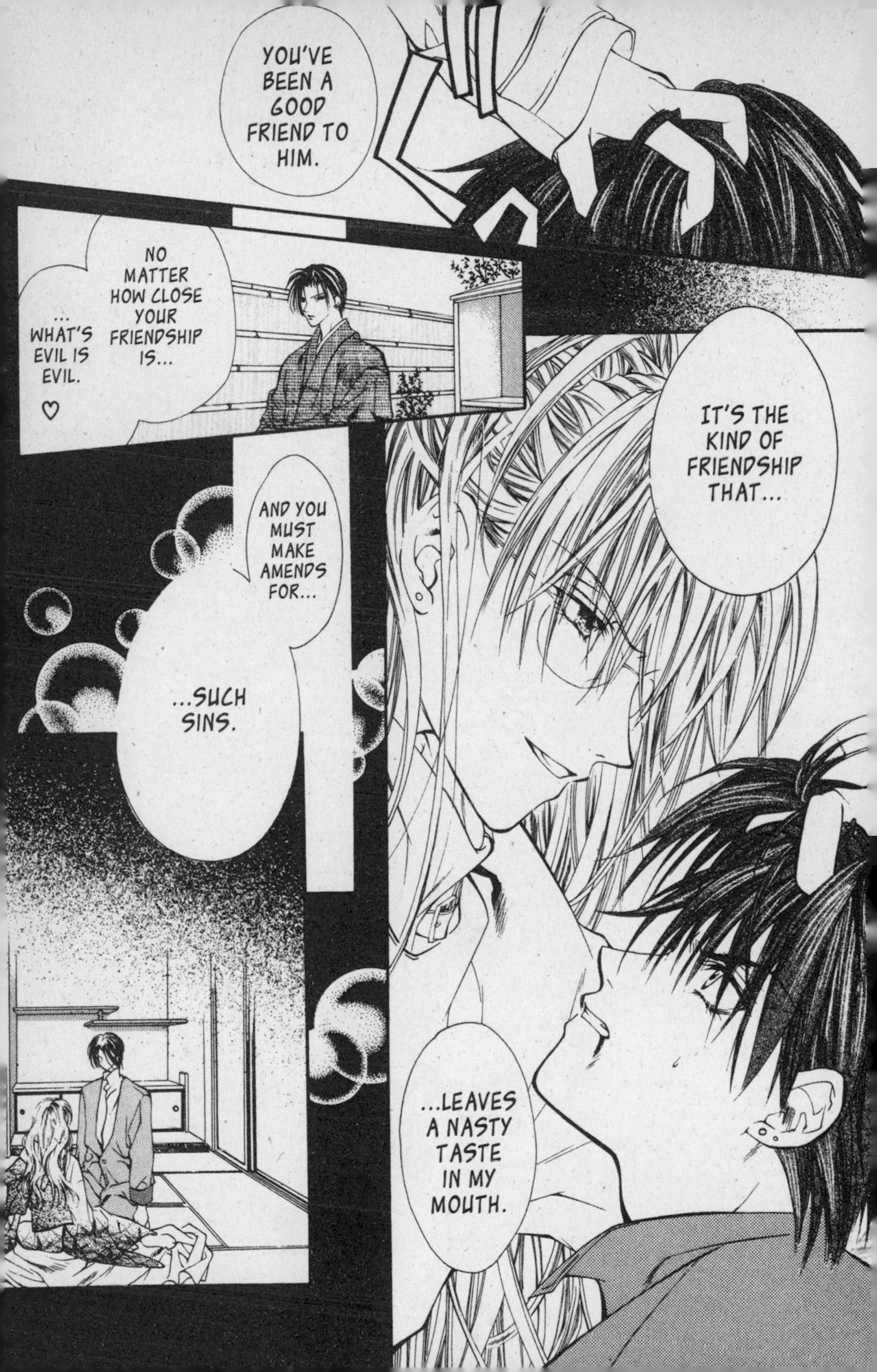
YOU'VE BEEN A GOOD FRIEND TO HIM.
IT'S THE KIND OF FRIENDSHIP THAT...
...LEAVES A NASTY TASTE IN MY MOUTH.
NO MATTER HOW CLOSE YOUR FRIENDSHIP IS...
...WHAT'S EVIL IS EVIL. ♡
AND YOU MUST MAKE AMENDS FOR...
...SUCH SINS.

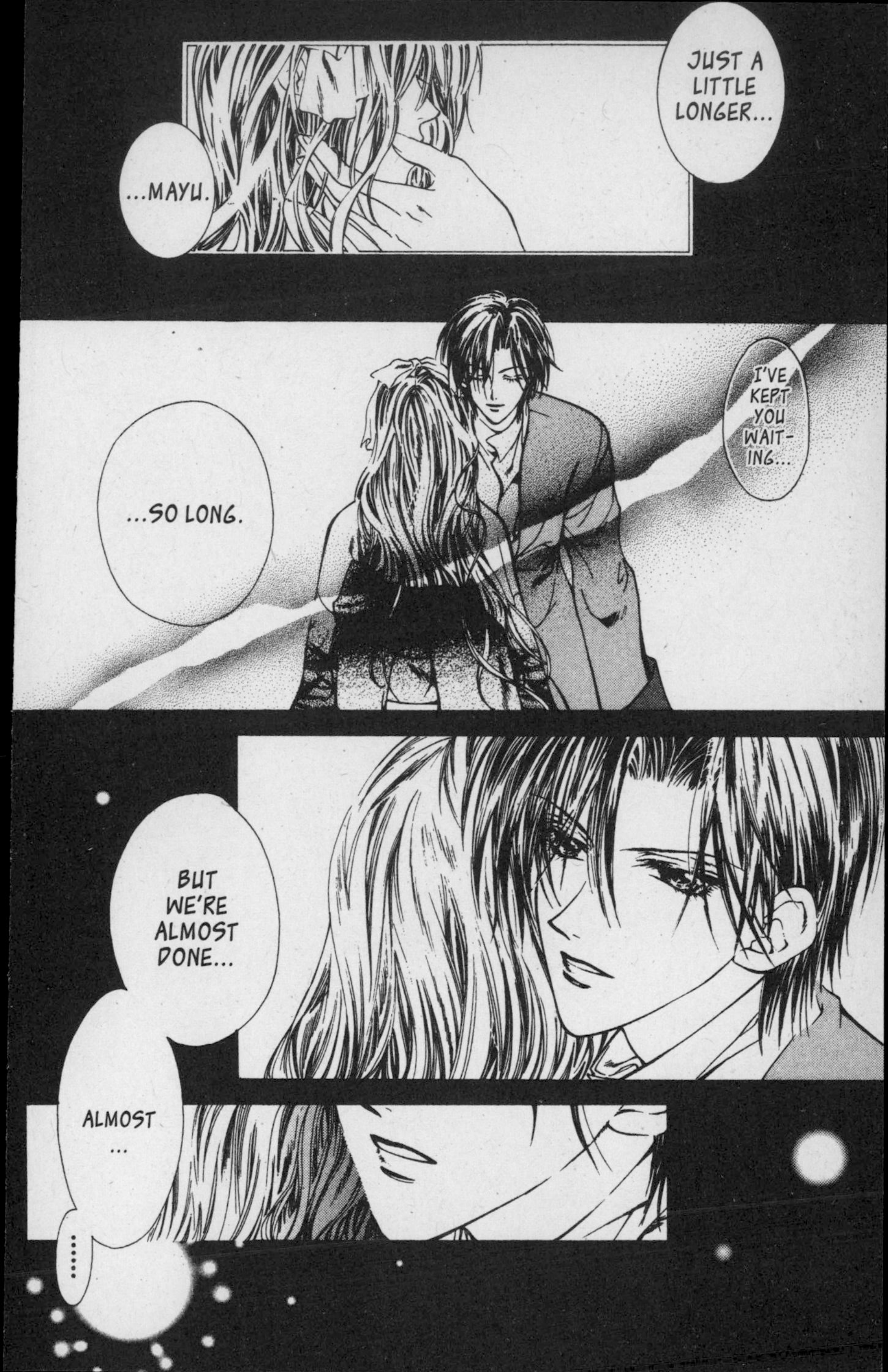
JUST A LITTLE LONGER...
...MAYU.
I'VE KEPT YOU WAIT-ING...
...SO LONG.
BUT WE'RE ALMOST DONE...
ALMOST ...
......

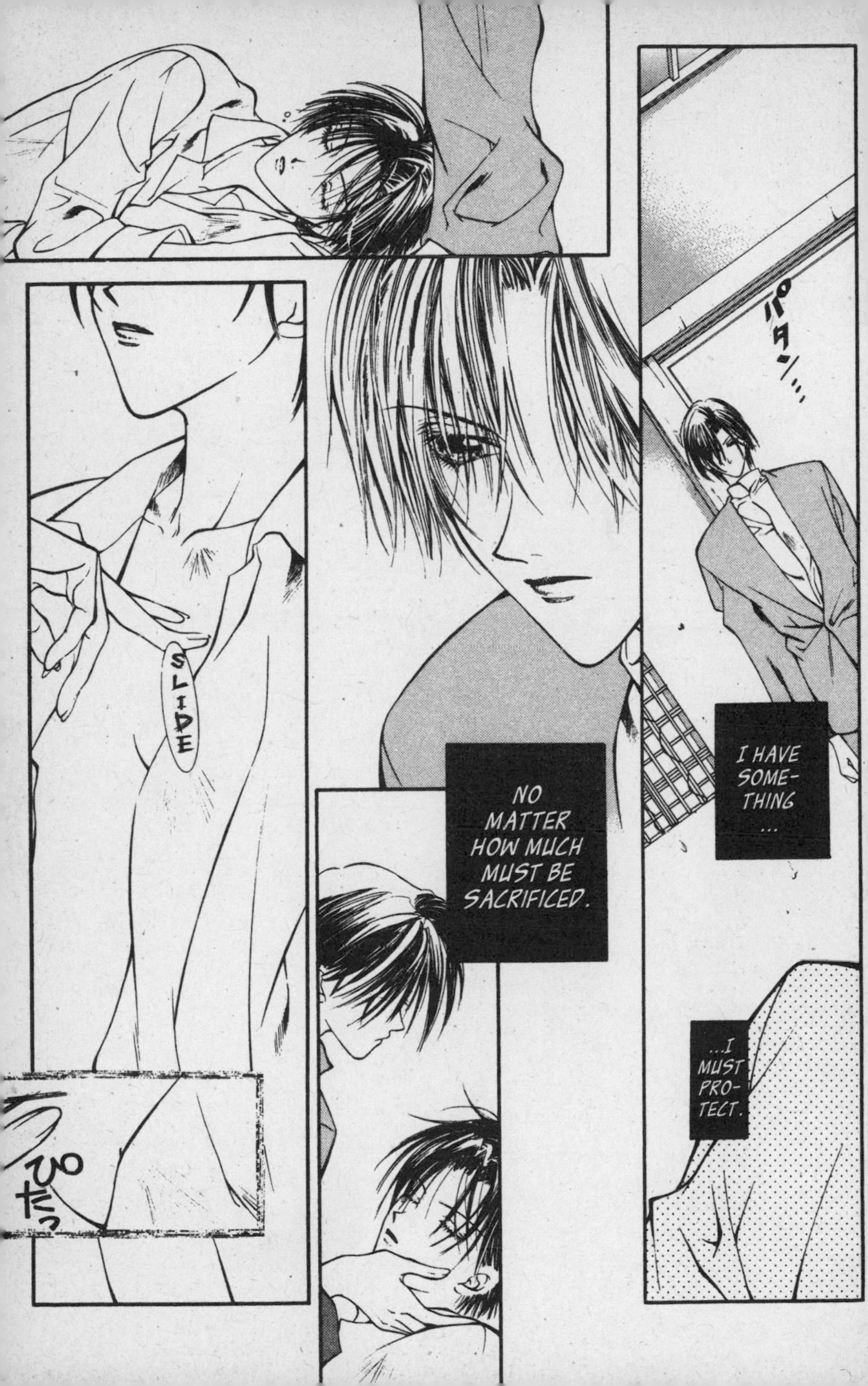
パタン…
I HAVE SOMETHING...
...I MUST PROTECT.
NO MATTER HOW MUCH MUST BE SACRIFICED.
SLIDE
ぴたっ

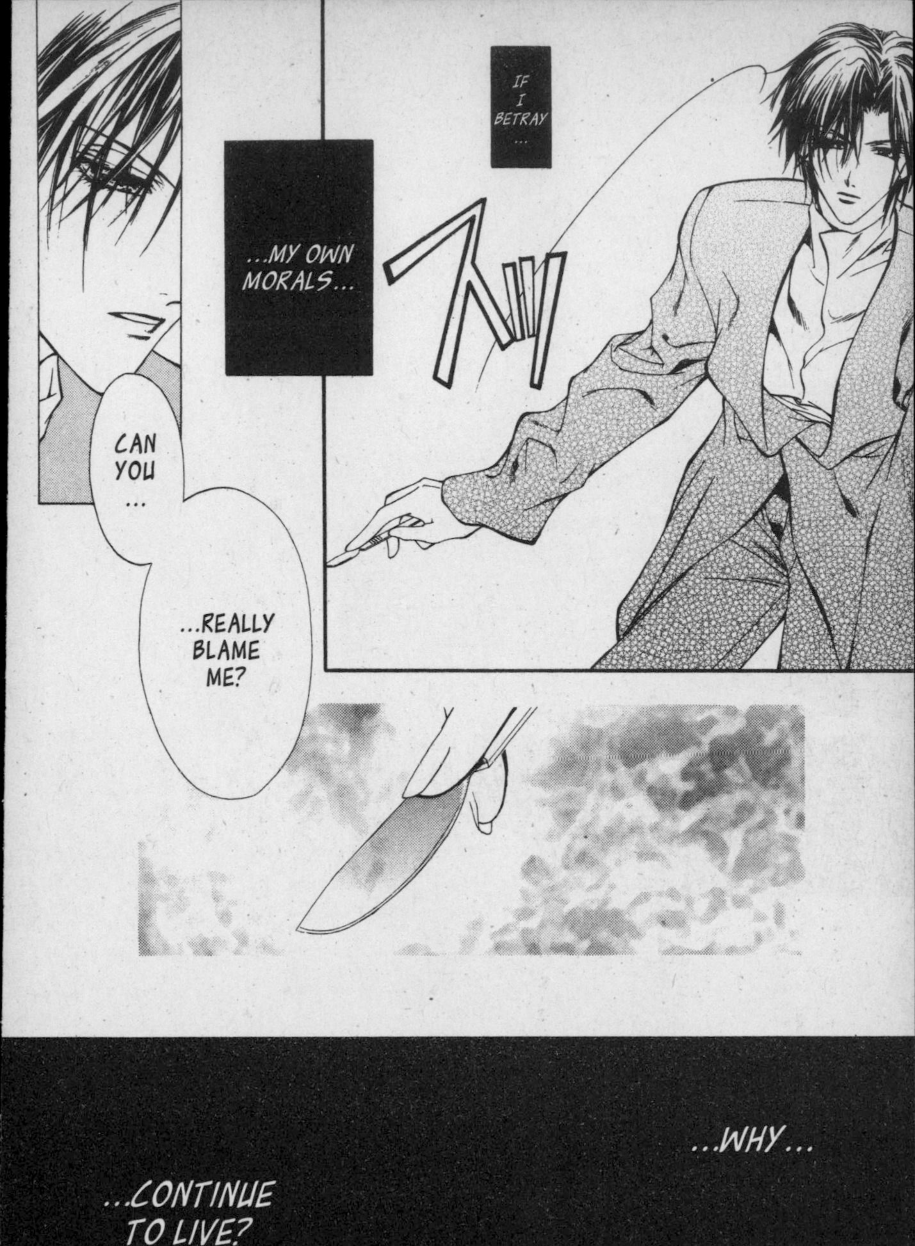
IF I BETRAY ...
...MY OWN MORALS...
CAN YOU ...
...REALLY BLAME ME?
...WHY...
...CONTINUE TO LIVE?

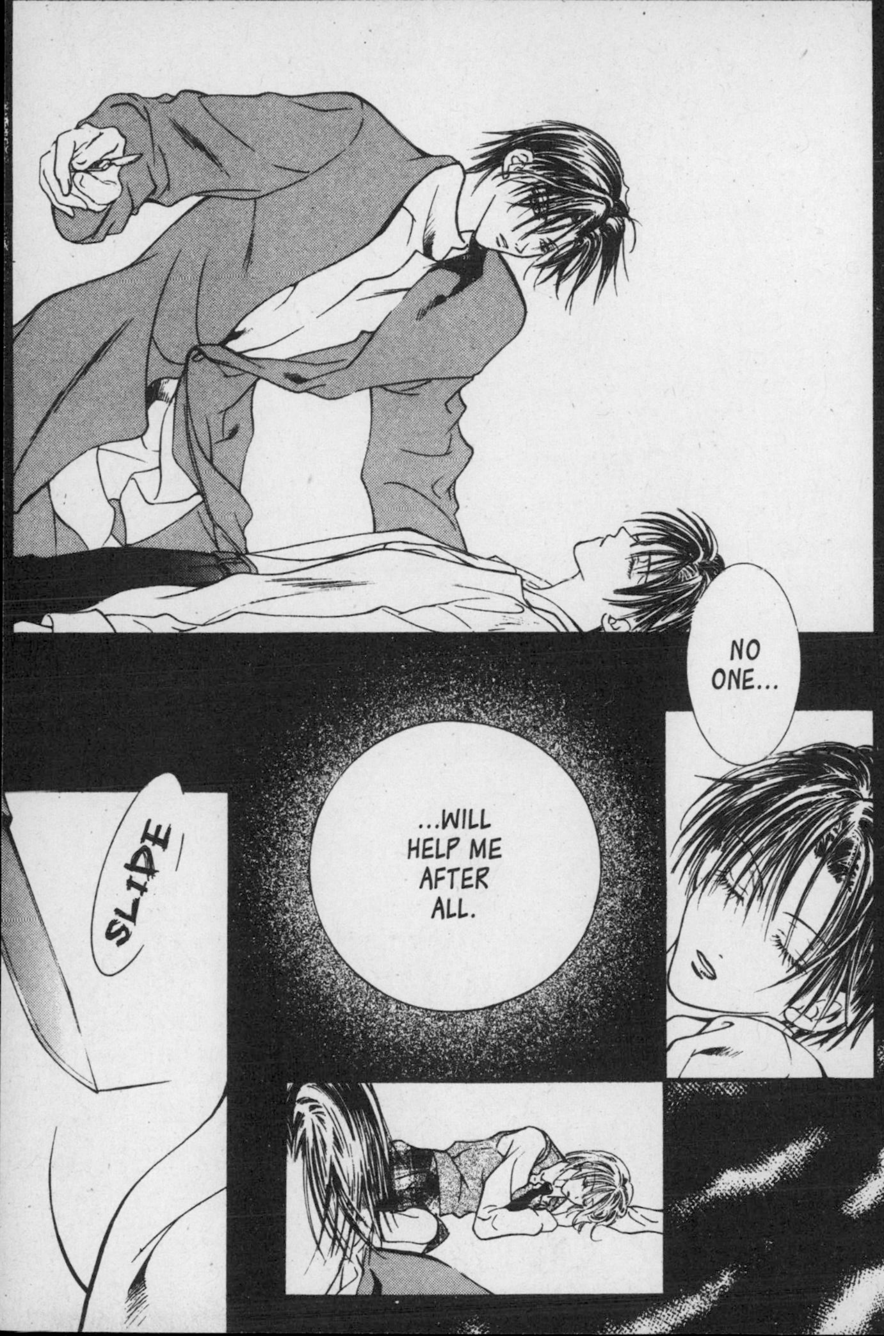
NO ONE...
...WILL HELP ME AFTER ALL.
SLIDE

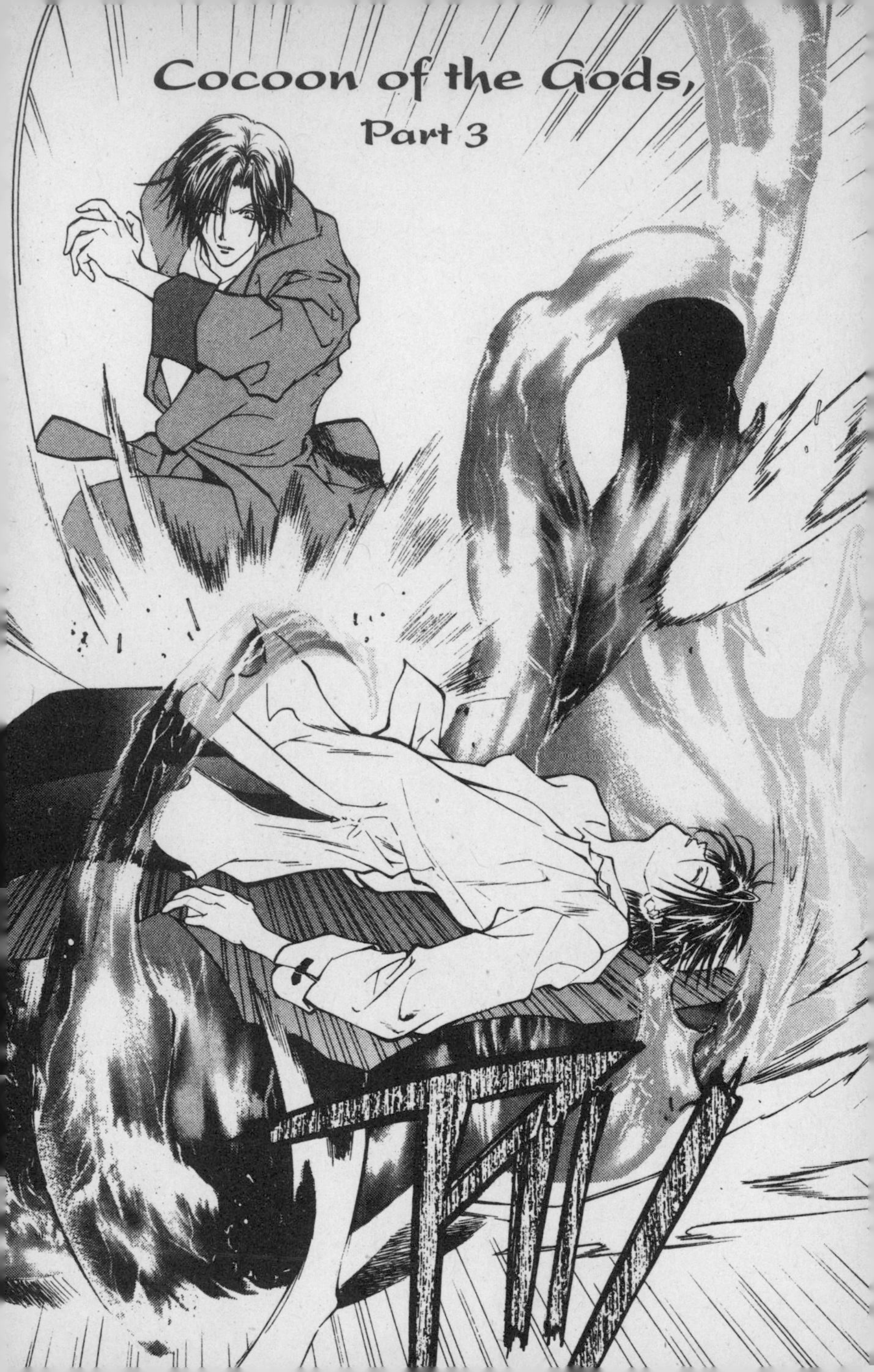
Cocoon of the Gods,
Part 3

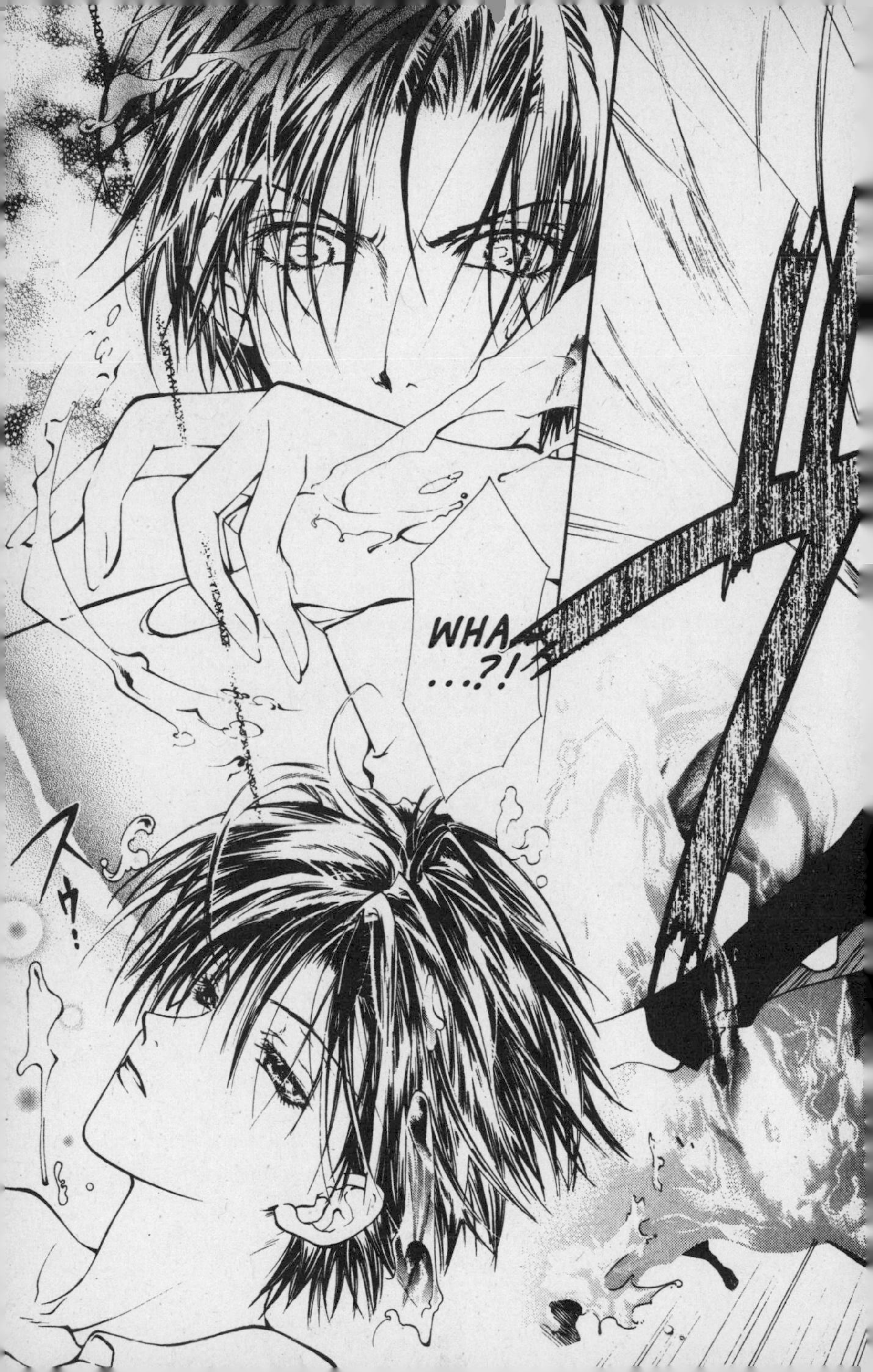
WHA ...?!
スゥ..

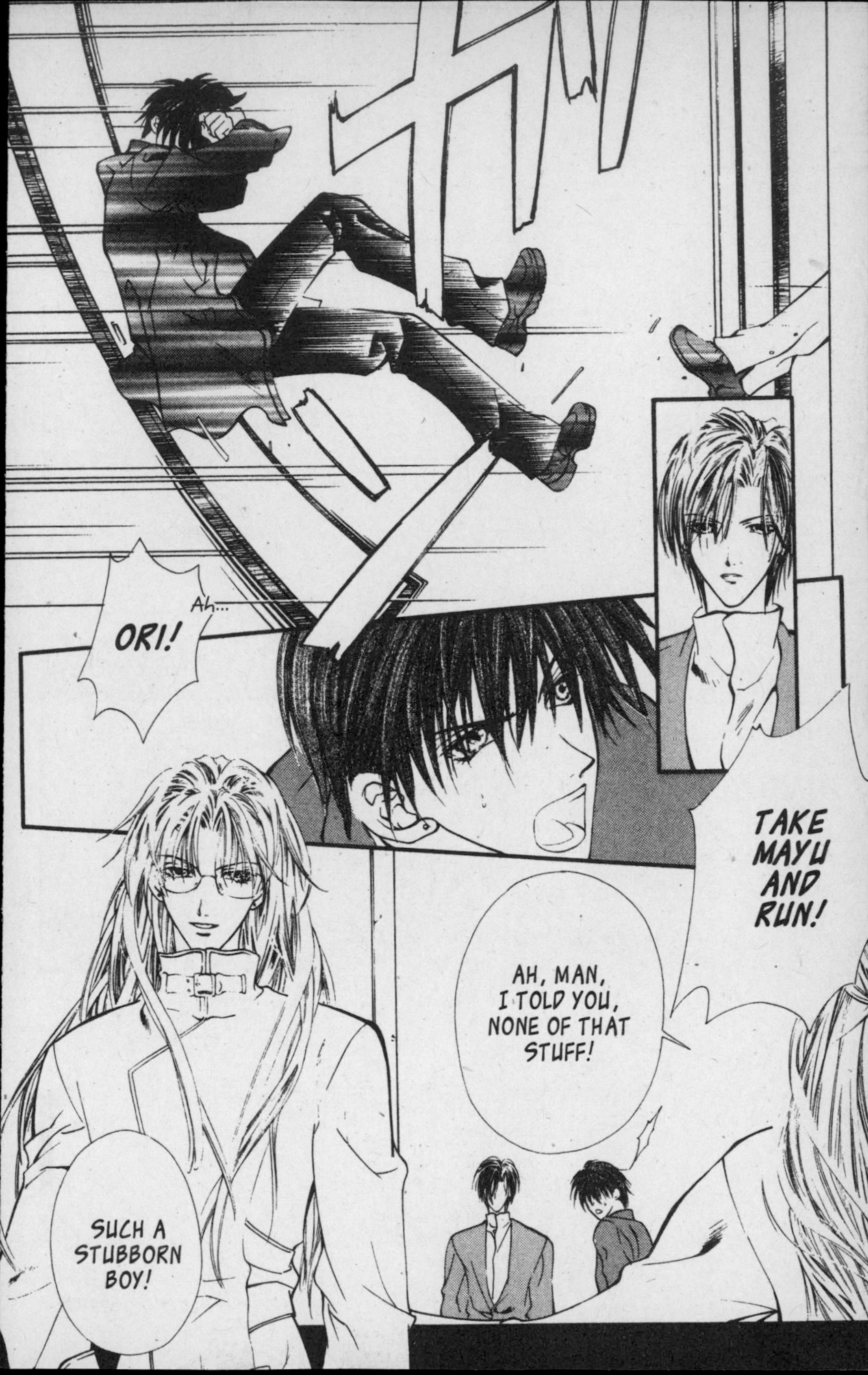
Ah...
ORI!
TAKE MAYU AND RUN!
AH, MAN, I TOLD YOU, NONE OF THAT STUFF!
SUCH A STUBBORN BOY!

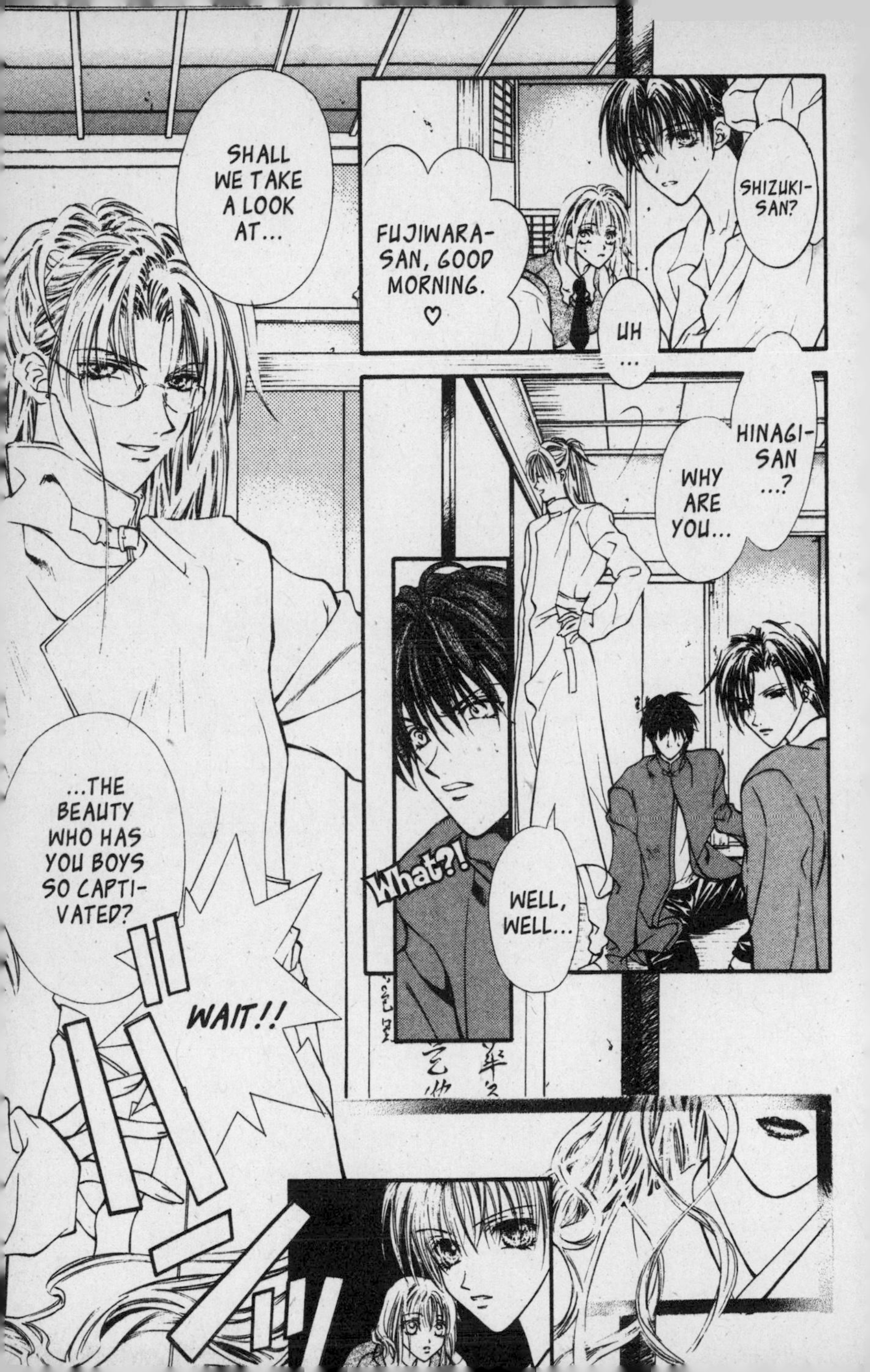
SHIZUKI-SAN?
UH ...
FUJIWARA-SAN, GOOD MORNING. ♡
HINAGI-SAN ...?
WHY ARE YOU...
What?!
WELL, WELL...
SHALL WE TAKE A LOOK AT...
...THE BEAUTY WHO HAS YOU BOYS SO CAPTIVATED?
WAIT!!

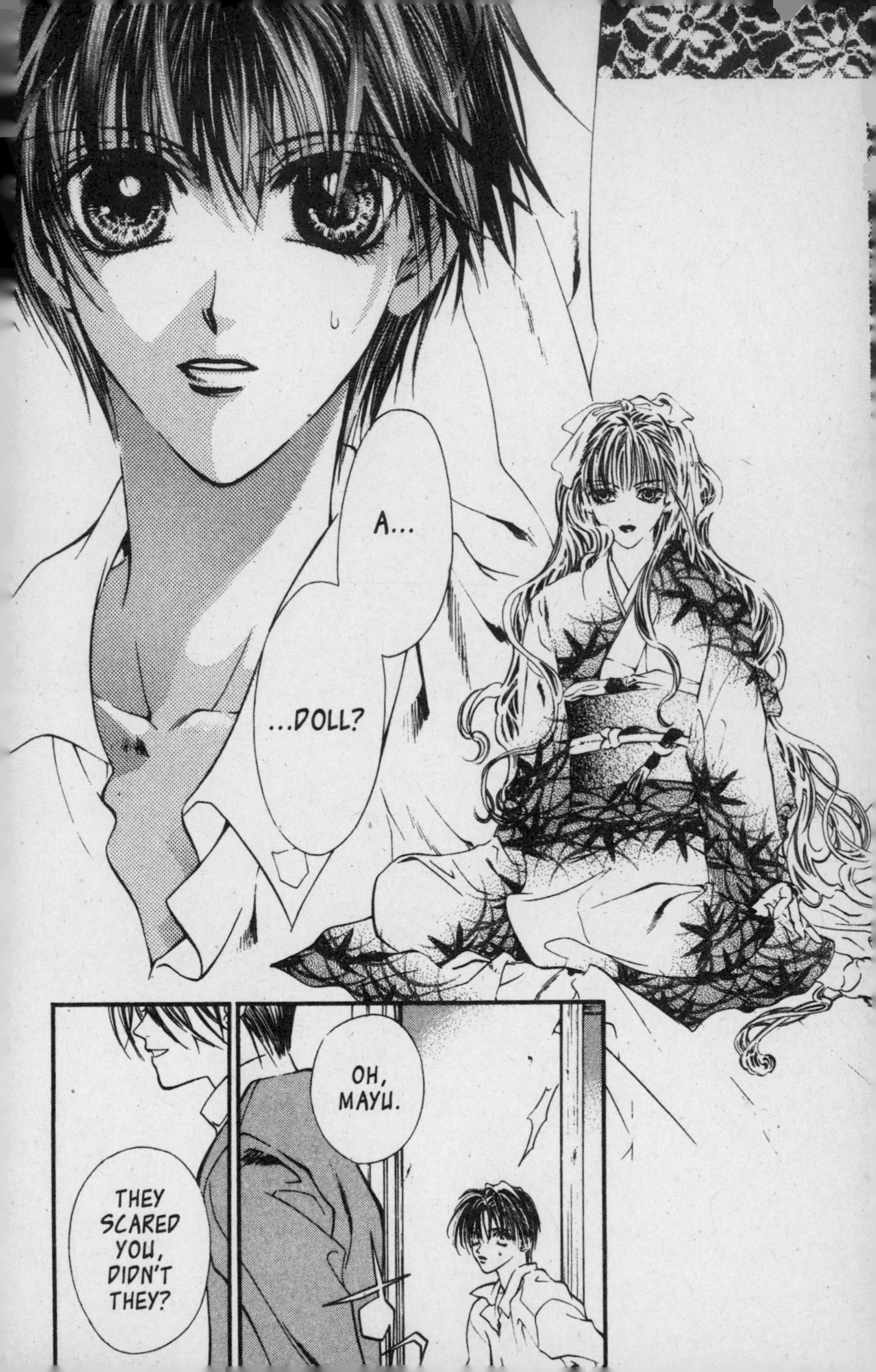
A...
...DOLL?
OH, MAYU.
THEY SCARED YOU, DIDN'T THEY?

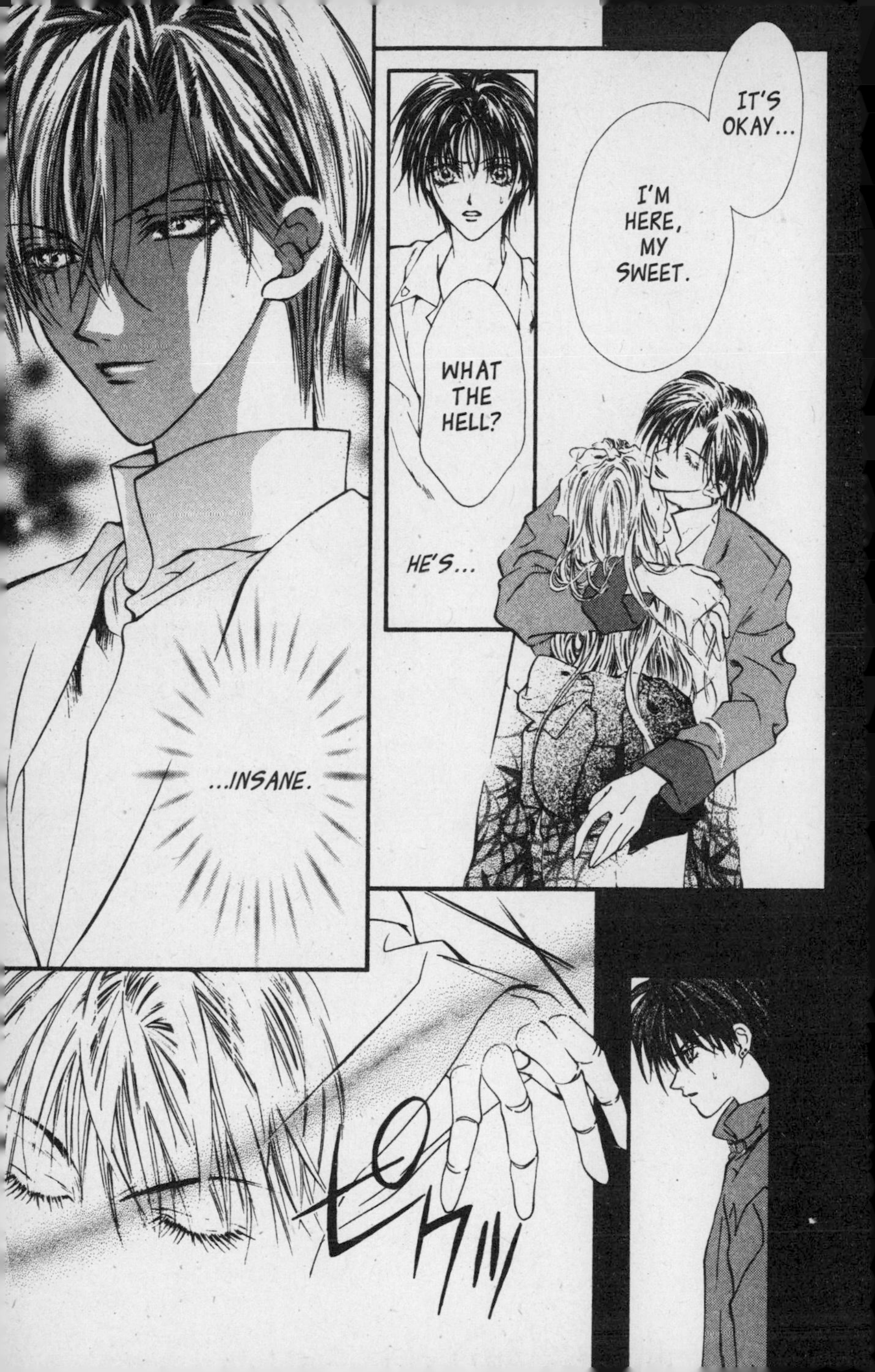
IT'S OKAY...
I'M HERE, MY SWEET.
WHAT THE HELL?
HE'S...
...INSANE.

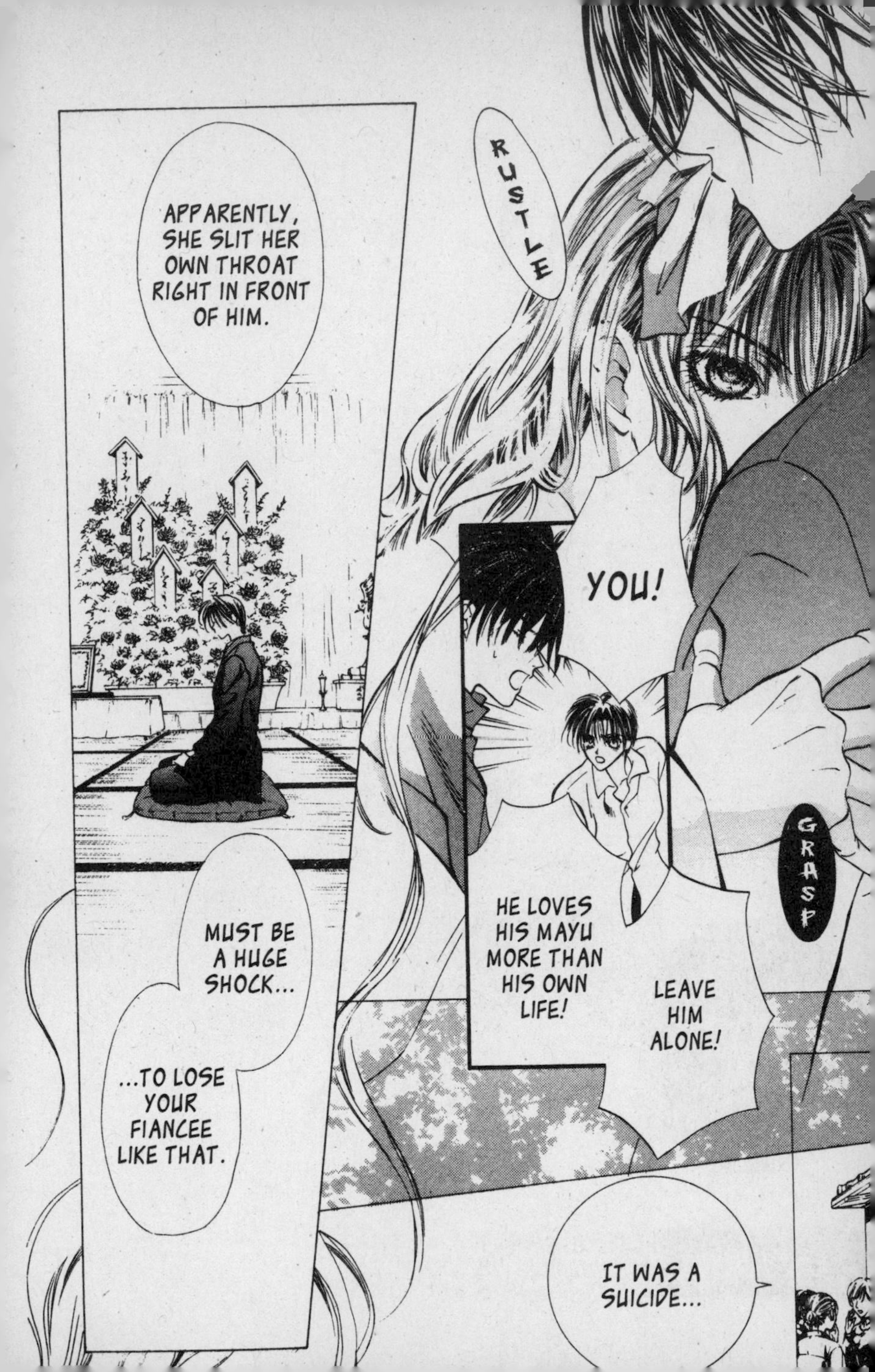
RUSTLE
YOU!
GRASP
HE LOVES HIS MAYU MORE THAN HIS OWN LIFE!
LEAVE HIM ALONE!
IT WAS A SUICIDE...
APPARENTLY, SHE SLIT HER OWN THROAT RIGHT IN FRONT OF HIM.
MUST BE A HUGE SHOCK...
...TO LOSE YOUR FIANCEE LIKE THAT.

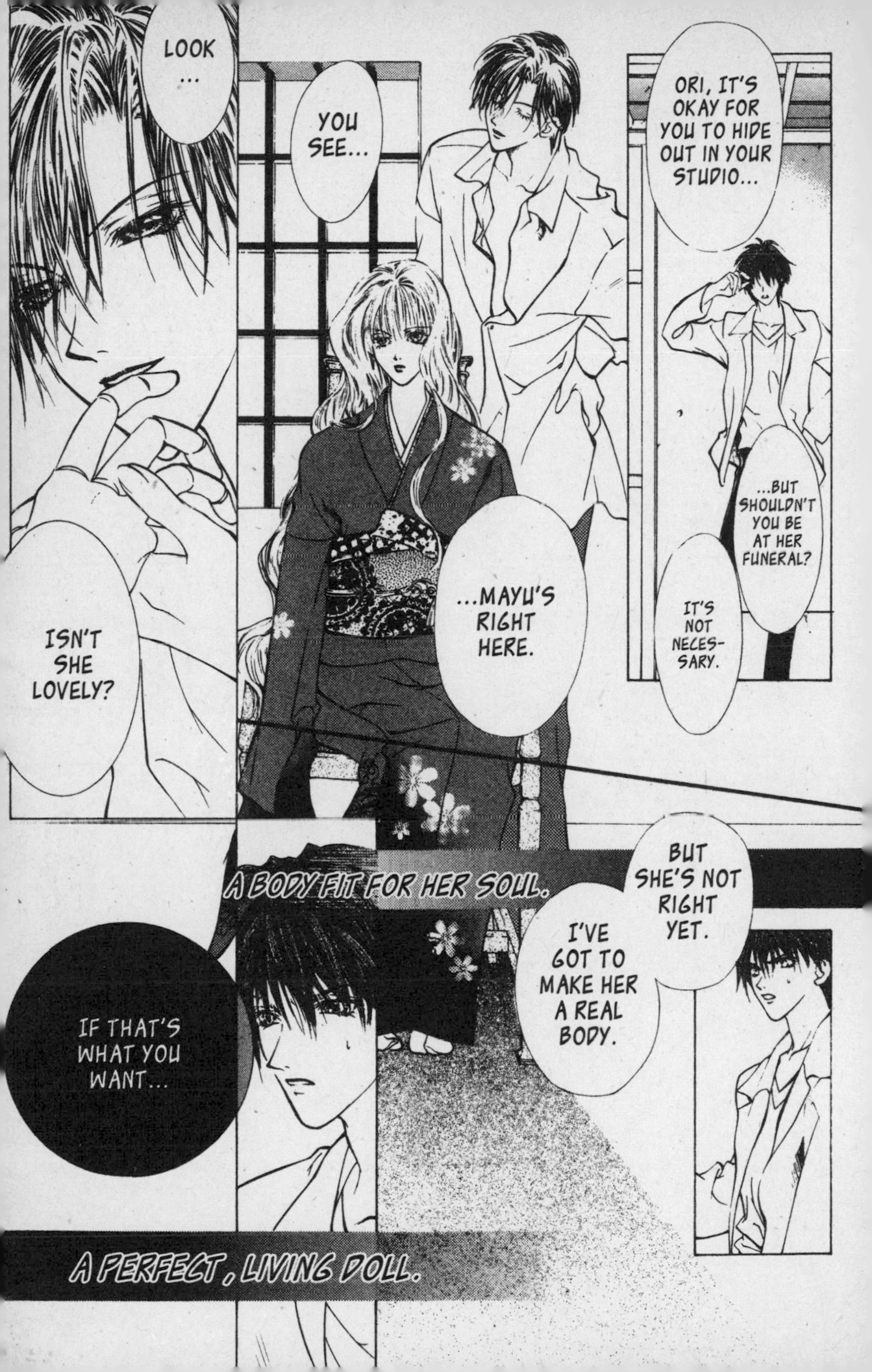
ORI, IT'S OKAY FOR YOU TO HIDE OUT IN YOUR STUDIO...
...BUT SHOULDN'T YOU BE AT HER FUNERAL?
IT'S NOT NECES-SARY.
YOU SEE...
...MAYU'S RIGHT HERE.
LOOK...
ISN'T SHE LOVELY?
BUT SHE'S NOT RIGHT YET.
I'VE GOT TO MAKE HER A REAL BODY.
A BODY FIT FOR HER SOUL.
IF THAT'S WHAT YOU WANT...
A PERFECT, LIVING DOLL.

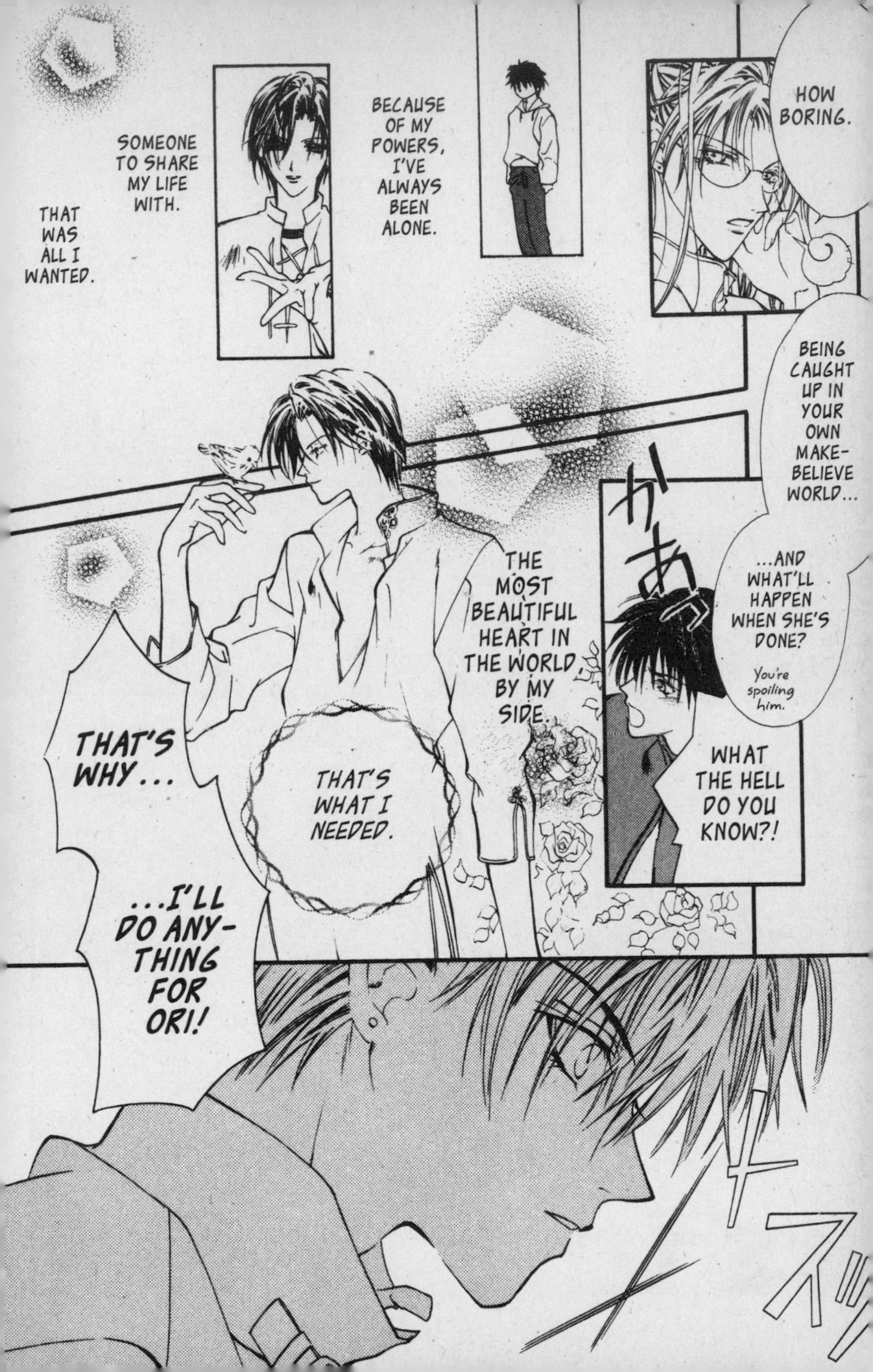
HOW BORING.
BECAUSE OF MY POWERS, I'VE ALWAYS BEEN ALONE.
SOMEONE TO SHARE MY LIFE WITH.
THAT WAS ALL I WANTED.
BEING CAUGHT UP IN YOUR OWN MAKE-BELIEVE WORLD...
...AND WHAT'LL HAPPEN WHEN SHE'S DONE?
You're spoiling him.
WHAT THE HELL DO YOU KNOW?!
THE MOST BEAUTIFUL HEART IN THE WORLD, BY MY SIDE.
THAT'S WHAT I NEEDED.
THAT'S WHY...
...I'LL DO ANYTHING FOR ORI!

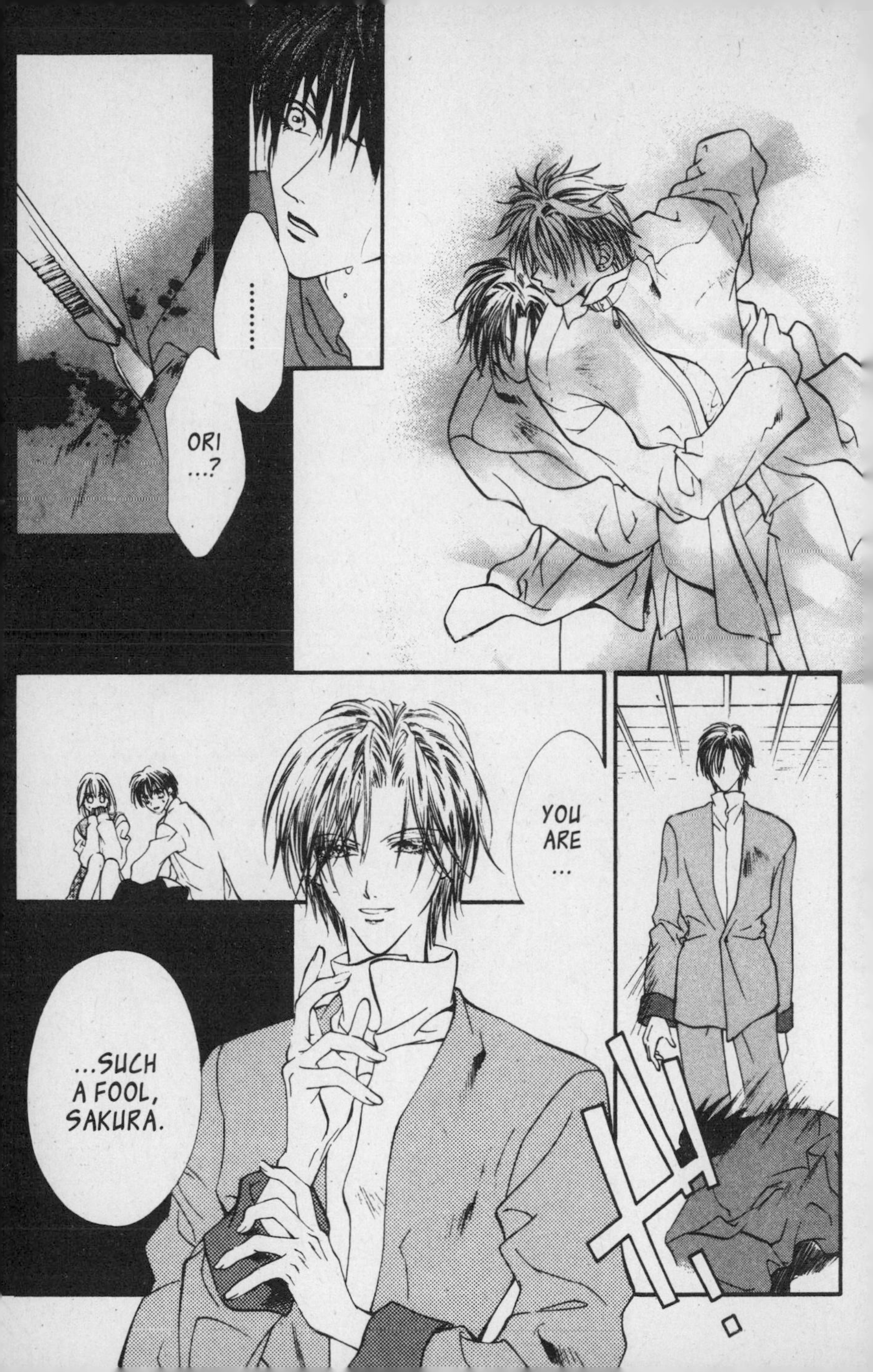
......
ORI ...?
YOU ARE ...
...SUCH A FOOL, SAKURA.

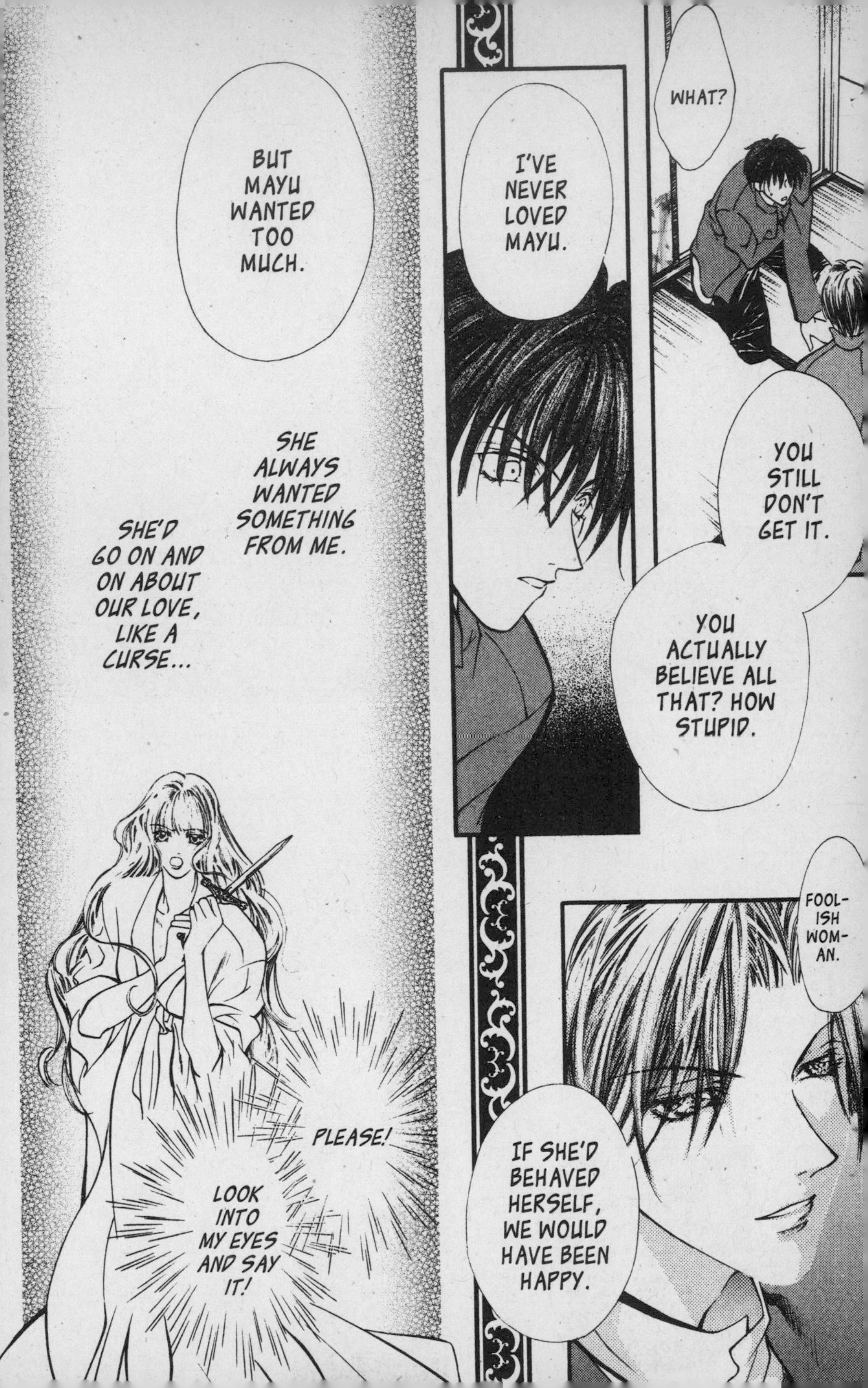
WHAT?
I'VE NEVER LOVED MAYU.
YOU STILL DON'T GET IT.
YOU ACTUALLY BELIEVE ALL THAT? HOW STUPID.
FOOL-ISH WOM-AN.
IF SHE'D BEHAVED HERSELF, WE WOULD HAVE BEEN HAPPY.
BUT MAYU WANTED TOO MUCH.
SHE ALWAYS WANTED SOMETHING FROM ME.
SHE'D GO ON AND ON ABOUT OUR LOVE, LIKE A CURSE...
PLEASE!
LOOK INTO MY EYES AND SAY IT!

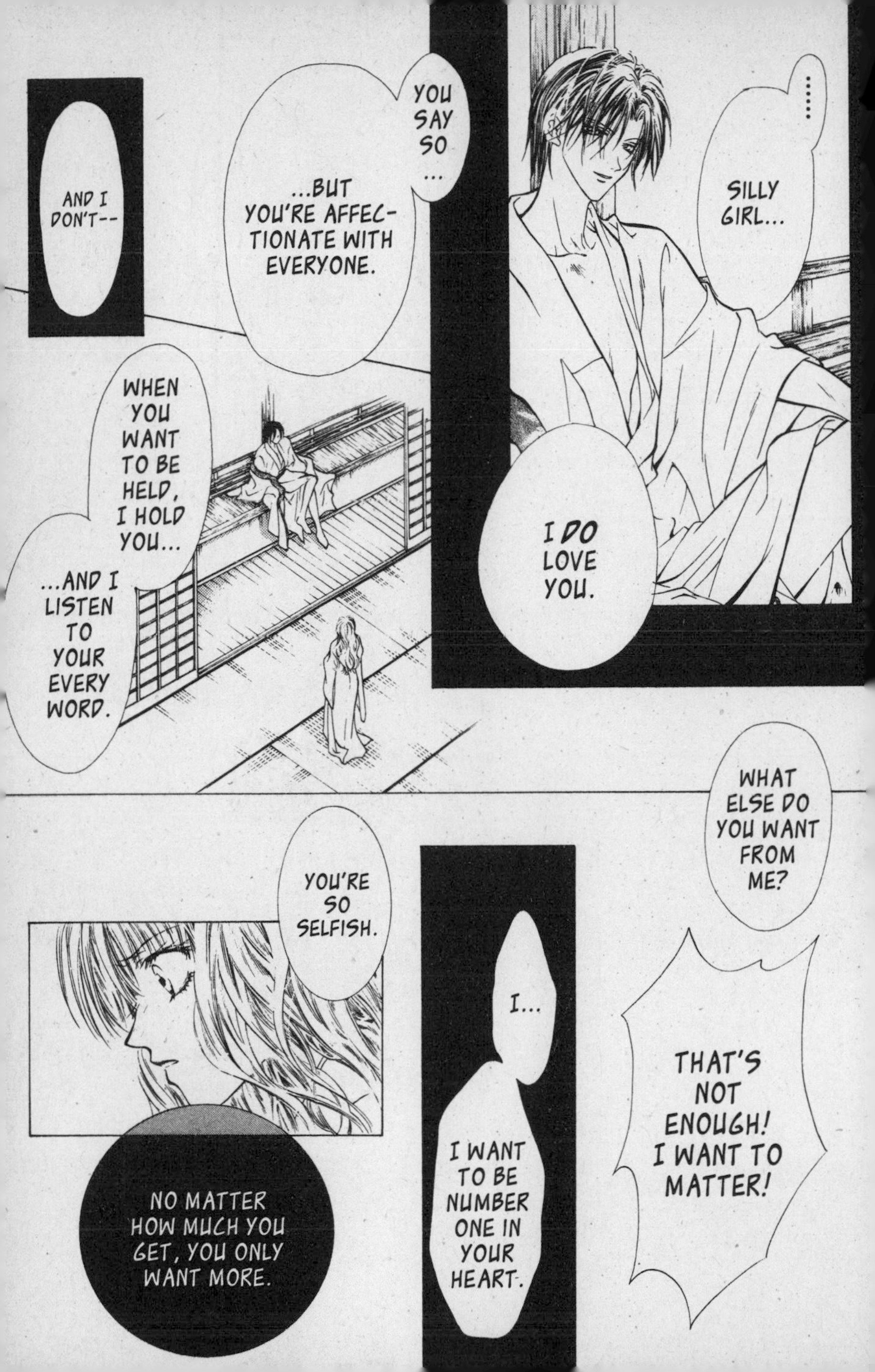
......
SILLY GIRL...
I DO LOVE YOU.
YOU SAY SO ...
...BUT YOU'RE AFFECTIONATE WITH EVERYONE.
AND I DON'T--
WHEN YOU WANT TO BE HELD, I HOLD YOU...
...AND I LISTEN TO YOUR EVERY WORD.
WHAT ELSE DO YOU WANT FROM ME?
THAT'S NOT ENOUGH! I WANT TO MATTER!
I...
I WANT TO BE NUMBER ONE IN YOUR HEART.
YOU'RE SO SELFISH.
NO MATTER HOW MUCH YOU GET, YOU ONLY WANT MORE.

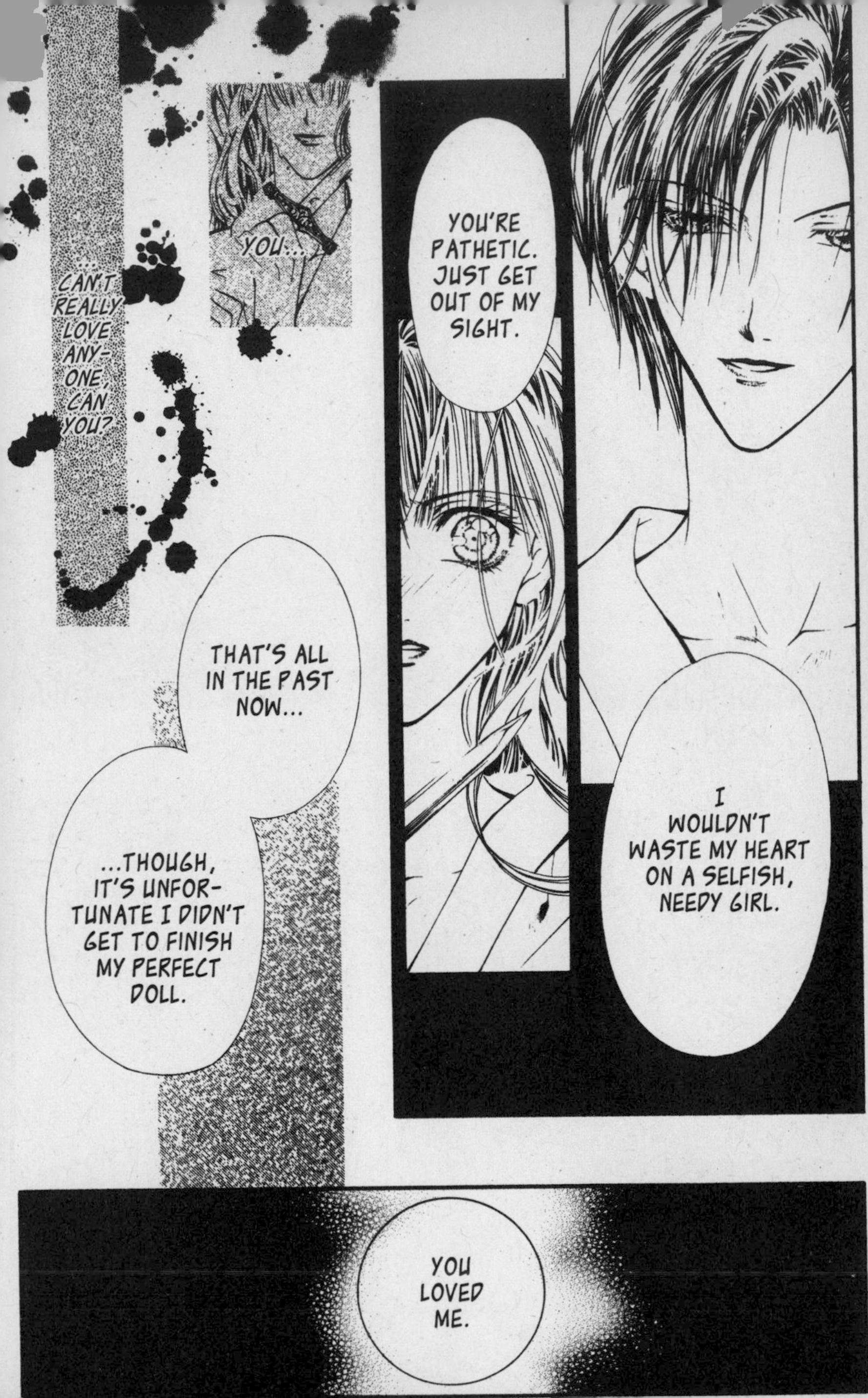
YOU'RE PATHETIC. JUST GET OUT OF MY SIGHT.
I WOULDN'T WASTE MY HEART ON A SELFISH, NEEDY GIRL.
YOU...
...CAN'T REALLY LOVE ANY-ONE, CAN YOU?
THAT'S ALL IN THE PAST NOW...
...THOUGH, IT'S UNFOR-TUNATE I DIDN'T GET TO FINISH MY PERFECT DOLL.
YOU LOVED ME.

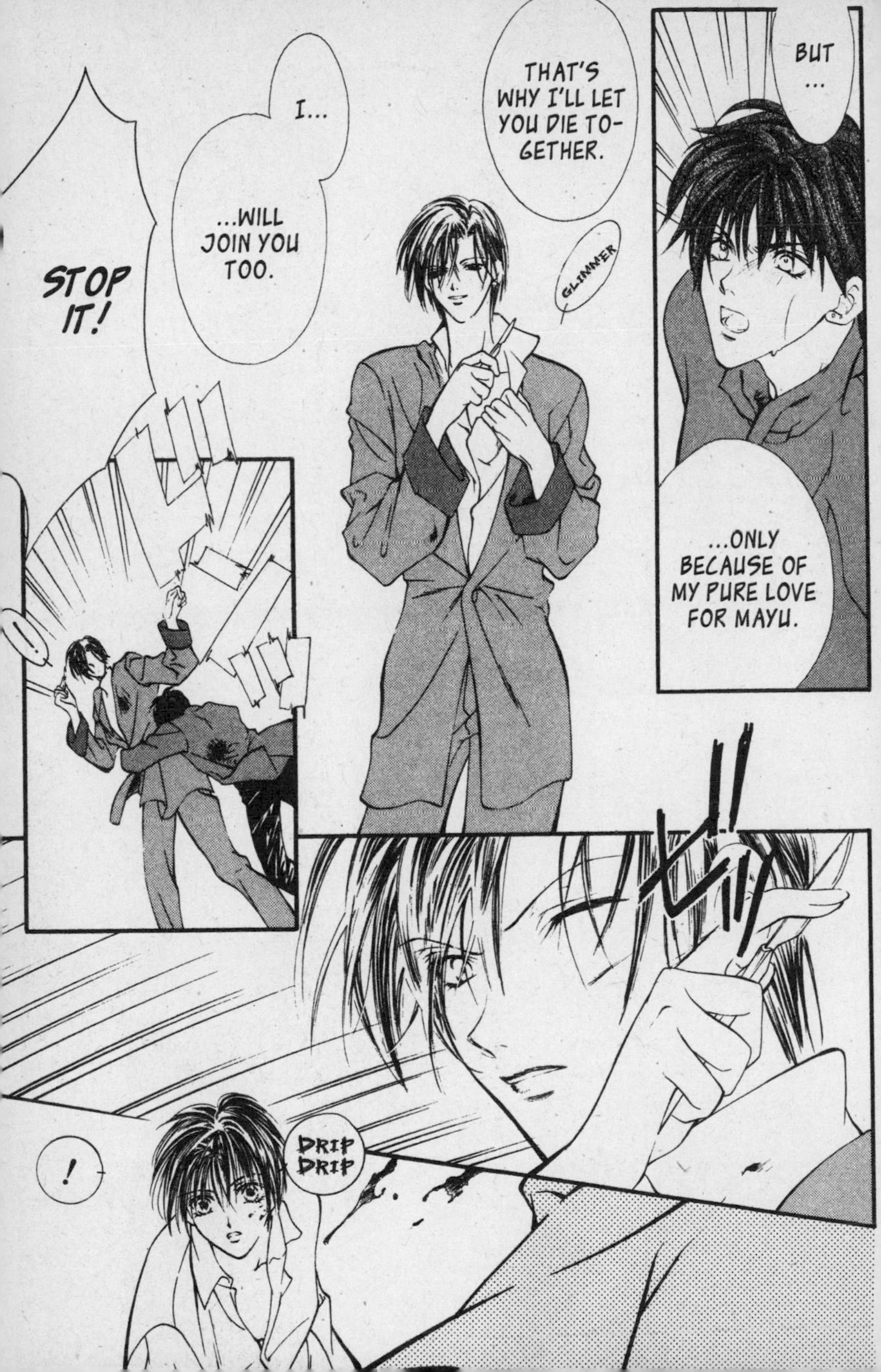
BUT ...
...ONLY BECAUSE OF MY PURE LOVE FOR MAYU.
THAT'S WHY I'LL LET YOU DIE TO-GETHER.
GLIMMER
I...
...WILL JOIN YOU TOO.
STOP IT!
DRIP DRIP
!

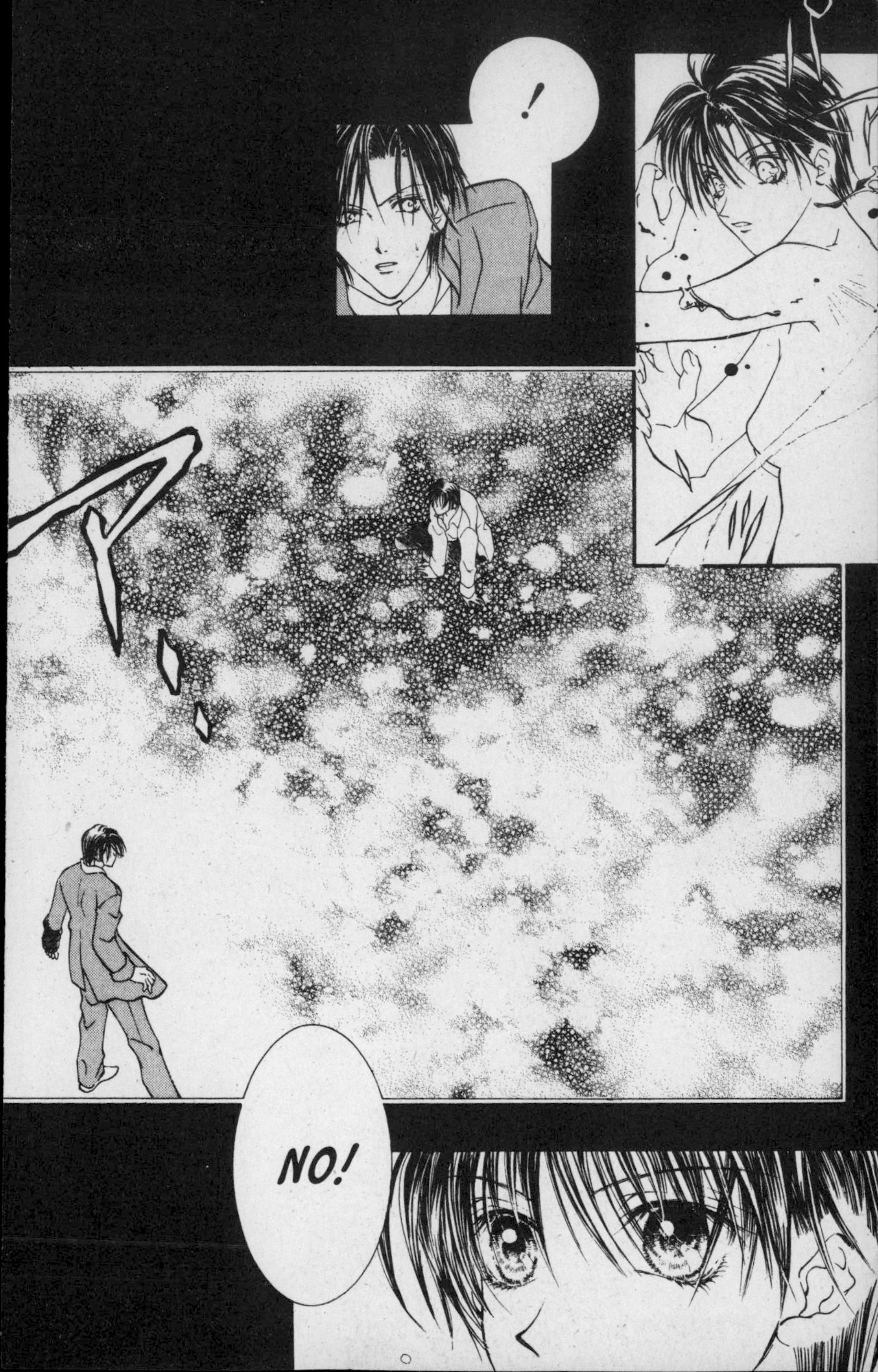
!
ア
NO!

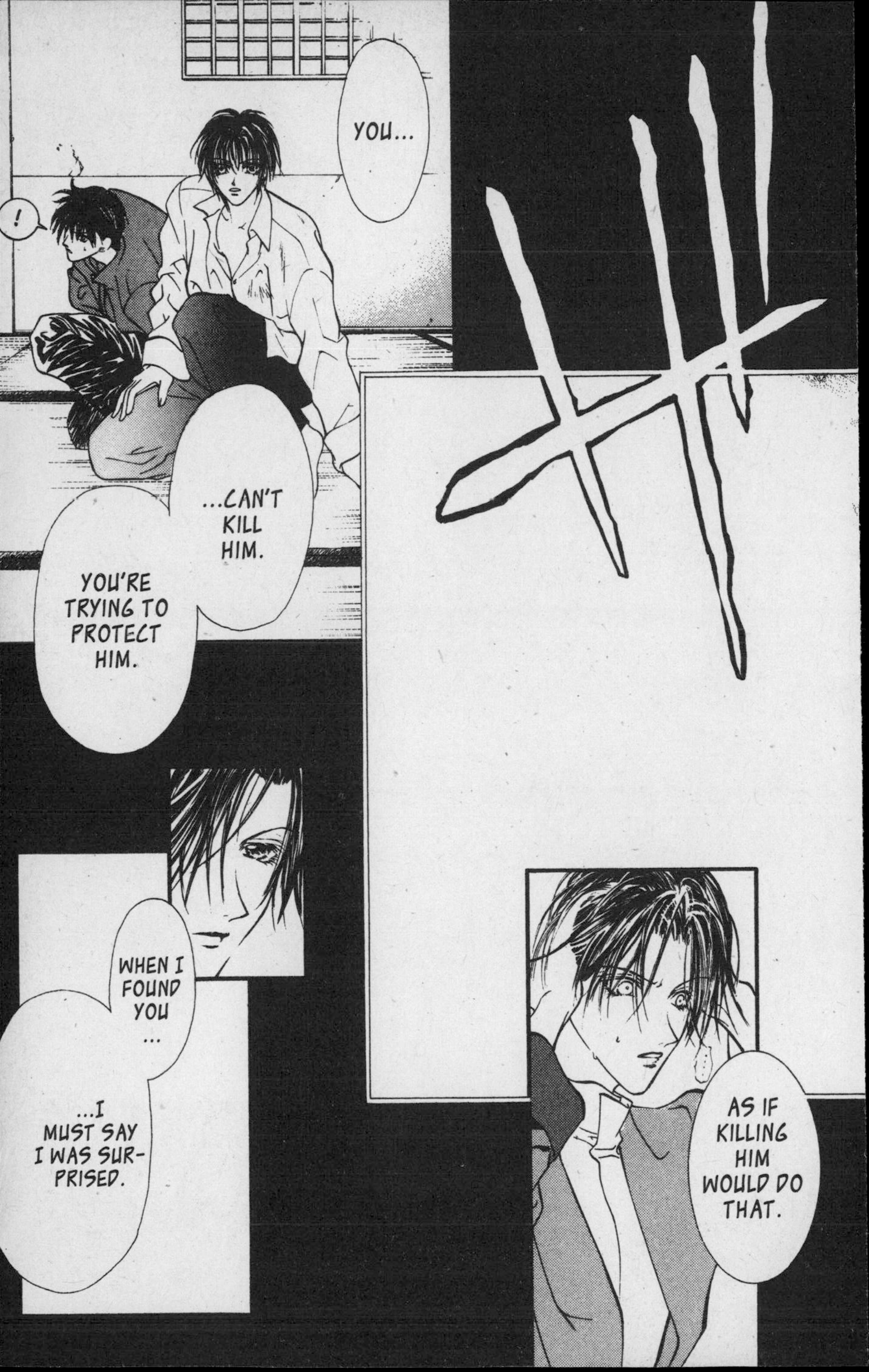
YOU...
!
...CAN'T KILL HIM.
YOU'RE TRYING TO PROTECT HIM.
AS IF KILLING HIM WOULD DO THAT.
WHEN I FOUND YOU ...
...I MUST SAY I WAS SUR-PRISED.

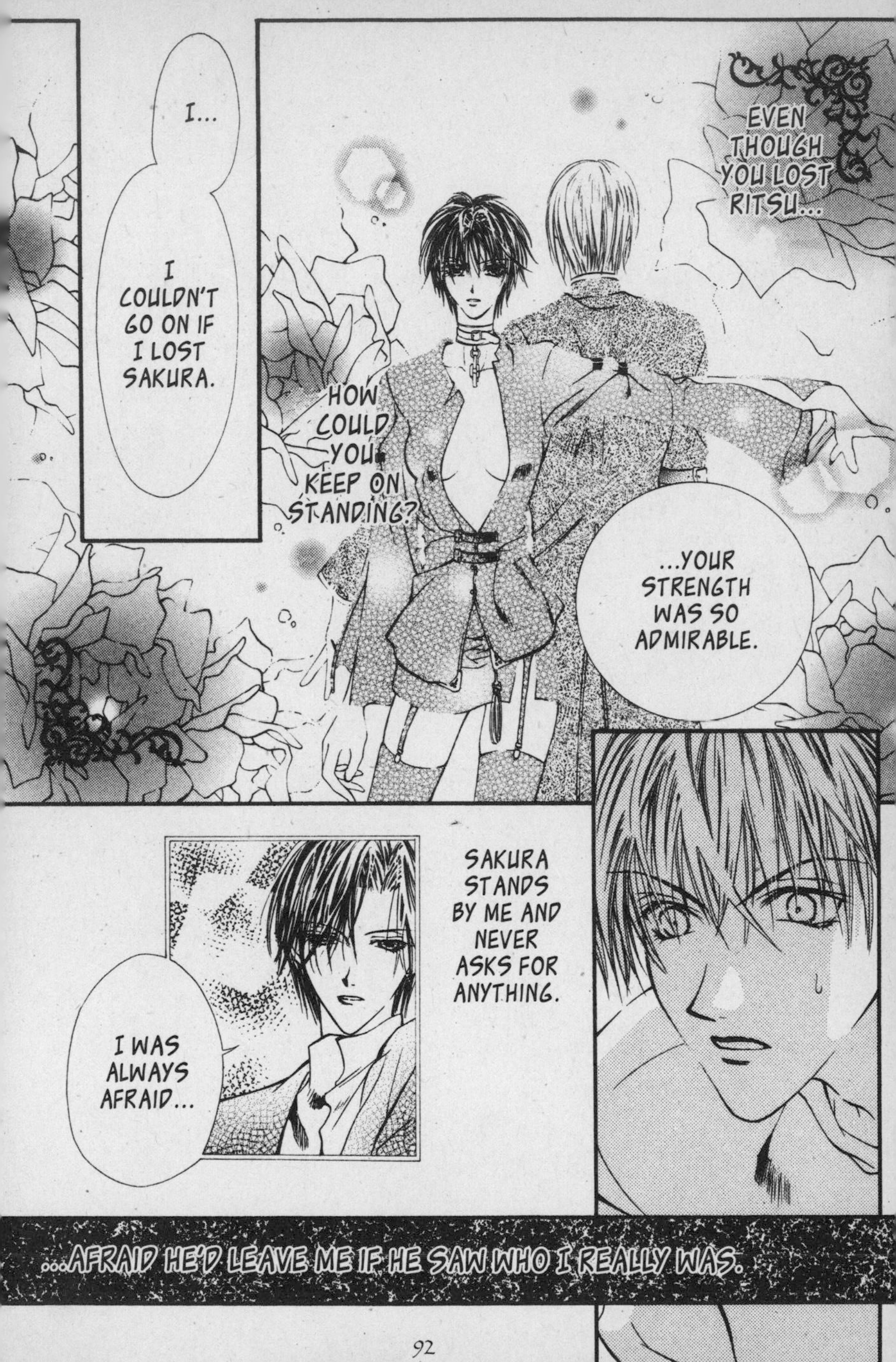
EVEN THOUGH YOU LOST RITSU...
HOW COULD YOU KEEP ON STANDING?
...YOUR STRENGTH WAS SO ADMIRABLE.
I...
I COULDN'T GO ON IF I LOST SAKURA.
SAKURA STANDS BY ME AND NEVER ASKS FOR ANYTHING.
I WAS ALWAYS AFRAID...
...AFRAID HE'D LEAVE ME IF HE SAW WHO I REALLY WAS.

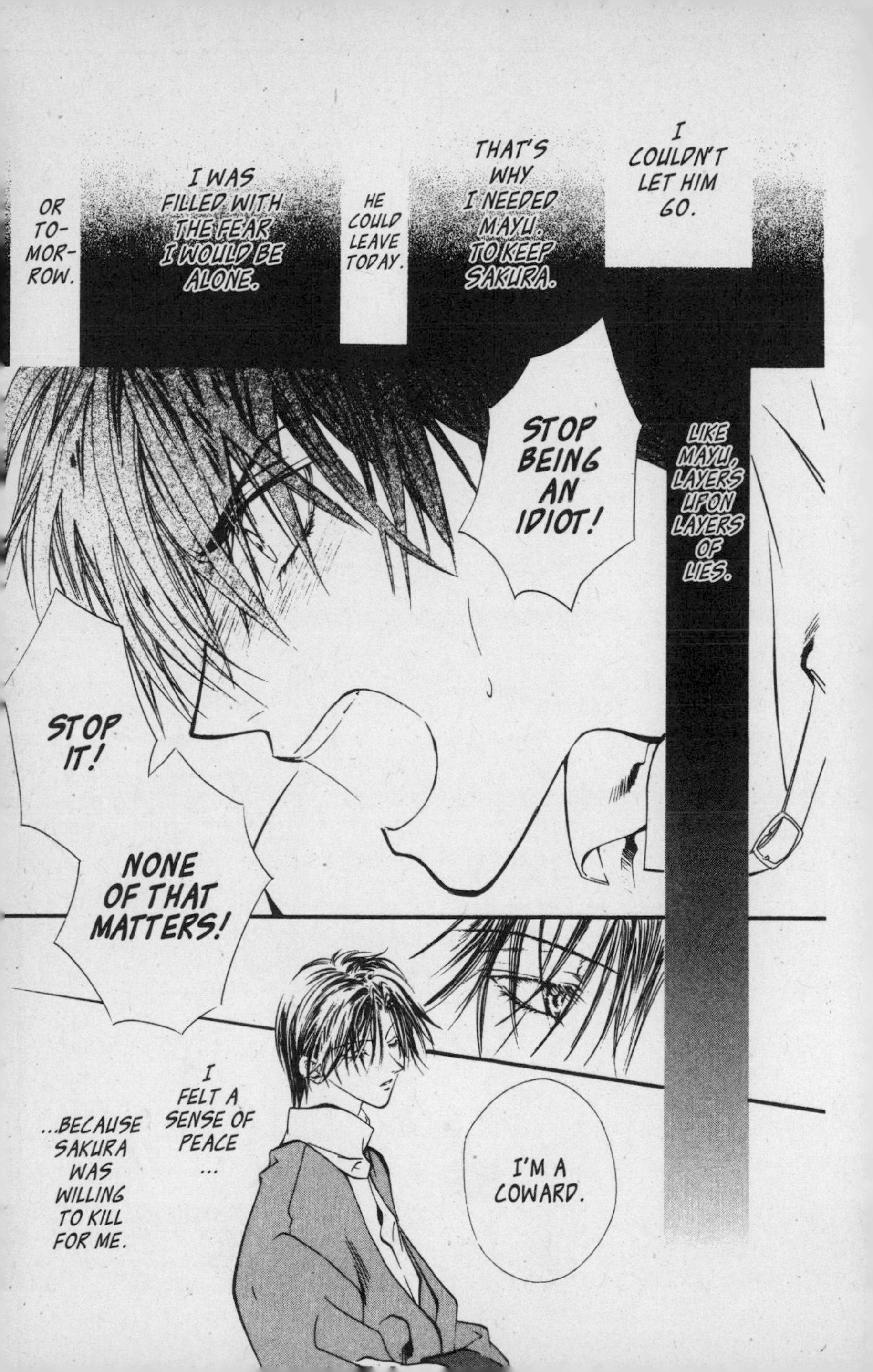
I COULDN'T LET HIM GO.
THAT'S WHY I NEEDED MAYU. TO KEEP SAKURA.
HE COULD LEAVE TODAY.
I WAS FILLED WITH THE FEAR I WOULD BE ALONE.
OR TO-MOR-ROW.
LIKE MAYU, LAYERS UPON LAYERS OF LIES.
STOP BEING AN IDIOT!
STOP IT!
NONE OF THAT MATTERS!
I'M A COWARD.
I FELT A SENSE OF PEACE...
...BECAUSE SAKURA WAS WILLING TO KILL FOR ME.

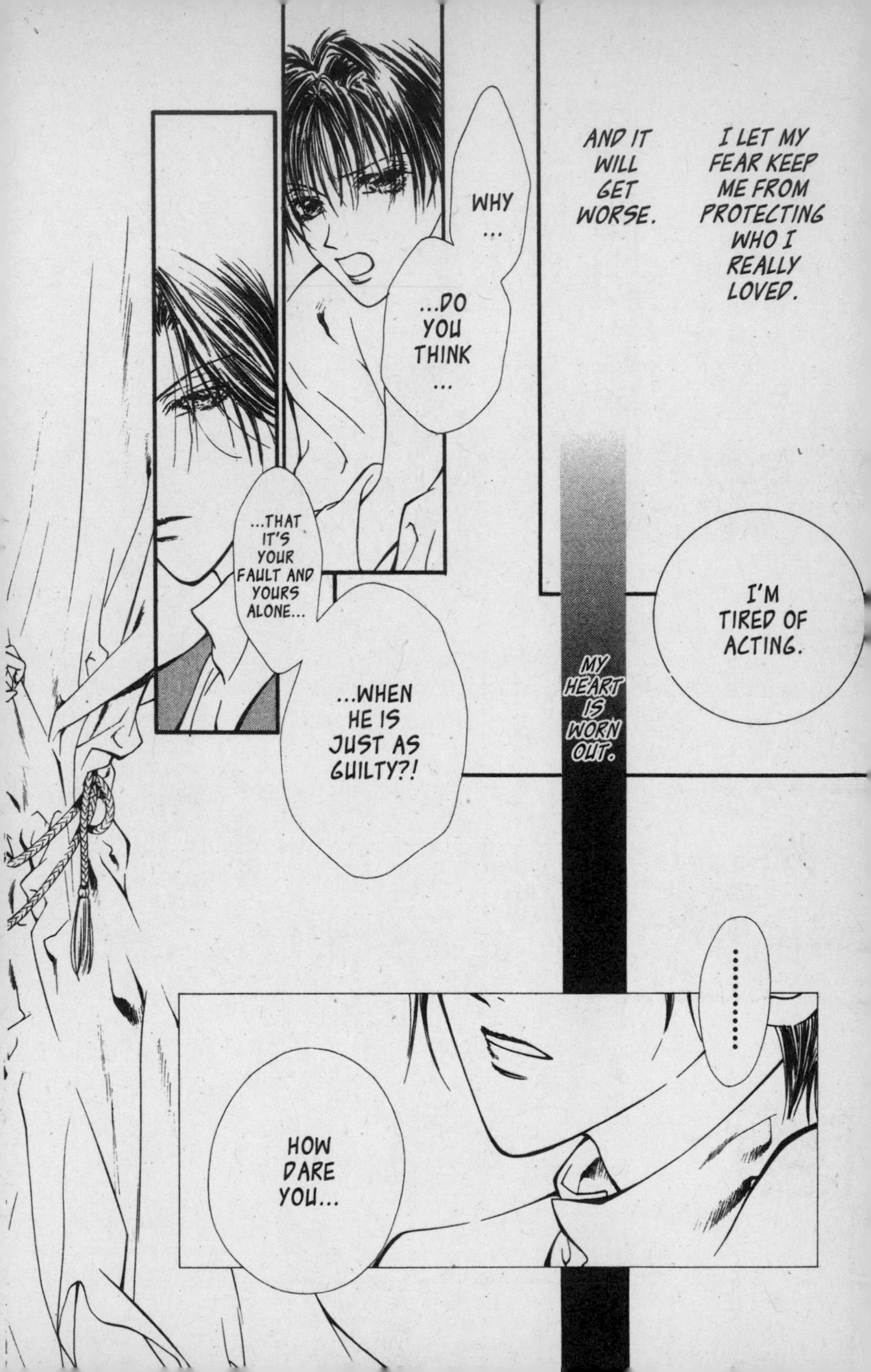

I LET MY FEAR KEEP ME FROM PROTECTING WHO I REALLY LOVED.
AND IT WILL GET WORSE.
I'M TIRED OF ACTING.
MY HEART IS WORN OUT.
WHY ...
...DO YOU THINK ...
...THAT IT'S YOUR FAULT AND YOURS ALONE...
...WHEN HE IS JUST AS GUILTY?!
......
HOW DARE YOU...

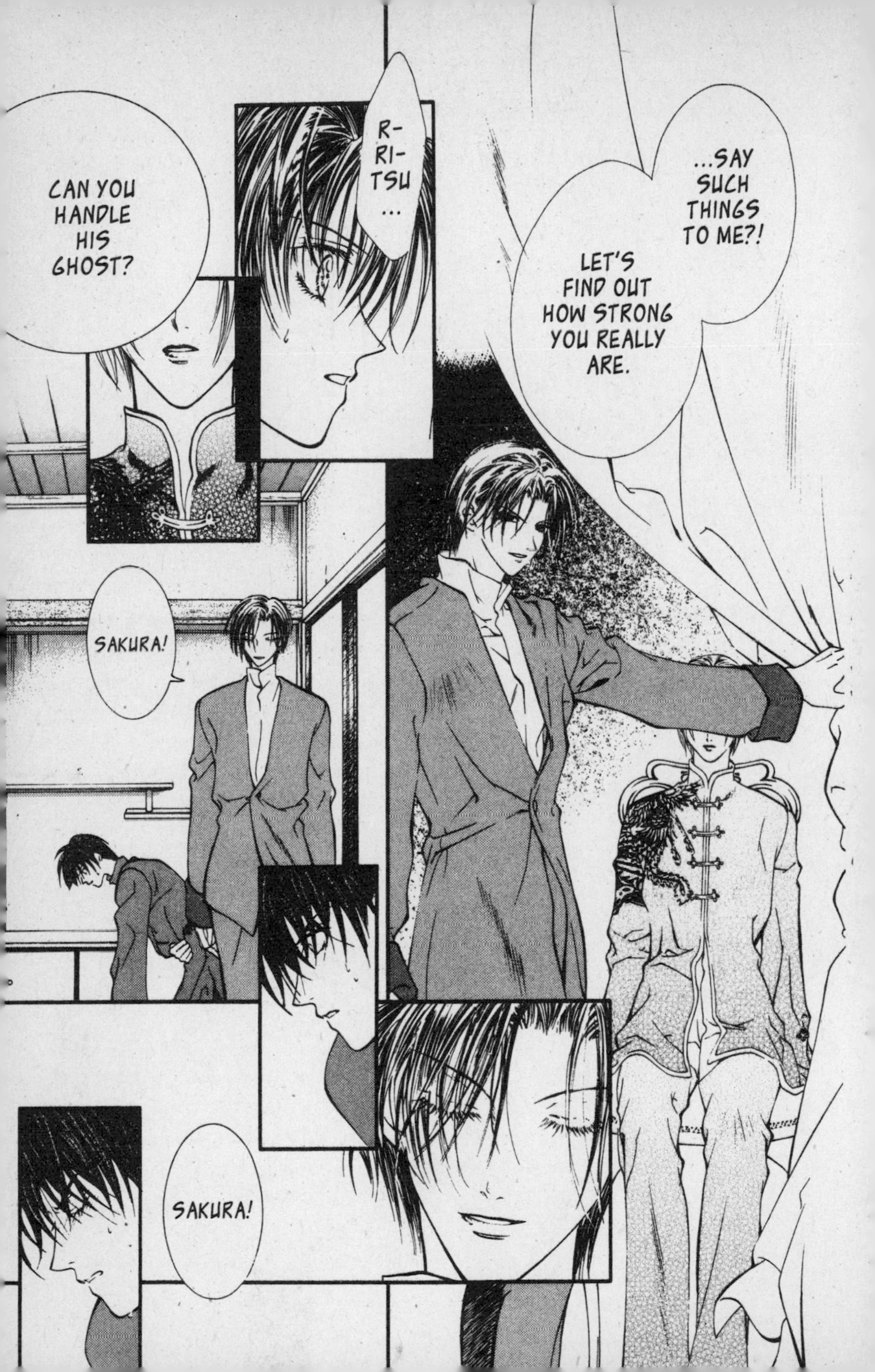
...SAY SUCH THINGS TO ME?!
LET'S FIND OUT HOW STRONG YOU REALLY ARE.
R-RI-TSU...
CAN YOU HANDLE HIS GHOST?
SAKURA!
SAKURA!

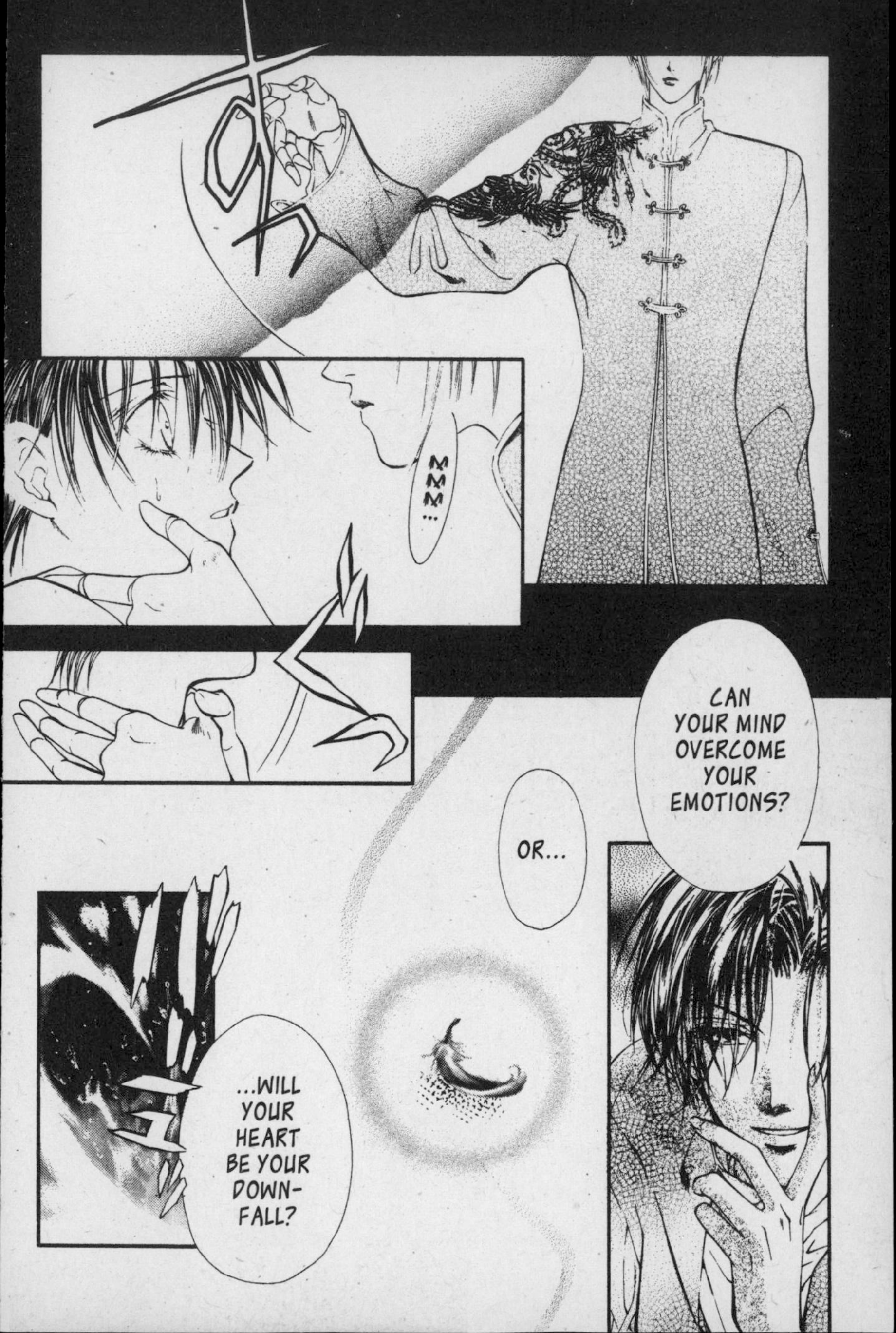
MMM...
CAN YOUR MIND OVERCOME YOUR EMOTIONS?
OR...
...WILL YOUR HEART BE YOUR DOWN-FALL?

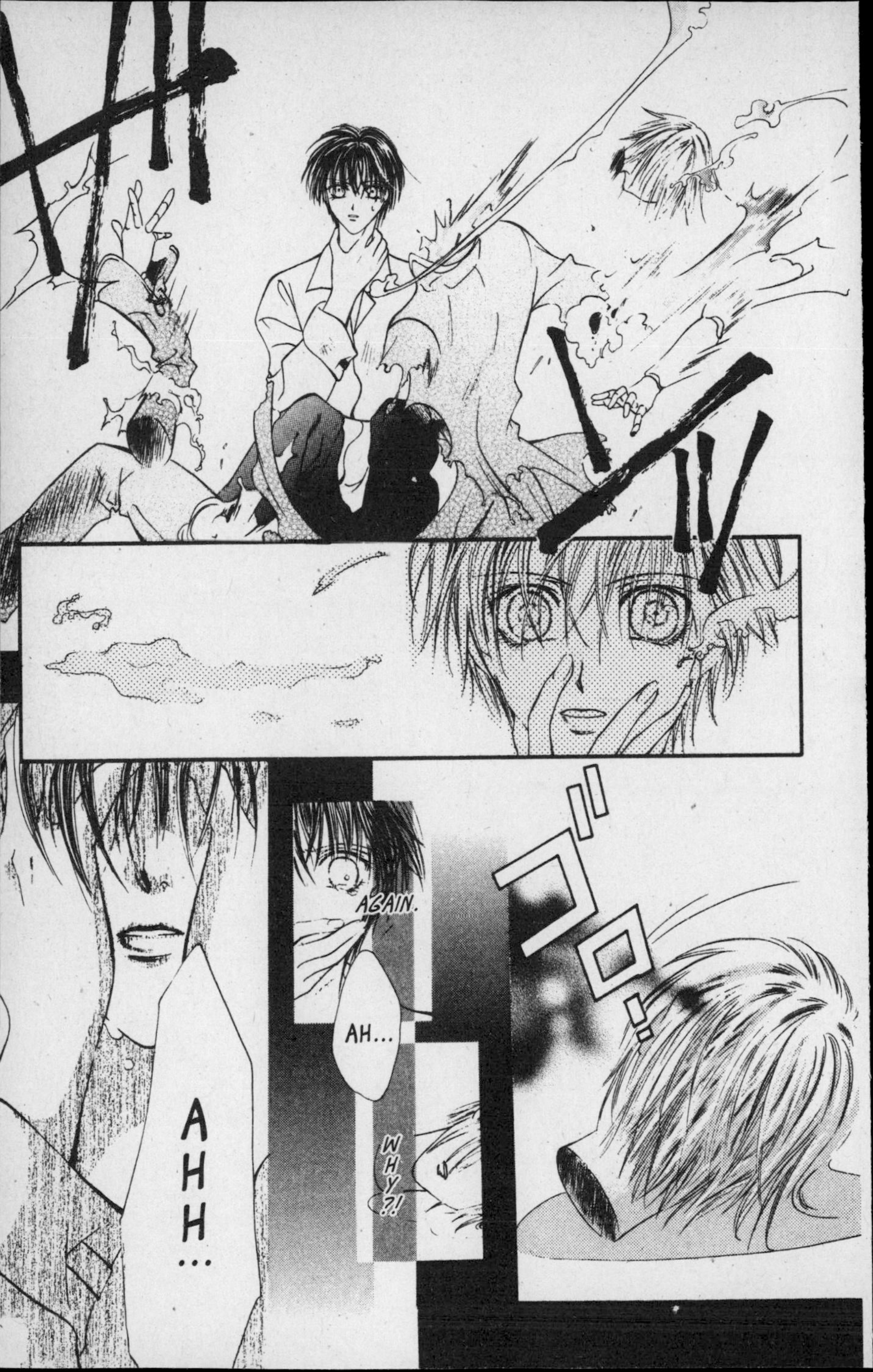
ゴロ!
AGAIN.
AH...
WHY?!
AHH...

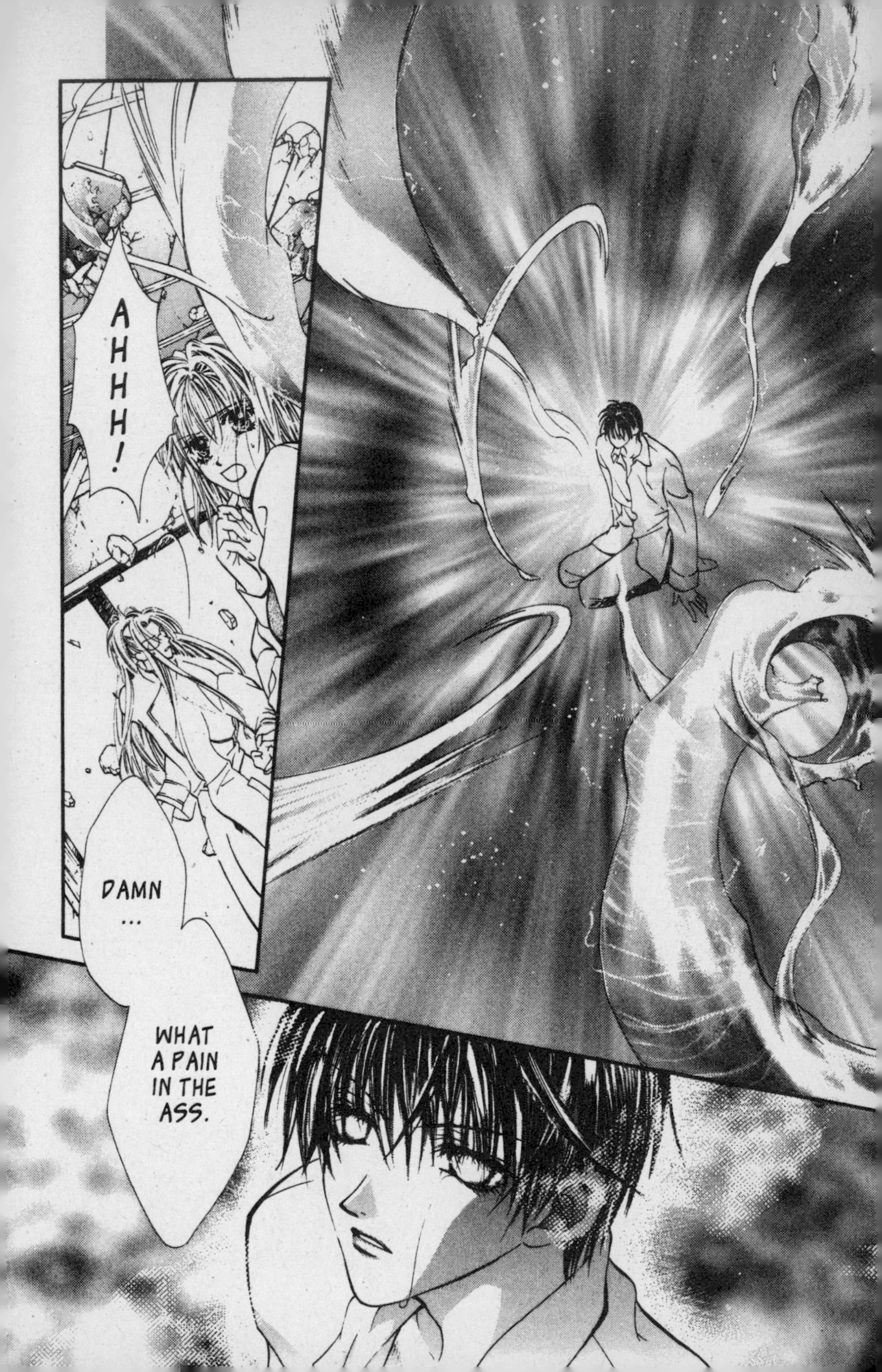
AHHHH!
DAMN ...
WHAT A PAIN IN THE ASS.

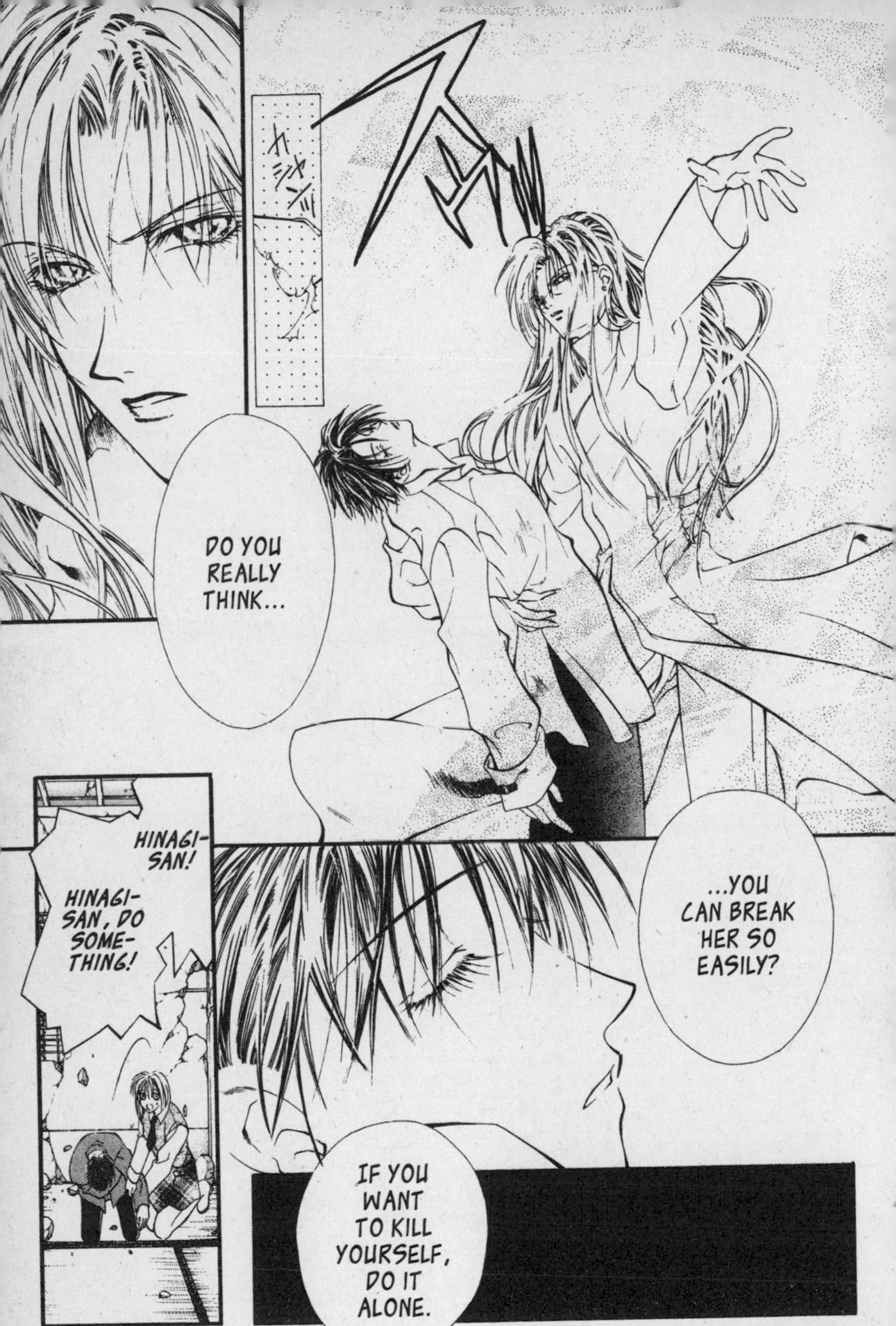
DO YOU REALLY THINK...
...YOU CAN BREAK HER SO EASILY?
IF YOU WANT TO KILL YOURSELF, DO IT ALONE.
HINAGI-SAN!
HINAGI-SAN, DO SOMETHING!

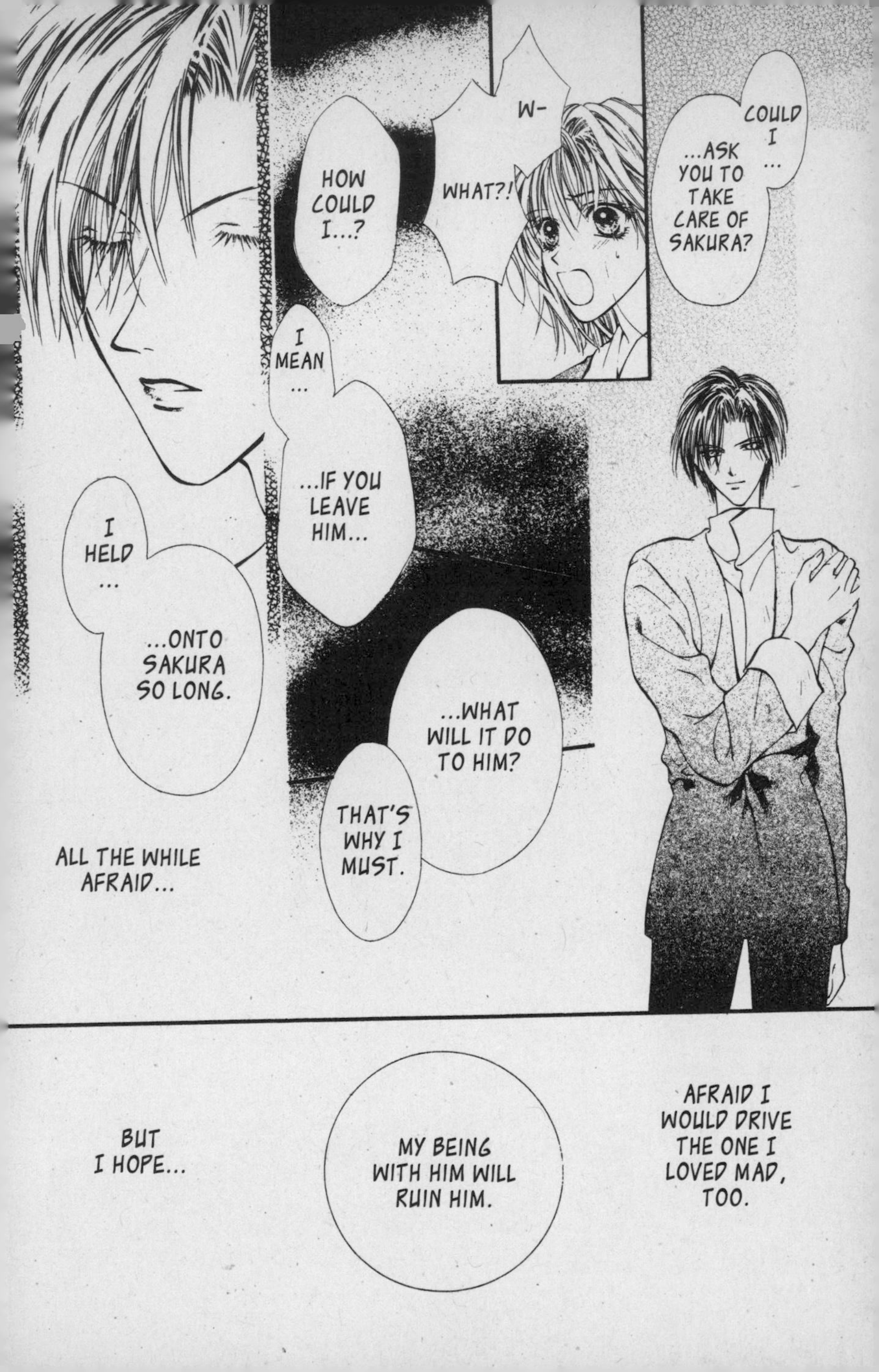
COULD I ...
...ASK YOU TO TAKE CARE OF SAKURA?
W-
WHAT?!
HOW COULD I...?
I MEAN ...
...IF YOU LEAVE HIM...
...WHAT WILL IT DO TO HIM?
THAT'S WHY I MUST.
I HELD ...
...ONTO SAKURA SO LONG.
ALL THE WHILE AFRAID...
AFRAID I WOULD DRIVE THE ONE I LOVED MAD, TOO.
MY BEING WITH HIM WILL RUIN HIM.
BUT I HOPE...

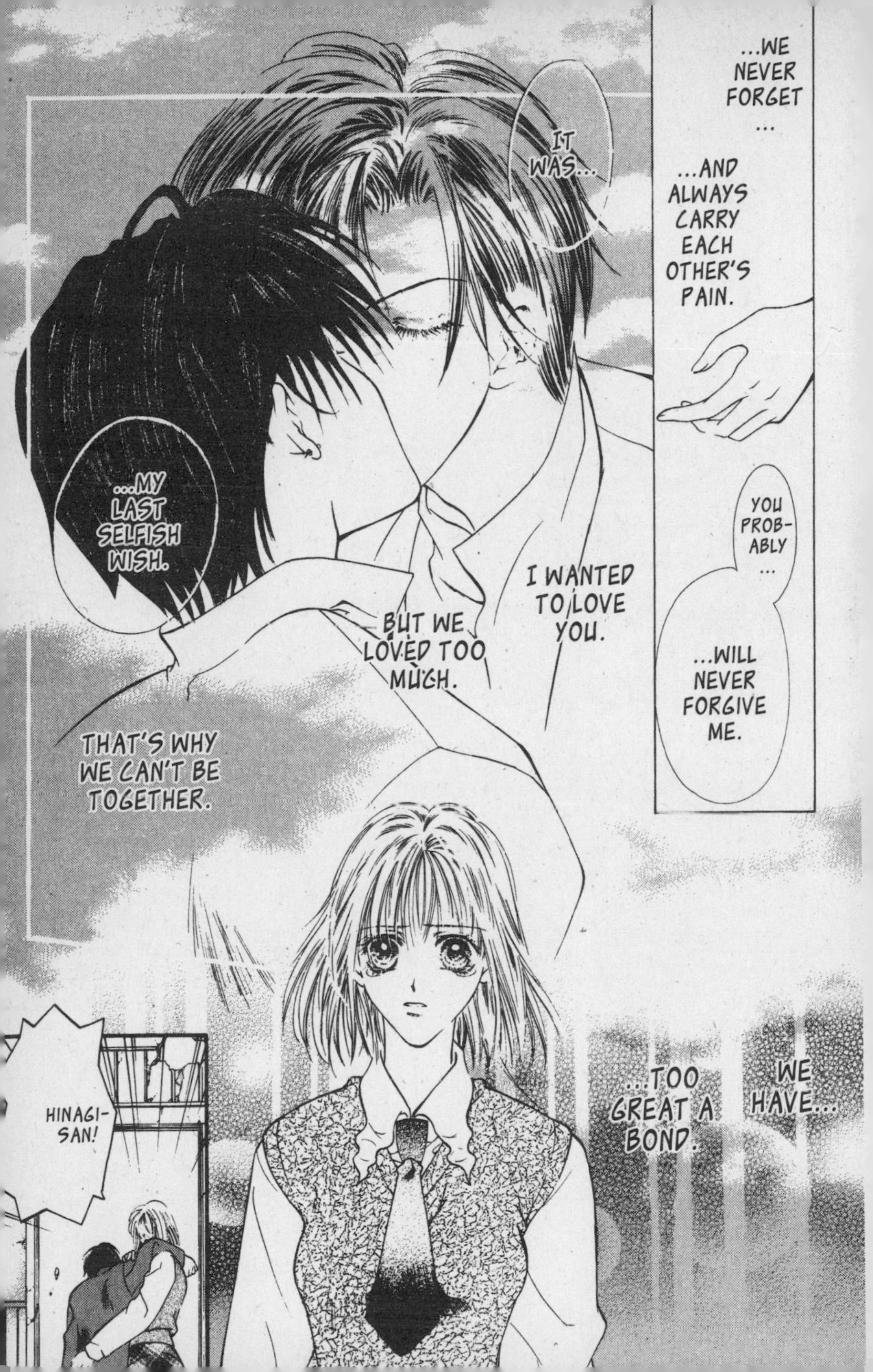
...WE NEVER FORGET ...
...AND ALWAYS CARRY EACH OTHER'S PAIN.
YOU PROBABLY ...
...WILL NEVER FORGIVE ME.
IT WAS...
...MY LAST SELFISH WISH.
I WANTED TO LOVE YOU.
BUT WE LOVED TOO MUCH.
THAT'S WHY WE CAN'T BE TOGETHER.
WE HAVE...
...TOO GREAT A BOND.
HINAGI-SAN!

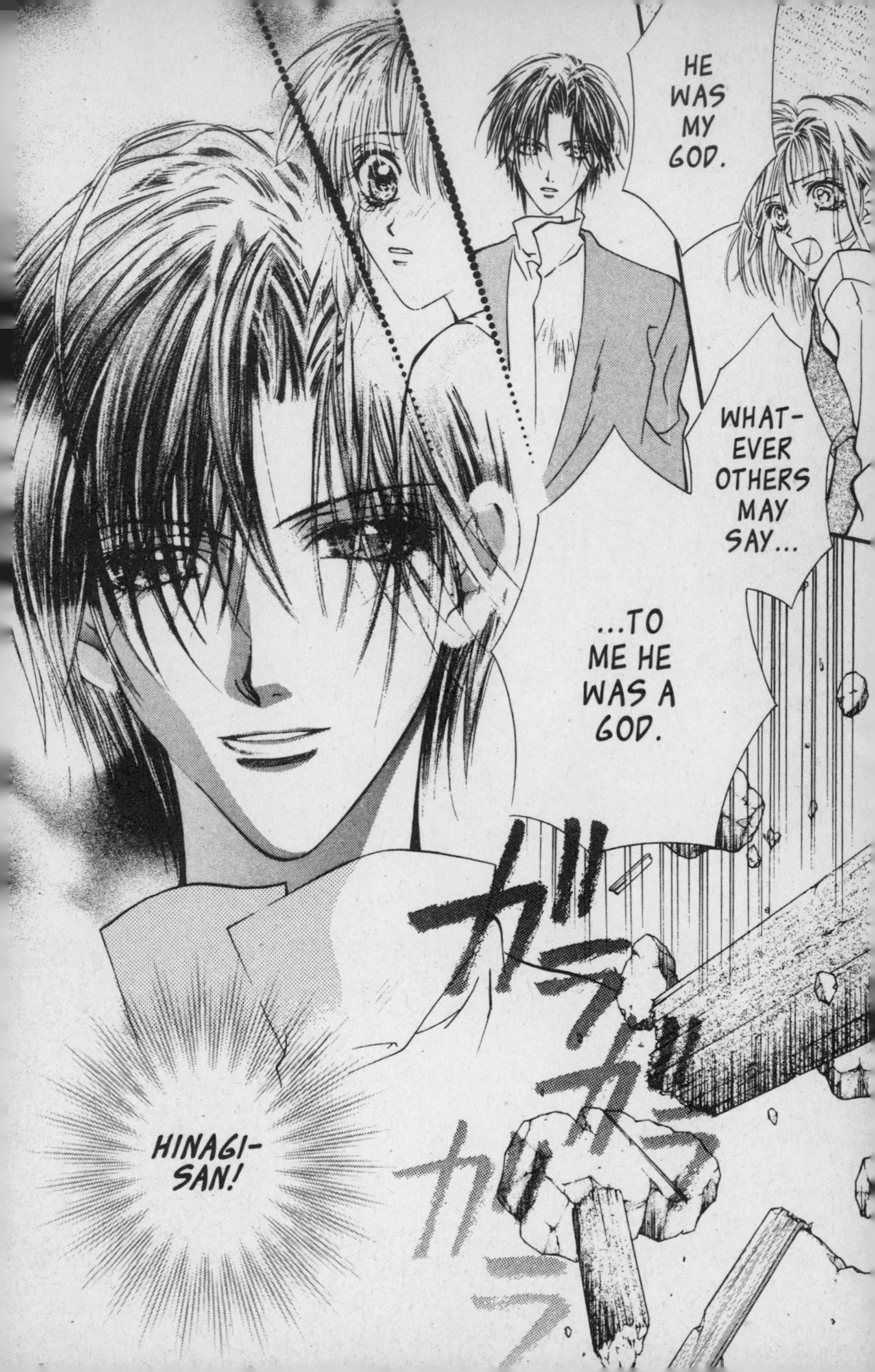
HE WAS MY GOD.
WHAT-EVER OTHERS MAY SAY...
...TO ME HE WAS A GOD.
ガラ
ガラ
HINAGI-SAN!

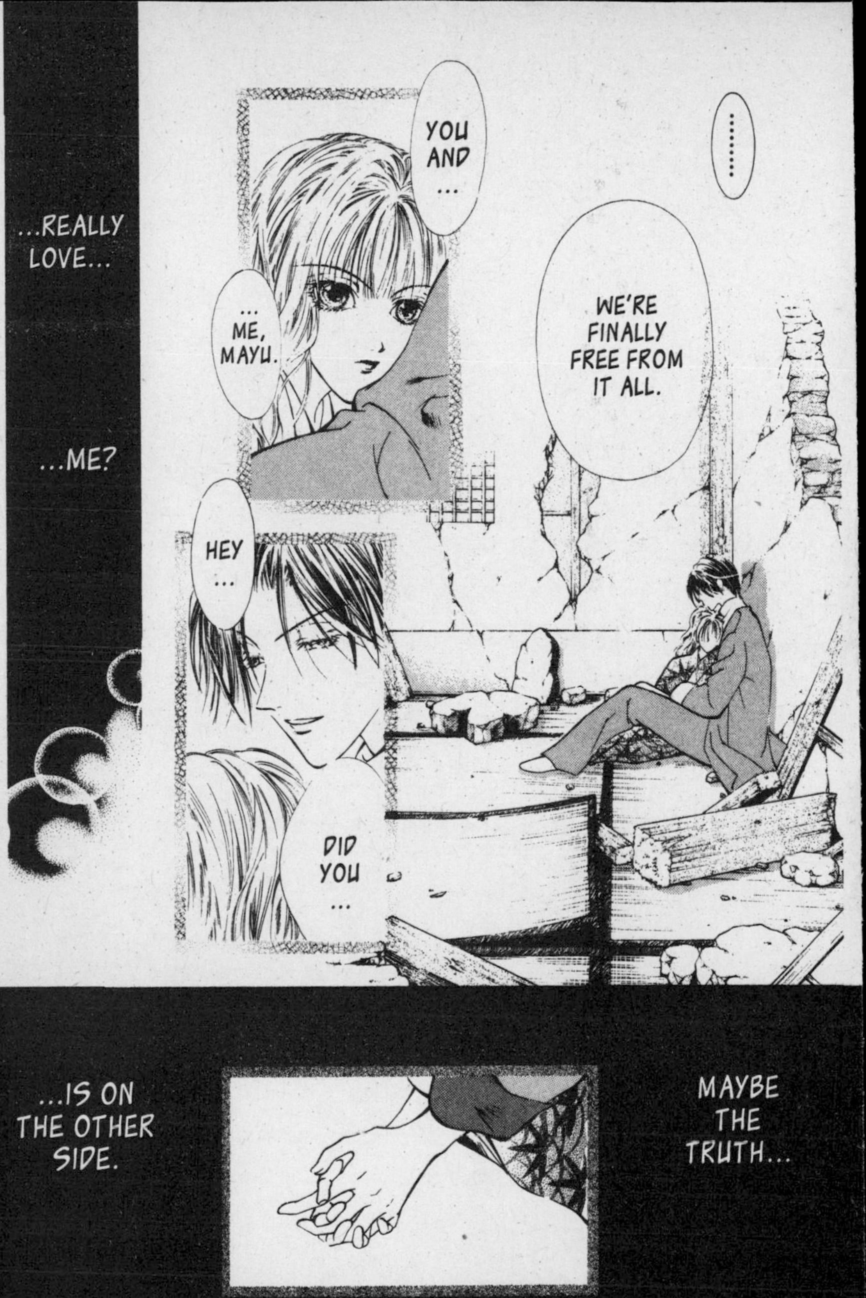
......
WE'RE FINALLY FREE FROM IT ALL.
YOU AND ...
... ME, MAYU.
HEY ...
DID YOU ...
...REALLY LOVE...
...ME?
MAYBE THE TRUTH...
...IS ON THE OTHER SIDE.

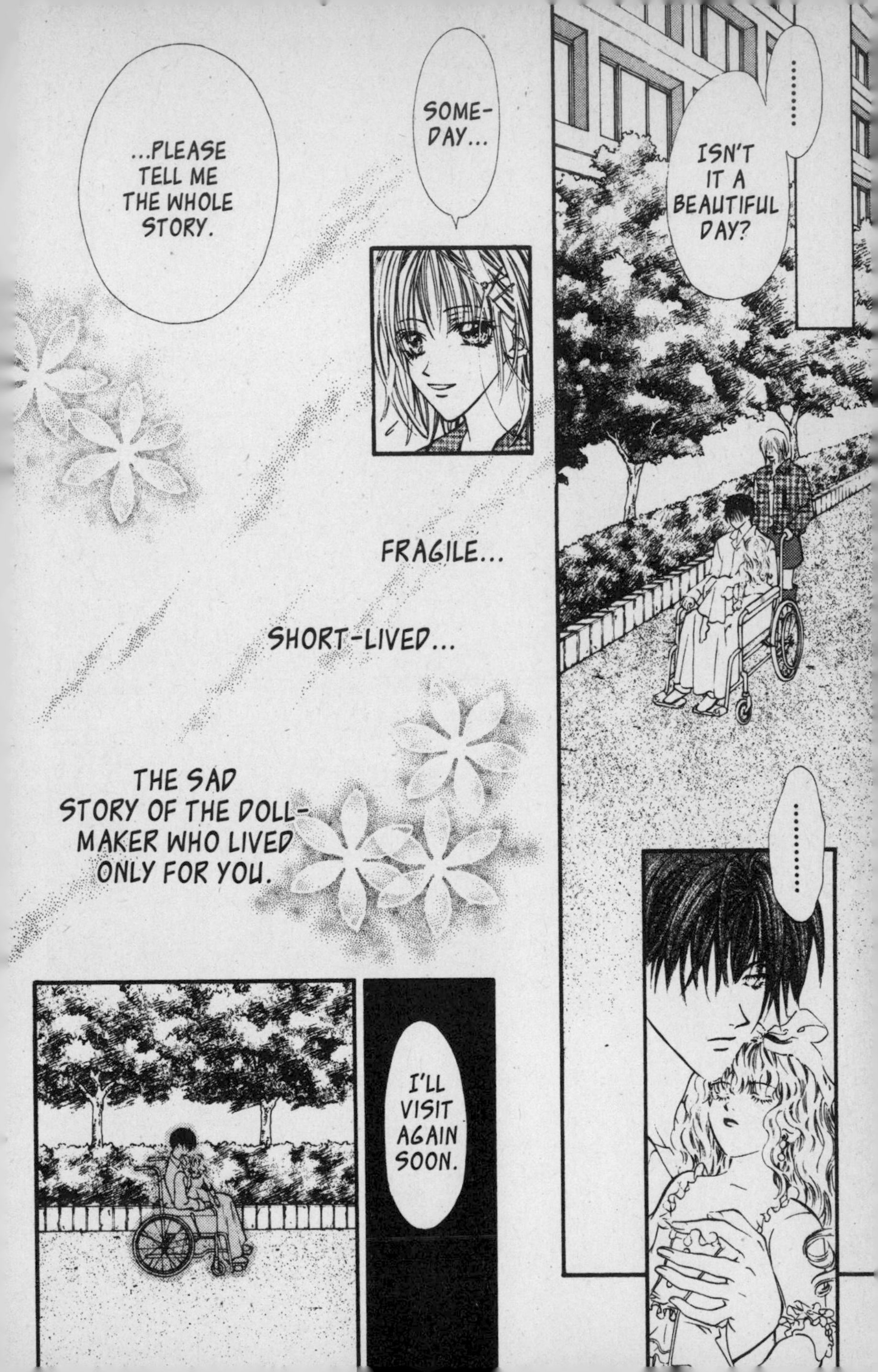
......
ISN'T IT A BEAUTIFUL DAY?
......
SOME-DAY...
...PLEASE TELL ME THE WHOLE STORY.
FRAGILE...
SHORT-LIVED...
THE SAD STORY OF THE DOLL-MAKER WHO LIVED ONLY FOR YOU.
I'LL VISIT AGAIN SOON.

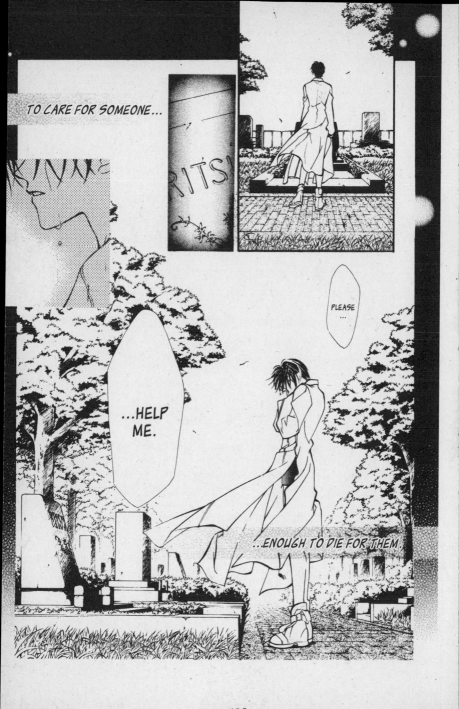

TO CARE FOR SOMEONE...

PLEASE ...

...HELP ME.

...ENOUGH TO DIE FOR THEM.

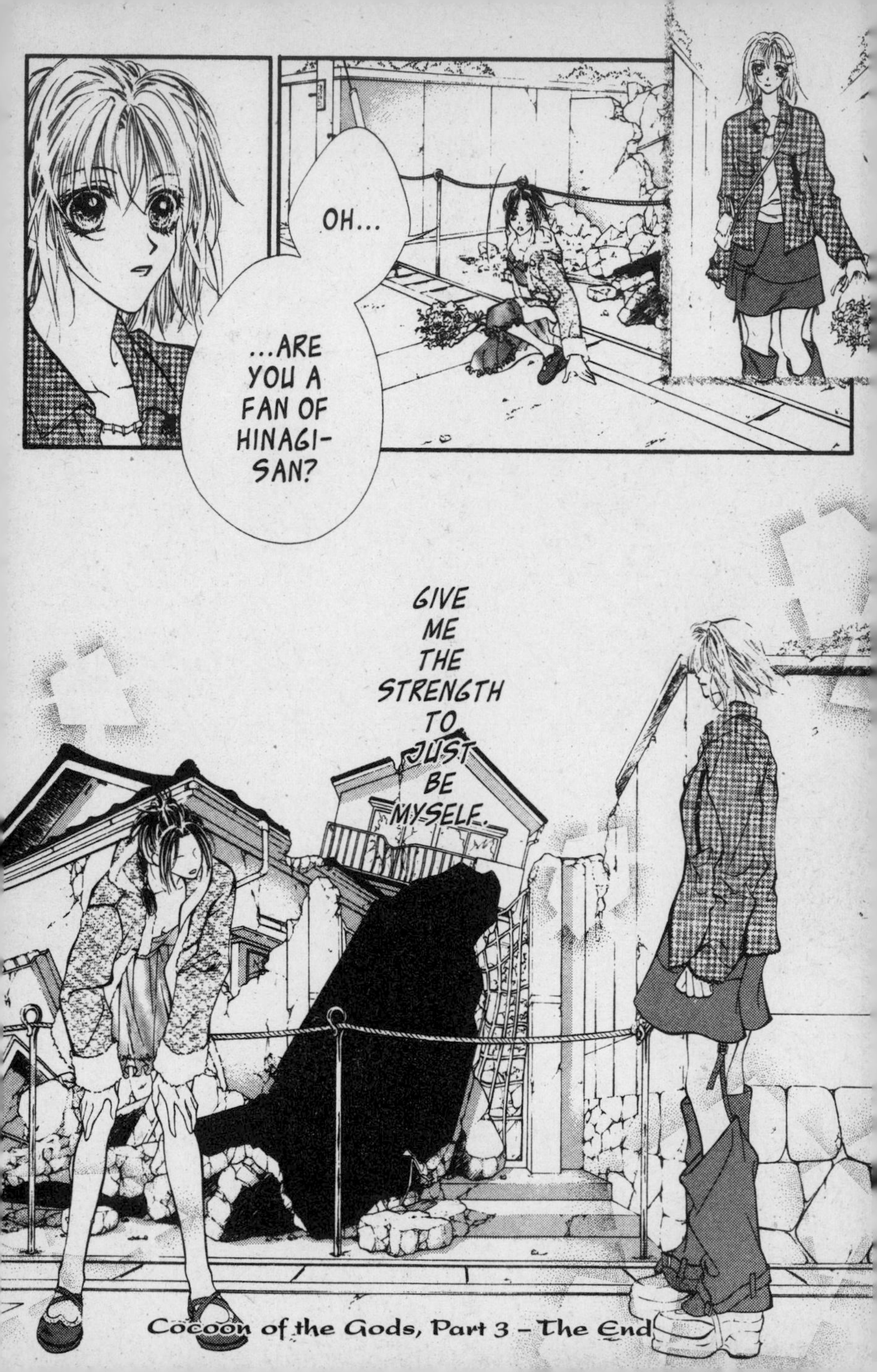
OH...
...ARE YOU A FAN OF HINAGI-SAN?
GIVE ME THE STRENGTH TO JUST BE MYSELF.
Cocoon of the Gods, Part 3 – The End

Bird Cage Princess

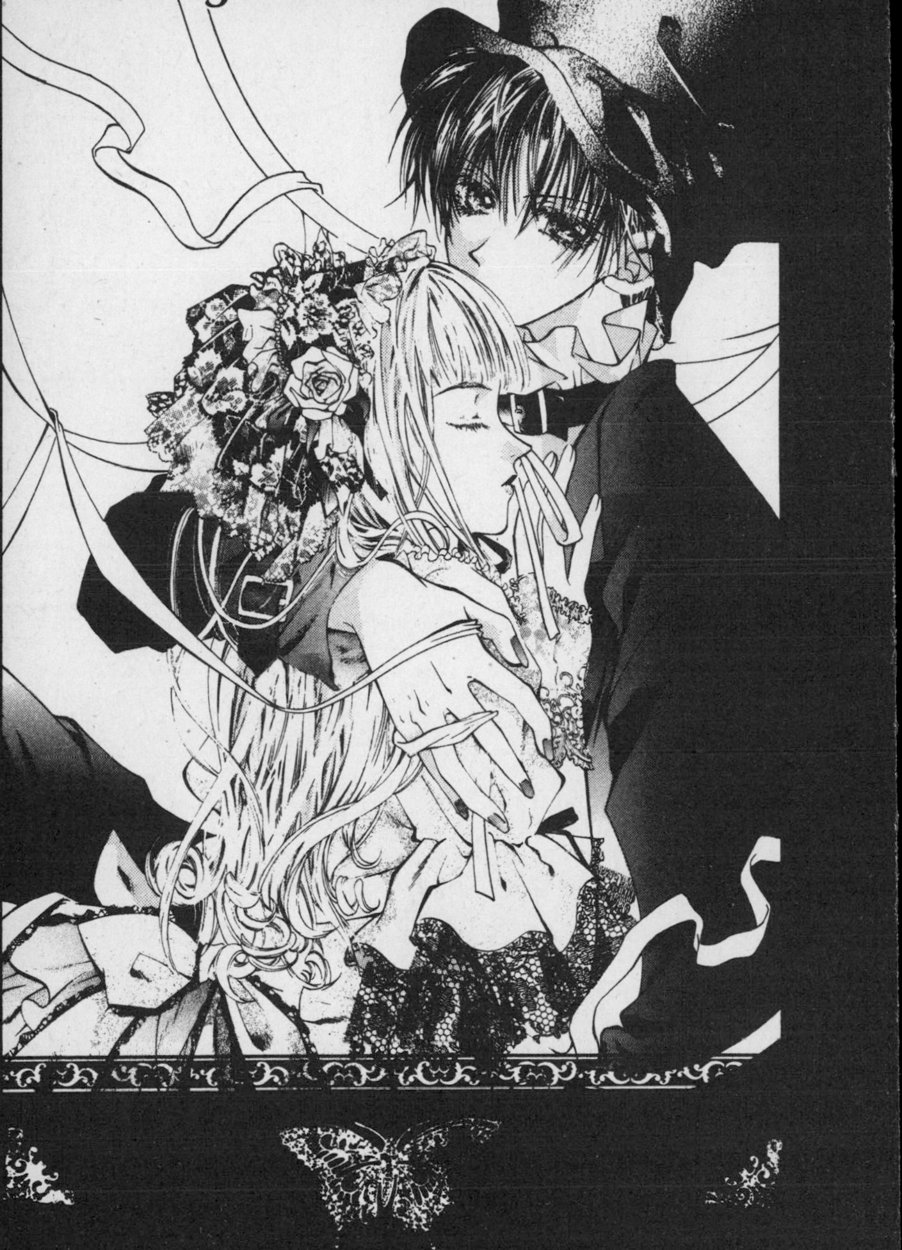

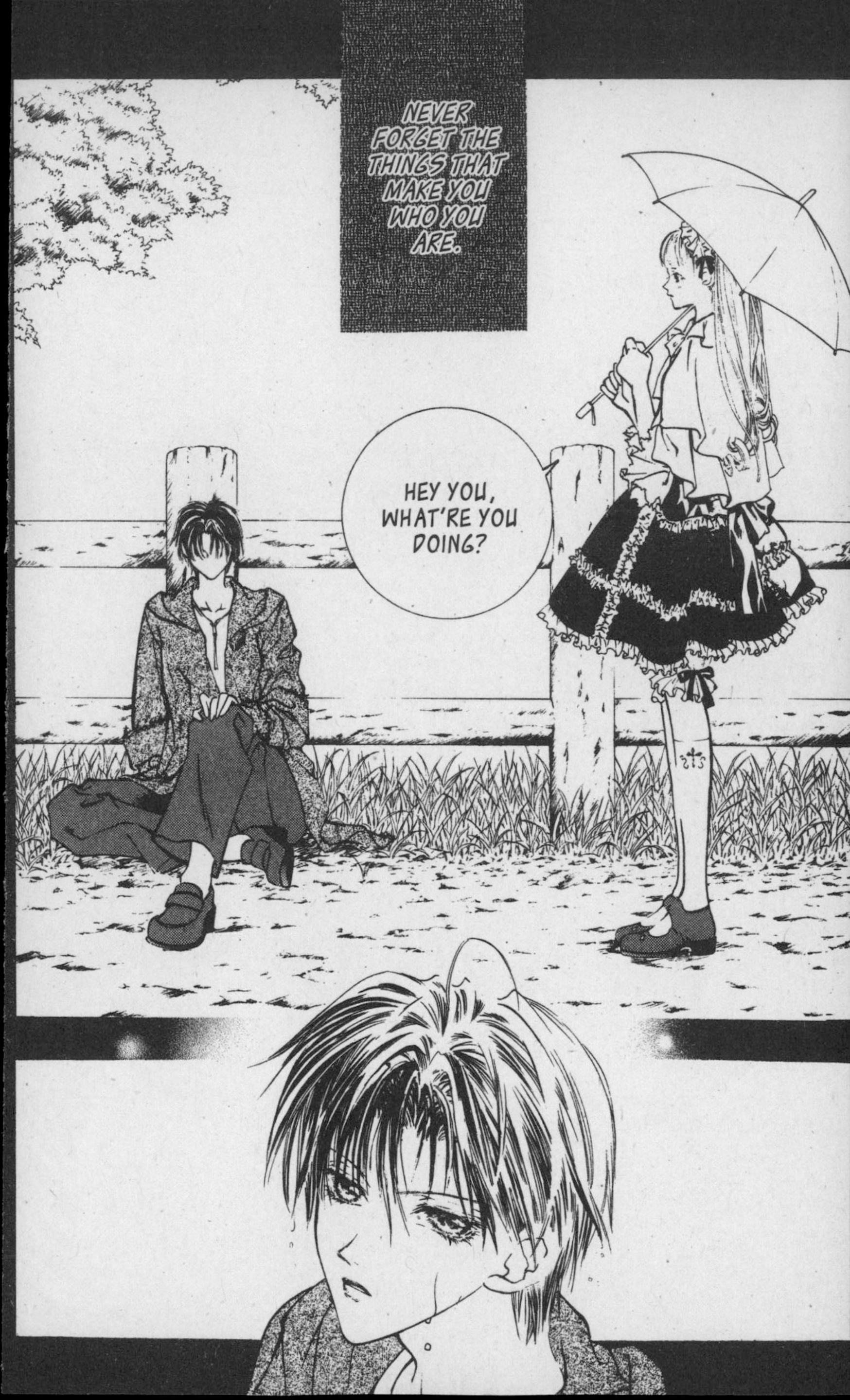
NEVER FORGET THE THINGS THAT MAKE YOU WHO YOU ARE.
HEY YOU, WHAT'RE YOU DOING?

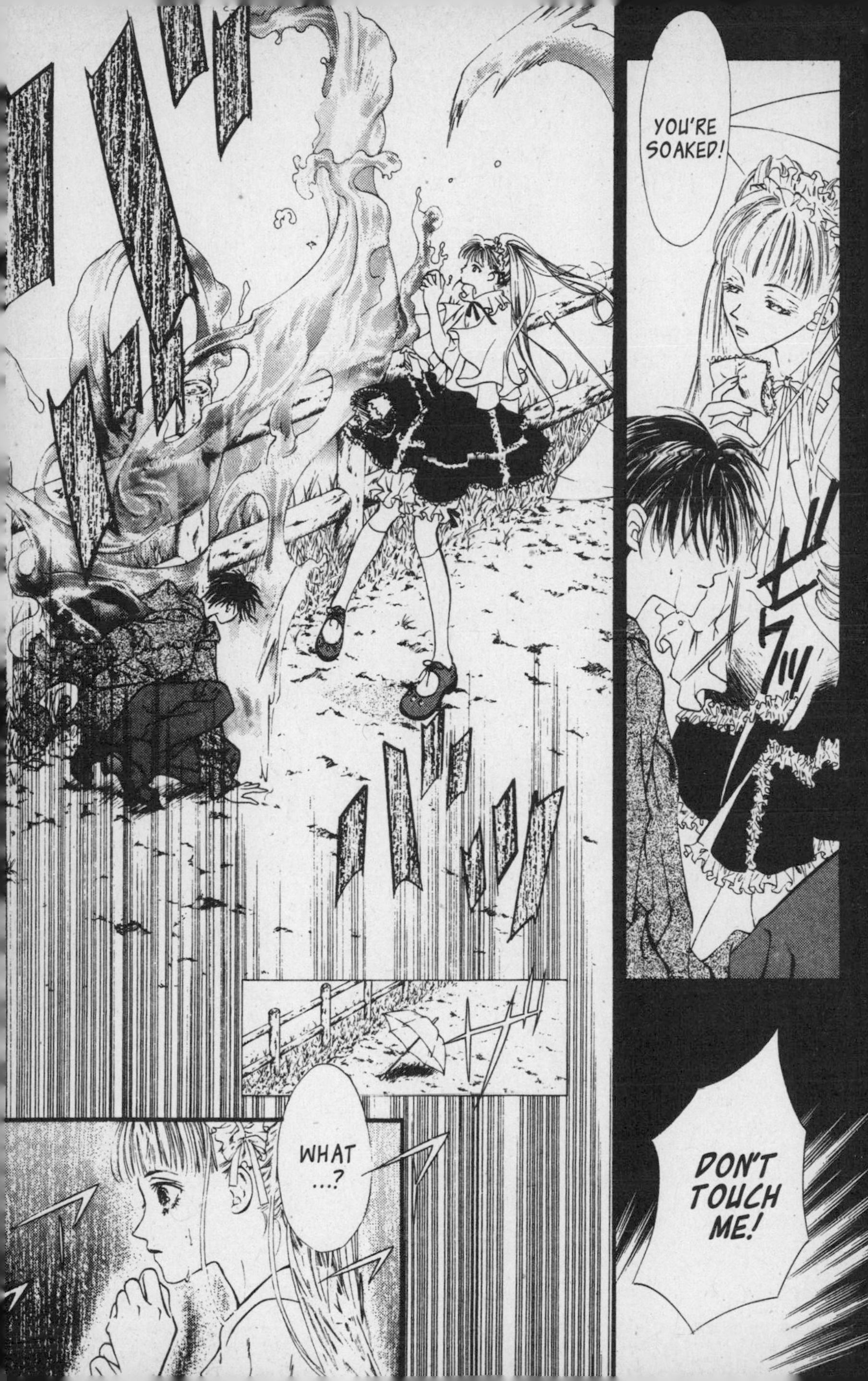
YOU'RE SOAKED!
DON'T TOUCH ME!
WHAT ...?

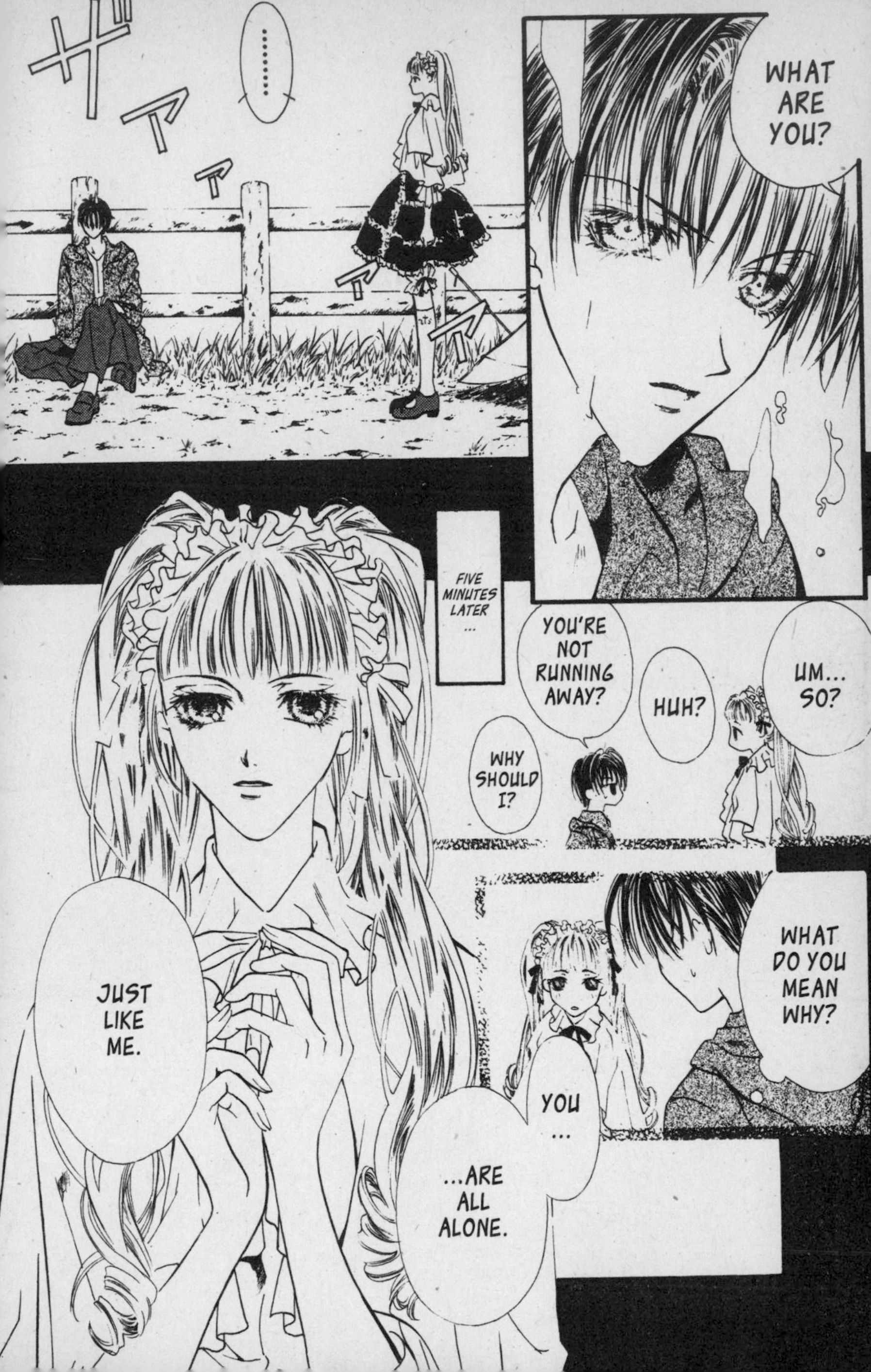
WHAT ARE YOU?
......
FIVE MINUTES LATER ...
UM... SO?
HUH?
YOU'RE NOT RUNNING AWAY?
WHY SHOULD I?
WHAT DO YOU MEAN WHY?
YOU ...
...ARE ALL ALONE.
JUST LIKE ME.

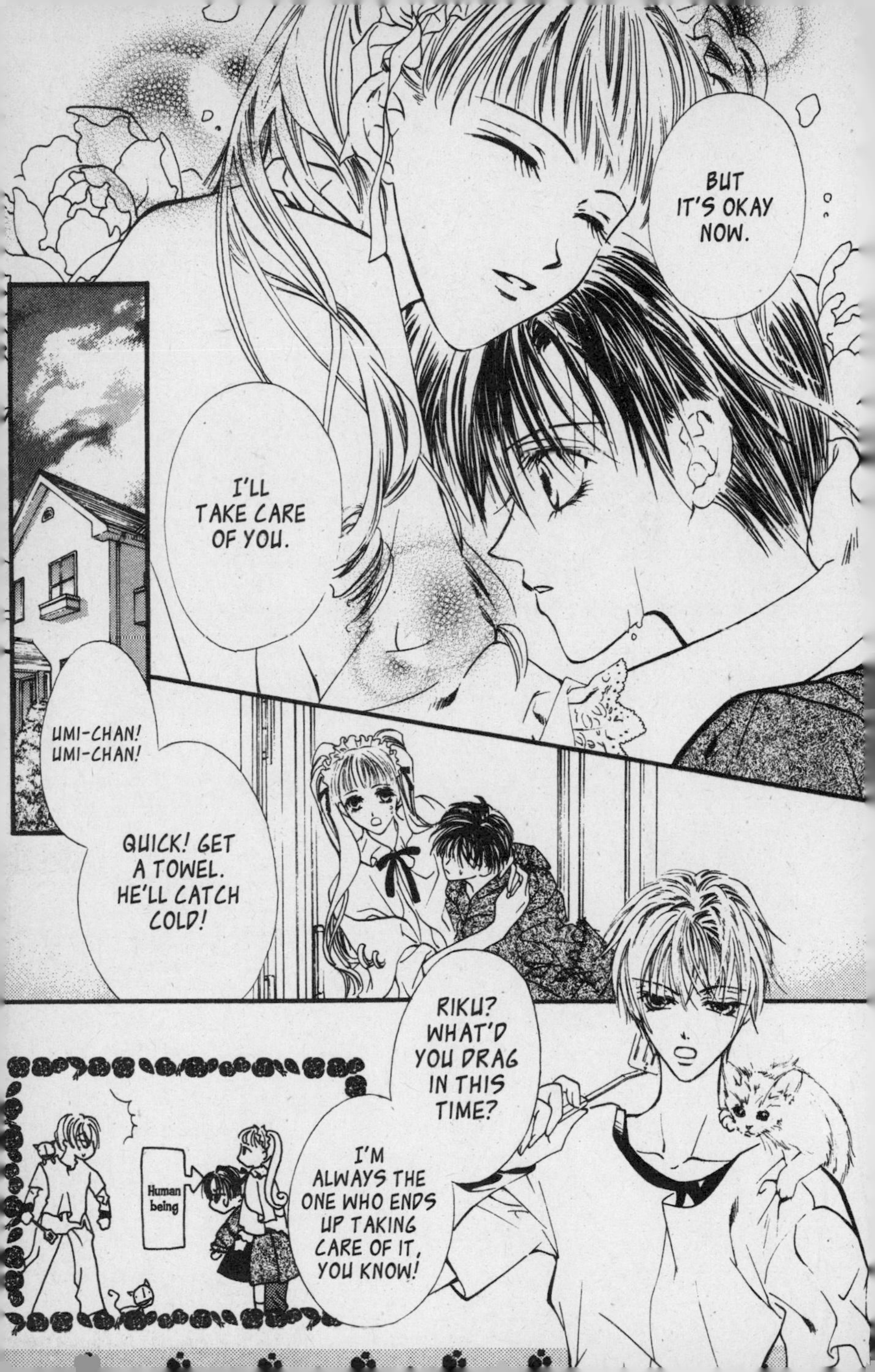

BUT IT'S OKAY NOW.
I'LL TAKE CARE OF YOU.
UMI-CHAN! UMI-CHAN!
QUICK! GET A TOWEL. HE'LL CATCH COLD!
RIKU? WHAT'D YOU DRAG IN THIS TIME?
I'M ALWAYS THE ONE WHO ENDS UP TAKING CARE OF IT, YOU KNOW!
Human being

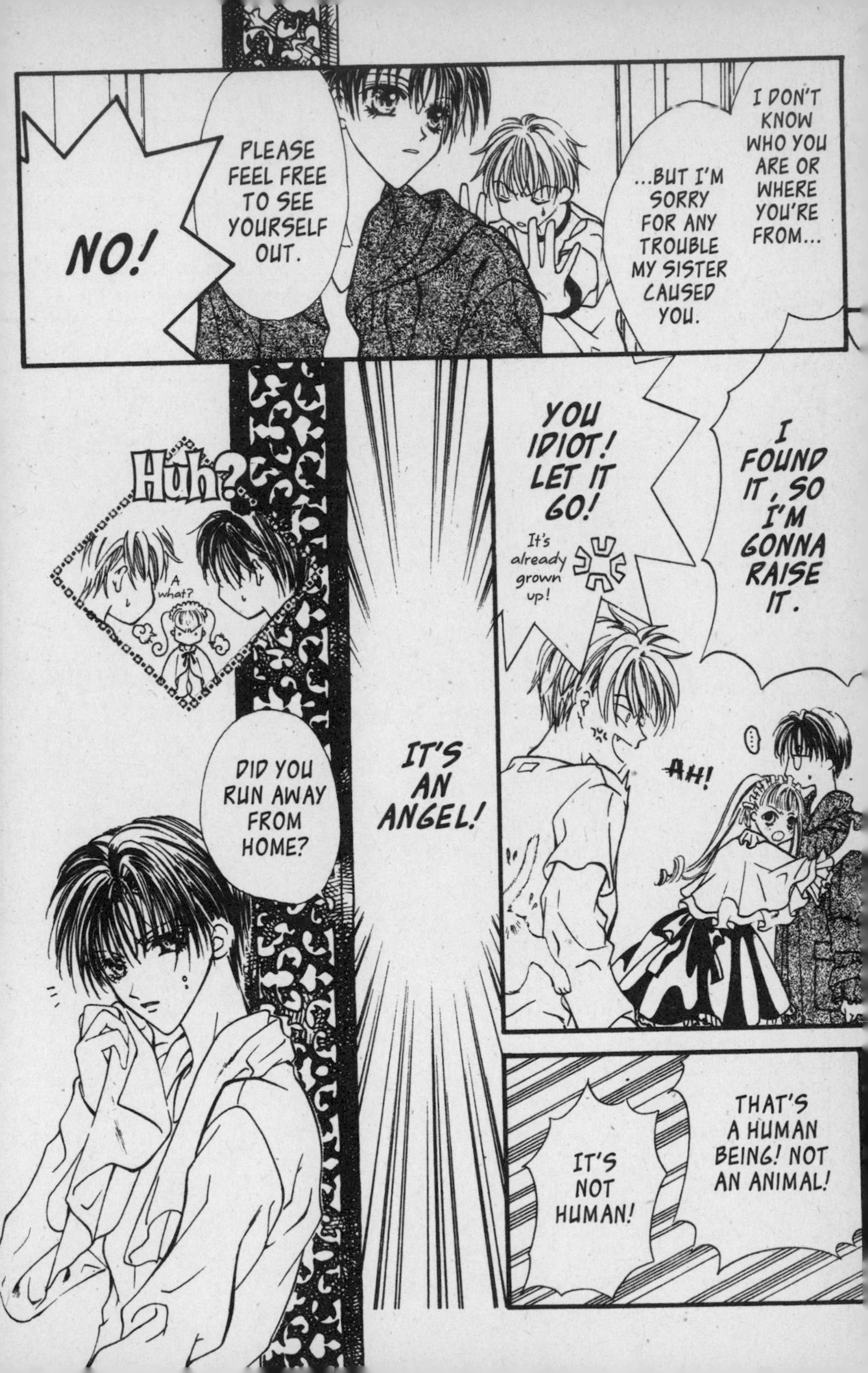
I DON'T KNOW WHO YOU ARE OR WHERE YOU'RE FROM...
...BUT I'M SORRY FOR ANY TROUBLE MY SISTER CAUSED YOU.
PLEASE FEEL FREE TO SEE YOURSELF OUT.
NO!
I FOUND IT, SO I'M GONNA RAISE IT.
YOU IDIOT! LET IT GO!
It's already grown up!
...
AH!
THAT'S A HUMAN BEING! NOT AN ANIMAL!
IT'S NOT HUMAN!
IT'S AN ANGEL!
Huh?
A what?
DID YOU RUN AWAY FROM HOME?

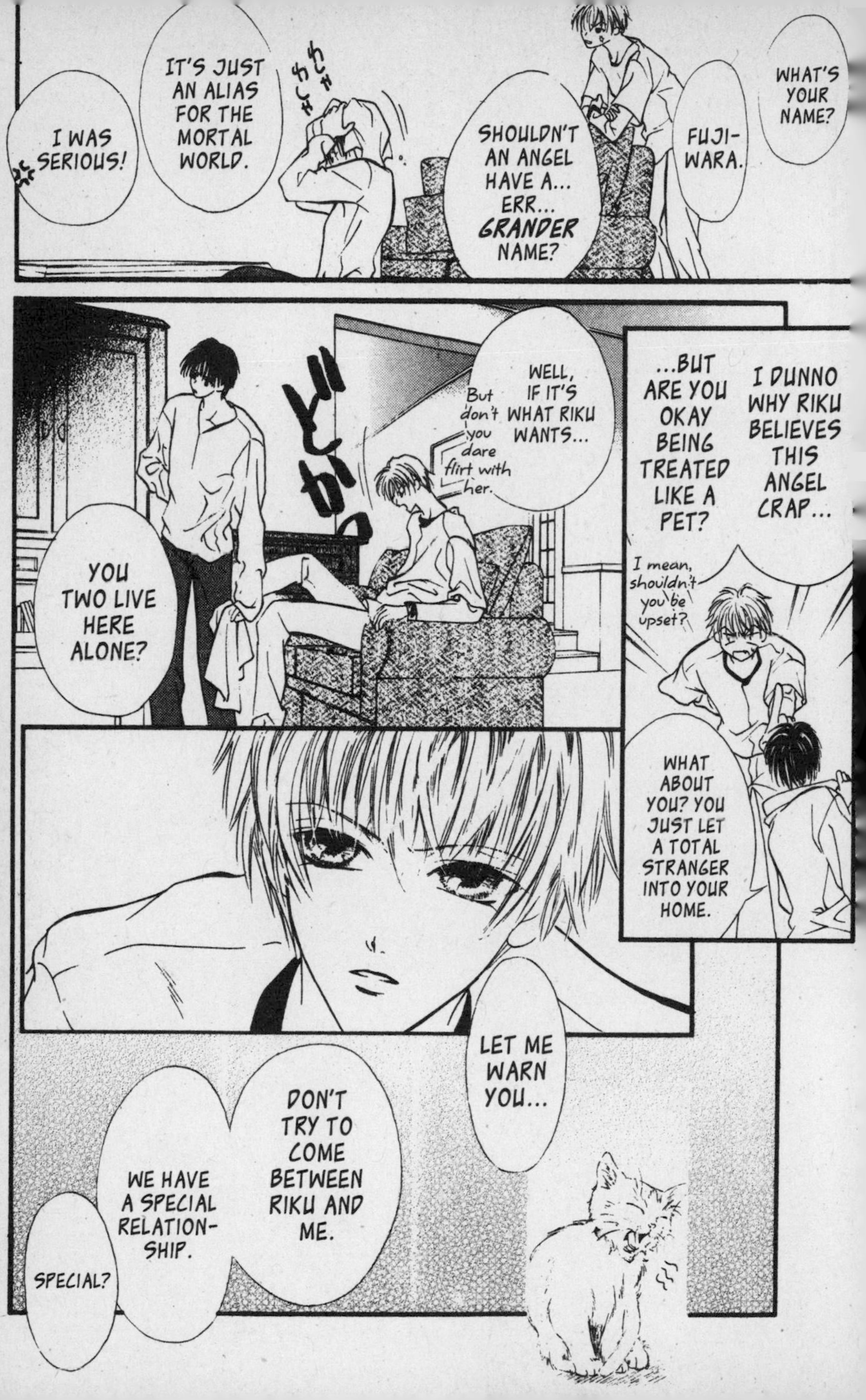
WHAT'S YOUR NAME?
FUJI-WARA.
SHOULDN'T AN ANGEL HAVE A... ERR... GRANDER NAME?
IT'S JUST AN ALIAS FOR THE MORTAL WORLD.
I WAS SERIOUS!
I DUNNO WHY RIKU BELIEVES THIS ANGEL CRAP...
...BUT ARE YOU OKAY BEING TREATED LIKE A PET?
I mean, shouldn't you be upset?
WHAT ABOUT YOU? YOU JUST LET A TOTAL STRANGER INTO YOUR HOME.
WELL, IF IT'S WHAT RIKU WANTS...
But don't you dare flirt with her.
YOU TWO LIVE HERE ALONE?
LET ME WARN YOU...
DON'T TRY TO COME BETWEEN RIKU AND ME.
WE HAVE A SPECIAL RELATION-SHIP.
SPECIAL?

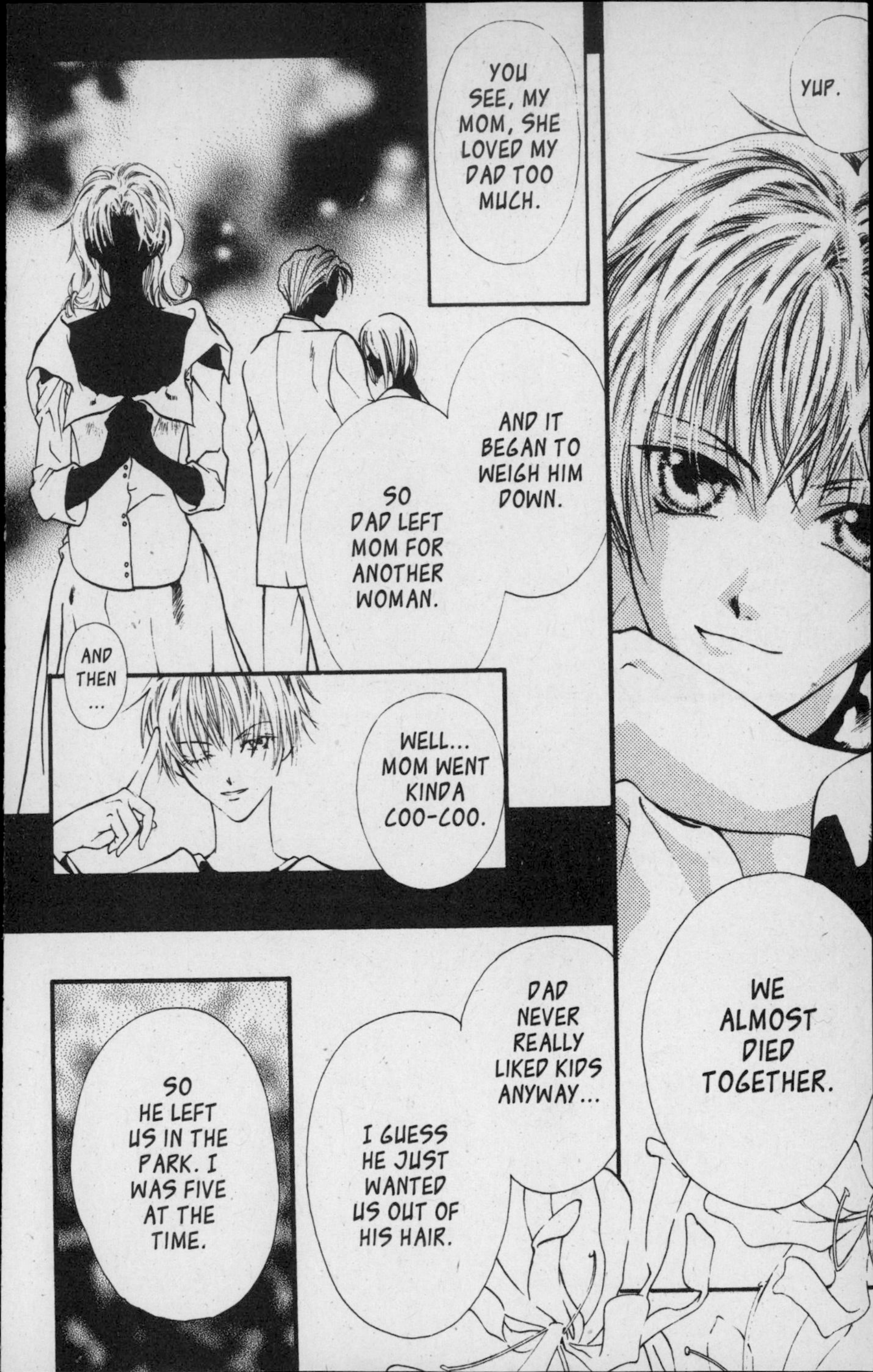
YUP.
YOU SEE, MY MOM, SHE LOVED MY DAD TOO MUCH.
AND IT BEGAN TO WEIGH HIM DOWN.
SO DAD LEFT MOM FOR ANOTHER WOMAN.
AND THEN...
WELL... MOM WENT KINDA COO-COO.
WE ALMOST DIED TOGETHER.
DAD NEVER REALLY LIKED KIDS ANYWAY...
I GUESS HE JUST WANTED US OUT OF HIS HAIR.
SO HE LEFT US IN THE PARK. I WAS FIVE AT THE TIME.

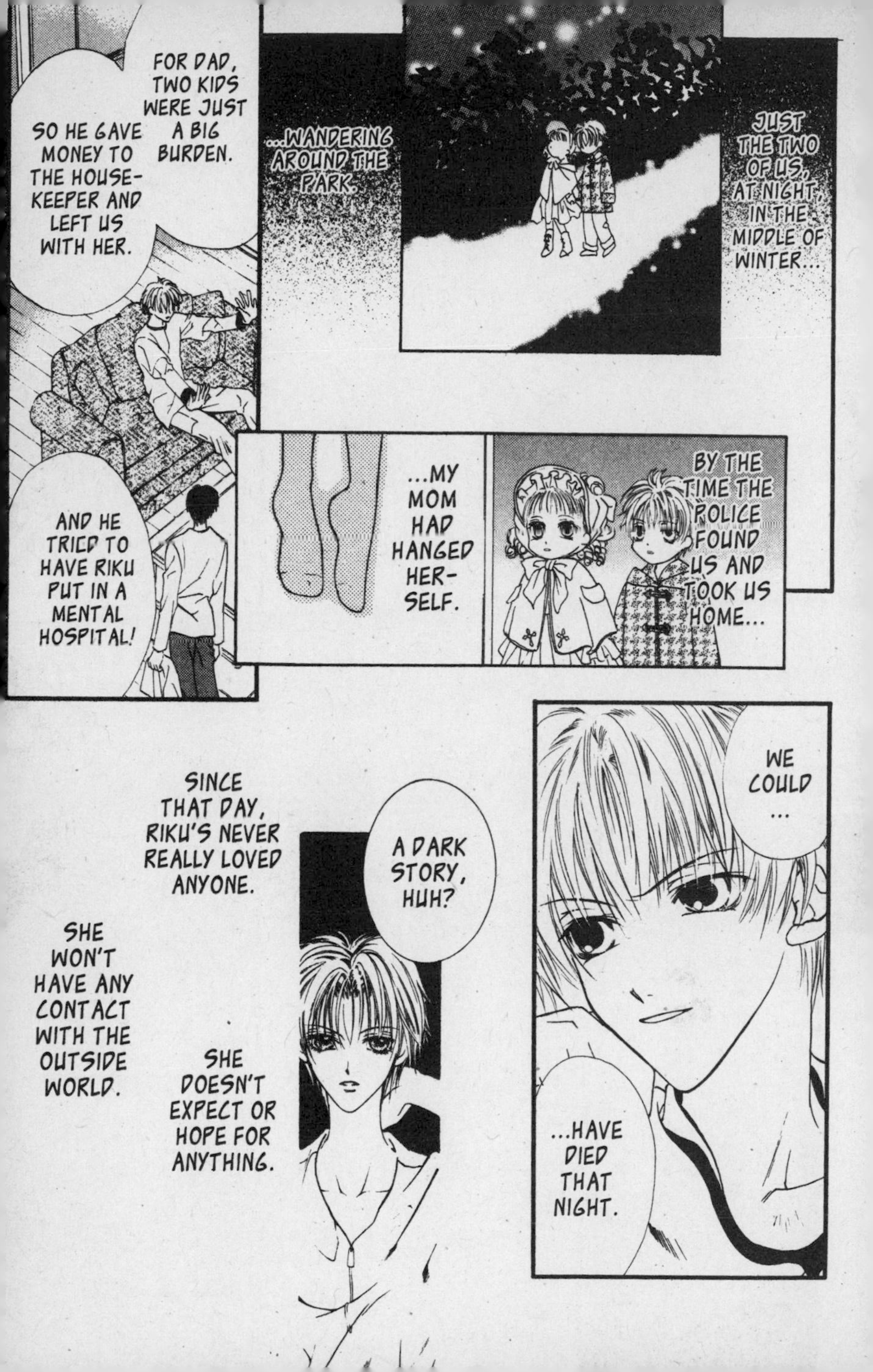
JUST THE TWO OF US, AT NIGHT, IN THE MIDDLE OF WINTER...
...WANDERING AROUND THE PARK.
BY THE TIME THE POLICE FOUND US AND TOOK US HOME...
...MY MOM HAD HANGED HERSELF.
FOR DAD, TWO KIDS WERE JUST A BIG BURDEN.
SO HE GAVE MONEY TO THE HOUSE-KEEPER AND LEFT US WITH HER.
AND HE TRIED TO HAVE RIKU PUT IN A MENTAL HOSPITAL!
WE COULD...
...HAVE DIED THAT NIGHT.
A DARK STORY, HUH?
SINCE THAT DAY, RIKU'S NEVER REALLY LOVED ANYONE.
SHE DOESN'T EXPECT OR HOPE FOR ANYTHING.
SHE WON'T HAVE ANY CONTACT WITH THE OUTSIDE WORLD.

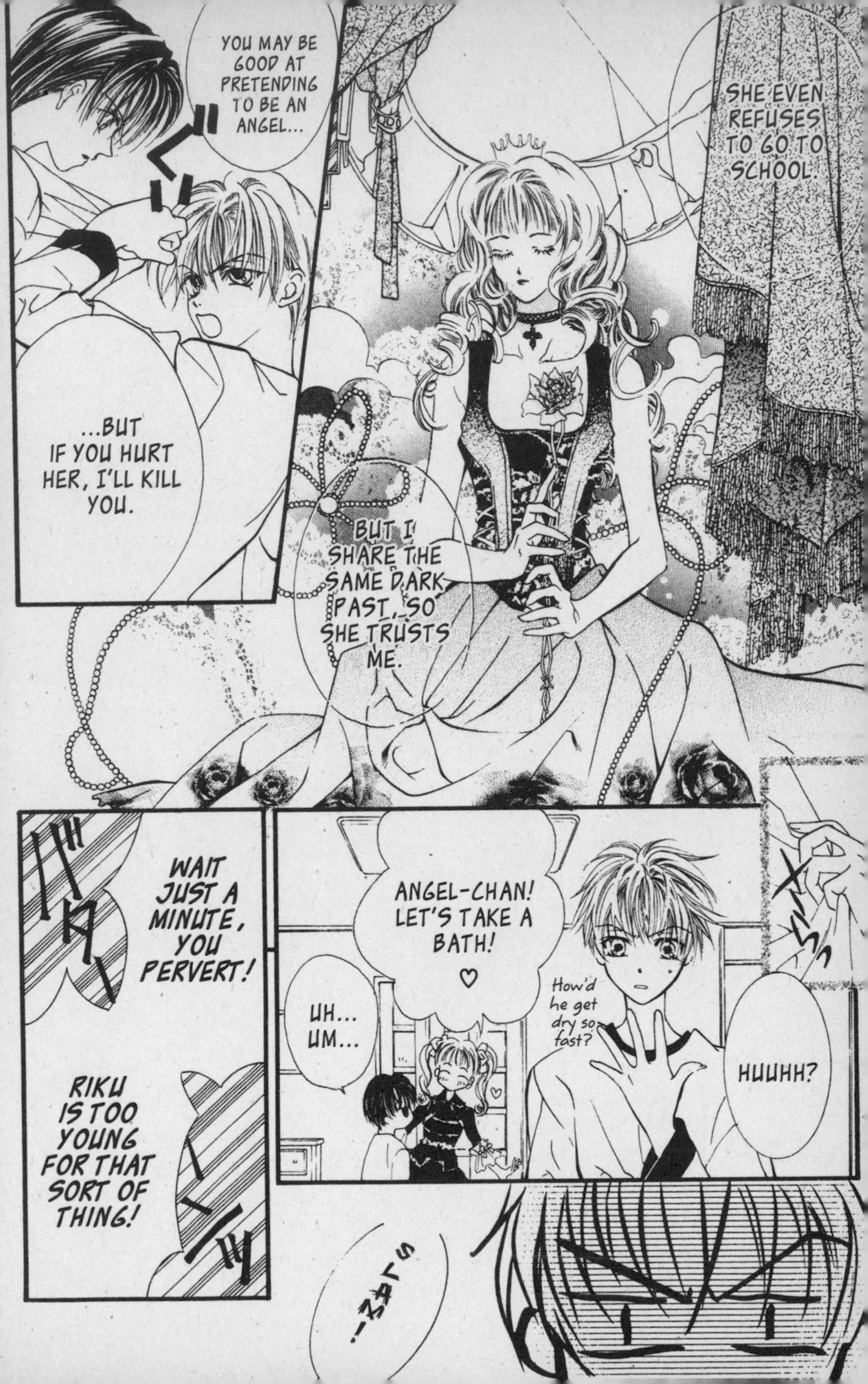
SHE EVEN REFUSES TO GO TO SCHOOL.
BUT I SHARE THE SAME DARK PAST, SO SHE TRUSTS ME.
YOU MAY BE GOOD AT PRETENDING TO BE AN ANGEL...
...BUT IF YOU HURT HER, I'LL KILL YOU.
HUUHH?
How'd he get dry so fast?
ANGEL-CHAN! LET'S TAKE A BATH! ♡
UH... UM...
SLAM!
WAIT JUST A MINUTE, YOU PERVERT!
RIKU IS TOO YOUNG FOR THAT SORT OF THING!

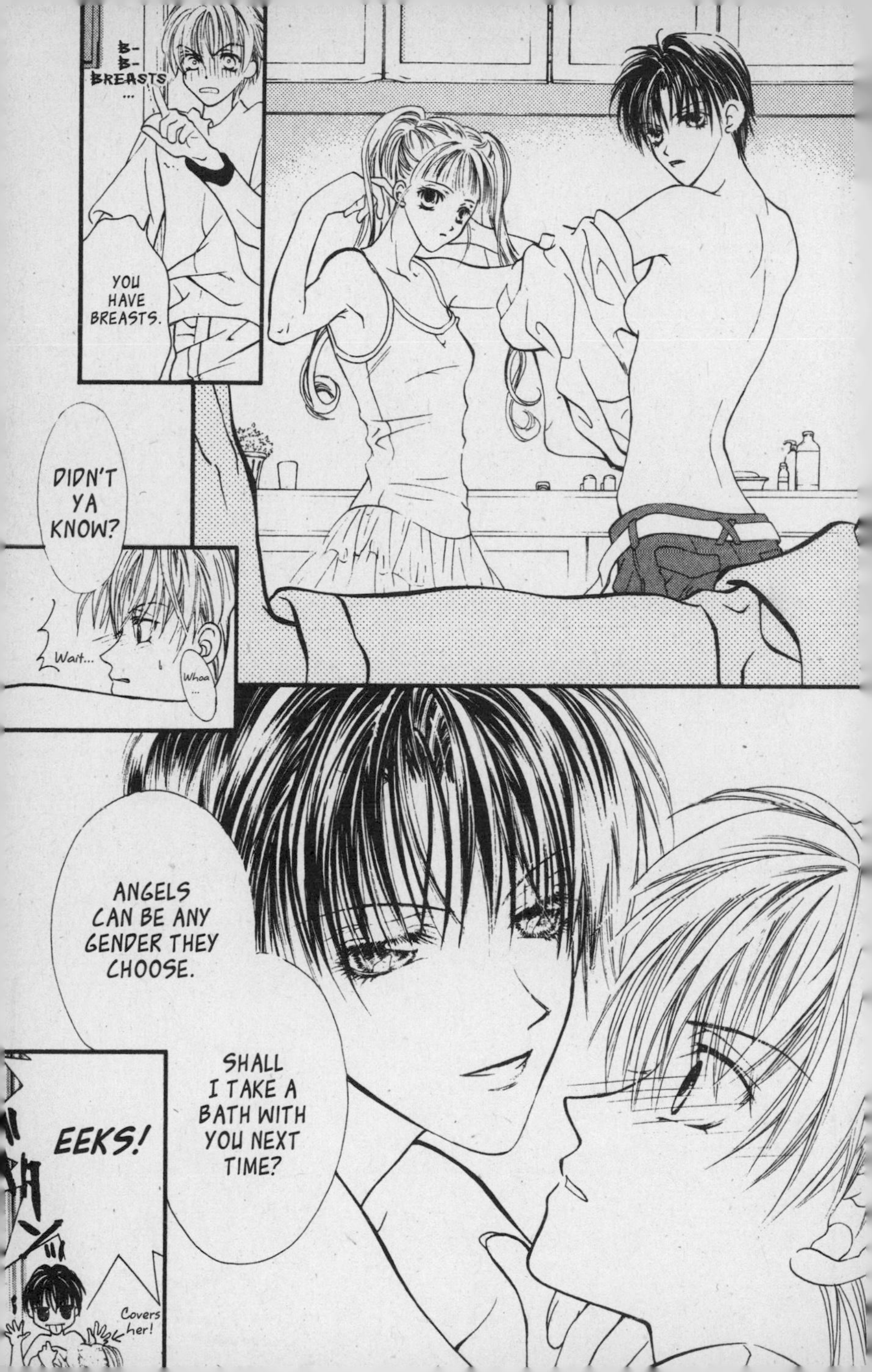

DIDN'T YA KNOW?
B-B-BREASTS...
YOU HAVE BREASTS.
Whoa...
Wait...
ANGELS CAN BE ANY GENDER THEY CHOOSE.
SHALL I TAKE A BATH WITH YOU NEXT TIME?
EEKS!
Covers her!

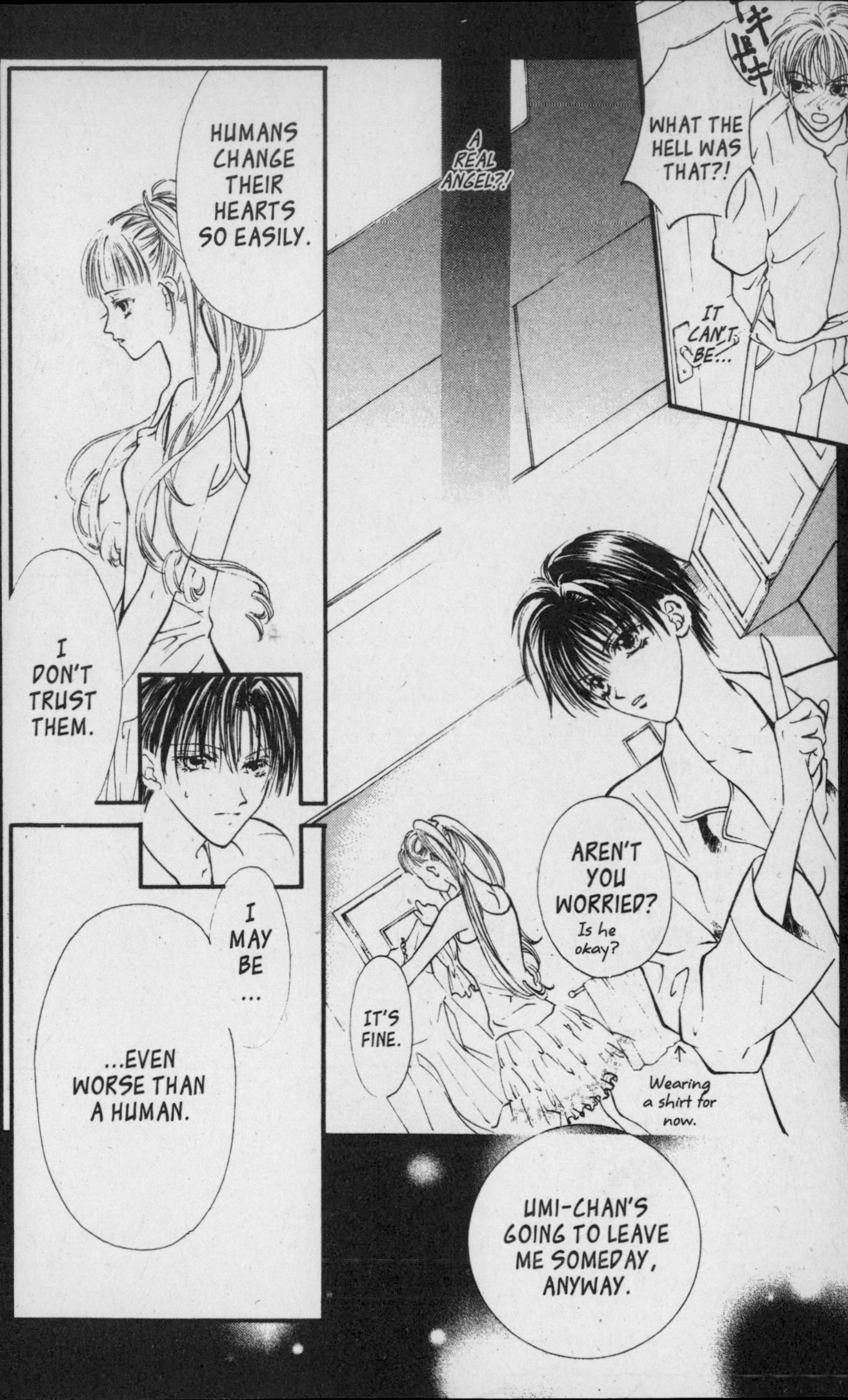

WHAT THE HELL WAS THAT?!
IT CAN'T BE...
A REAL ANGEL?!
AREN'T YOU WORRIED?
Is he okay?
IT'S FINE.
Wearing a shirt for now.
UMI-CHAN'S GOING TO LEAVE ME SOMEDAY, ANYWAY.
HUMANS CHANGE THEIR HEARTS SO EASILY.
I DON'T TRUST THEM.
I MAY BE...
...EVEN WORSE THAN A HUMAN.

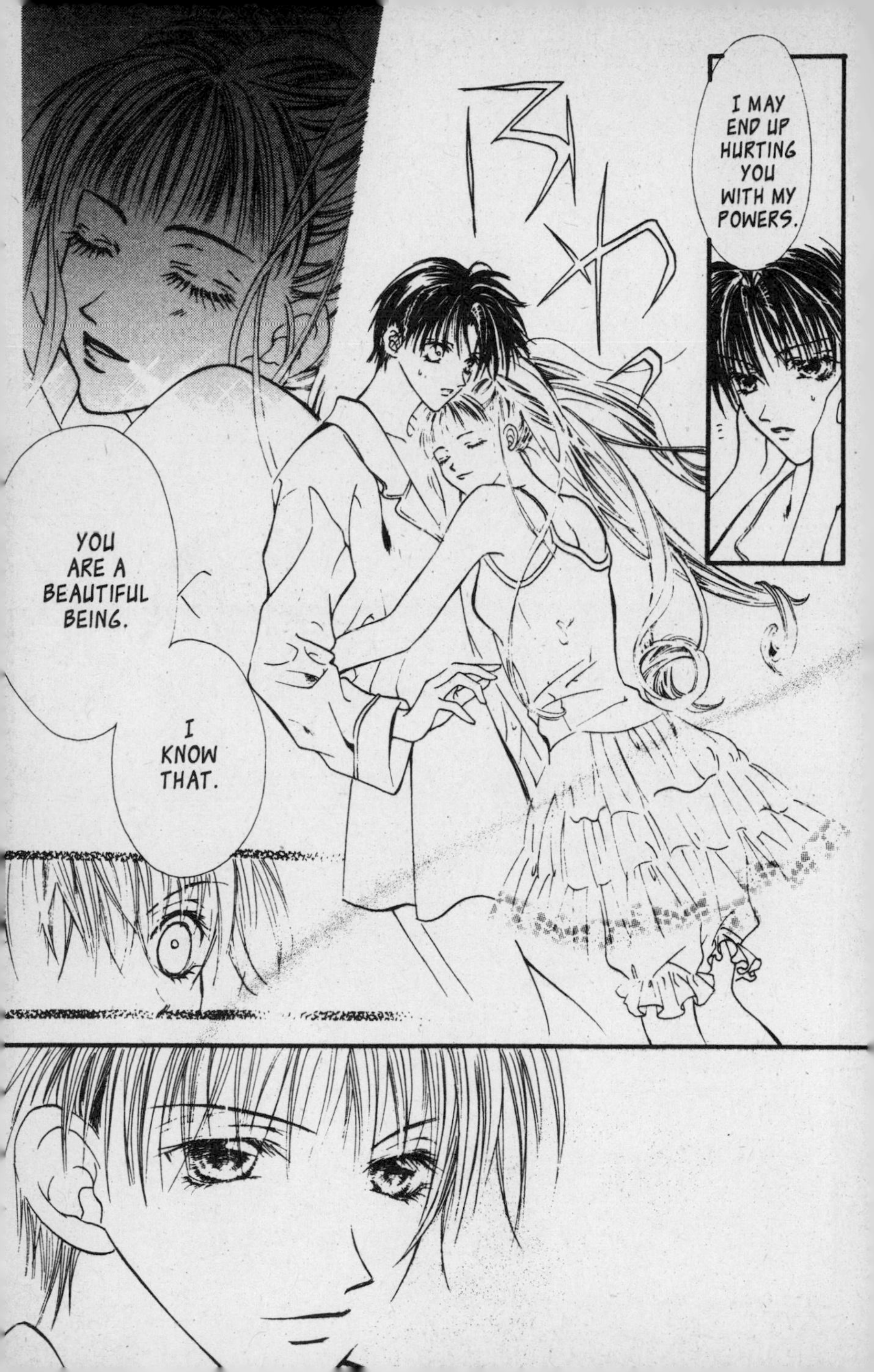
I MAY END UP HURTING YOU WITH MY POWERS.
YOU ARE A BEAUTIFUL BEING.
I KNOW THAT.

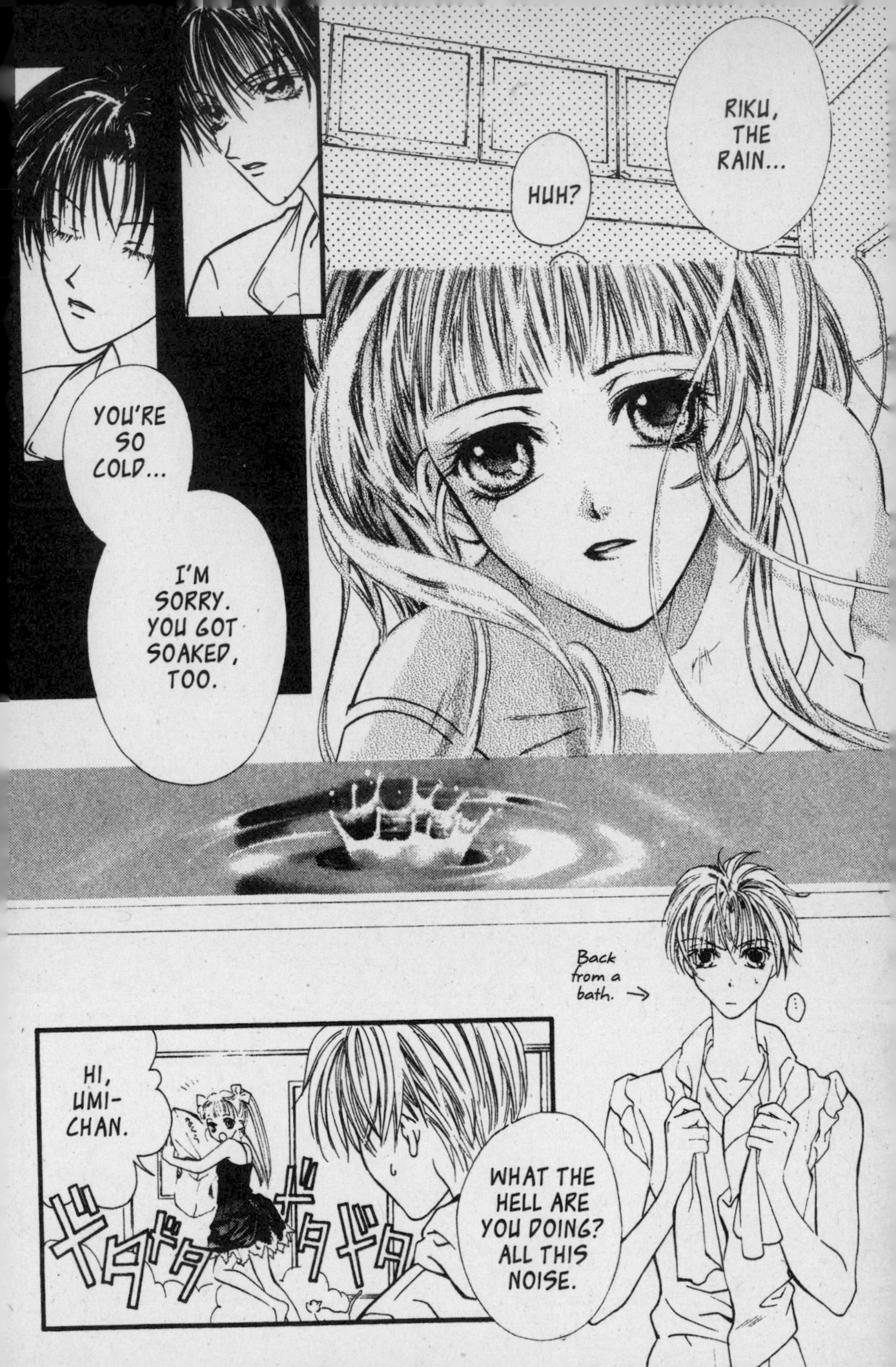
RIKU, THE RAIN...
HUH?
YOU'RE SO COLD...
I'M SORRY. YOU GOT SOAKED, TOO.
Back from a bath.
...
WHAT THE HELL ARE YOU DOING? ALL THIS NOISE.
HI, UMI-CHAN.

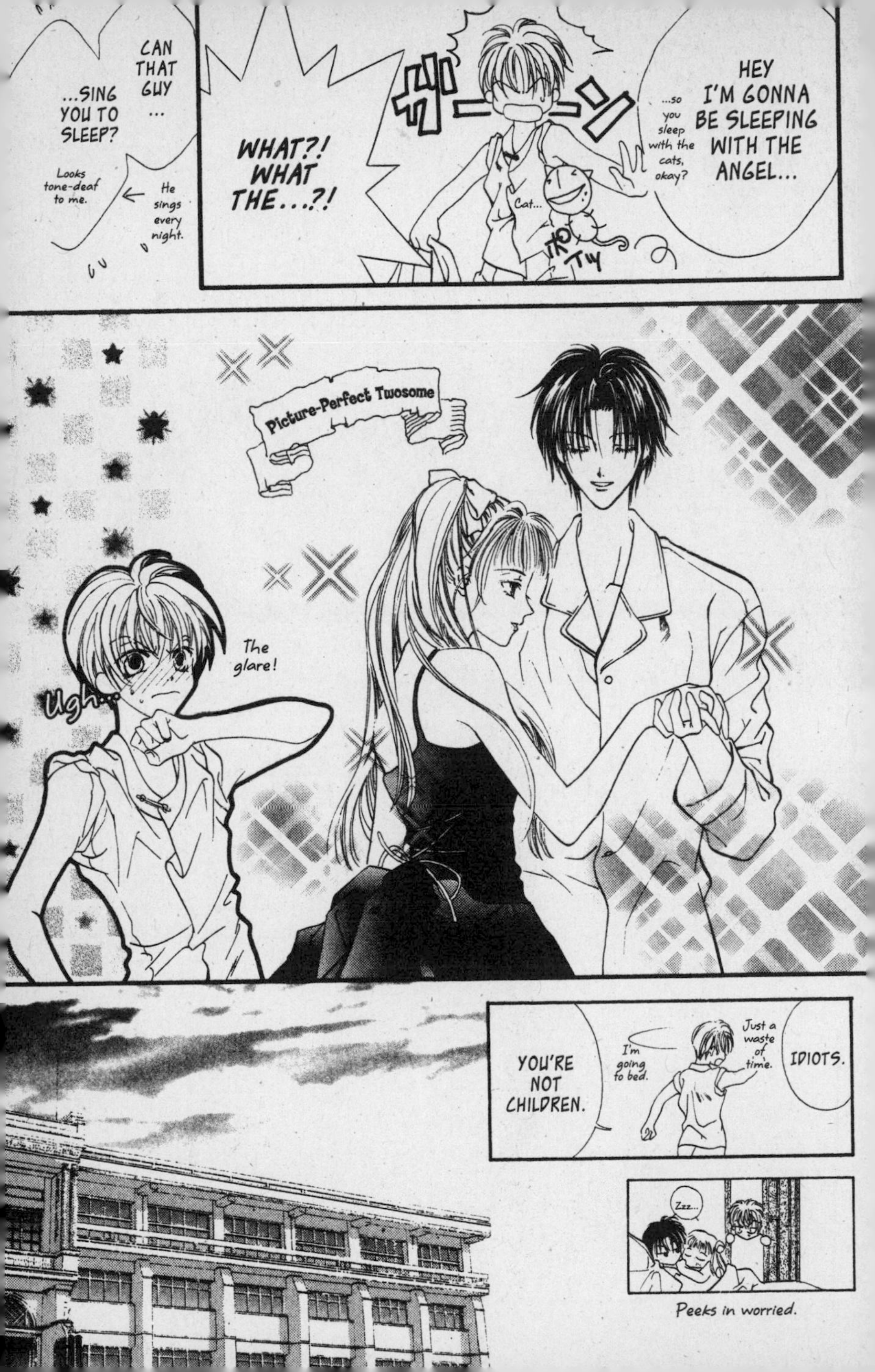
HEY I'M GONNA BE SLEEPING WITH THE ANGEL...
...so you sleep with the cats, okay?
Cat...
WHAT?! WHAT THE...?!
CAN THAT GUY...
...SING YOU TO SLEEP?
He sings every night.
Looks tone-deaf to me.
Picture-Perfect Twosome
The glare!
Ugh...
IDIOTS.
Just a waste of time.
I'm going to bed.
YOU'RE NOT CHILDREN.
Zzz...
Peeks in worried.

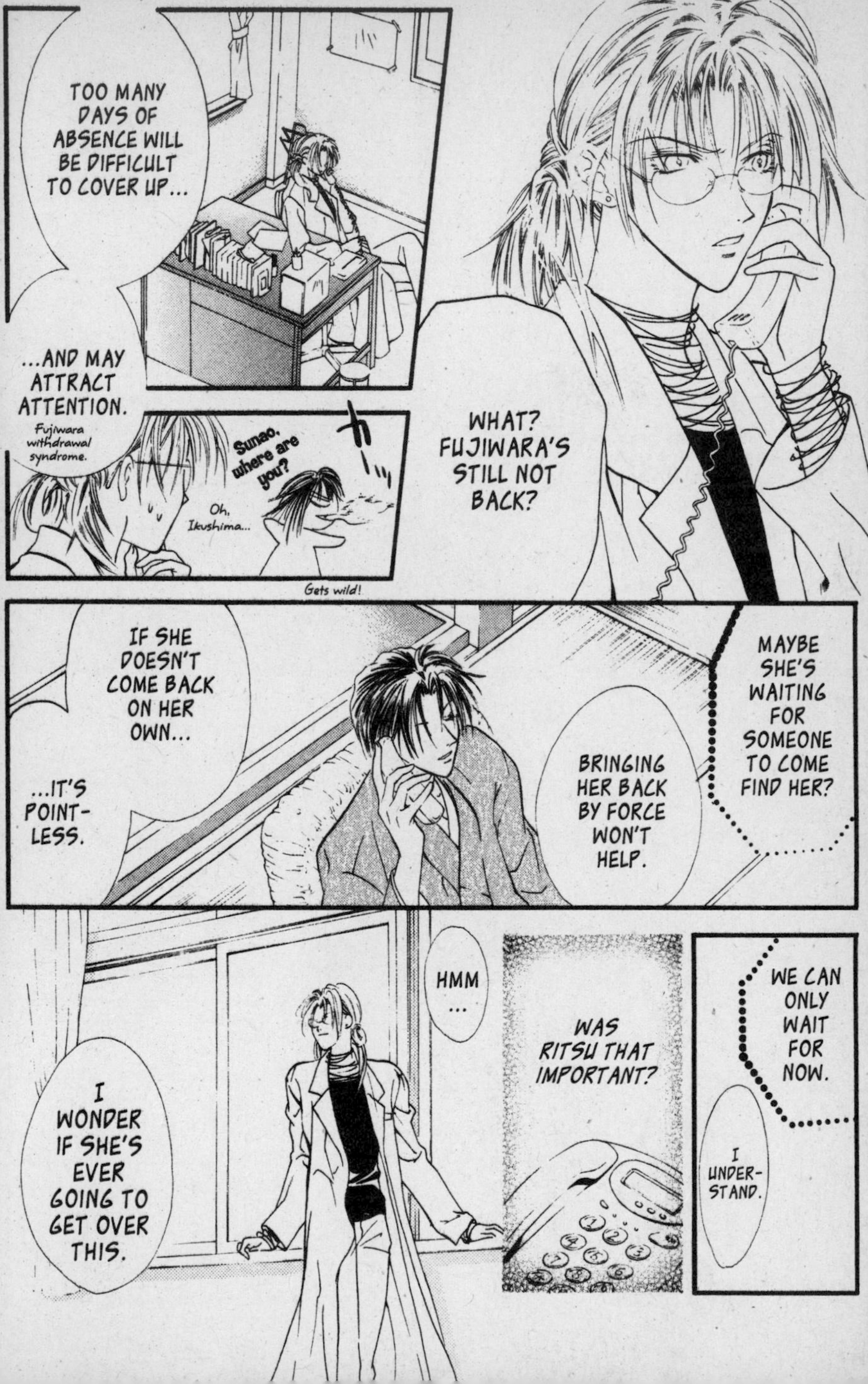
WHAT? FUJIWARA'S STILL NOT BACK?
TOO MANY DAYS OF ABSENCE WILL BE DIFFICULT TO COVER UP...
...AND MAY ATTRACT ATTENTION.
Sunao, where are you?
Oh, Ikushima...
Fujiwara withdrawal syndrome.
Gets wild!
MAYBE SHE'S WAITING FOR SOMEONE TO COME FIND HER?
BRINGING HER BACK BY FORCE WON'T HELP.
IF SHE DOESN'T COME BACK ON HER OWN...
...IT'S POINT-LESS.
WE CAN ONLY WAIT FOR NOW.
I UNDER-STAND.
WAS RITSU THAT IMPORTANT?
HMM...
I WONDER IF SHE'S EVER GOING TO GET OVER THIS.

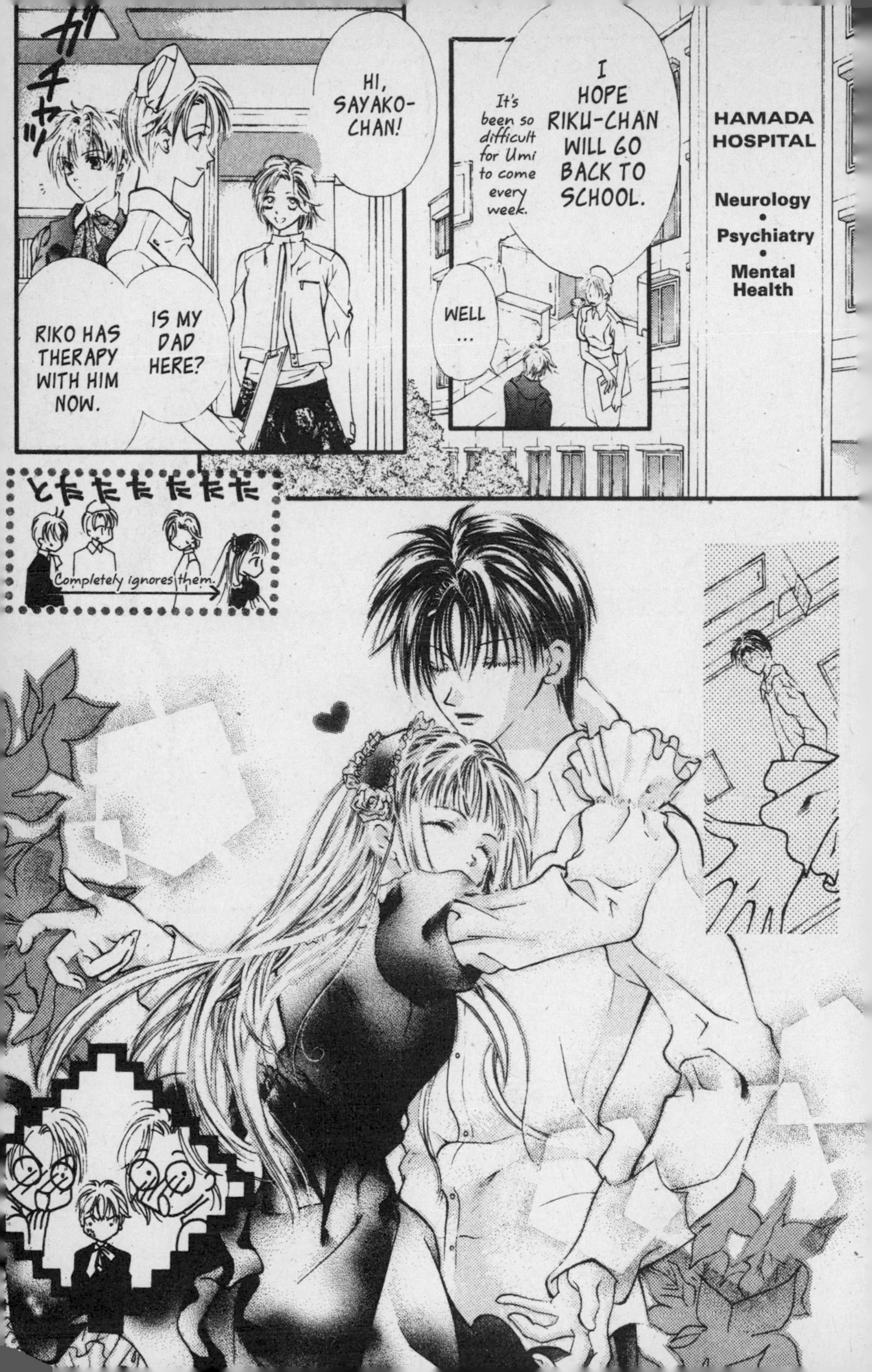
HAMADA HOSPITAL
Neurology • Psychiatry • Mental Health
I HOPE RIKU-CHAN WILL GO BACK TO SCHOOL.
It's been so difficult for Umi to come every week.
WELL ...
ガチャッ
HI, SAYAKO-CHAN!
IS MY DAD HERE?
RIKO HAS THERAPY WITH HIM NOW.
とたたた たたた
Completely ignores them.

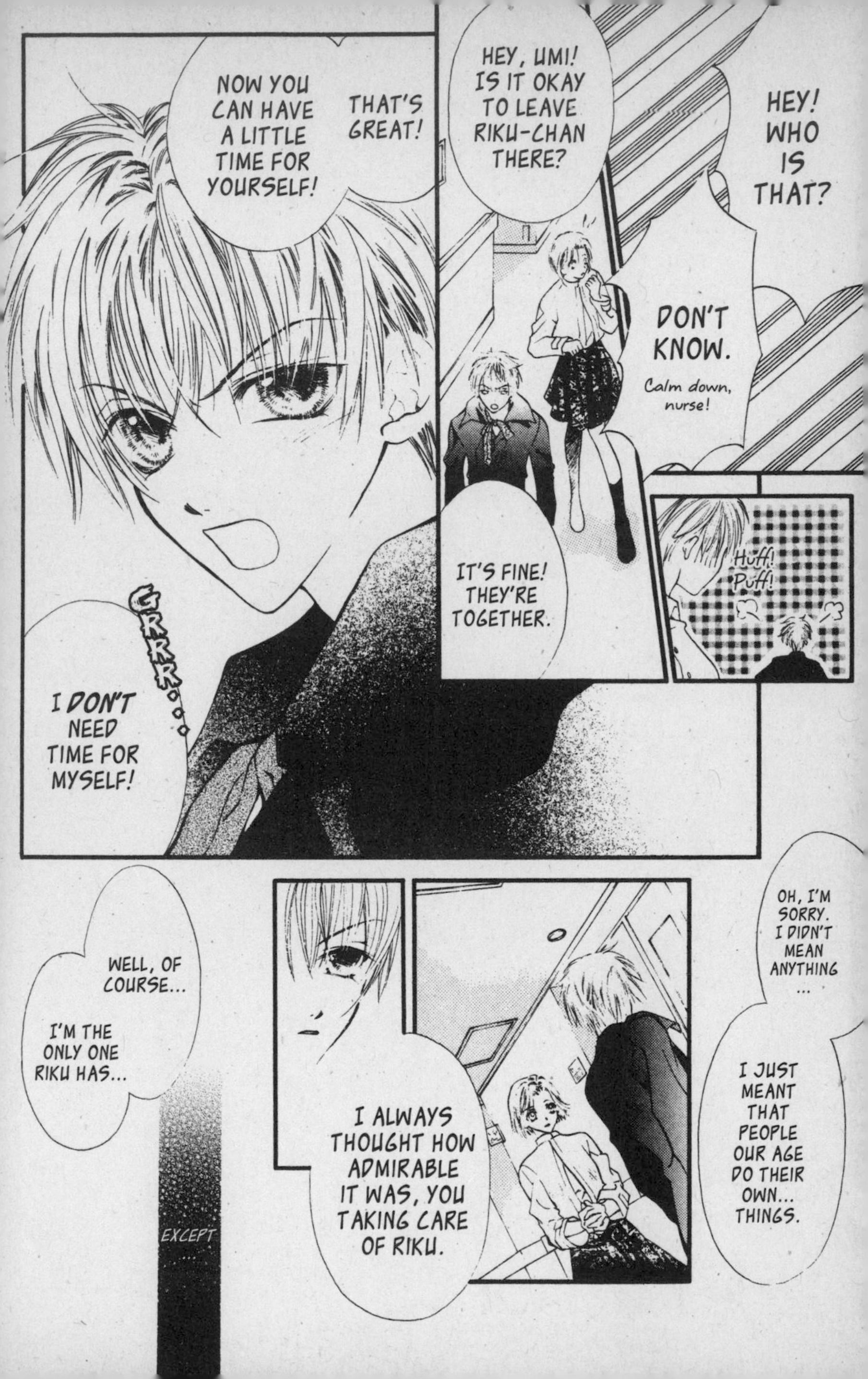
HEY! WHO IS THAT?
DON'T KNOW.
Calm down, nurse!
HEY, UMI! IS IT OKAY TO LEAVE RIKU-CHAN THERE?
IT'S FINE! THEY'RE TOGETHER.
Huff! Puff!
THAT'S GREAT!
NOW YOU CAN HAVE A LITTLE TIME FOR YOURSELF!
GRRR...
I DON'T NEED TIME FOR MYSELF!
OH, I'M SORRY. I DIDN'T MEAN ANYTHING ...
I JUST MEANT THAT PEOPLE OUR AGE DO THEIR OWN... THINGS.
I ALWAYS THOUGHT HOW ADMIRABLE IT WAS, YOU TAKING CARE OF RIKU.
WELL, OF COURSE...
I'M THE ONLY ONE RIKU HAS...
EXCEPT ...

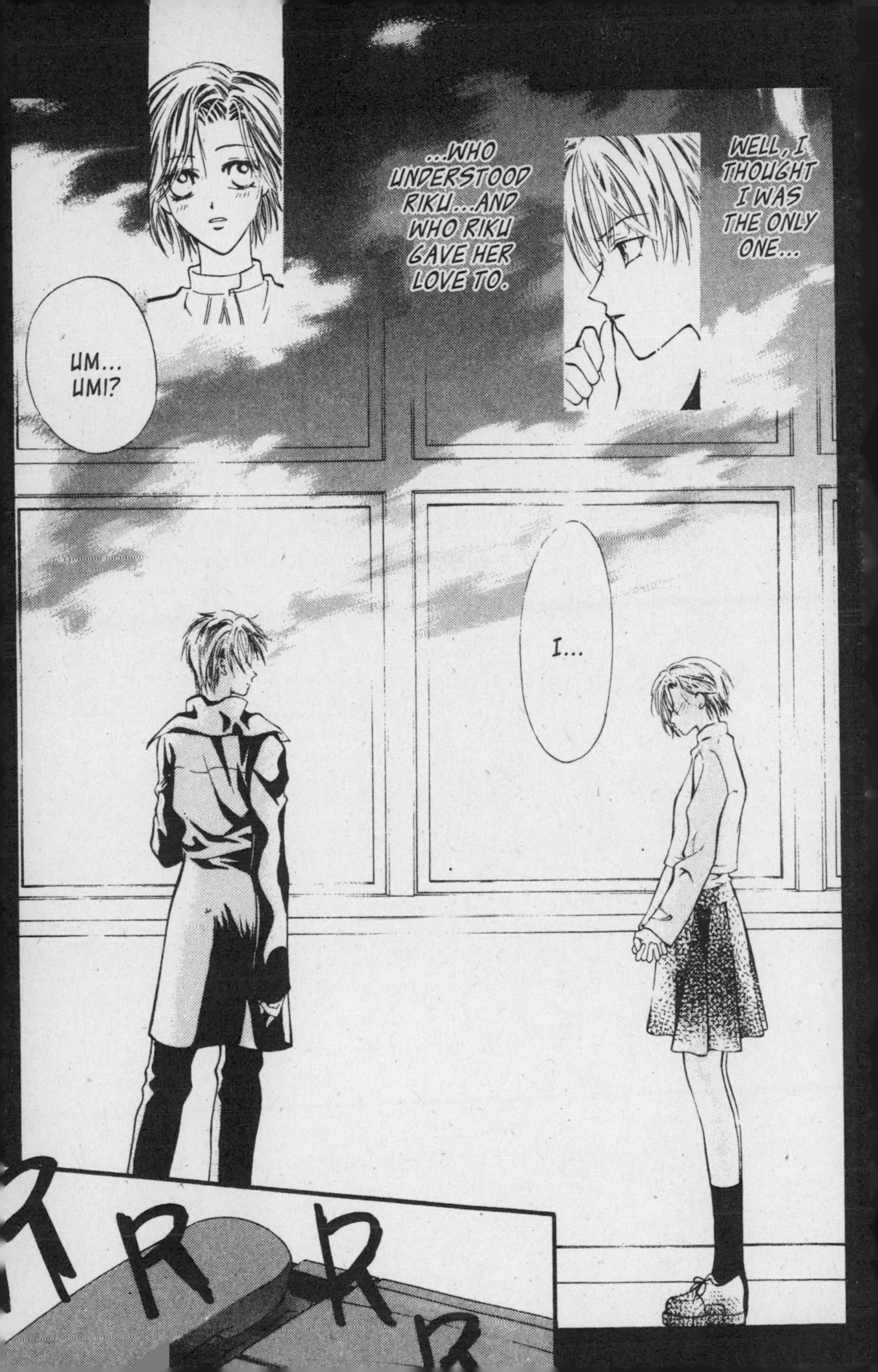
WELL, I THOUGHT I WAS THE ONLY ONE...
...WHO UNDERSTOOD RIKU...AND WHO RIKU GAVE HER LOVE TO.
UM... UMI?
I...

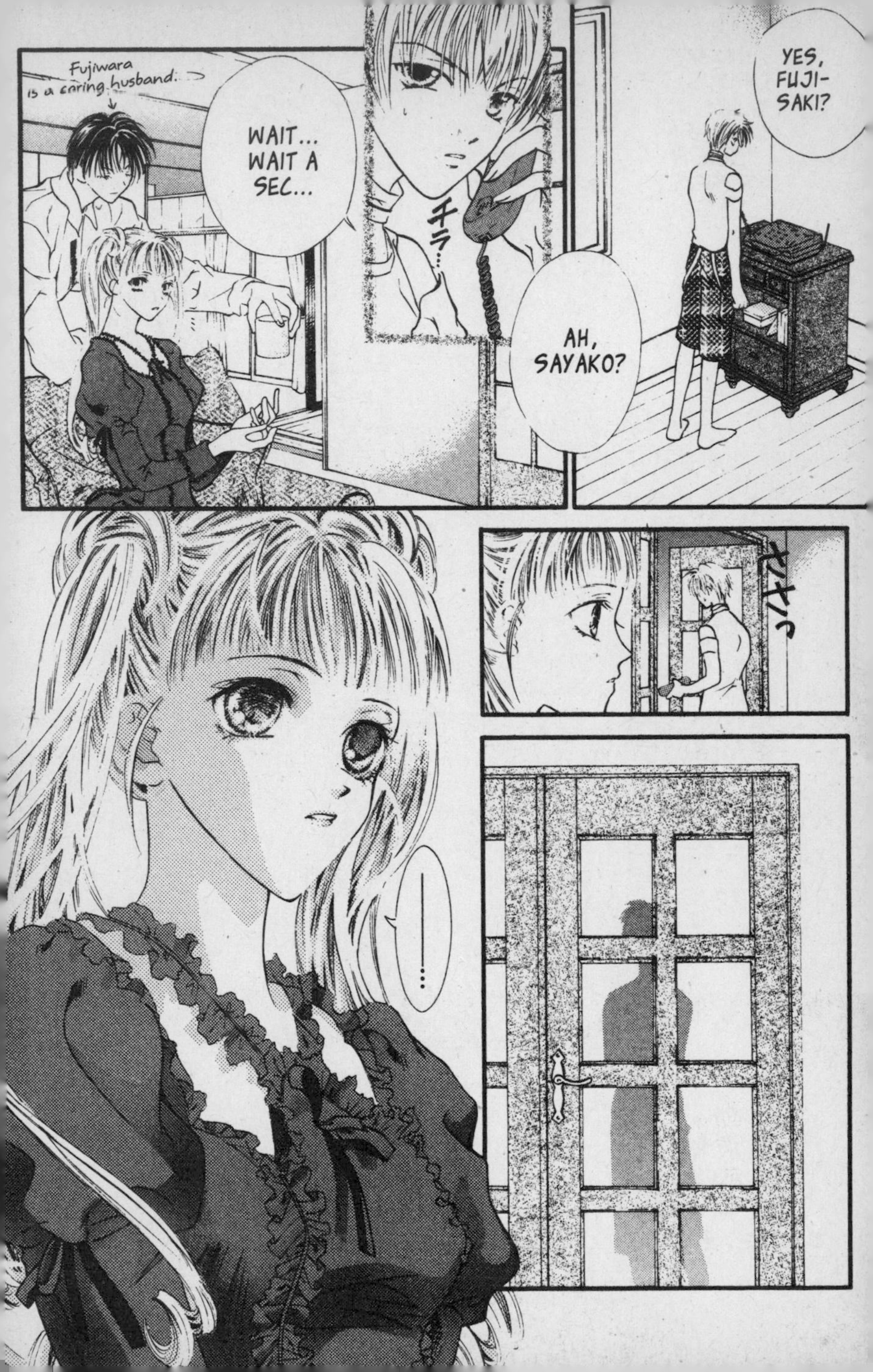
YES, FUJI-SAKI?
AH, SAYAKO?
チラ…
WAIT... WAIT A SEC...
Fujiwara is a caring husband.
さっ
—......

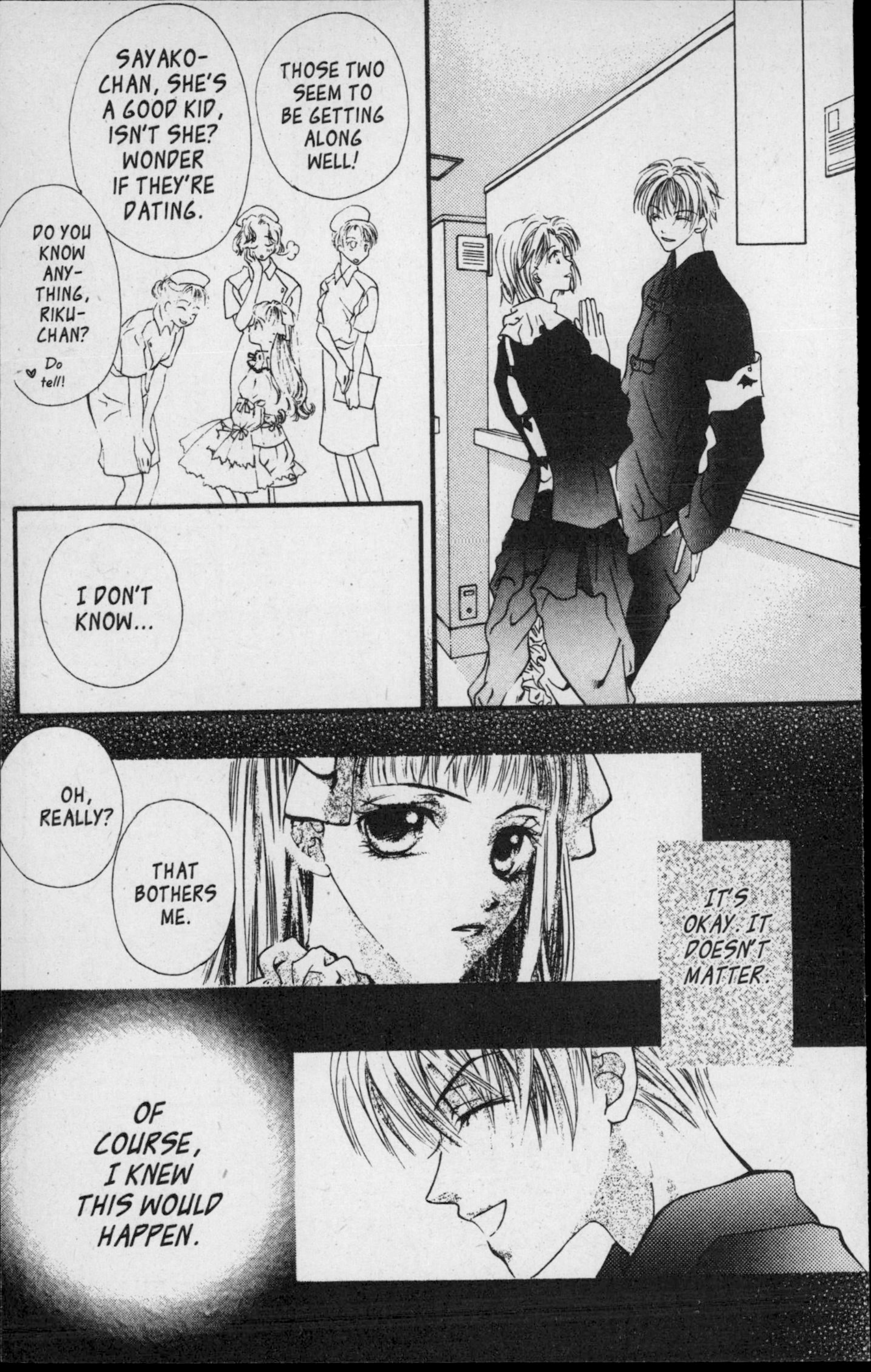
THOSE TWO SEEM TO BE GETTING ALONG WELL!
SAYAKO-CHAN, SHE'S A GOOD KID, ISN'T SHE? WONDER IF THEY'RE DATING.
DO YOU KNOW ANYTHING, RIKU-CHAN?
Do tell!
I DON'T KNOW...
OH, REALLY?
THAT BOTHERS ME.
IT'S OKAY. IT DOESN'T MATTER.
OF COURSE, I KNEW THIS WOULD HAPPEN.

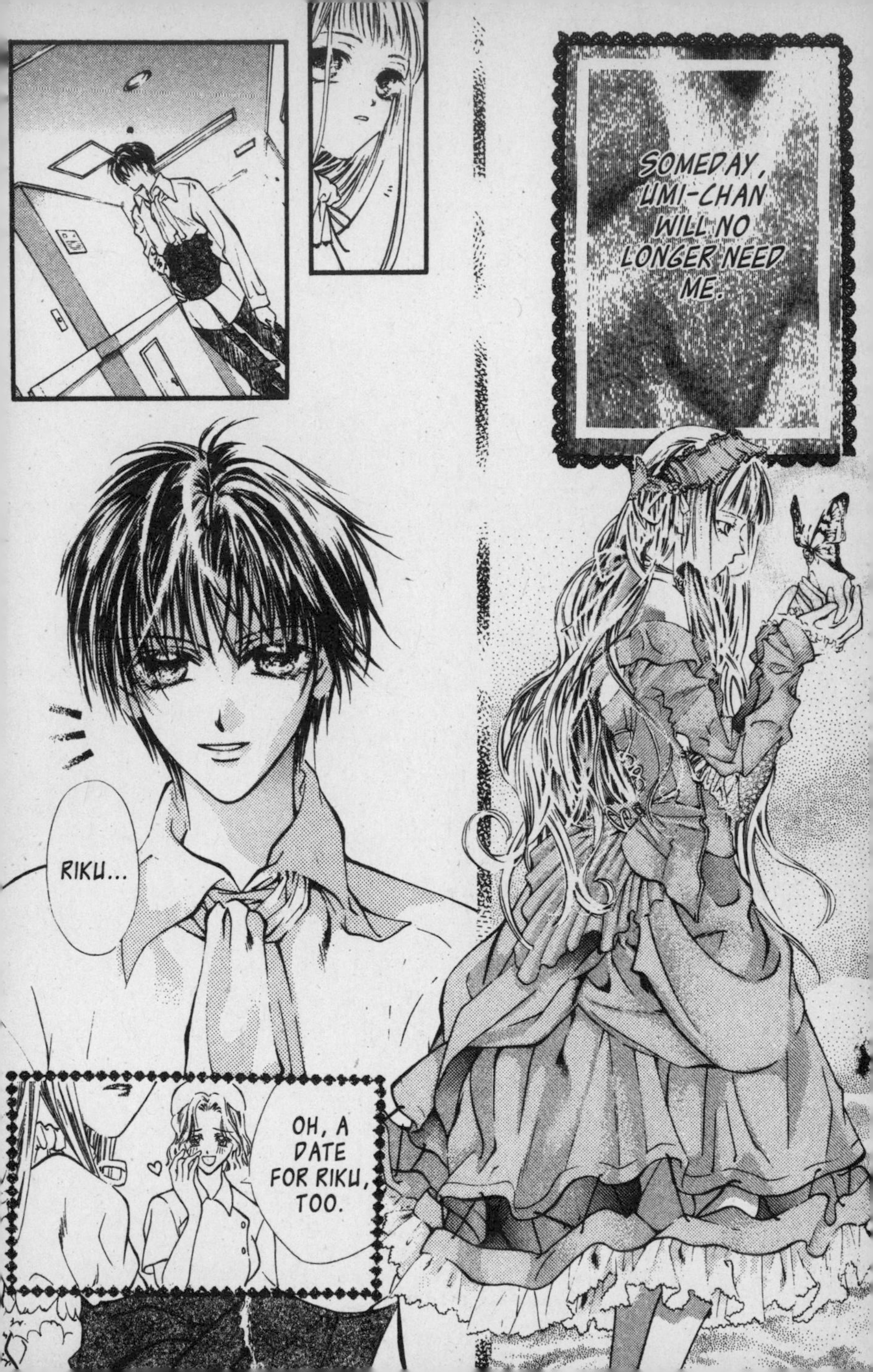
SOMEDAY, UMI-CHAN WILL NO LONGER NEED ME.
RIKU...
OH, A DATE FOR RIKU, TOO.

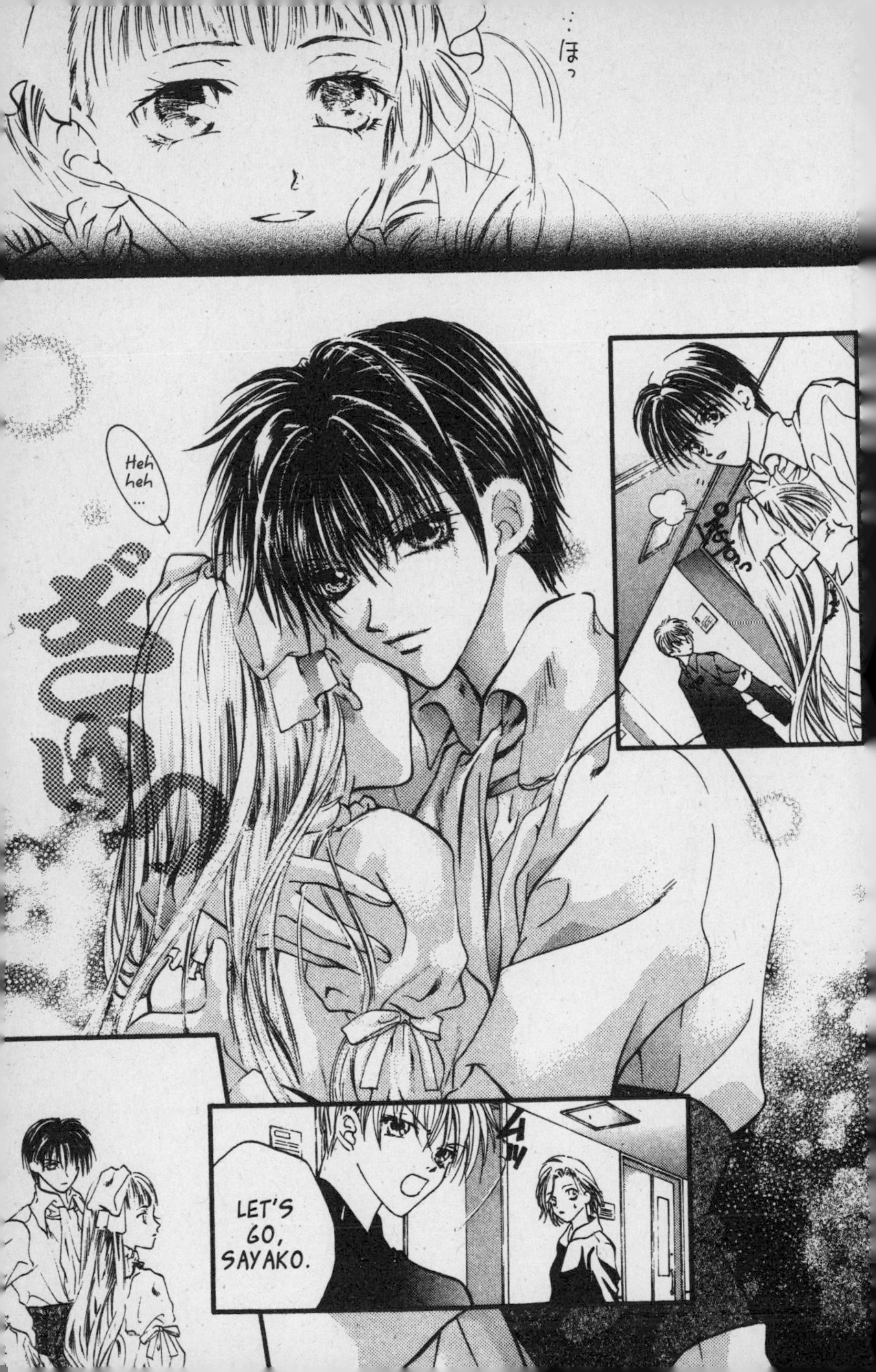
…ほっ
Heh heh ...
LET'S GO, SAYAKO.

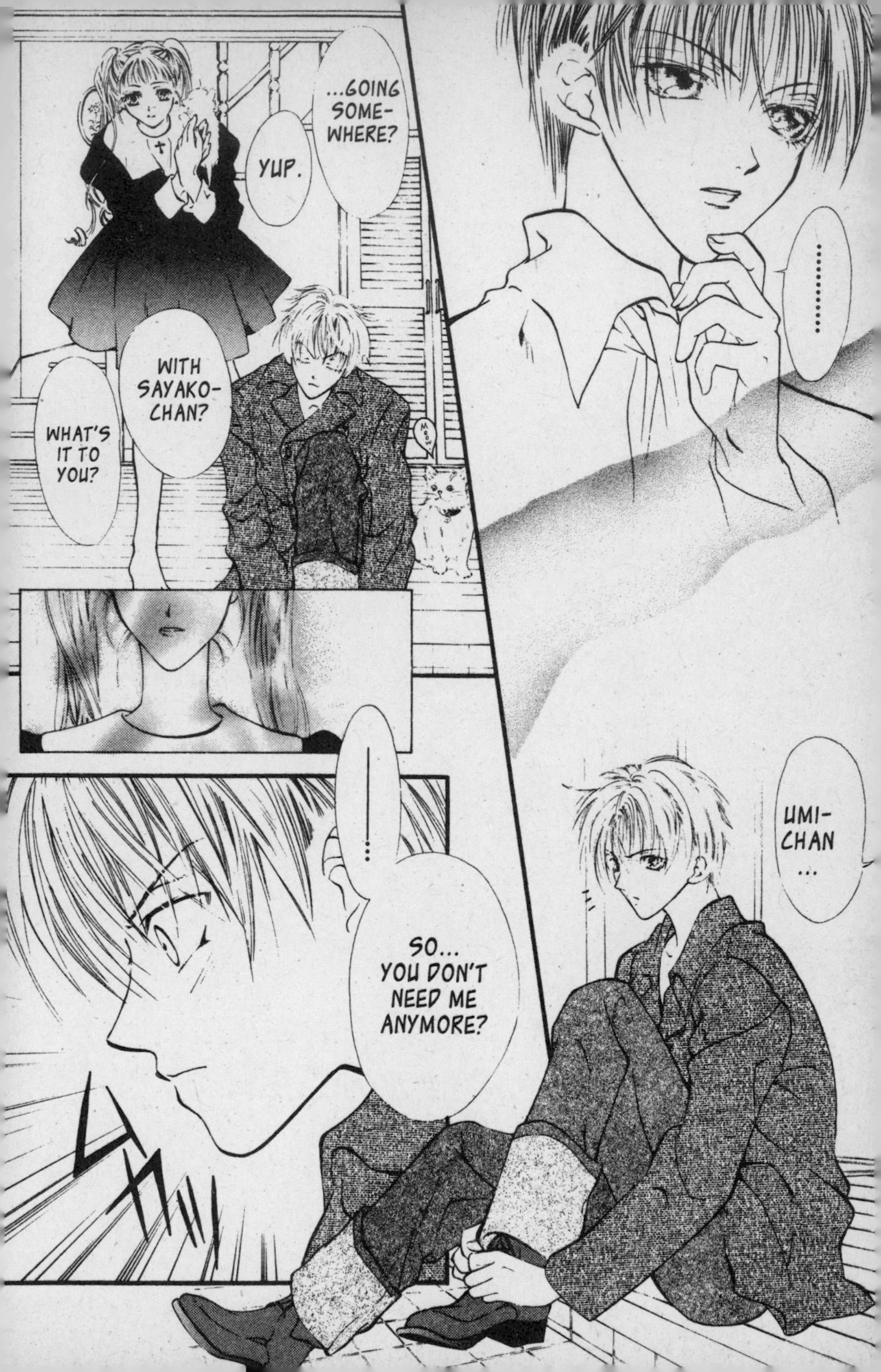
......
UMI-CHAN...
...GOING SOMEWHERE?
YUP.
WITH SAYAKO-CHAN?
WHAT'S IT TO YOU?
MEOW
......
SO... YOU DON'T NEED ME ANYMORE?

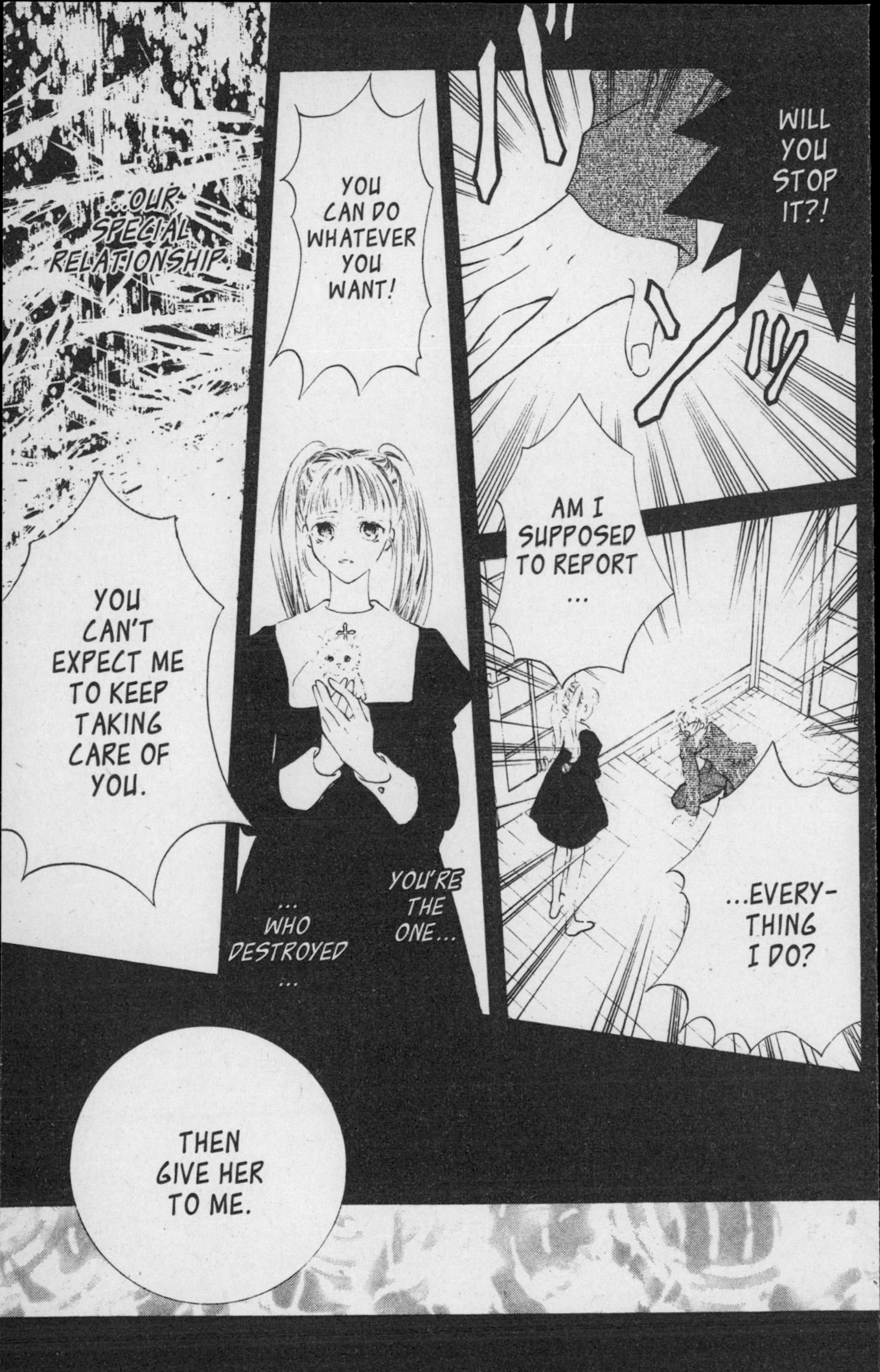
WILL YOU STOP IT?!
AM I SUPPOSED TO REPORT ...
...EVERY-THING I DO?
YOU CAN DO WHATEVER YOU WANT!
YOU'RE THE ONE...
...WHO DESTROYED...
...OUR SPECIAL RELATIONSHIP.
YOU CAN'T EXPECT ME TO KEEP TAKING CARE OF YOU.
THEN GIVE HER TO ME.

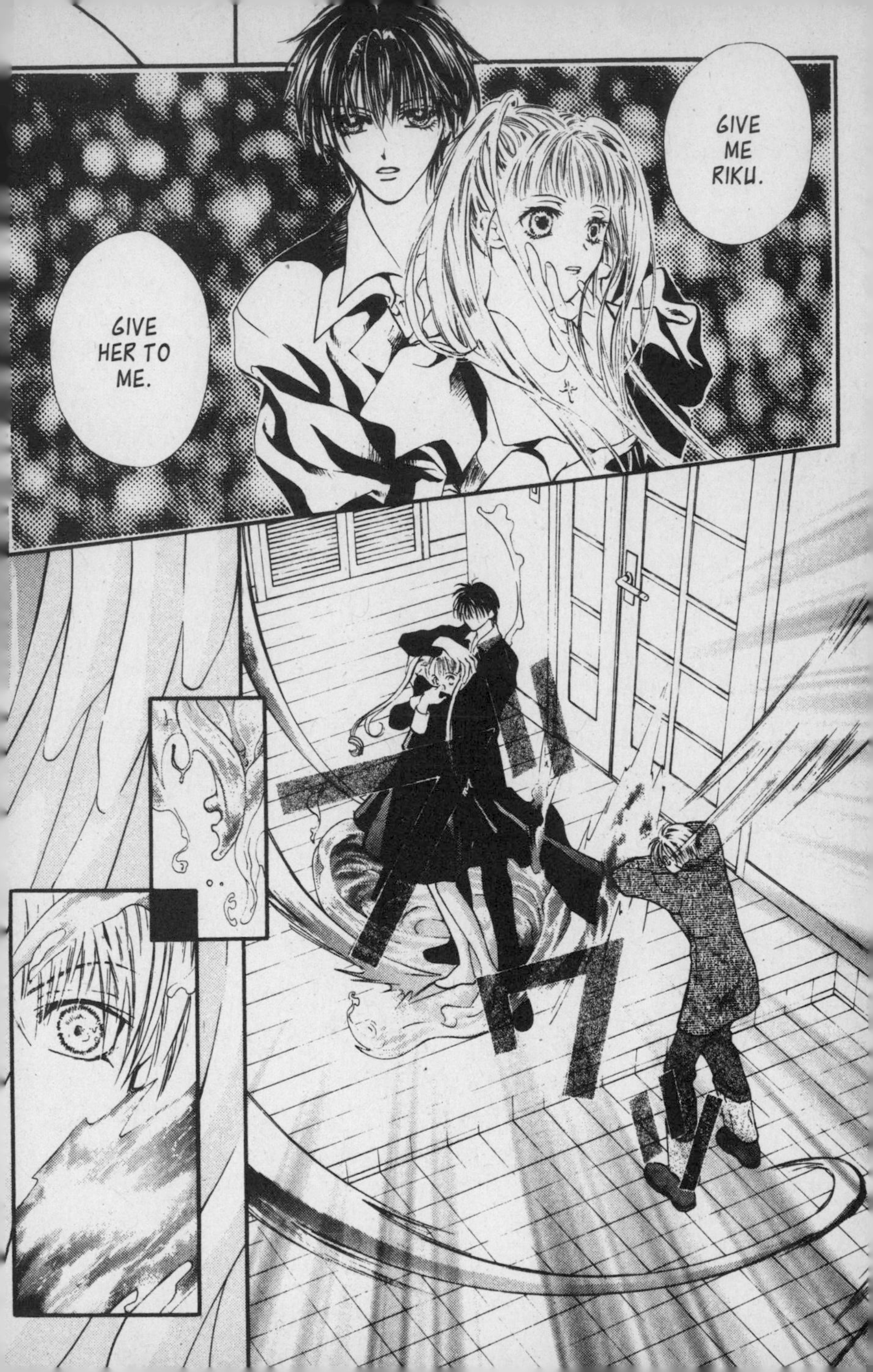
GIVE ME RIKU.
GIVE HER TO ME.

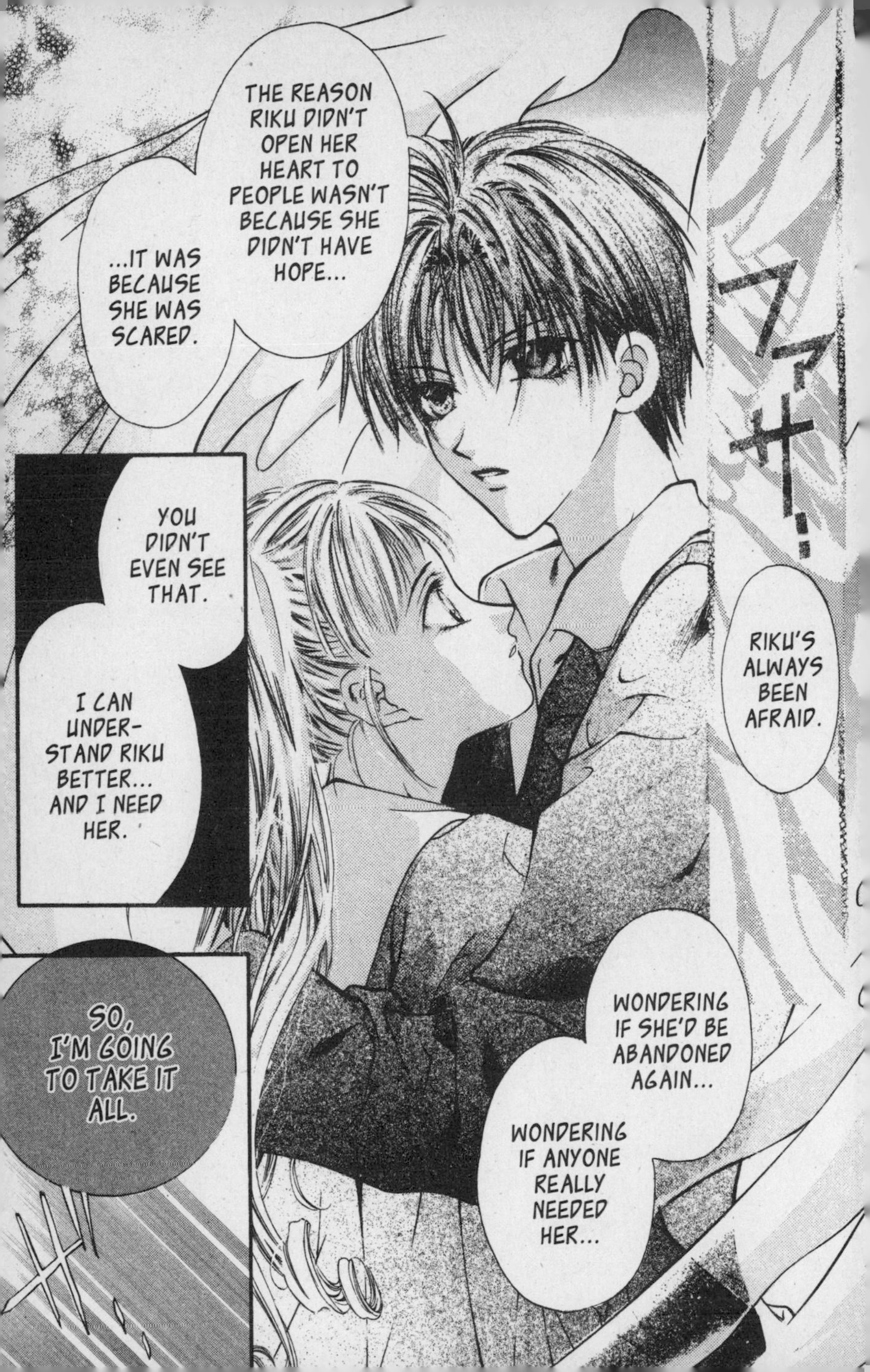

THE REASON RIKU DIDN'T OPEN HER HEART TO PEOPLE WASN'T BECAUSE SHE DIDN'T HAVE HOPE...
...IT WAS BECAUSE SHE WAS SCARED.
ファサー!!
RIKU'S ALWAYS BEEN AFRAID.
WONDERING IF SHE'D BE ABANDONED AGAIN...
WONDERING IF ANYONE REALLY NEEDED HER...
YOU DIDN'T EVEN SEE THAT.
I CAN UNDER-STAND RIKU BETTER... AND I NEED HER.
SO, I'M GOING TO TAKE IT ALL.

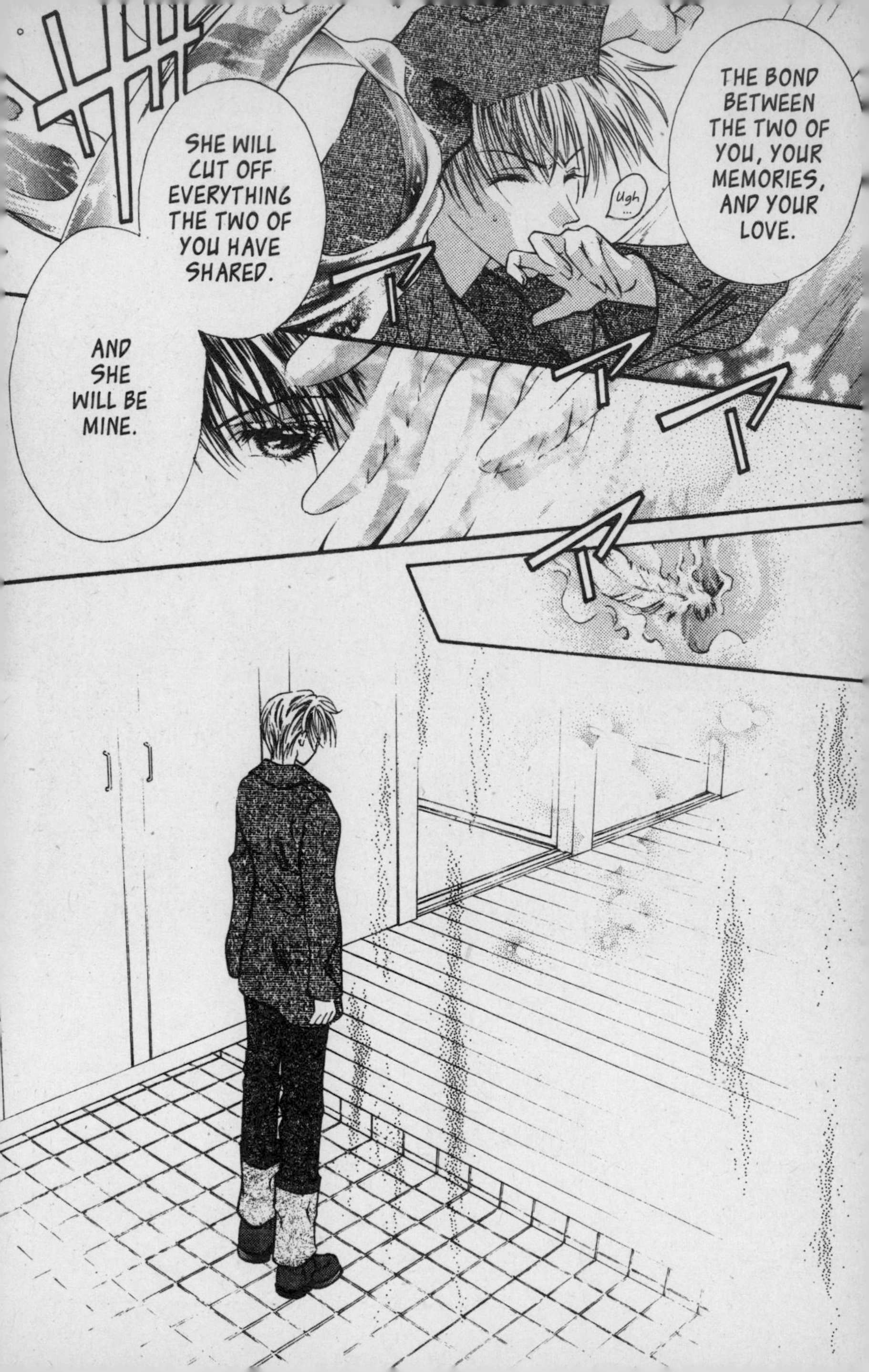
THE BOND BETWEEN THE TWO OF YOU, YOUR MEMORIES, AND YOUR LOVE.
Ugh...
SHE WILL CUT OFF EVERYTHING THE TWO OF YOU HAVE SHARED.
AND SHE WILL BE MINE.

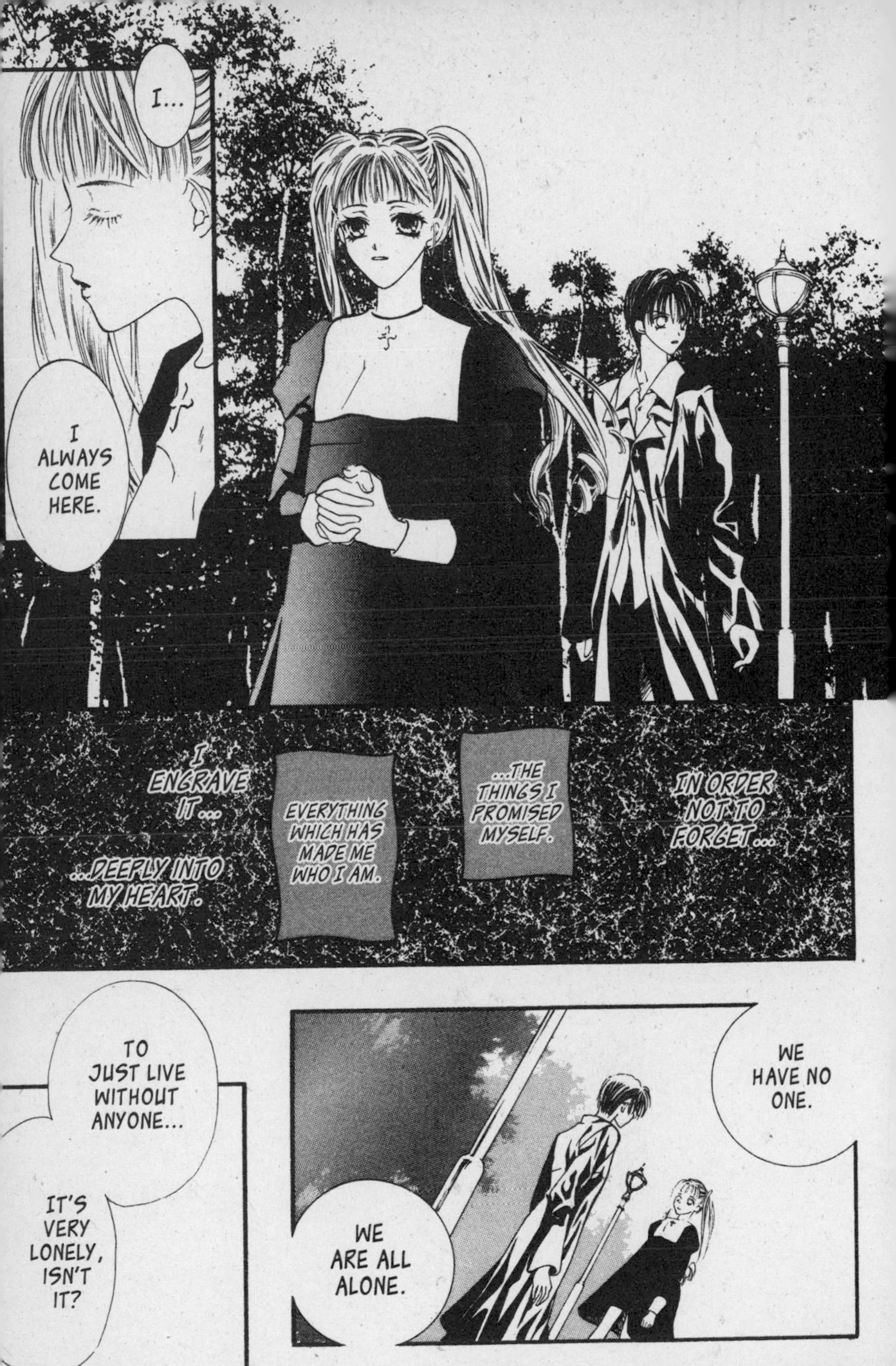
I...
I ALWAYS COME HERE.
IN ORDER NOT TO FORGET...
...THE THINGS I PROMISED MYSELF.
EVERYTHING WHICH HAS MADE ME WHO I AM.
I ENGRAVE IT...
...DEEPLY INTO MY HEART.
WE HAVE NO ONE.
WE ARE ALL ALONE.
TO JUST LIVE WITHOUT ANYONE...
IT'S VERY LONELY, ISN'T IT?

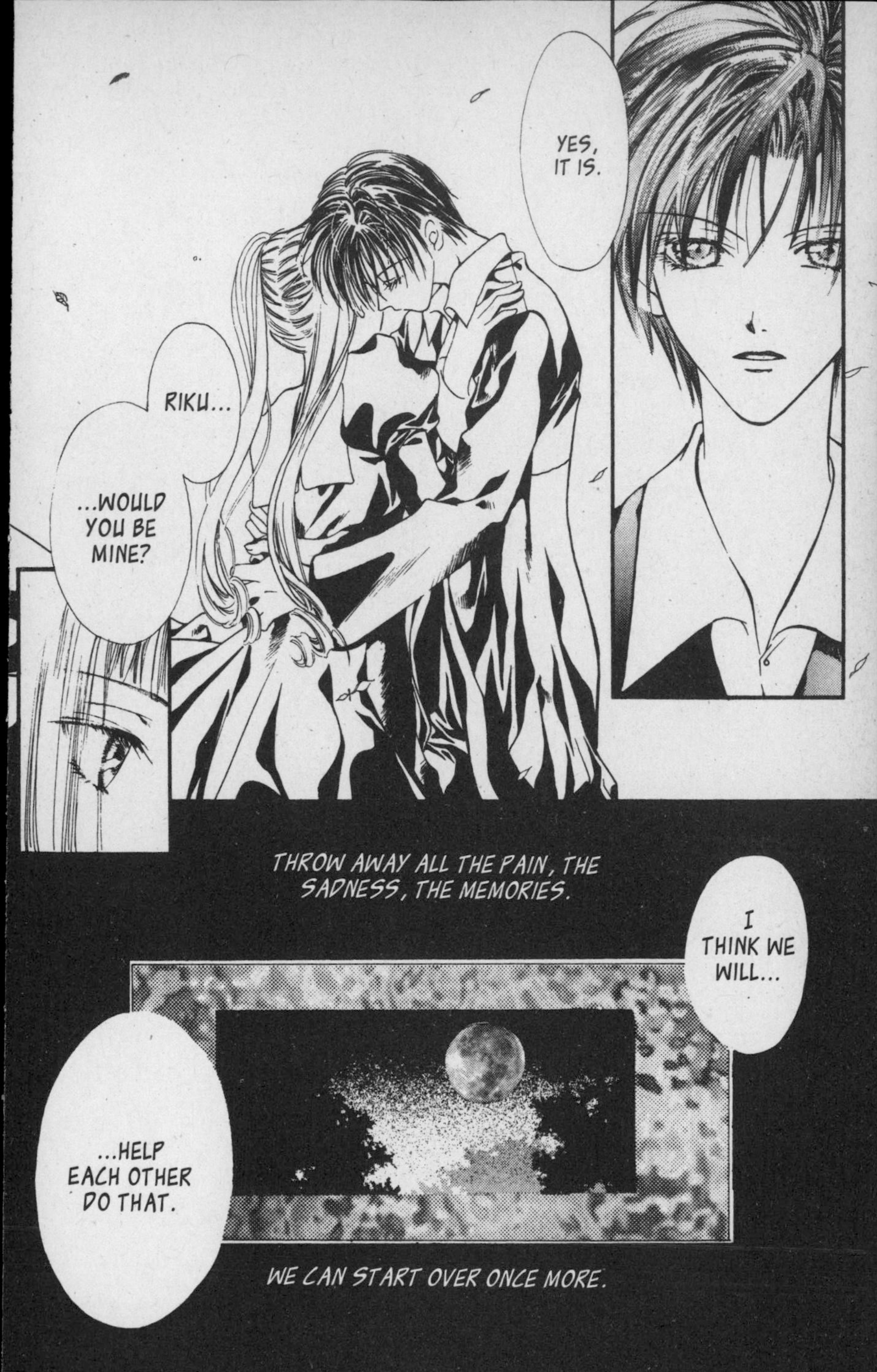
YES, IT IS.
RIKU...
...WOULD YOU BE MINE?
THROW AWAY ALL THE PAIN, THE SADNESS, THE MEMORIES.
I THINK WE WILL...
...HELP EACH OTHER DO THAT.
WE CAN START OVER ONCE MORE.

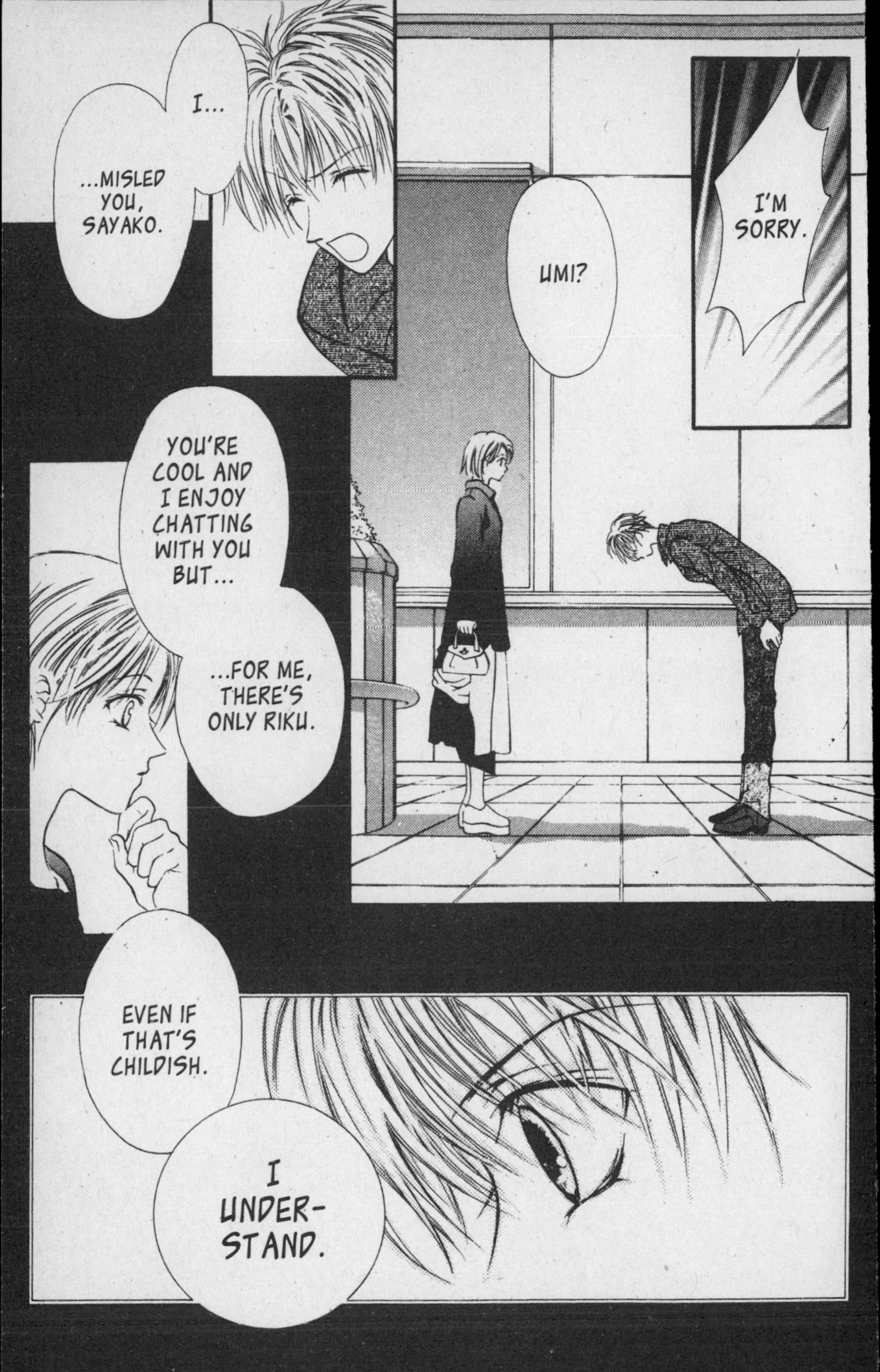
I'M SORRY.
UMI?
I...
...MISLED YOU, SAYAKO.
YOU'RE COOL AND I ENJOY CHATTING WITH YOU BUT...
...FOR ME, THERE'S ONLY RIKU.
EVEN IF THAT'S CHILDISH.
I UNDER-STAND.

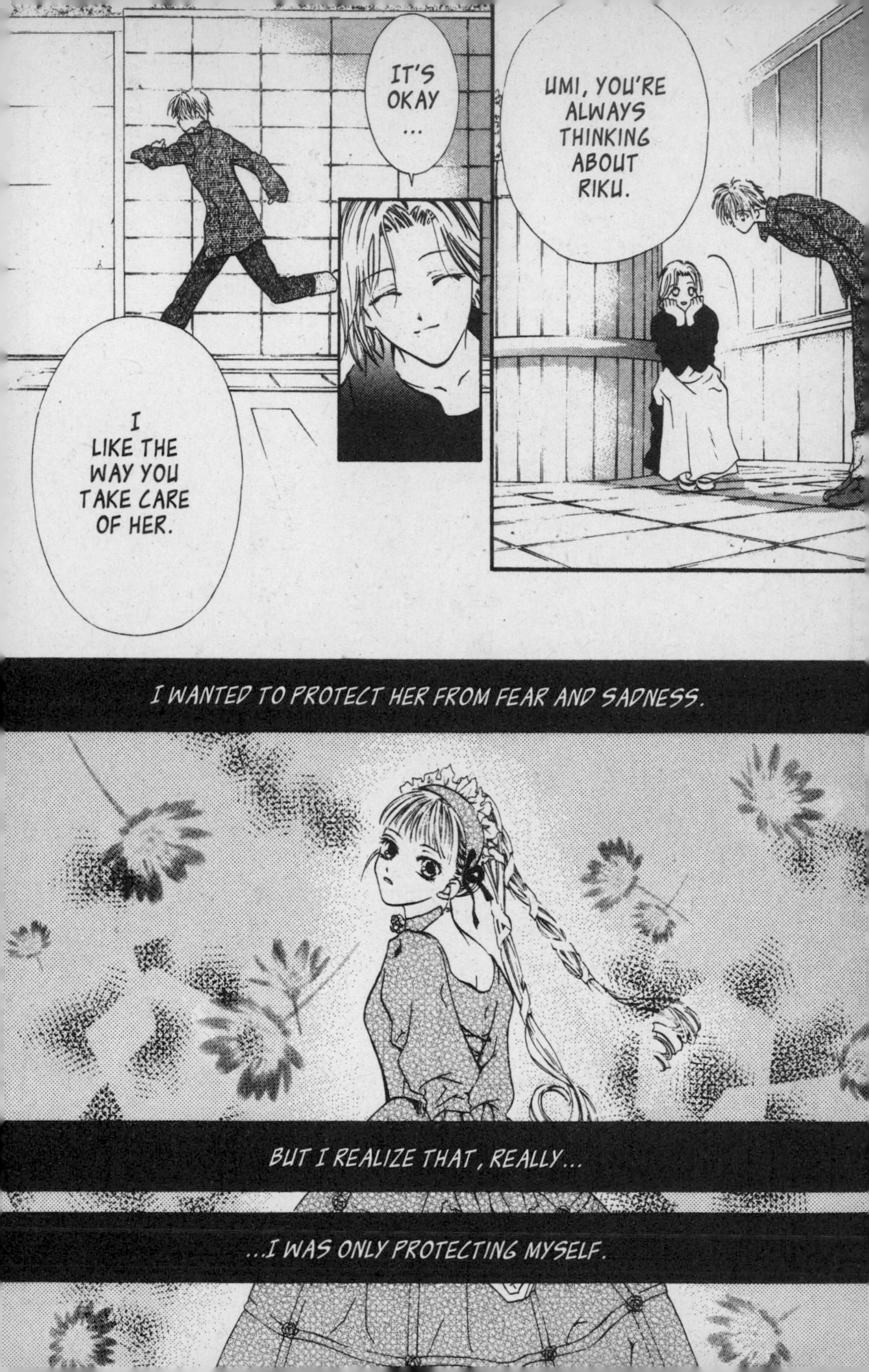
UMI, YOU'RE ALWAYS THINKING ABOUT RIKU.
IT'S OKAY ...
I LIKE THE WAY YOU TAKE CARE OF HER.
I WANTED TO PROTECT HER FROM FEAR AND SADNESS.
BUT I REALIZE THAT, REALLY...
...I WAS ONLY PROTECTING MYSELF.

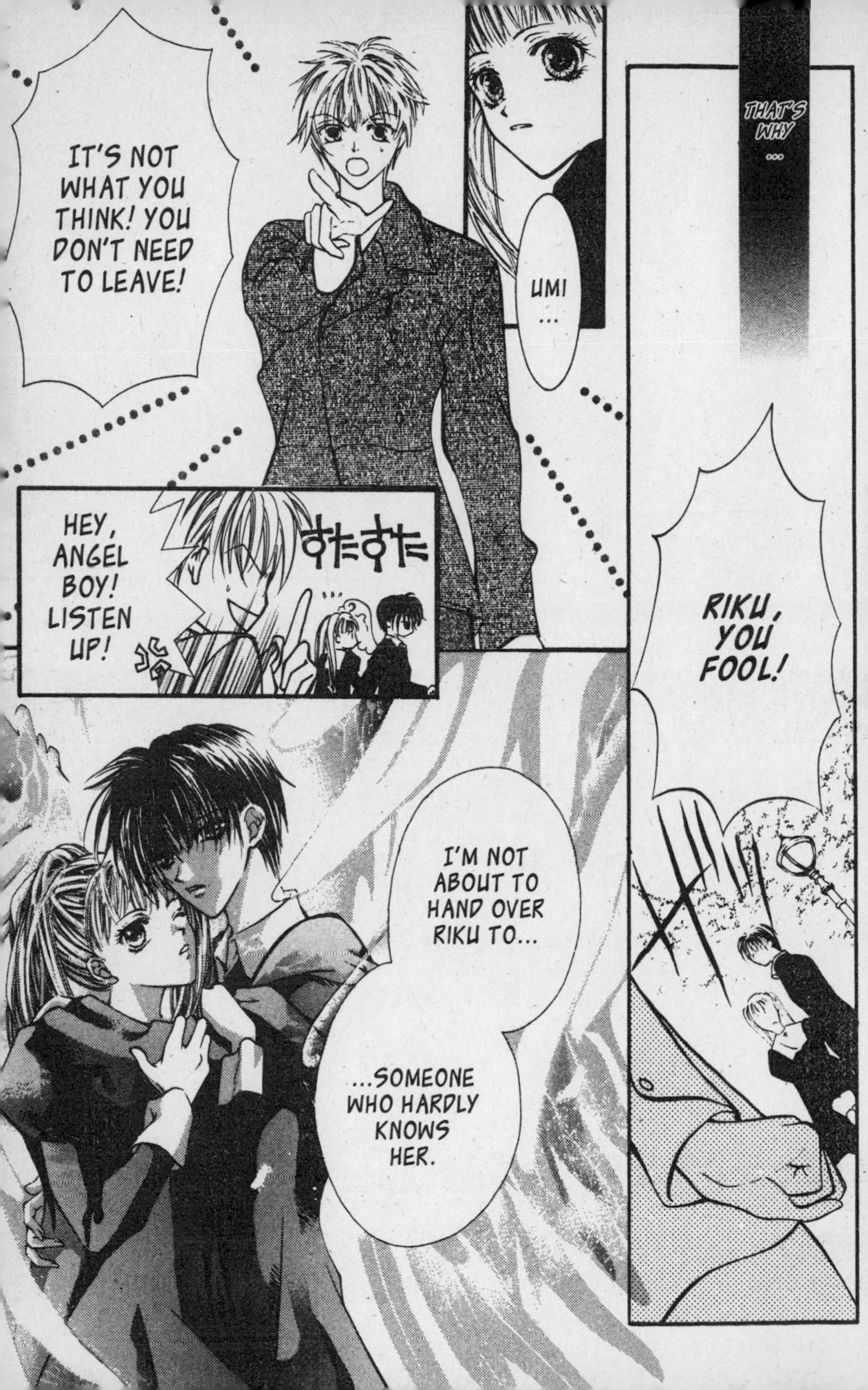
THAT'S WHY ...
RIKU, YOU FOOL!
UMI ...
IT'S NOT WHAT YOU THINK! YOU DON'T NEED TO LEAVE!
すたすた
HEY, ANGEL BOY! LISTEN UP!
I'M NOT ABOUT TO HAND OVER RIKU TO...
...SOMEONE WHO HARDLY KNOWS HER.

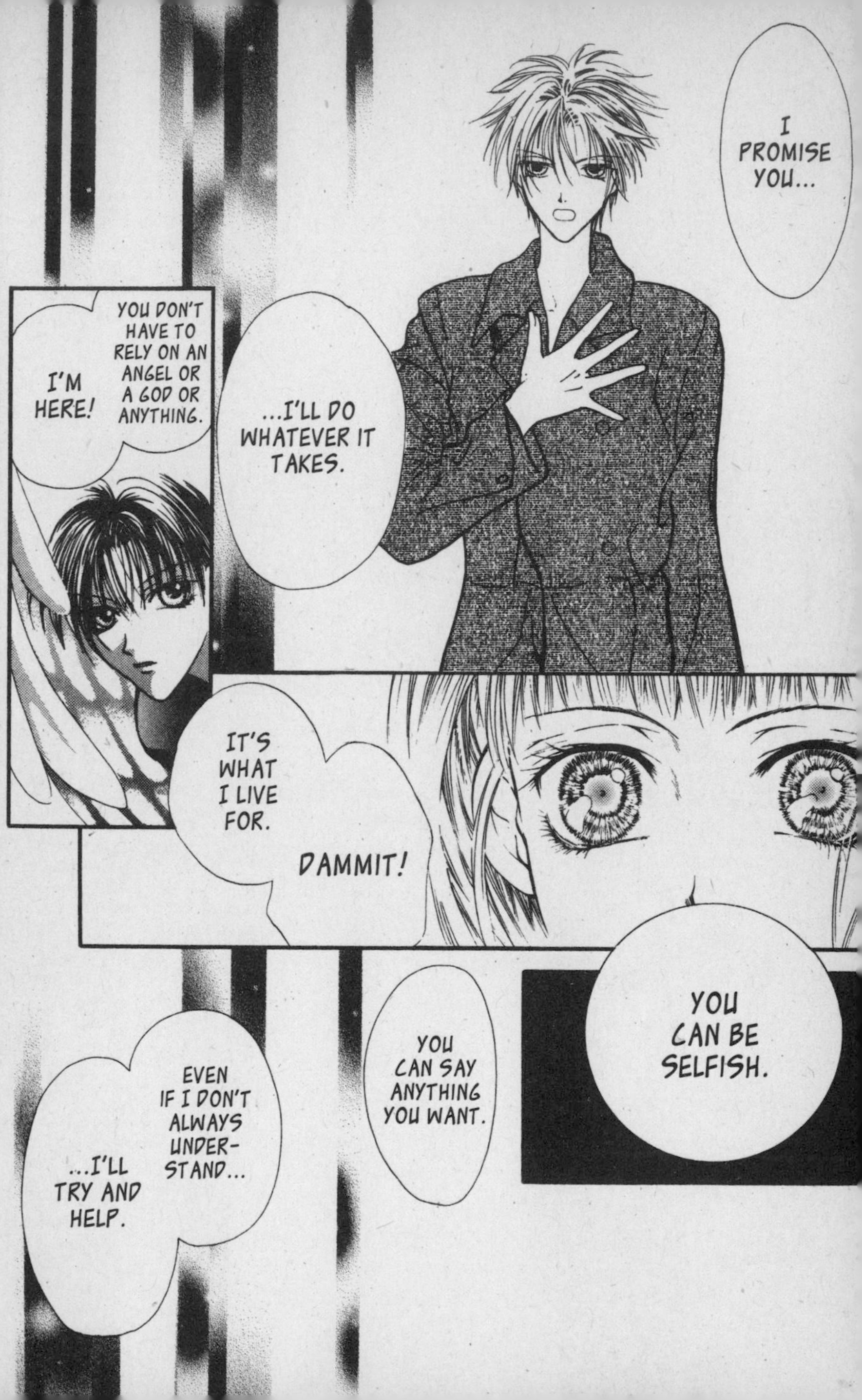
I PROMISE YOU...
...I'LL DO WHATEVER IT TAKES.
YOU DON'T HAVE TO RELY ON AN ANGEL OR A GOD OR ANYTHING.
I'M HERE!
IT'S WHAT I LIVE FOR.
DAMMIT!
YOU CAN BE SELFISH.
YOU CAN SAY ANYTHING YOU WANT.
EVEN IF I DON'T ALWAYS UNDER-STAND...
...I'LL TRY AND HELP.

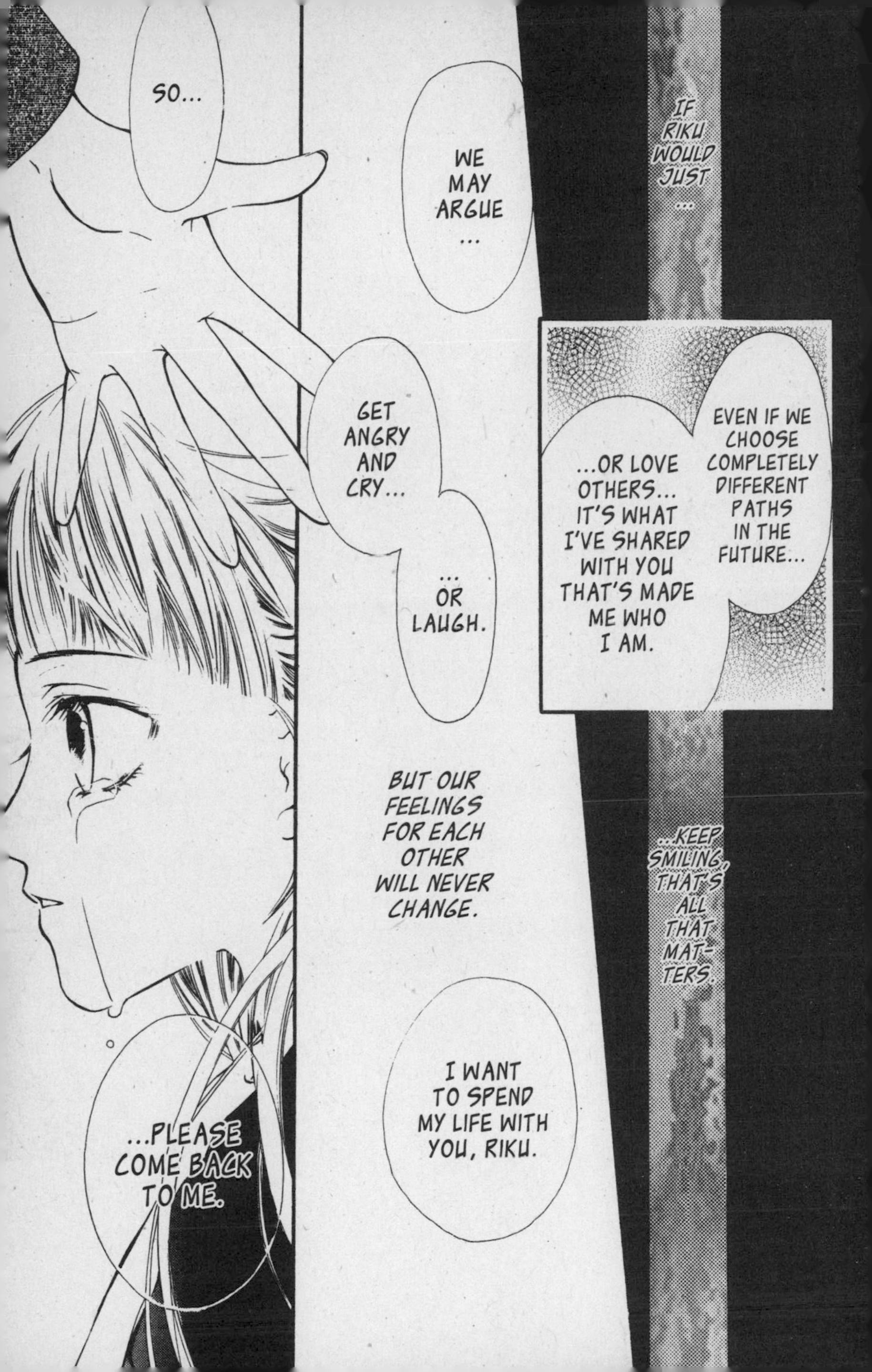
IF RIKU WOULD JUST...
EVEN IF WE CHOOSE COMPLETELY DIFFERENT PATHS IN THE FUTURE...
...OR LOVE OTHERS... IT'S WHAT I'VE SHARED WITH YOU THAT'S MADE ME WHO I AM.
...KEEP SMILING, THAT'S ALL THAT MAT-TERS.
WE MAY ARGUE...
GET ANGRY AND CRY...
...OR LAUGH.
BUT OUR FEELINGS FOR EACH OTHER WILL NEVER CHANGE.
I WANT TO SPEND MY LIFE WITH YOU, RIKU.
SO...
...PLEASE COME BACK TO ME.

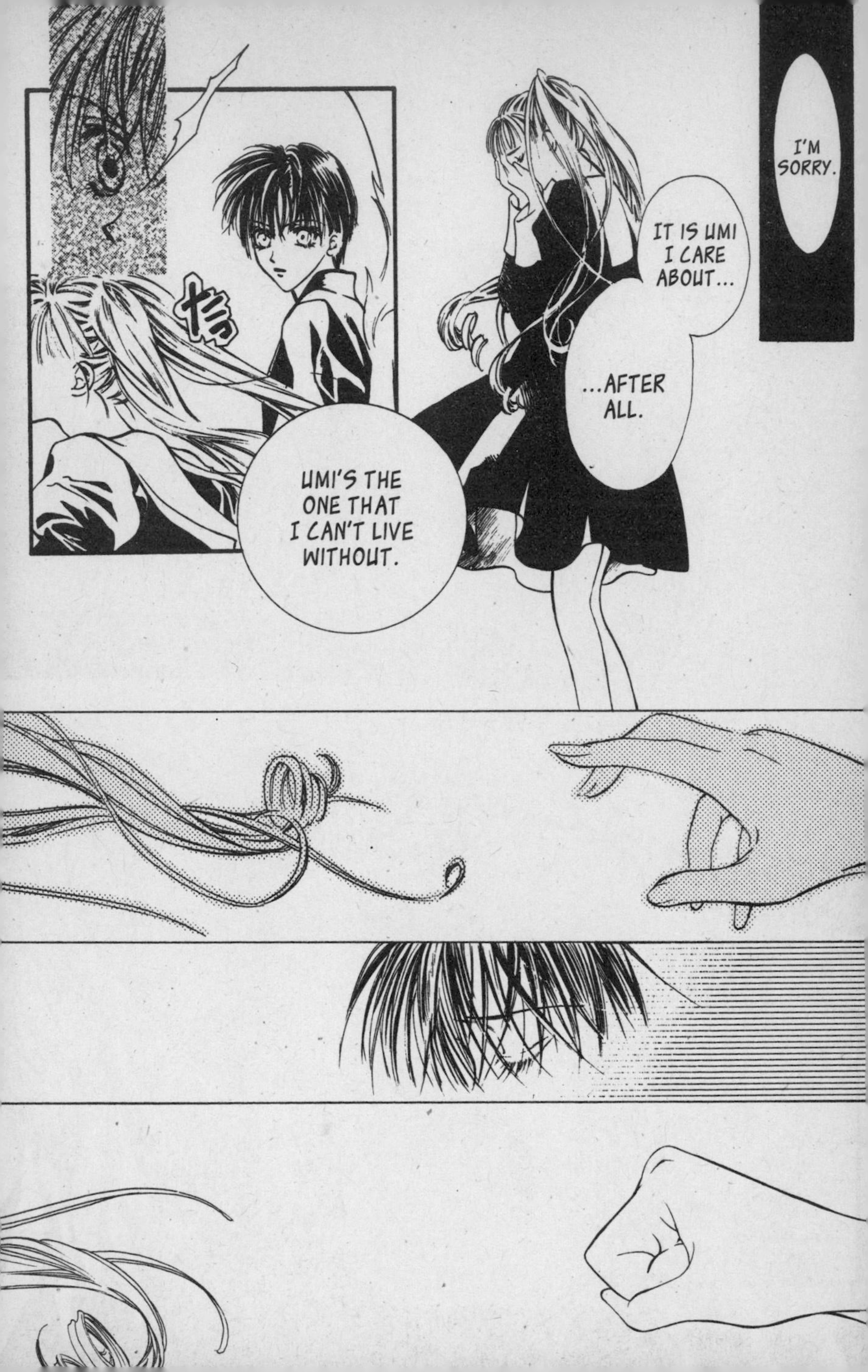
I'M SORRY.
IT IS UMI I CARE ABOUT...
...AFTER ALL.
UMI'S THE ONE THAT I CAN'T LIVE WITHOUT.

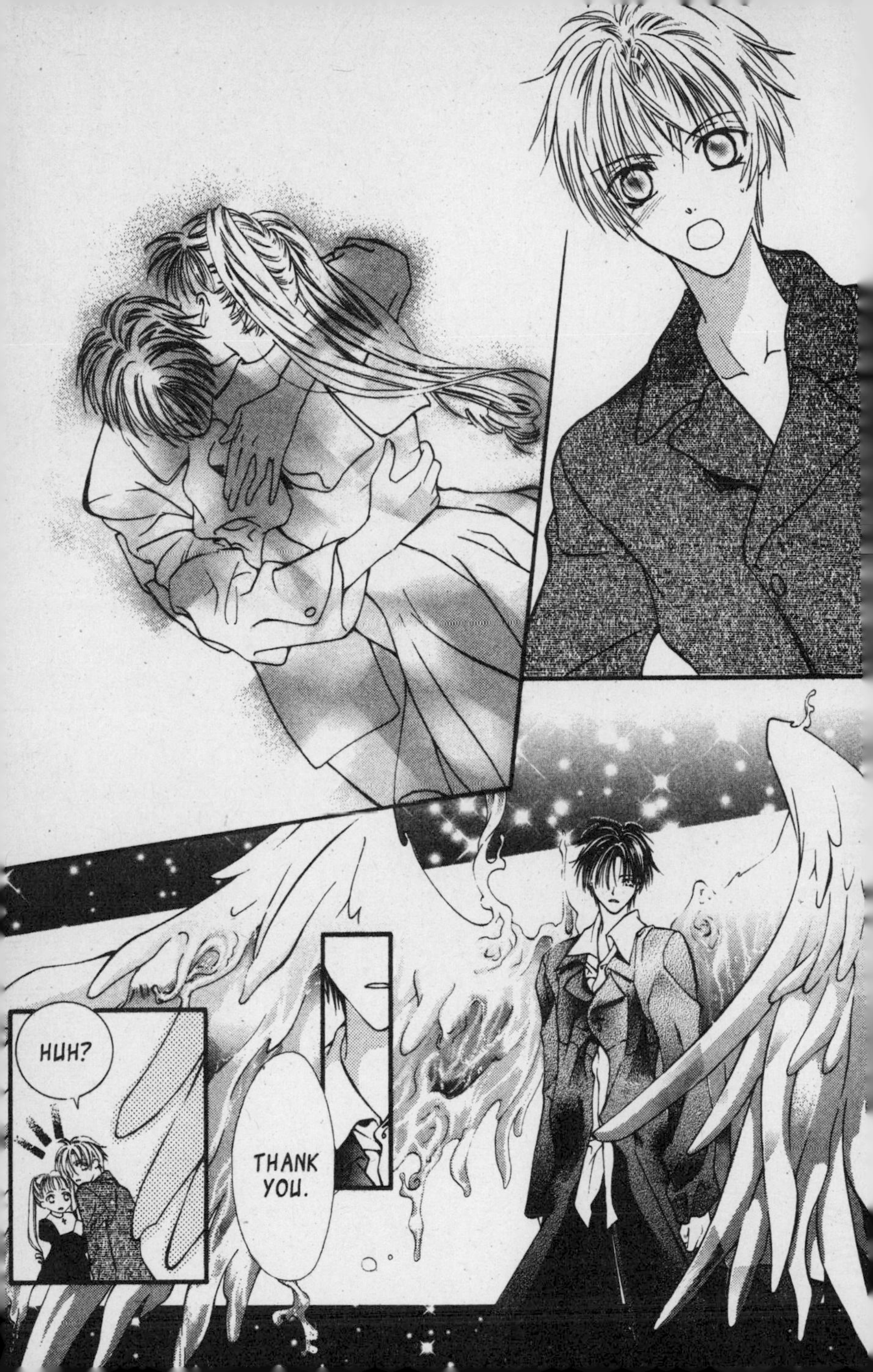
THANK YOU.
HUH?

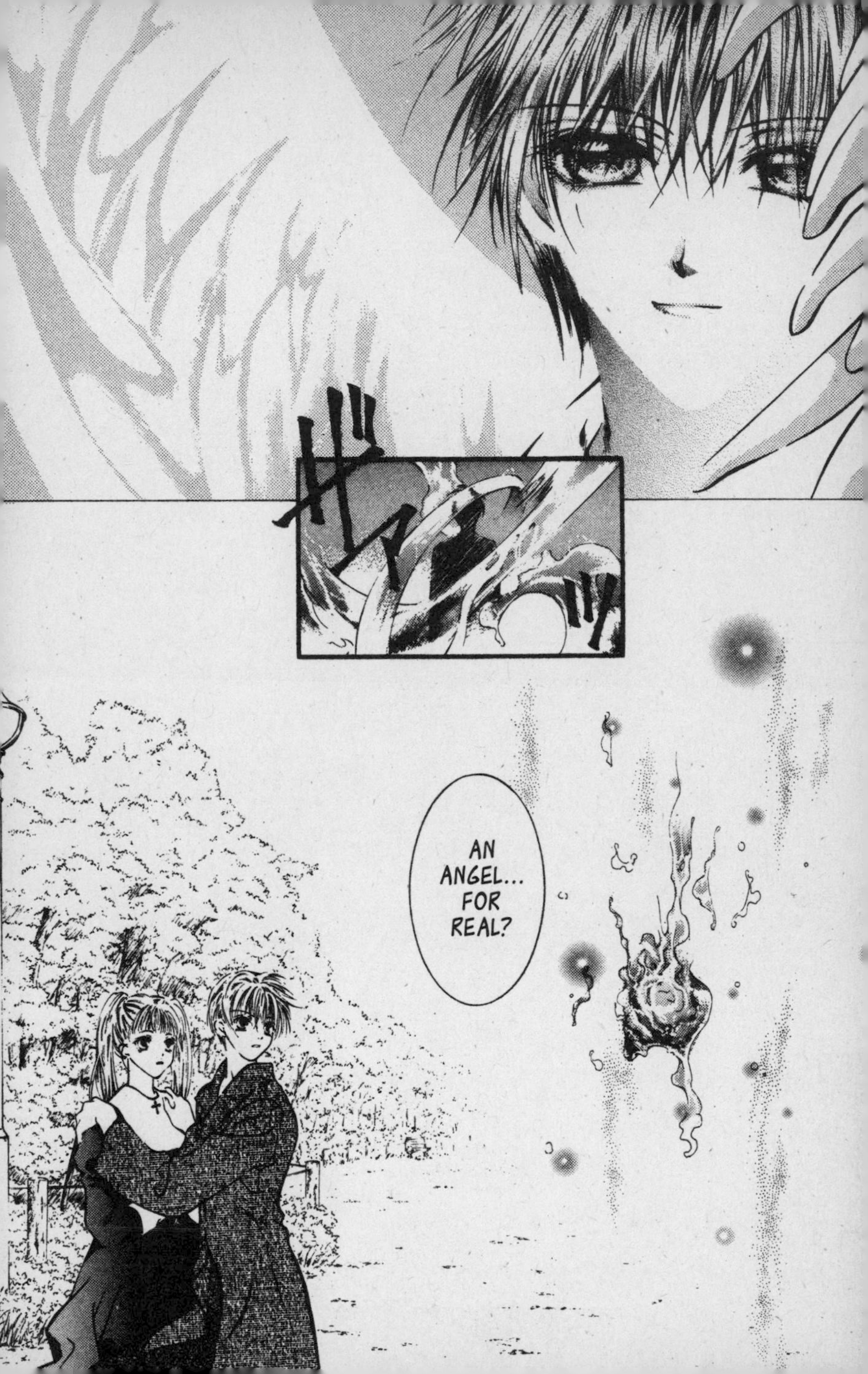
AN ANGEL... FOR REAL?

IT'S ALL RIGHT.

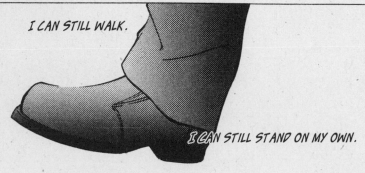

I CAN STILL WALK.

I CAN STILL STAND ON MY OWN.

I CAN LIVE FACING THIS WORLD...

...WHICH HAS MADE ME WHO I AM.

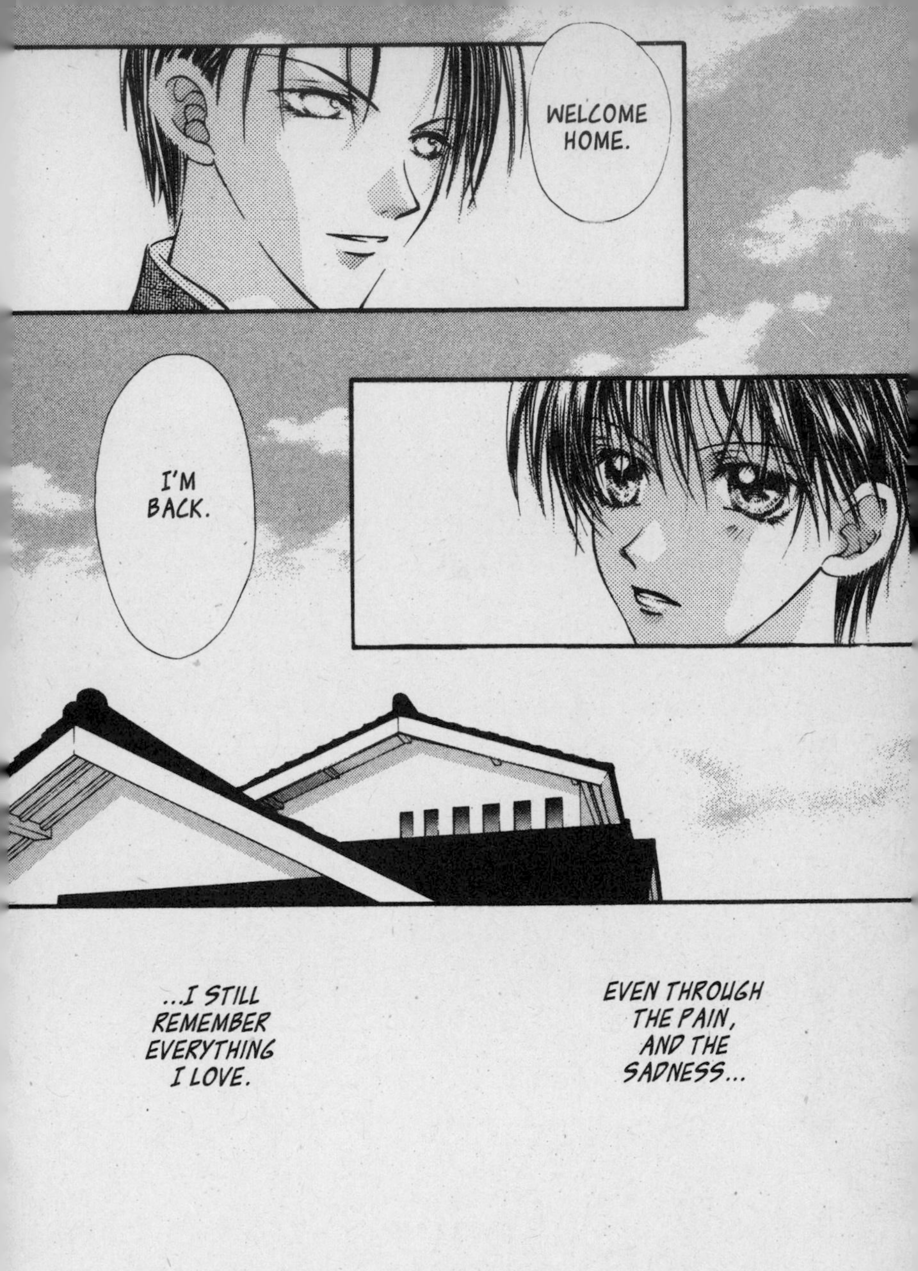
WELCOME HOME.
I'M BACK.
EVEN THROUGH THE PAIN, AND THE SADNESS...
...I STILL REMEMBER EVERYTHING I LOVE.

Bird Cage Princess – The End

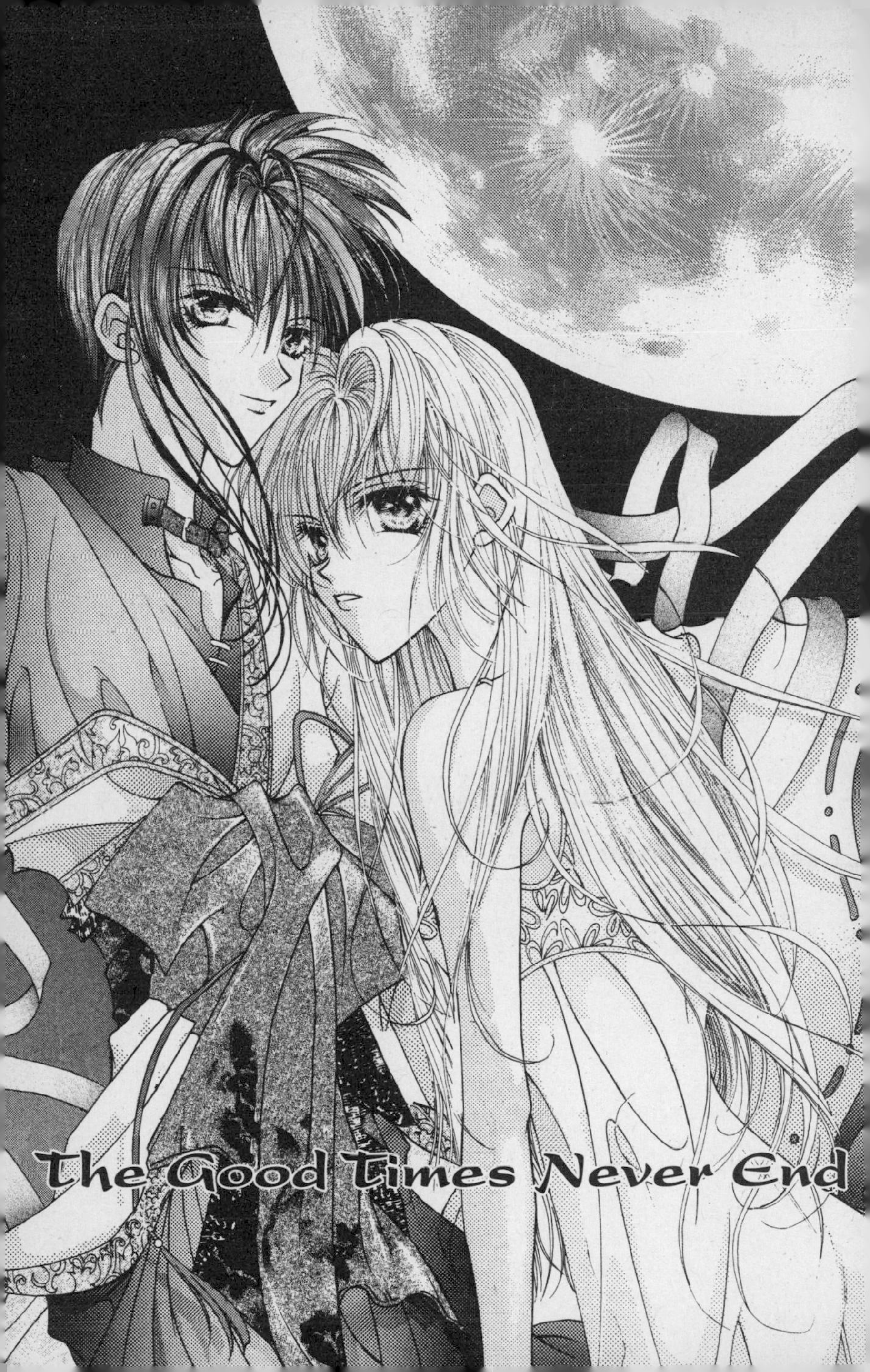
The Good Times Never End

38 points

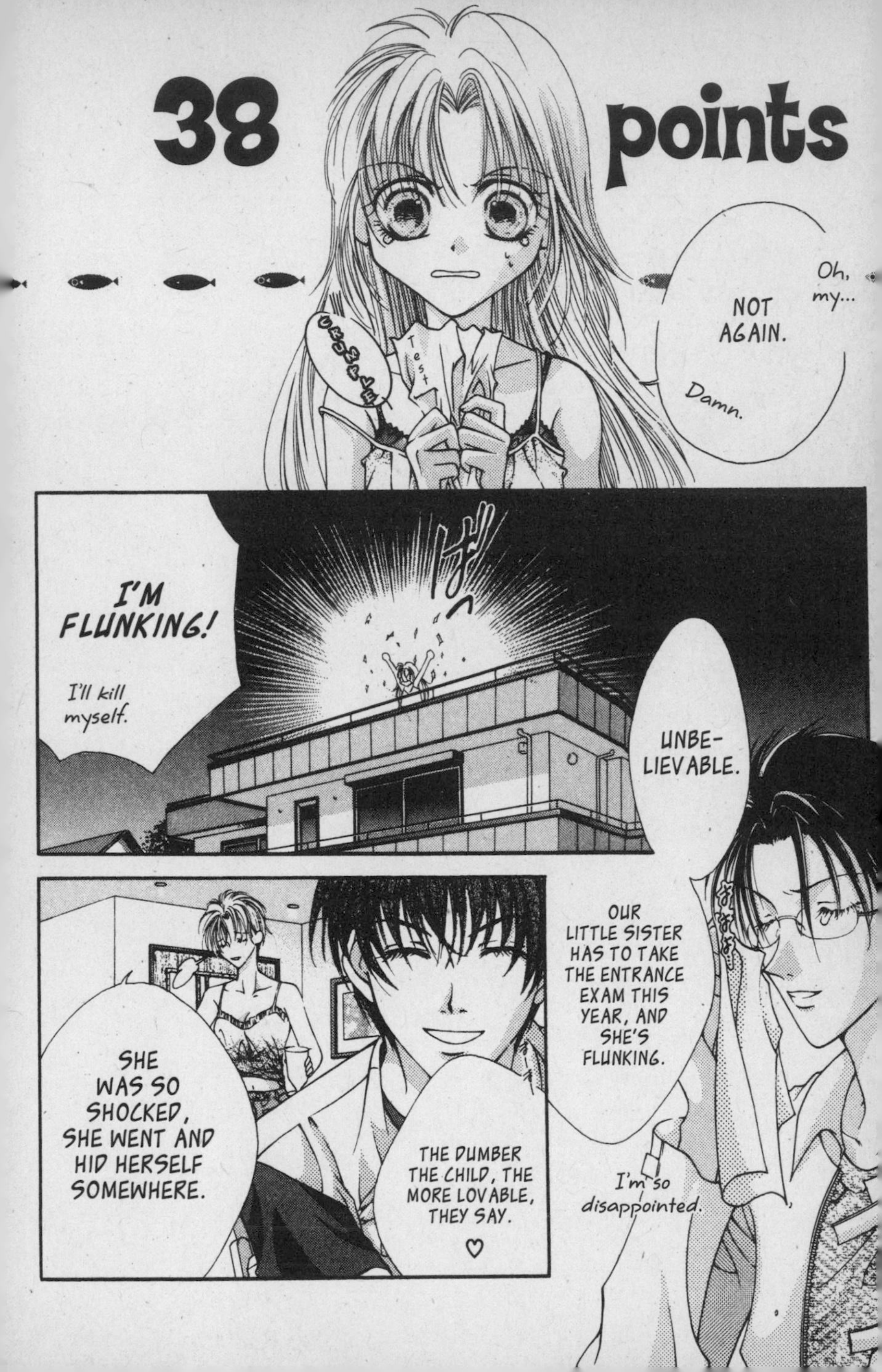

Oh, my... NOT AGAIN. Damn.
CRUMPLE
Test
I'M FLUNKING!
I'll kill myself.
UNBE-LIEVABLE.
OUR LITTLE SISTER HAS TO TAKE THE ENTRANCE EXAM THIS YEAR, AND SHE'S FLUNKING.
I'm so disappointed.
THE DUMBER THE CHILD, THE MORE LOVABLE, THEY SAY. ♡
SHE WAS SO SHOCKED, SHE WENT AND HID HERSELF SOMEWHERE.

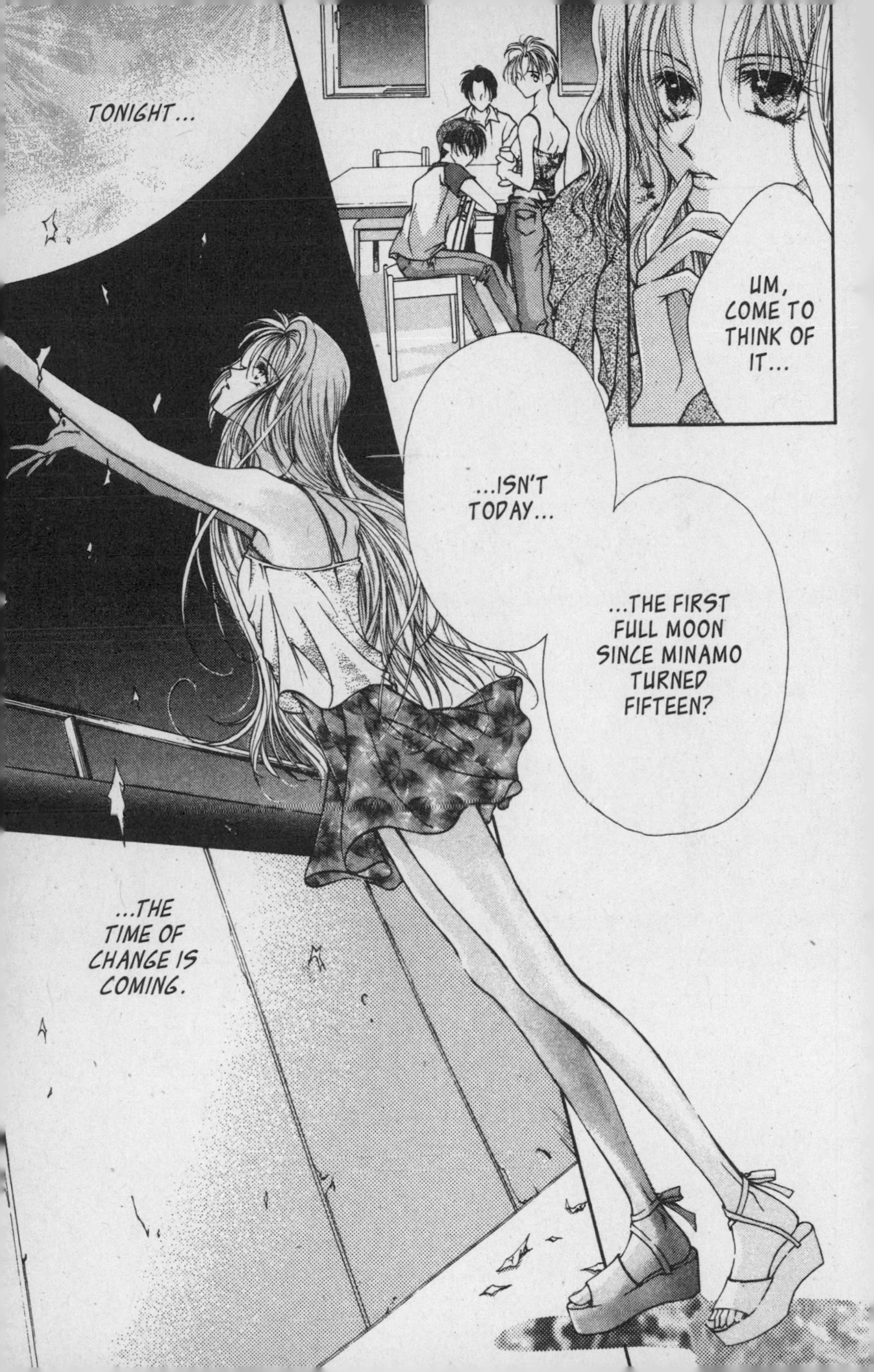
UM, COME TO THINK OF IT...
...ISN'T TODAY...
...THE FIRST FULL MOON SINCE MINAMO TURNED FIFTEEN?
TONIGHT...
...THE TIME OF CHANGE IS COMING.

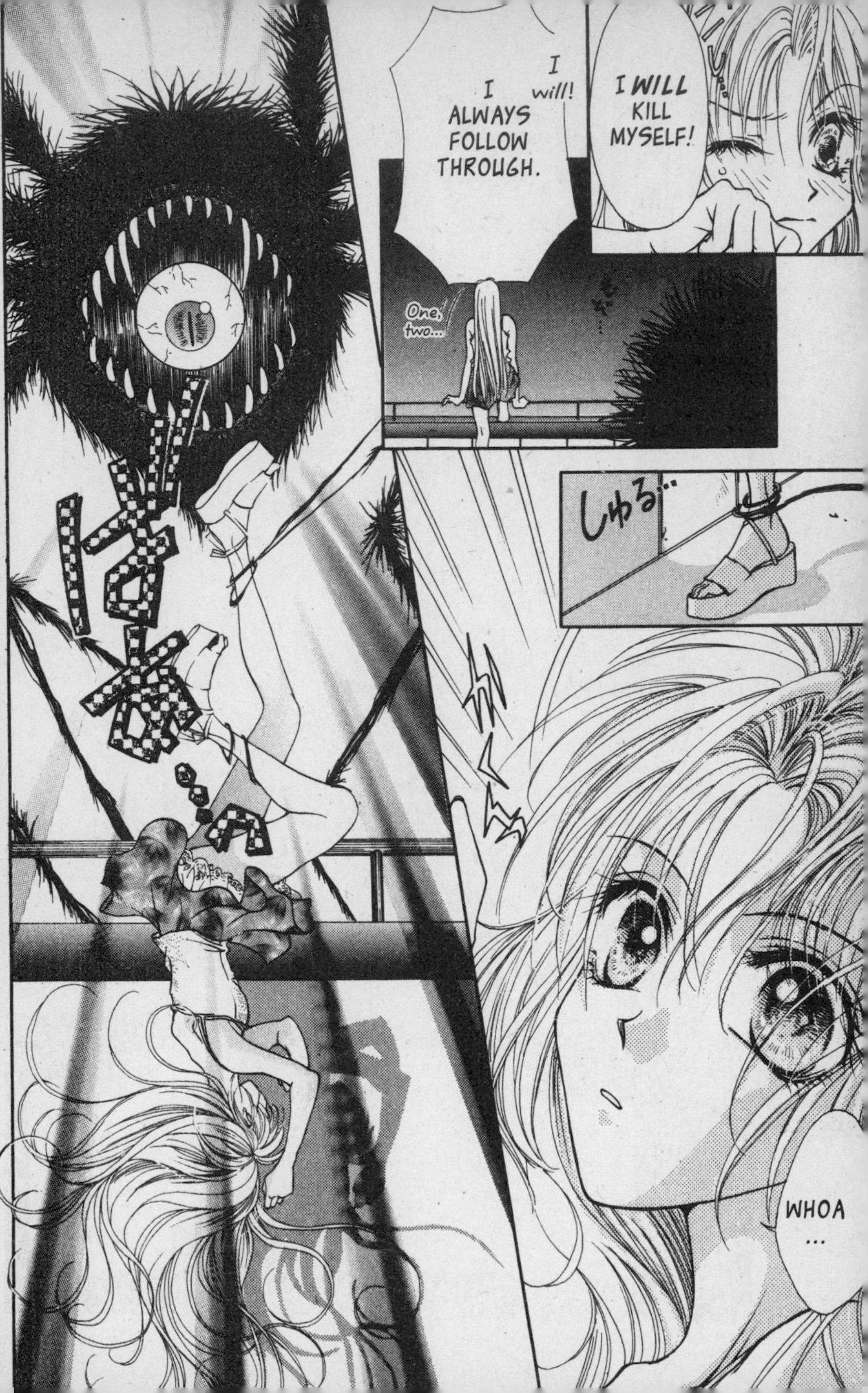
I WILL KILL MYSELF!
I will!
I ALWAYS FOLLOW THROUGH.
One, two...
しゅる…
WHOA ...

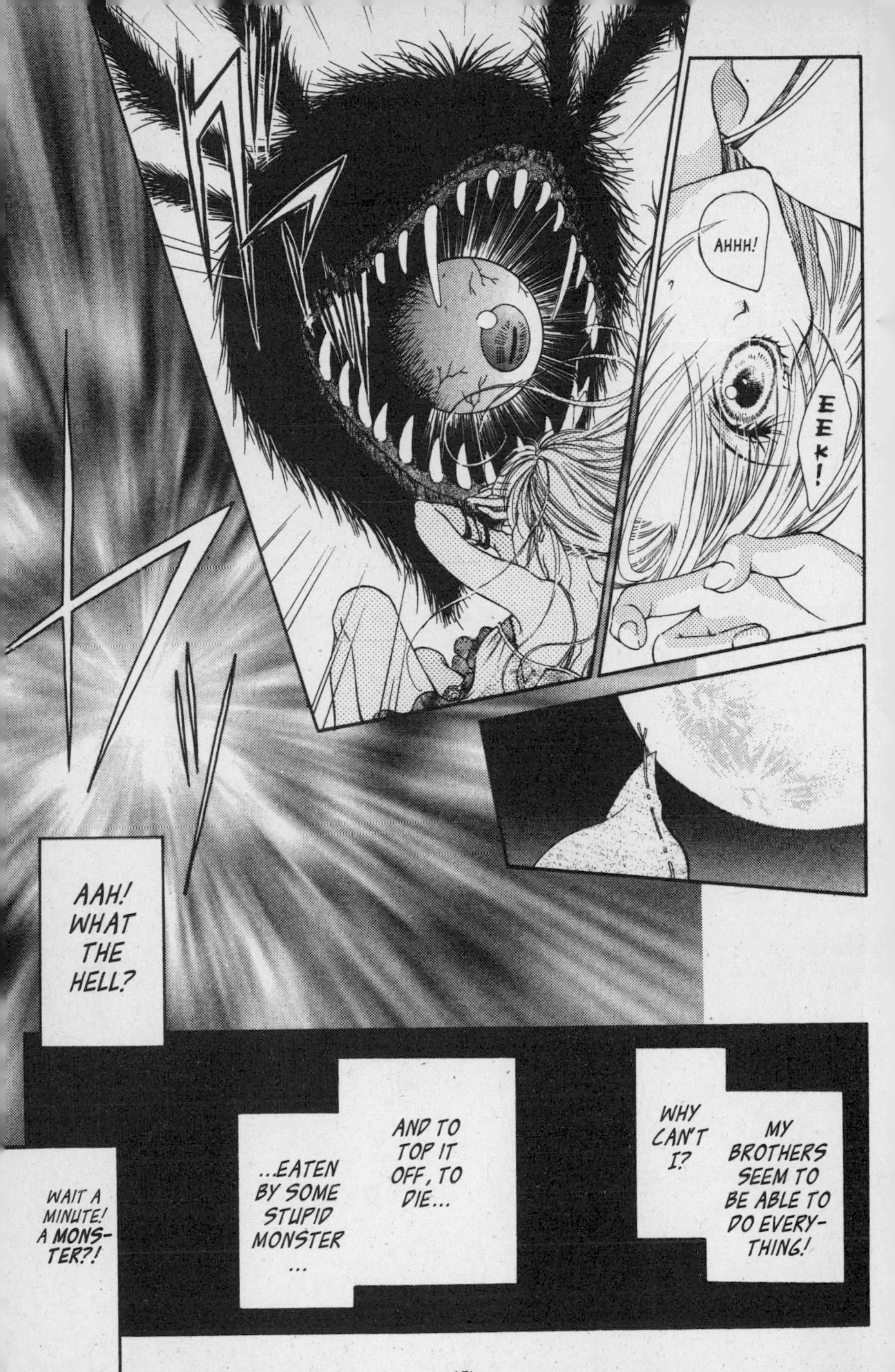
AHHH!
EEK!
AAH! WHAT THE HELL?
MY BROTHERS SEEM TO BE ABLE TO DO EVERY-THING!
WHY CAN'T I?
AND TO TOP IT OFF, TO DIE...
...EATEN BY SOME STUPID MONSTER ...
WAIT A MINUTE! A MONS-TER?!

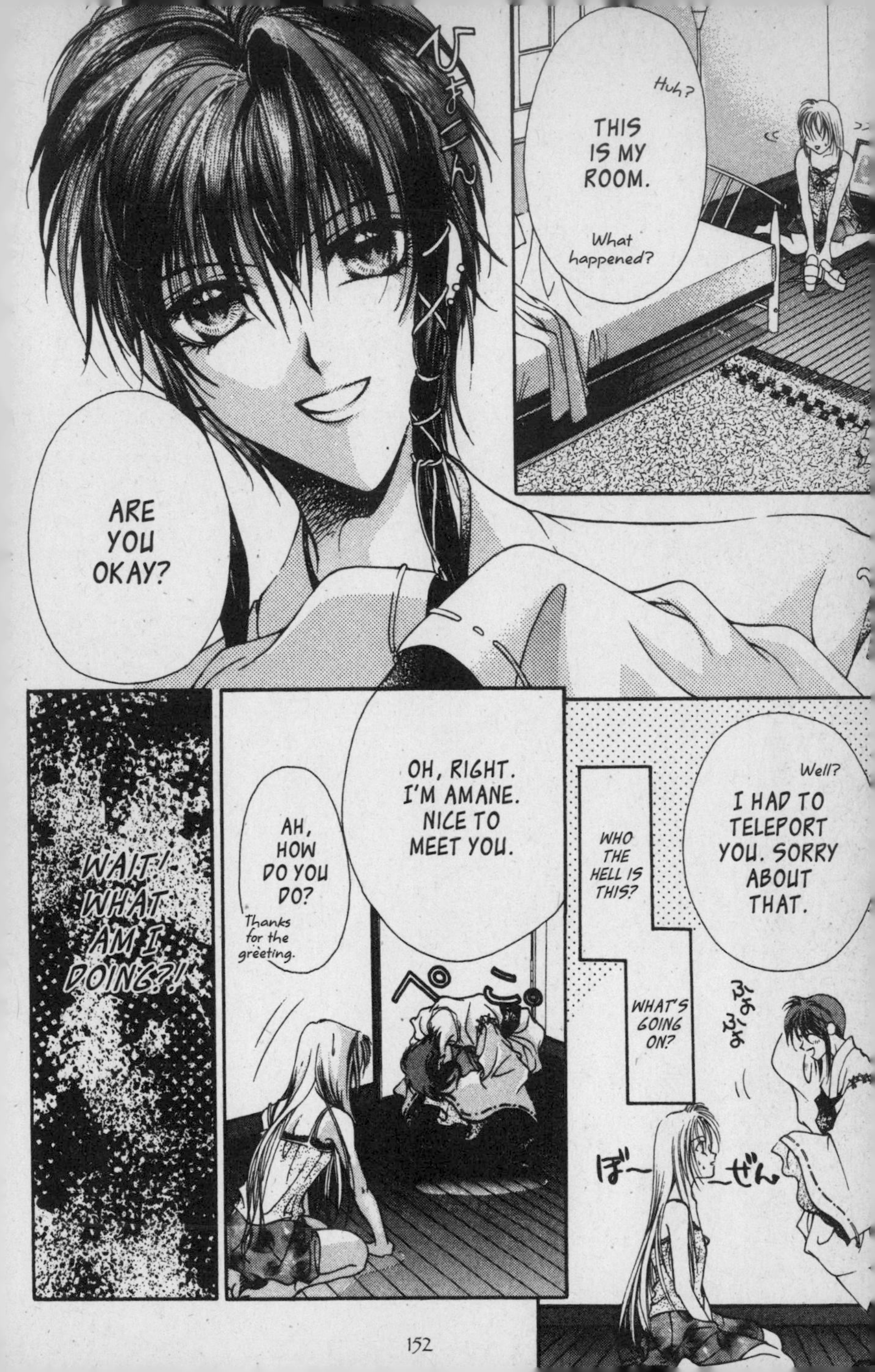
Huh?
THIS IS MY ROOM.
What happened?
ARE YOU OKAY?
Well?
I HAD TO TELEPORT YOU. SORRY ABOUT THAT.
ぼ〜ぜん
WHO THE HELL IS THIS?
WHAT'S GOING ON?
OH, RIGHT. I'M AMANE. NICE TO MEET YOU.
AH, HOW DO YOU DO?
Thanks for the greeting.
WAIT! WHAT AM I DOING?!

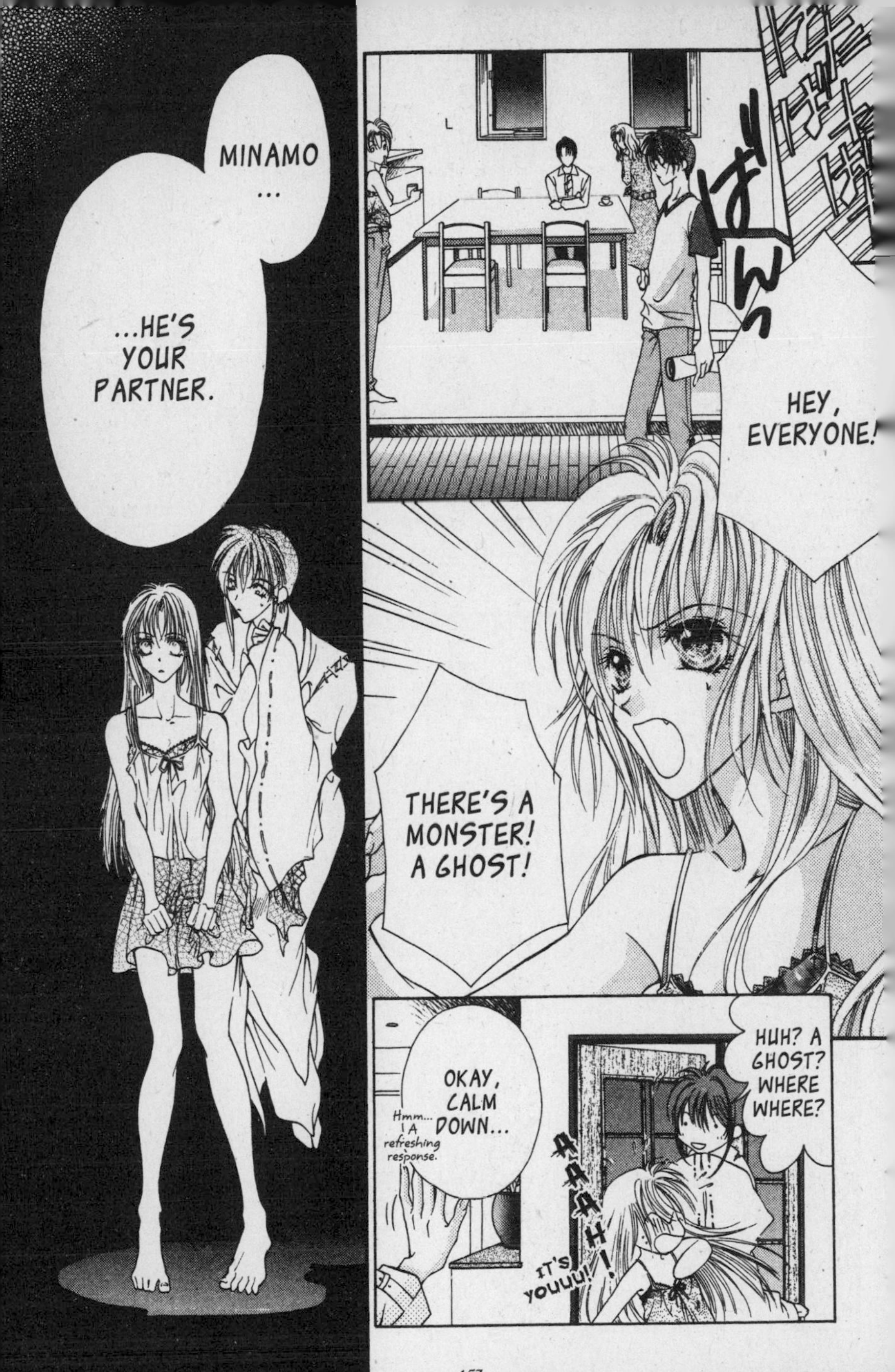
ばんっ
HEY, EVERYONE!
THERE'S A MONSTER! A GHOST!
HUH? A GHOST? WHERE WHERE?
AAAH!
IT'S YOUUU!
OKAY, CALM DOWN...
Hmm... A refreshing response.
MINAMO ...
...HE'S YOUR PARTNER.

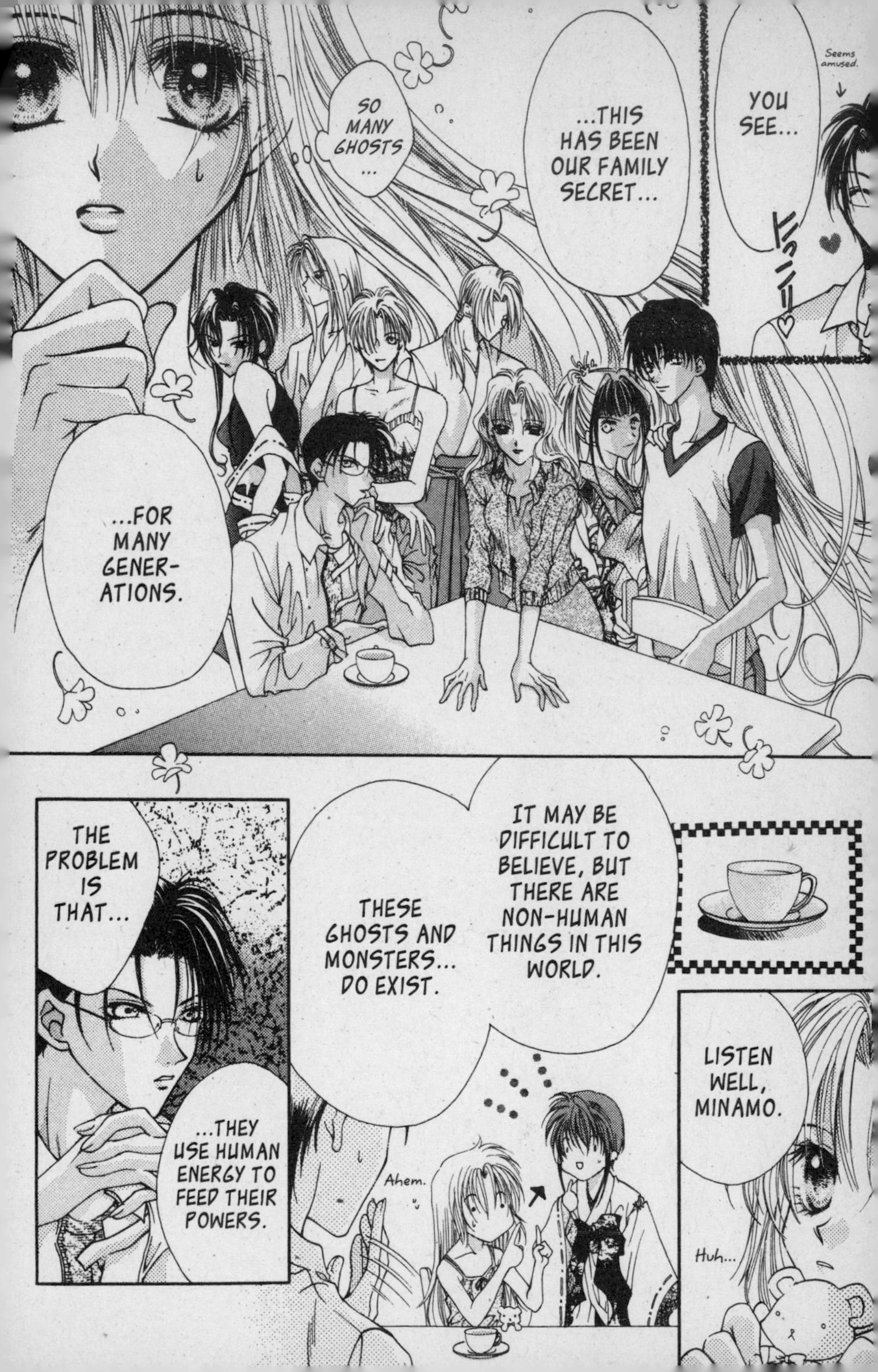
Seems amused.
YOU SEE...
...THIS HAS BEEN OUR FAMILY SECRET...
SO MANY GHOSTS...
...FOR MANY GENERATIONS.
LISTEN WELL, MINAMO.
Huh...
IT MAY BE DIFFICULT TO BELIEVE, BUT THERE ARE NON-HUMAN THINGS IN THIS WORLD.
THESE GHOSTS AND MONSTERS... DO EXIST.
Ahem.
THE PROBLEM IS THAT...
...THEY USE HUMAN ENERGY TO FEED THEIR POWERS.

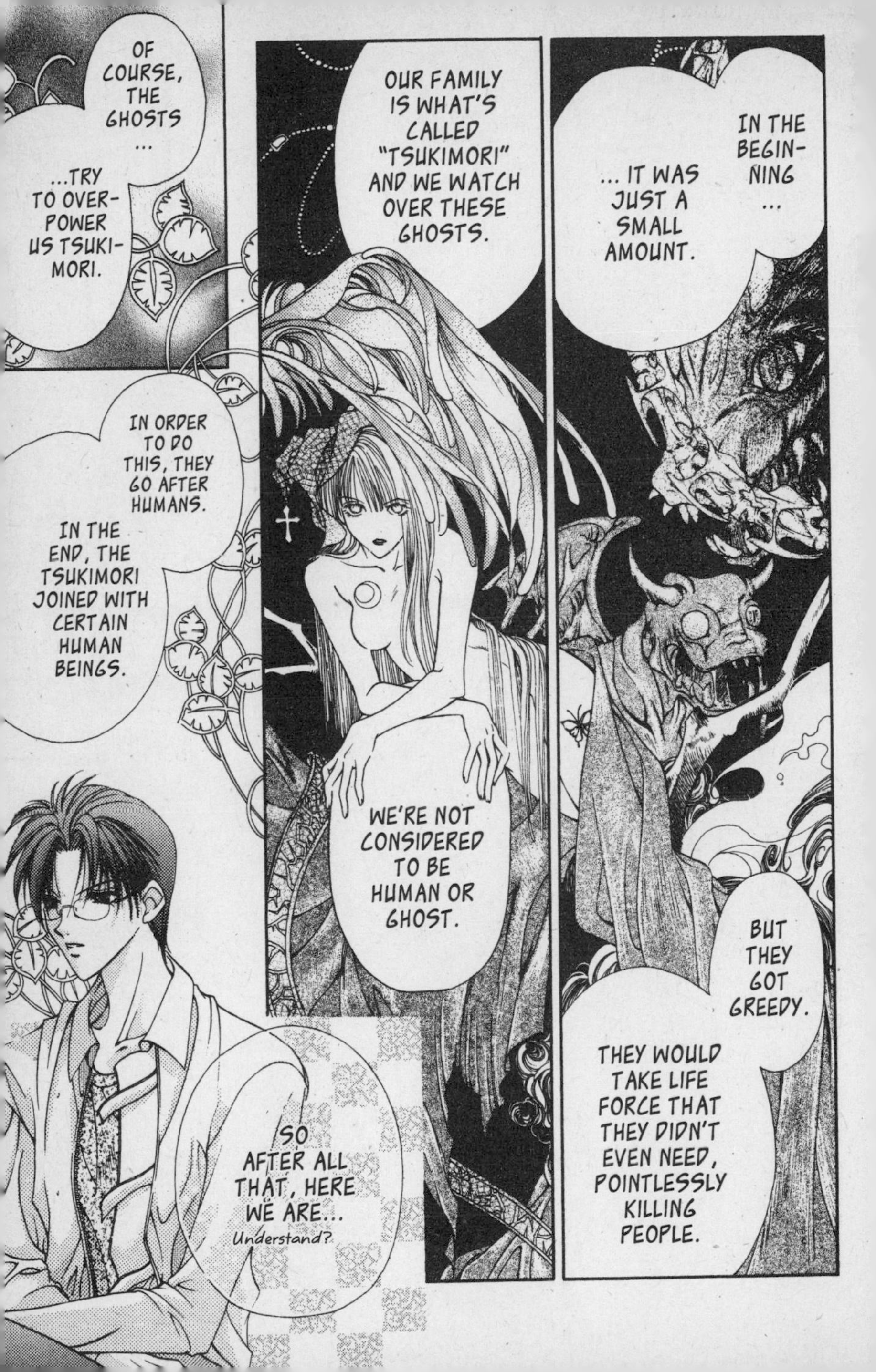
IN THE BEGINNING ...
... IT WAS JUST A SMALL AMOUNT.
BUT THEY GOT GREEDY.
THEY WOULD TAKE LIFE FORCE THAT THEY DIDN'T EVEN NEED, POINTLESSLY KILLING PEOPLE.
OUR FAMILY IS WHAT'S CALLED "TSUKIMORI" AND WE WATCH OVER THESE GHOSTS.
WE'RE NOT CONSIDERED TO BE HUMAN OR GHOST.
OF COURSE, THE GHOSTS ...
...TRY TO OVERPOWER US TSUKIMORI.
IN ORDER TO DO THIS, THEY GO AFTER HUMANS.
IN THE END, THE TSUKIMORI JOINED WITH CERTAIN HUMAN BEINGS.
SO AFTER ALL THAT, HERE WE ARE...
Understand?

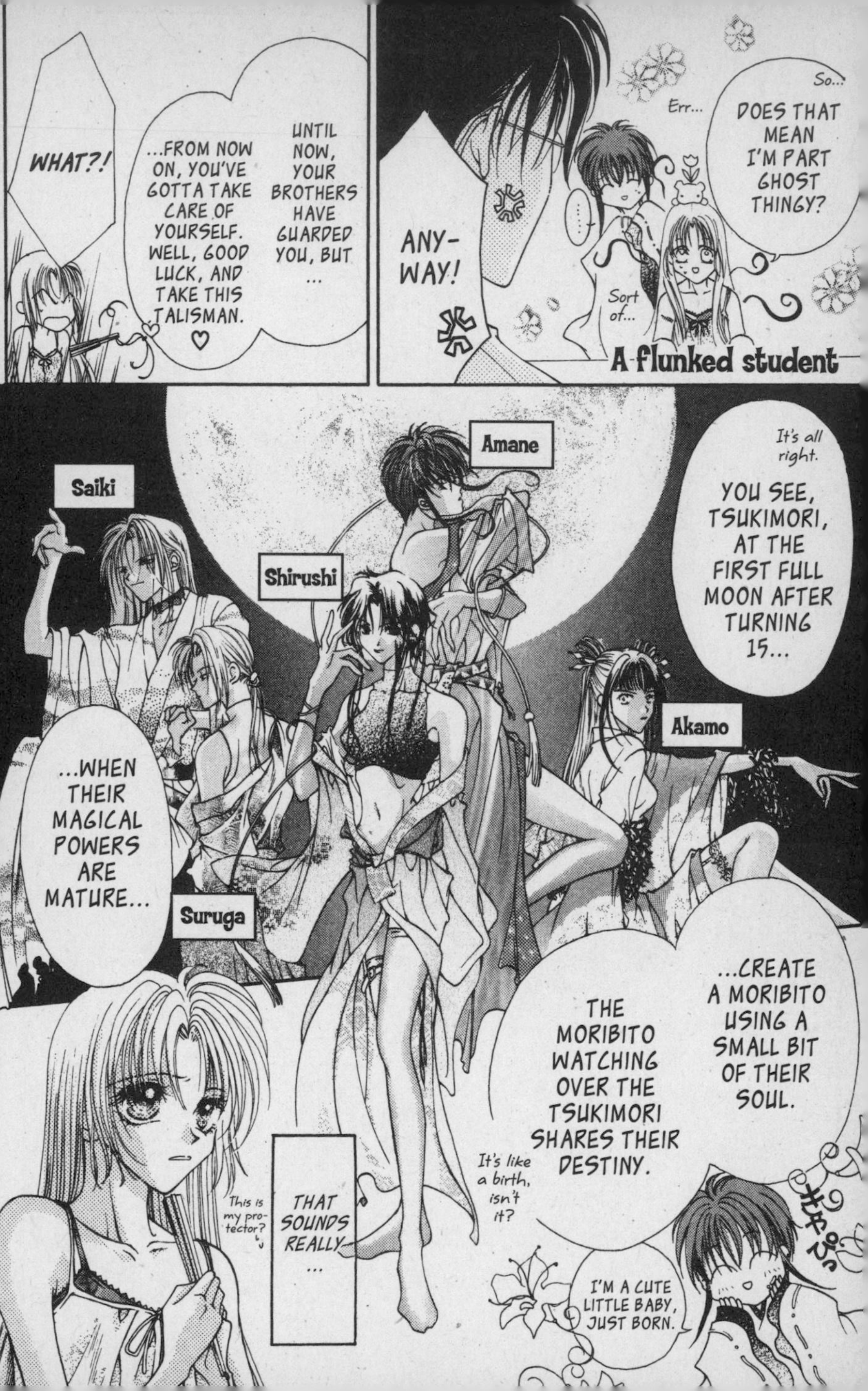
So...
DOES THAT MEAN I'M PART GHOST THINGY?
Err...
...
Sort of...
ANY-WAY!
A flunked student
UNTIL NOW, YOUR BROTHERS HAVE GUARDED YOU, BUT ...
...FROM NOW ON, YOU'VE GOTTA TAKE CARE OF YOURSELF. WELL, GOOD LUCK, AND TAKE THIS TALISMAN. ♡
WHAT?!
It's all right.
YOU SEE, TSUKIMORI, AT THE FIRST FULL MOON AFTER TURNING 15...
Amane
Saiki
Shirushi
Akamo
Suruga
...WHEN THEIR MAGICAL POWERS ARE MATURE...
...CREATE A MORIBITO USING A SMALL BIT OF THEIR SOUL.
THE MORIBITO WATCHING OVER THE TSUKIMORI SHARES THEIR DESTINY.
It's like a birth, isn't it?
きゃぴっ
I'M A CUTE LITTLE BABY, JUST BORN.
THAT SOUNDS REALLY ...
This is my protector?

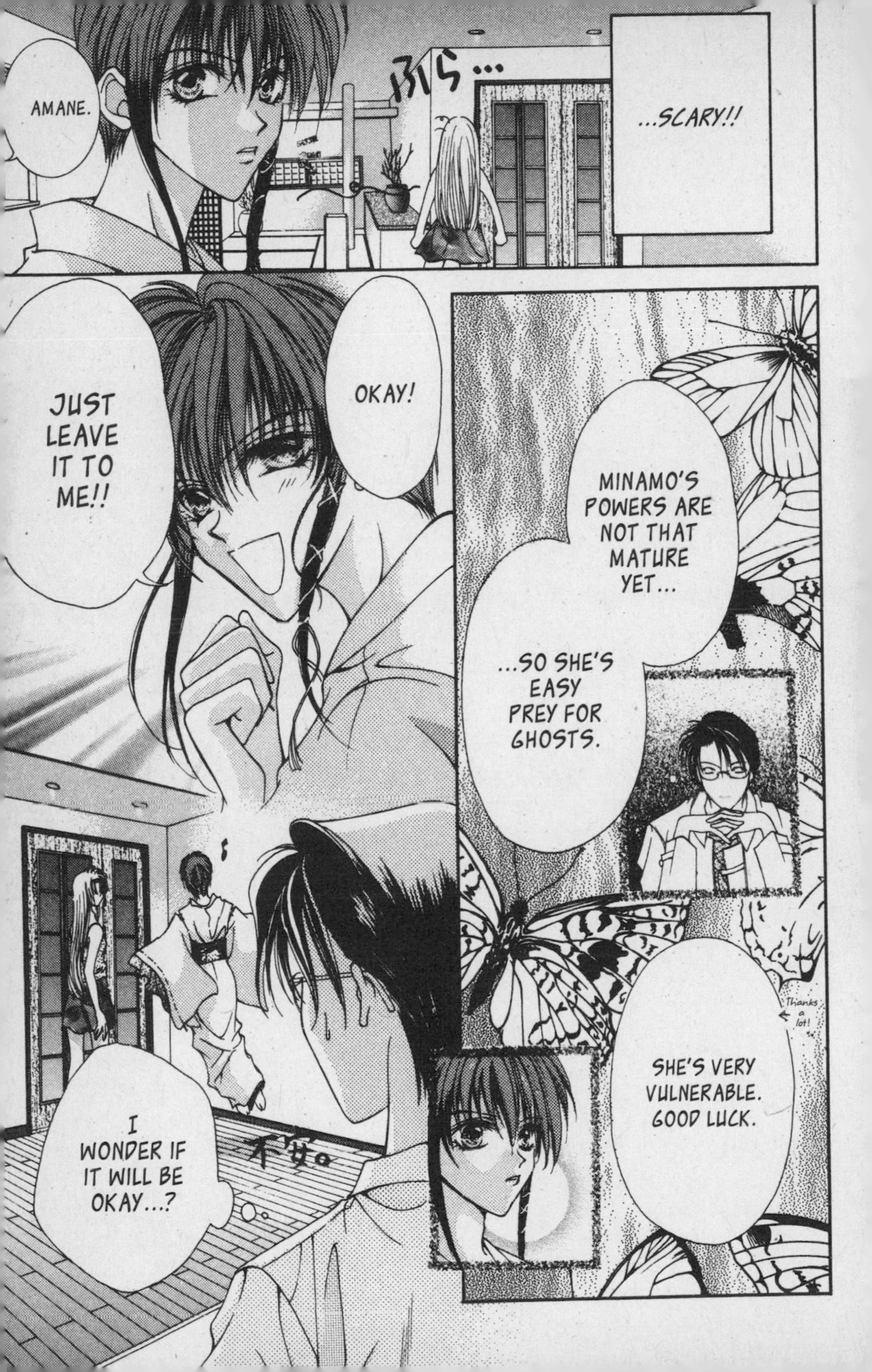
...SCARY!!
AMANE.
MINAMO'S POWERS ARE NOT THAT MATURE YET...
...SO SHE'S EASY PREY FOR GHOSTS.
SHE'S VERY VULNERABLE. GOOD LUCK.
Thanks a lot!
OKAY!
JUST LEAVE IT TO ME!!
I WONDER IF IT WILL BE OKAY...?

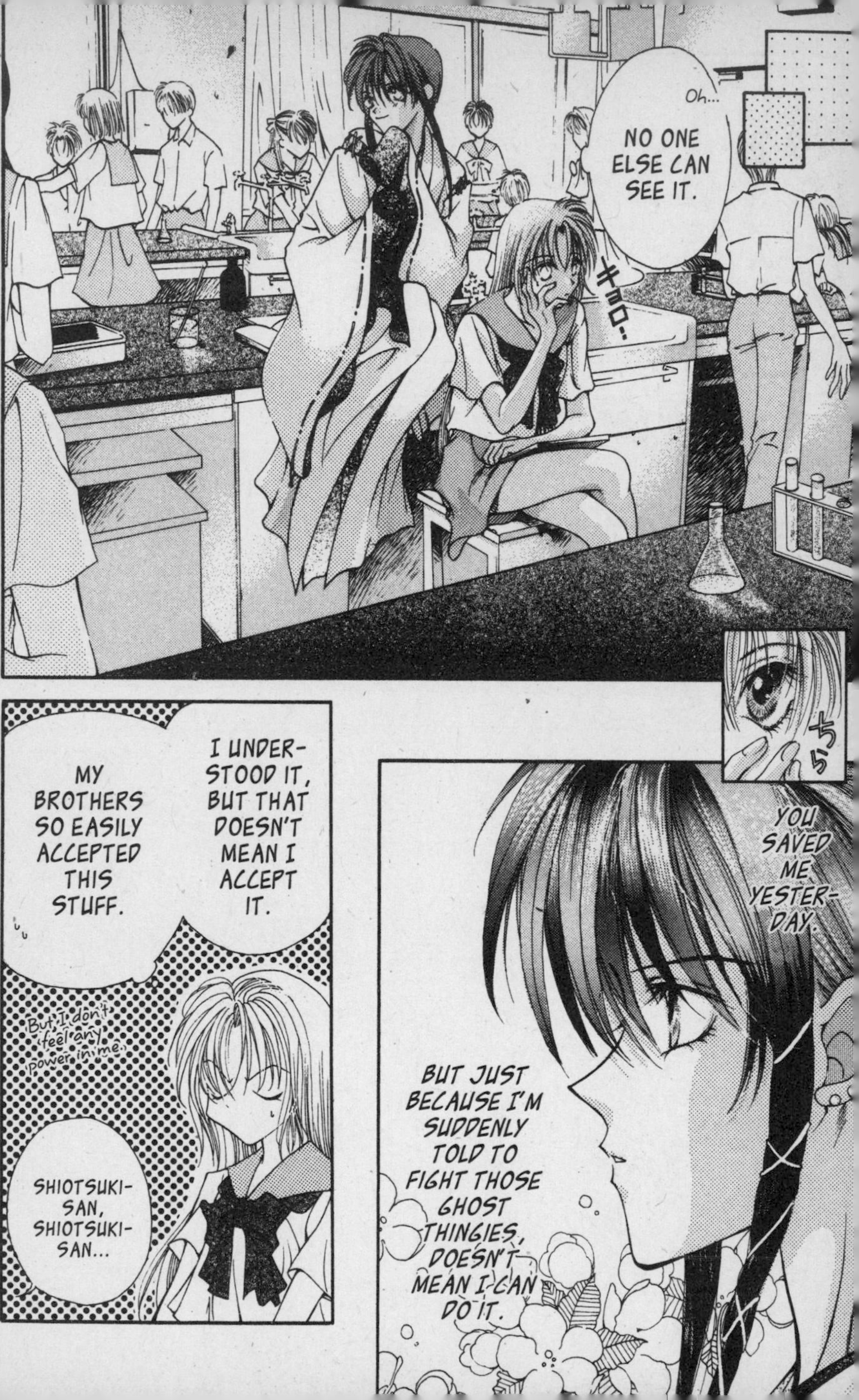
Oh...
NO ONE ELSE CAN SEE IT.
キョロ…
ちら
YOU SAVED ME YESTER-DAY.
BUT JUST BECAUSE I'M SUDDENLY TOLD TO FIGHT THOSE GHOST THINGIES, DOESN'T MEAN I CAN DO IT.
I UNDER-STOOD IT, BUT THAT DOESN'T MEAN I ACCEPT IT.
MY BROTHERS SO EASILY ACCEPTED THIS STUFF.
But I don't feel any power in me.
SHIOTSUKI-SAN, SHIOTSUKI-SAN...

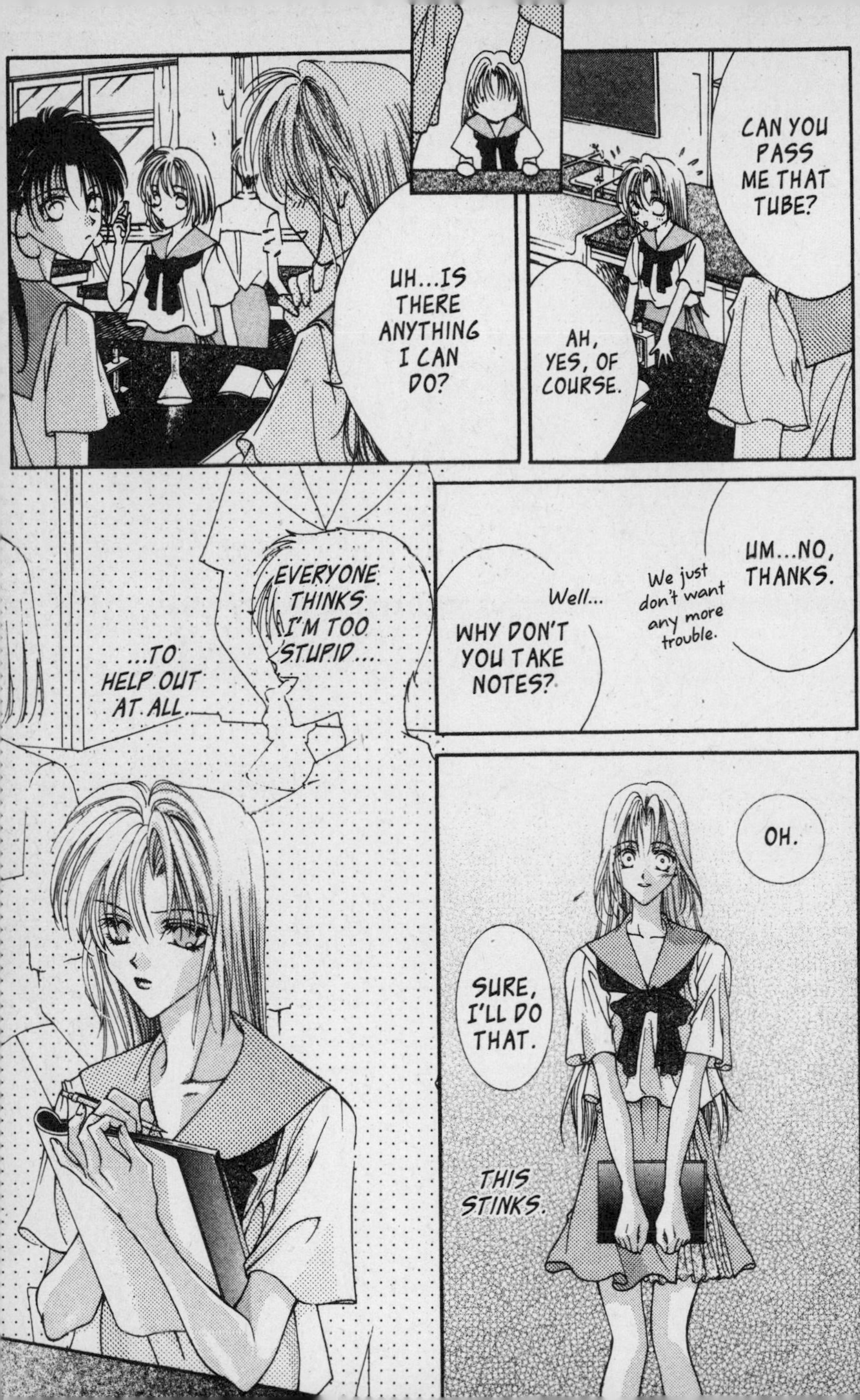
CAN YOU PASS ME THAT TUBE?
AH, YES, OF COURSE.
UH...IS THERE ANYTHING I CAN DO?
UM...NO, THANKS.
We just don't want any more trouble.
Well...
WHY DON'T YOU TAKE NOTES?
OH.
SURE, I'LL DO THAT.
THIS STINKS.
EVERYONE THINKS I'M TOO STUPID...
...TO HELP OUT AT ALL.

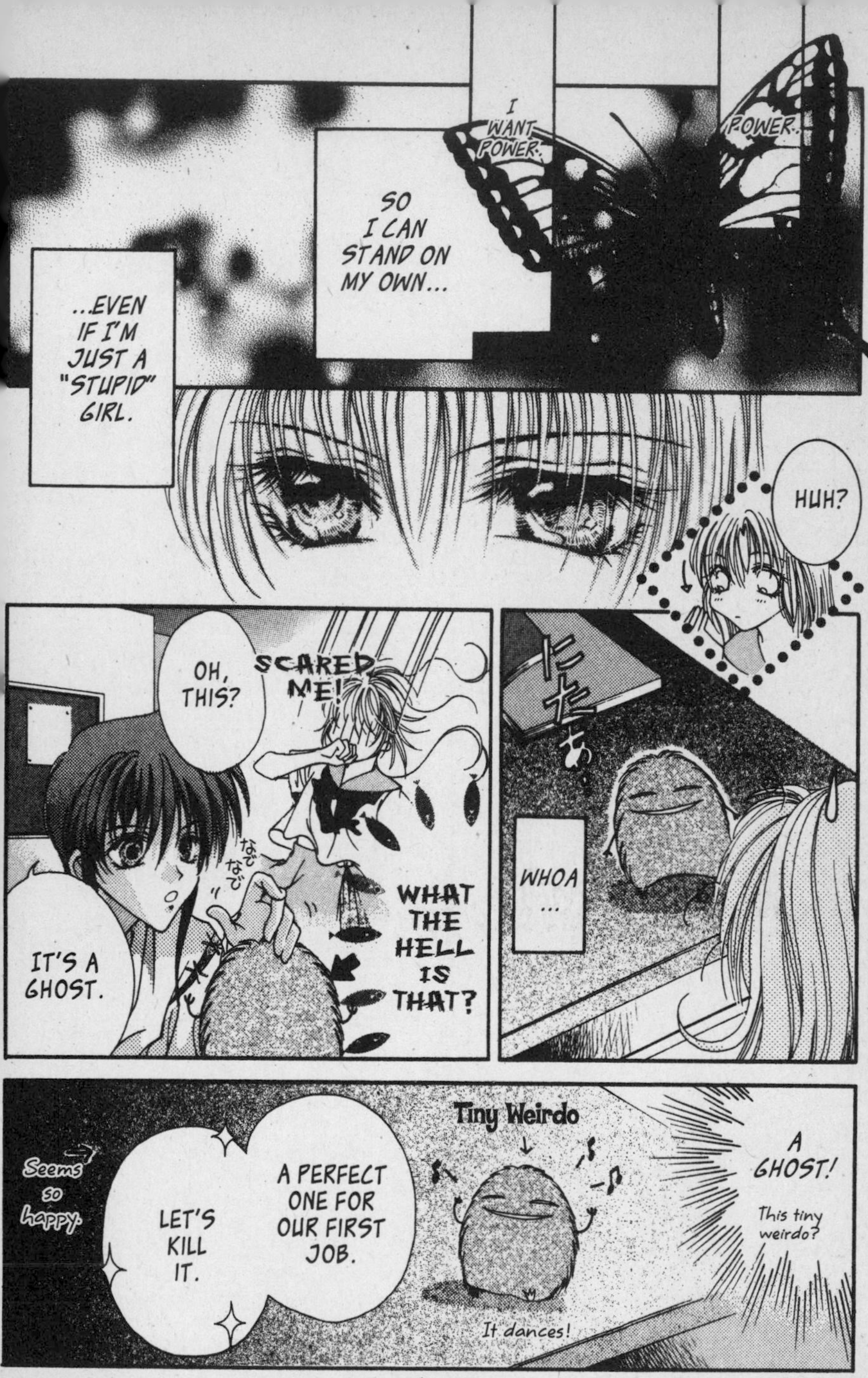
I WANT POWER.
POWER.
SO I CAN STAND ON MY OWN...
...EVEN IF I'M JUST A "STUPID" GIRL.
HUH?
WHOA...
SCARED ME!
OH, THIS?
WHAT THE HELL IS THAT?
なで なで
IT'S A GHOST.
A GHOST!
This tiny weirdo?
Tiny Weirdo
It dances!
A PERFECT ONE FOR OUR FIRST JOB.
LET'S KILL IT.
Seems so happy.

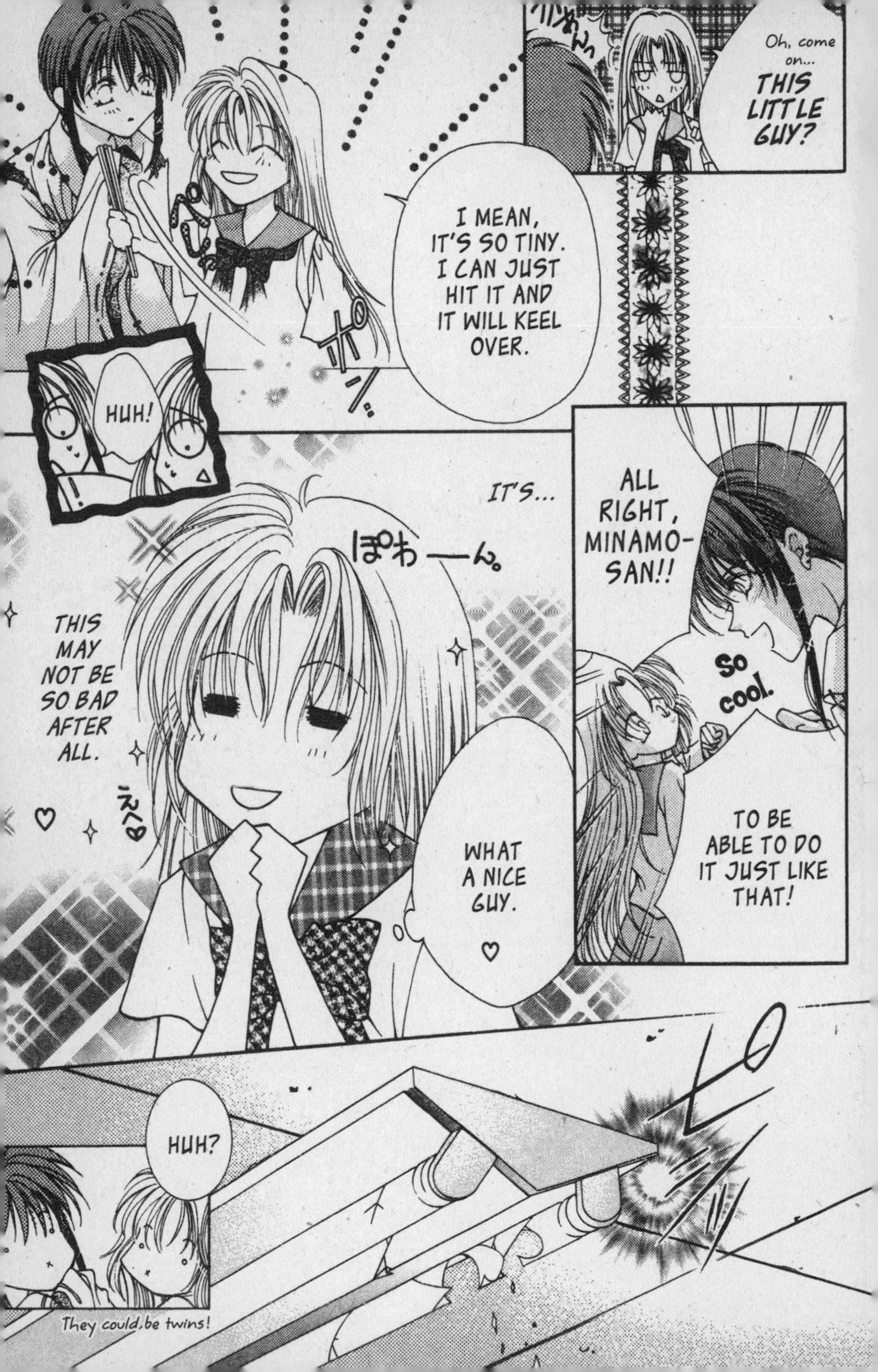
Oh, come on... THIS LITTLE GUY?
I MEAN, IT'S SO TINY. I CAN JUST HIT IT AND IT WILL KEEL OVER.
HUH!
ALL RIGHT, MINAMO-SAN!!
So cool.
TO BE ABLE TO DO IT JUST LIKE THAT!
IT'S...
ぽわーん。
WHAT A NICE GUY.
THIS MAY NOT BE SO BAD AFTER ALL.
えへ♥
HUH?
They could be twins!

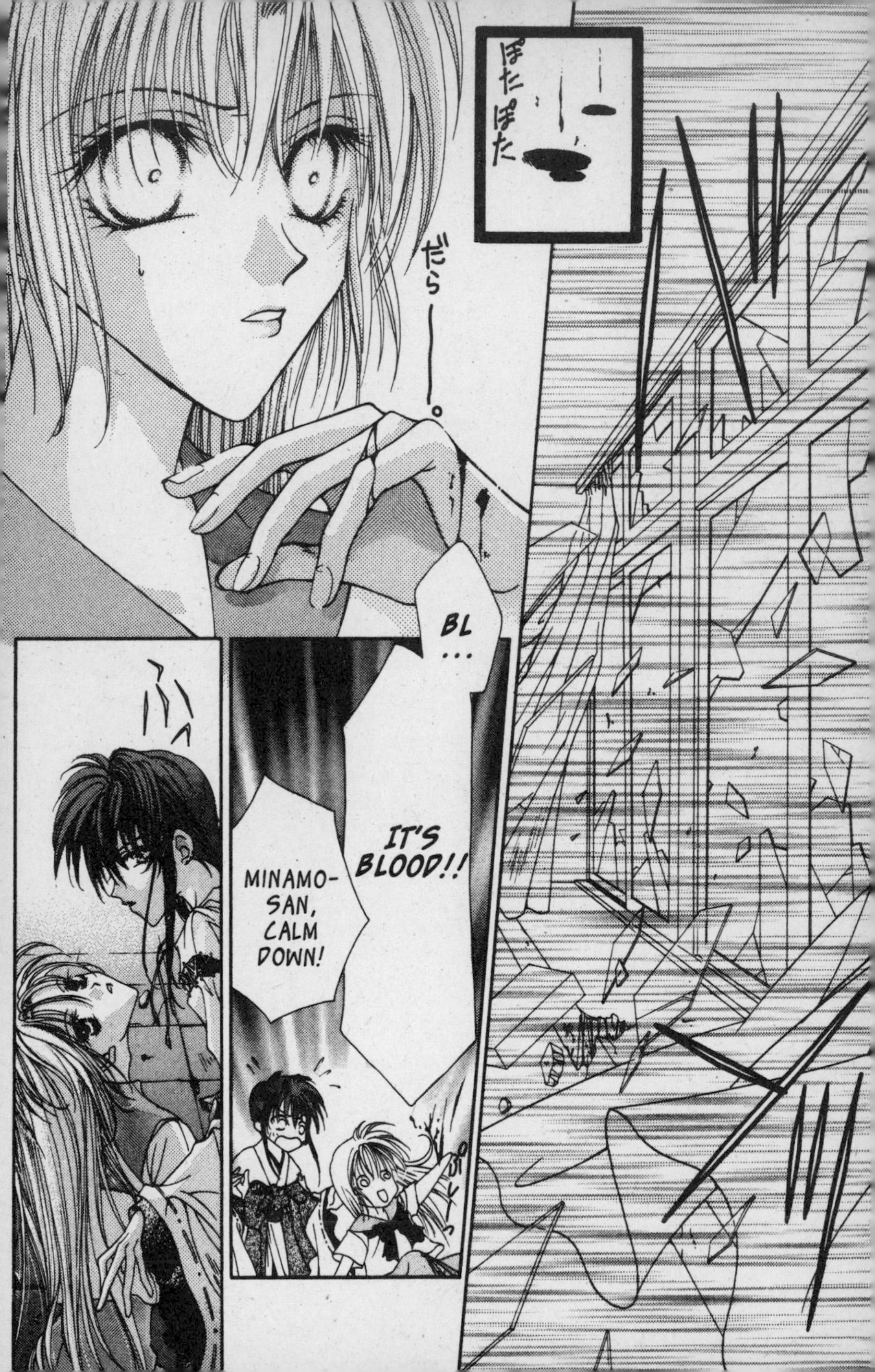
ぽたぽた
だらーー。
BL...
IT'S BLOOD!!
MINAMO-SAN, CALM DOWN!

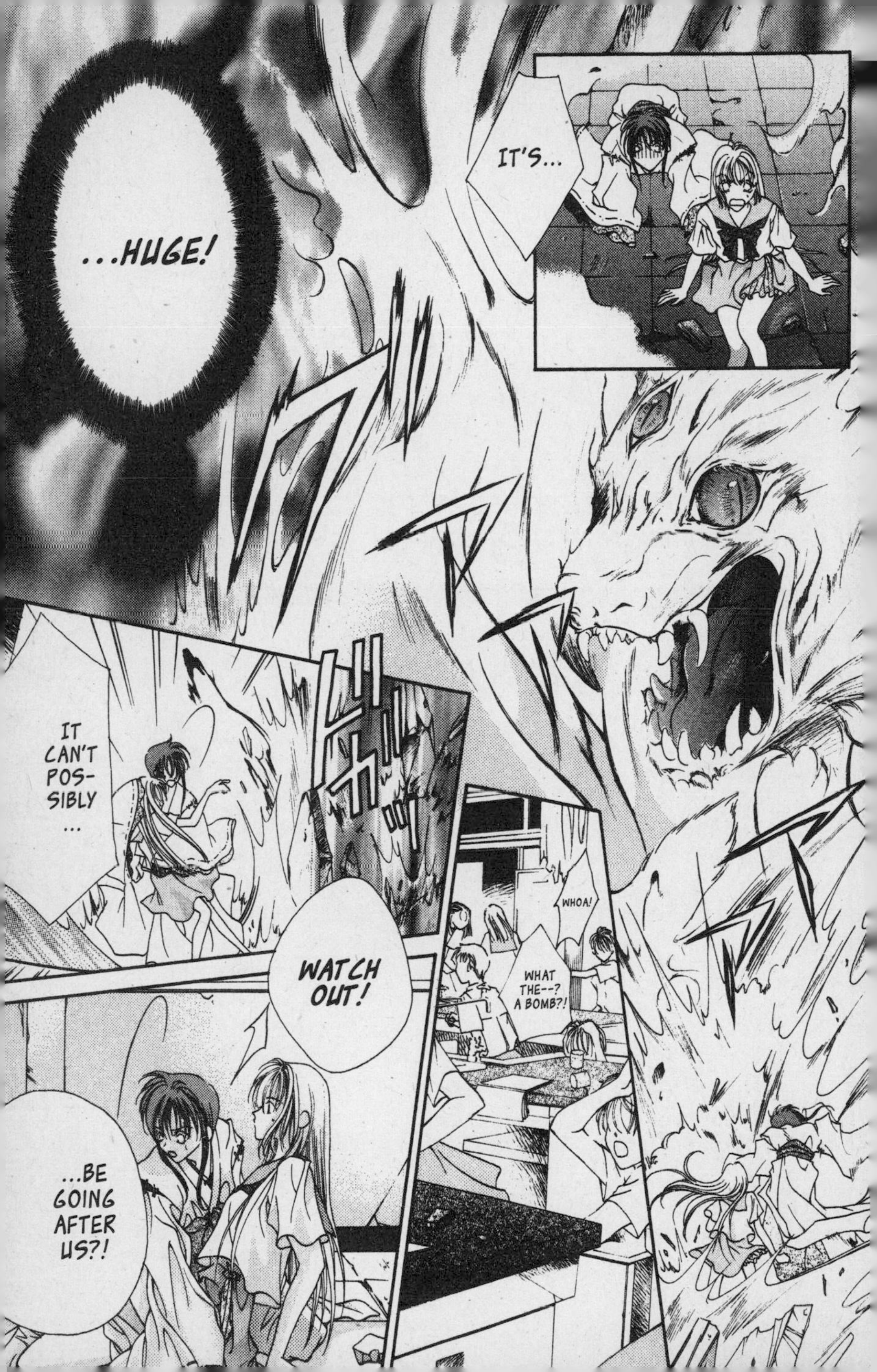
IT'S...
...HUGE!
WHOA!
WHAT THE--? A BOMB?!
WATCH OUT!
IT CAN'T POSSIBLY ...
...BE GOING AFTER US?!

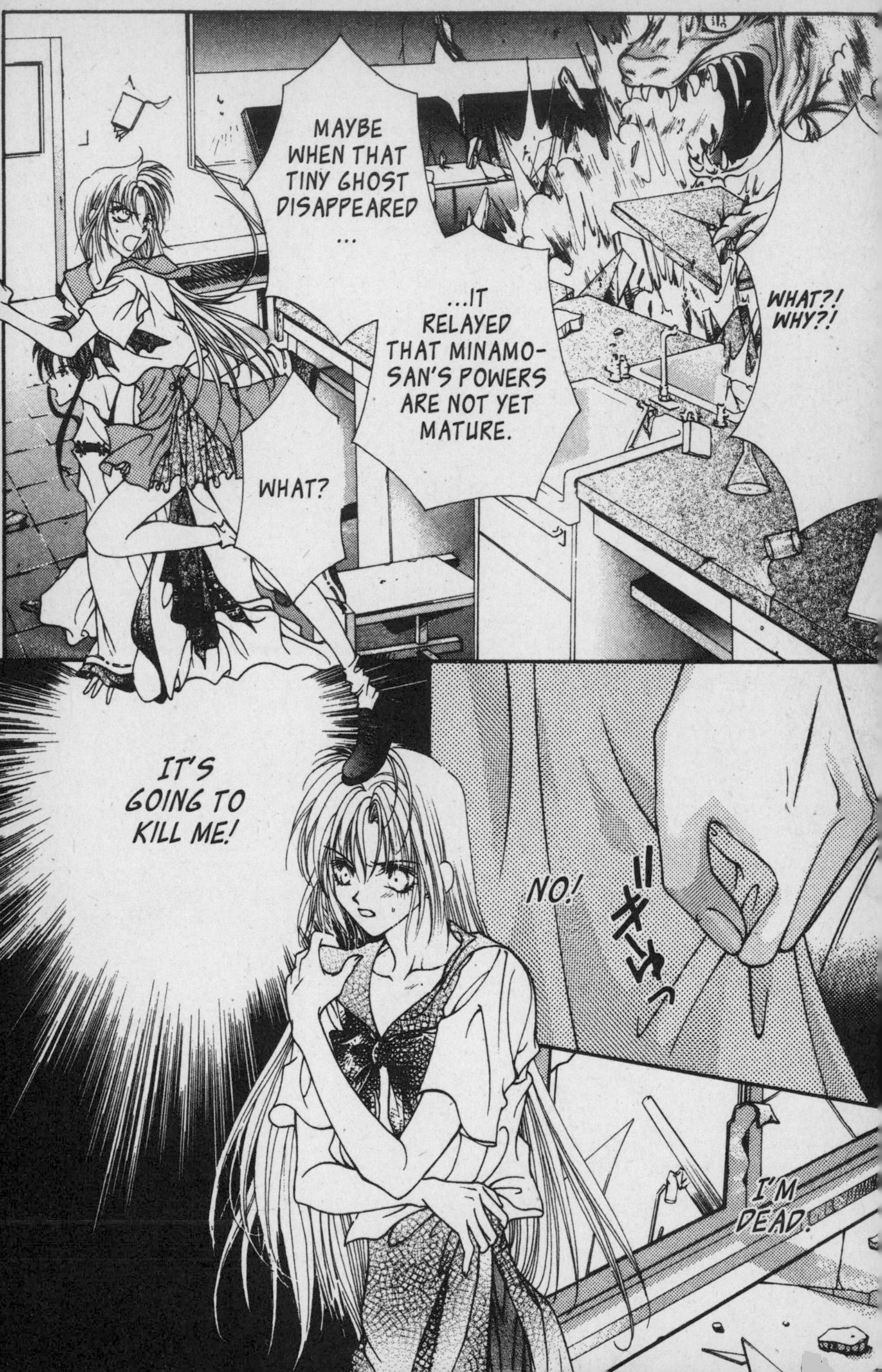
WHAT?! WHY?!
MAYBE WHEN THAT TINY GHOST DISAPPEARED ...
...IT RELAYED THAT MINAMO-SAN'S POWERS ARE NOT YET MATURE.
WHAT?
IT'S GOING TO KILL ME!
NO!
I'M DEAD.

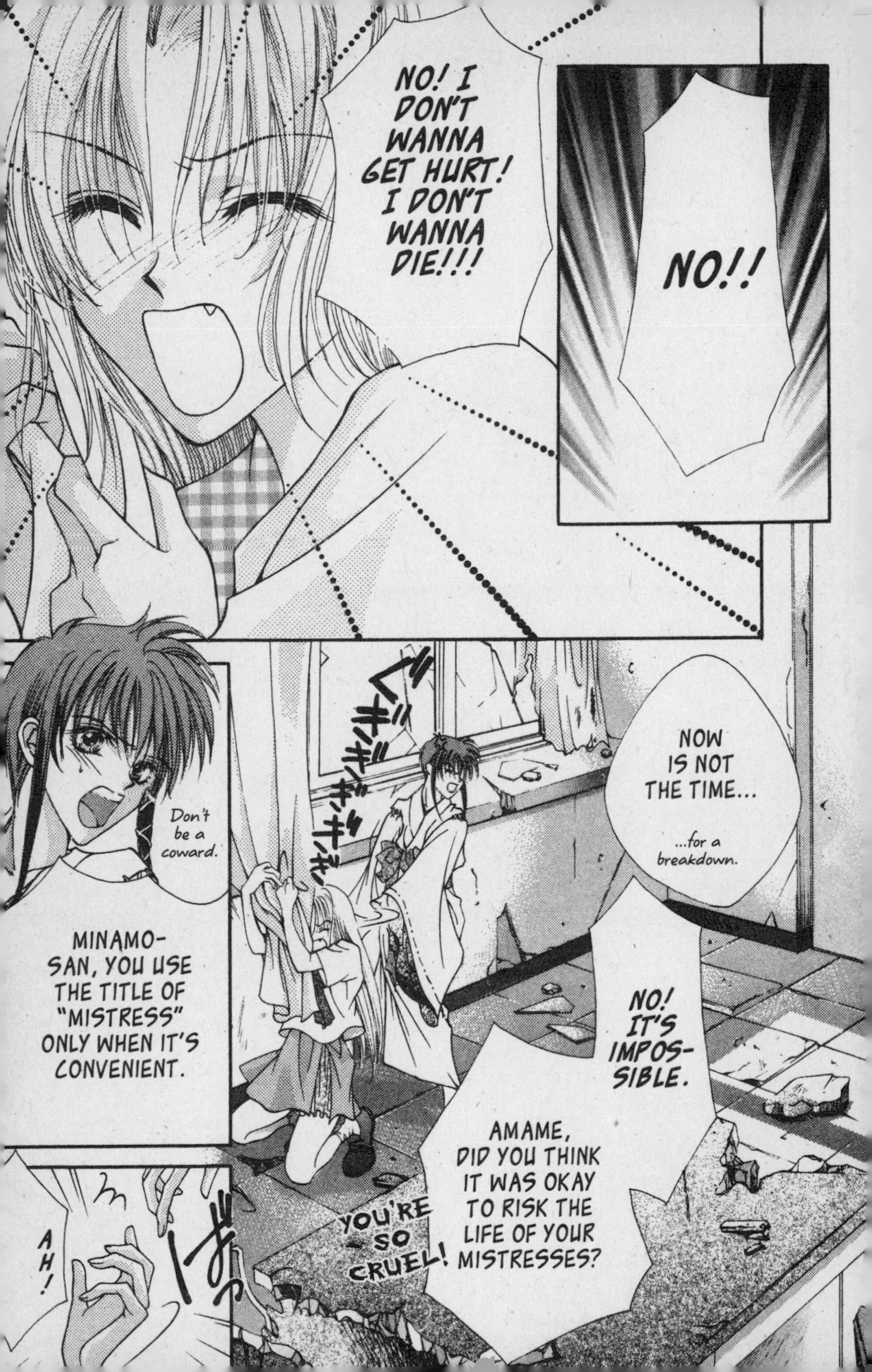

NO!!
NO! I DON'T WANNA GET HURT! I DON'T WANNA DIE!!!
NOW IS NOT THE TIME...
...for a breakdown.
NO! IT'S IMPOS-SIBLE.
AMAME, DID YOU THINK IT WAS OKAY TO RISK THE LIFE OF YOUR MISTRESSES?
YOU'RE SO CRUEL!
Don't be a coward.
MINAMO-SAN, YOU USE THE TITLE OF "MISTRESS" ONLY WHEN IT'S CONVENIENT.
AH!

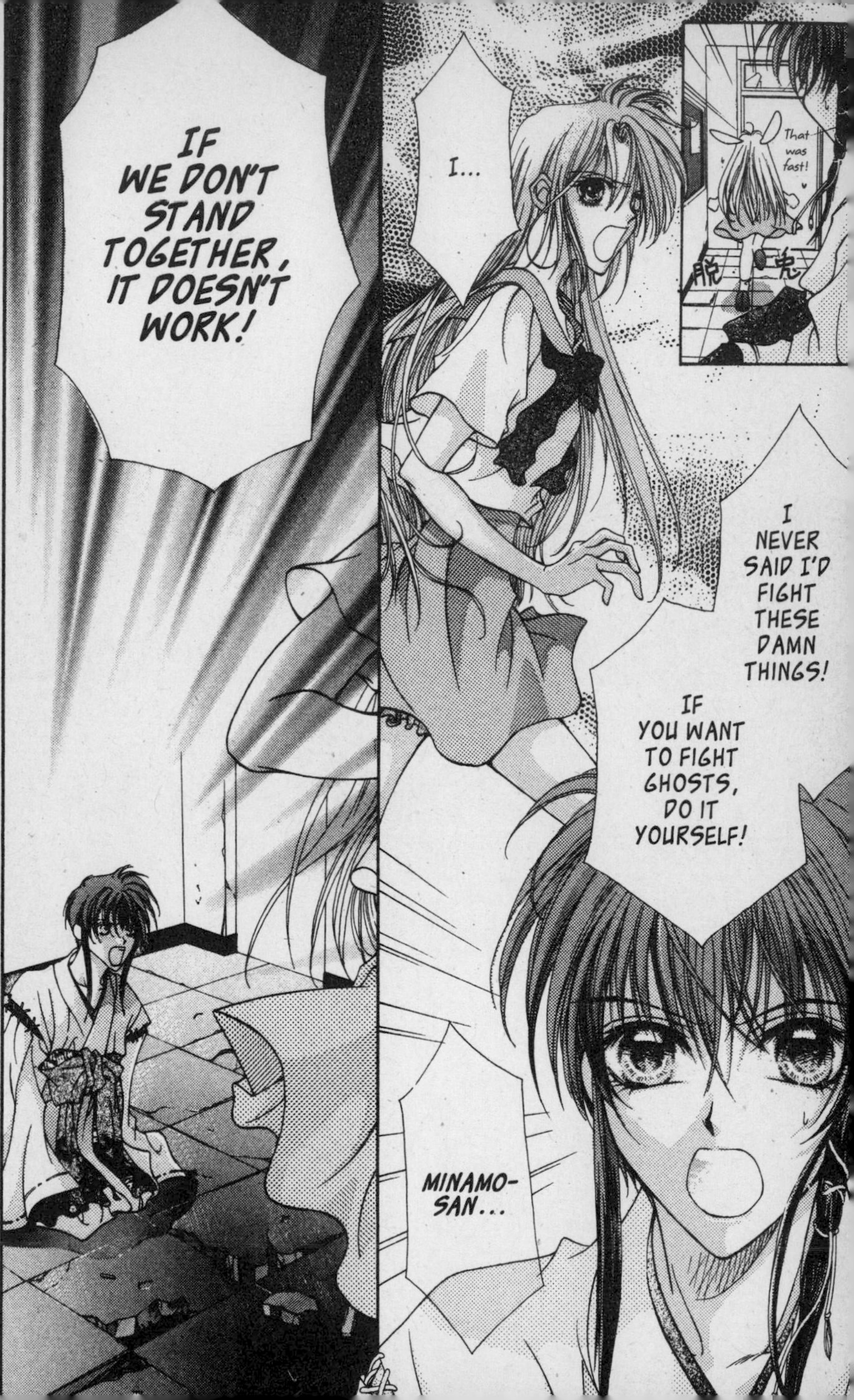
That was fast!
脱兎
I...
I NEVER SAID I'D FIGHT THESE DAMN THINGS!
IF YOU WANT TO FIGHT GHOSTS, DO IT YOURSELF!
MINAMO-SAN...
IF WE DON'T STAND TOGETHER, IT DOESN'T WORK!

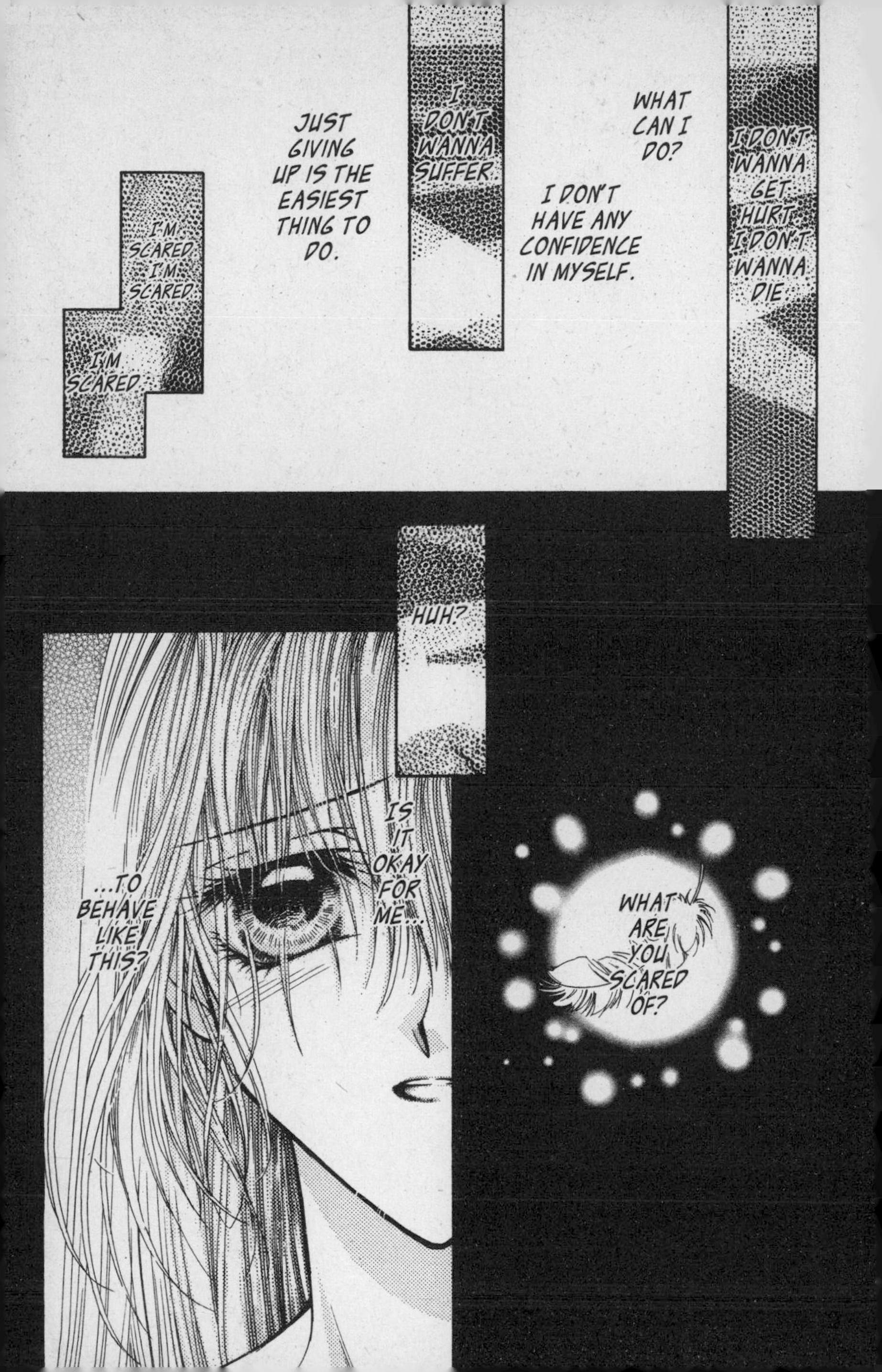
I DON'T WANNA GET HURT
I DON'T WANNA DIE
WHAT CAN I DO?
I DON'T HAVE ANY CONFIDENCE IN MYSELF.
I DON'T WANNA SUFFER
JUST GIVING UP IS THE EASIEST THING TO DO.
I'M SCARED I'M SCARED
I'M SCARED
HUH?
WHAT ARE YOU SCARED OF?
IS IT OKAY FOR ME...
...TO BEHAVE LIKE THIS?

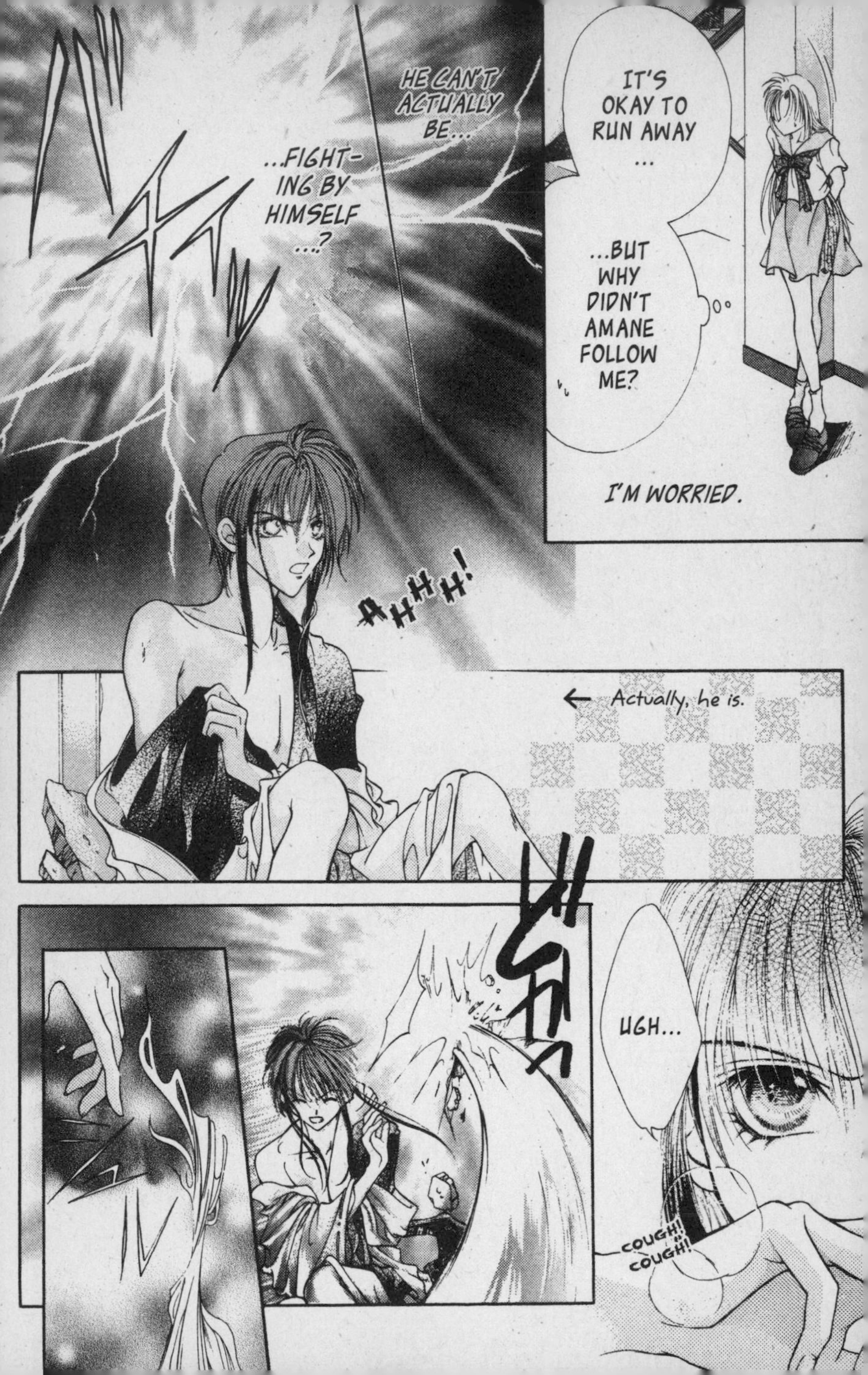
IT'S OKAY TO RUN AWAY ...
...BUT WHY DIDN'T AMANE FOLLOW ME?
I'M WORRIED.
HE CAN'T ACTUALLY BE...
...FIGHTING BY HIMSELF ...?
AHHHH!
← Actually, he is.
UGH...
COUGH! COUGH!

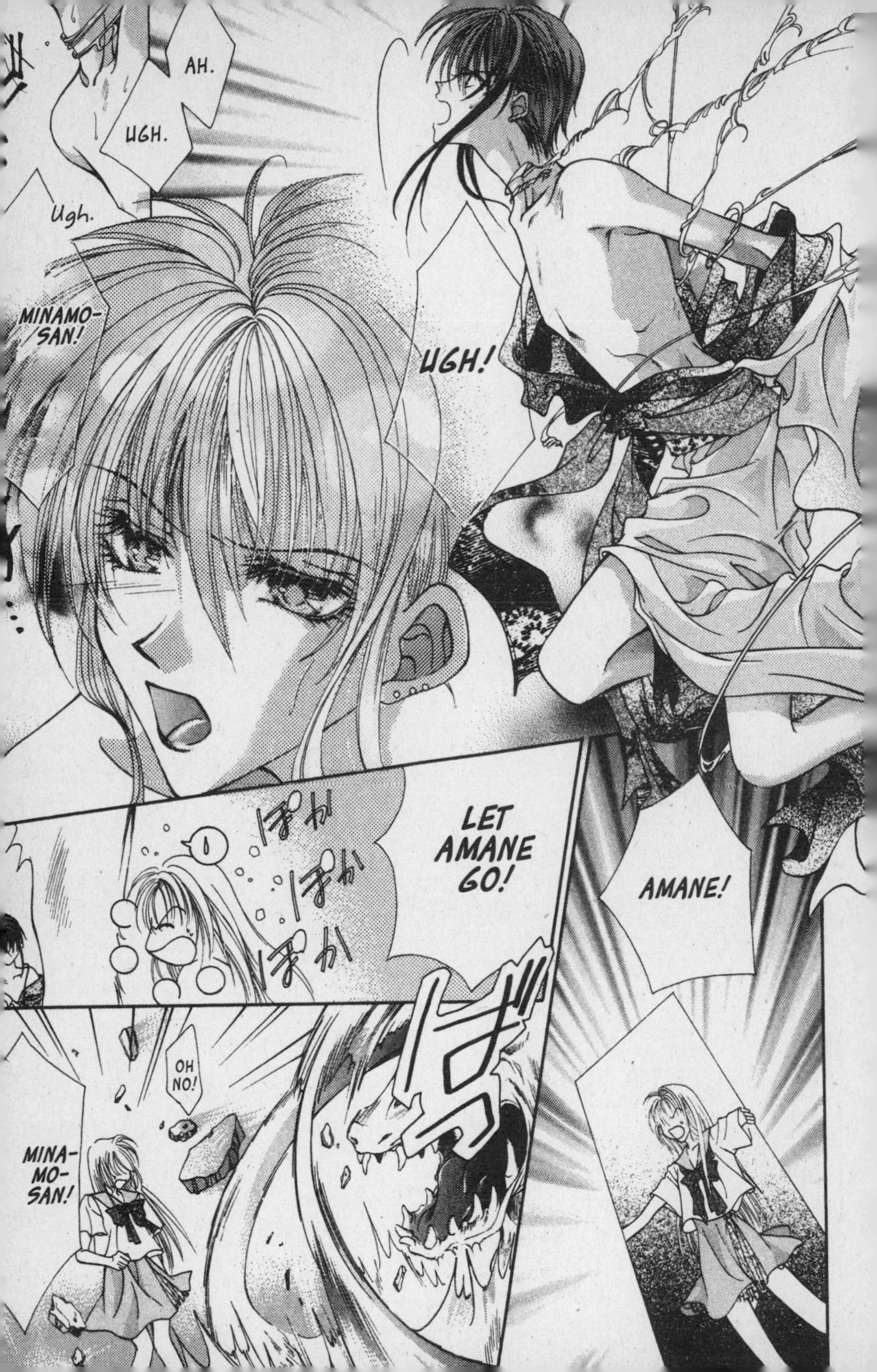
UGH!
AH.
UGH.
Ugh.
MINAMO-SAN!
AMANE!
LET AMANE GO!
ぽか
ぽか
ぽか
ばっ
OH NO!
MINA-MO-SAN!

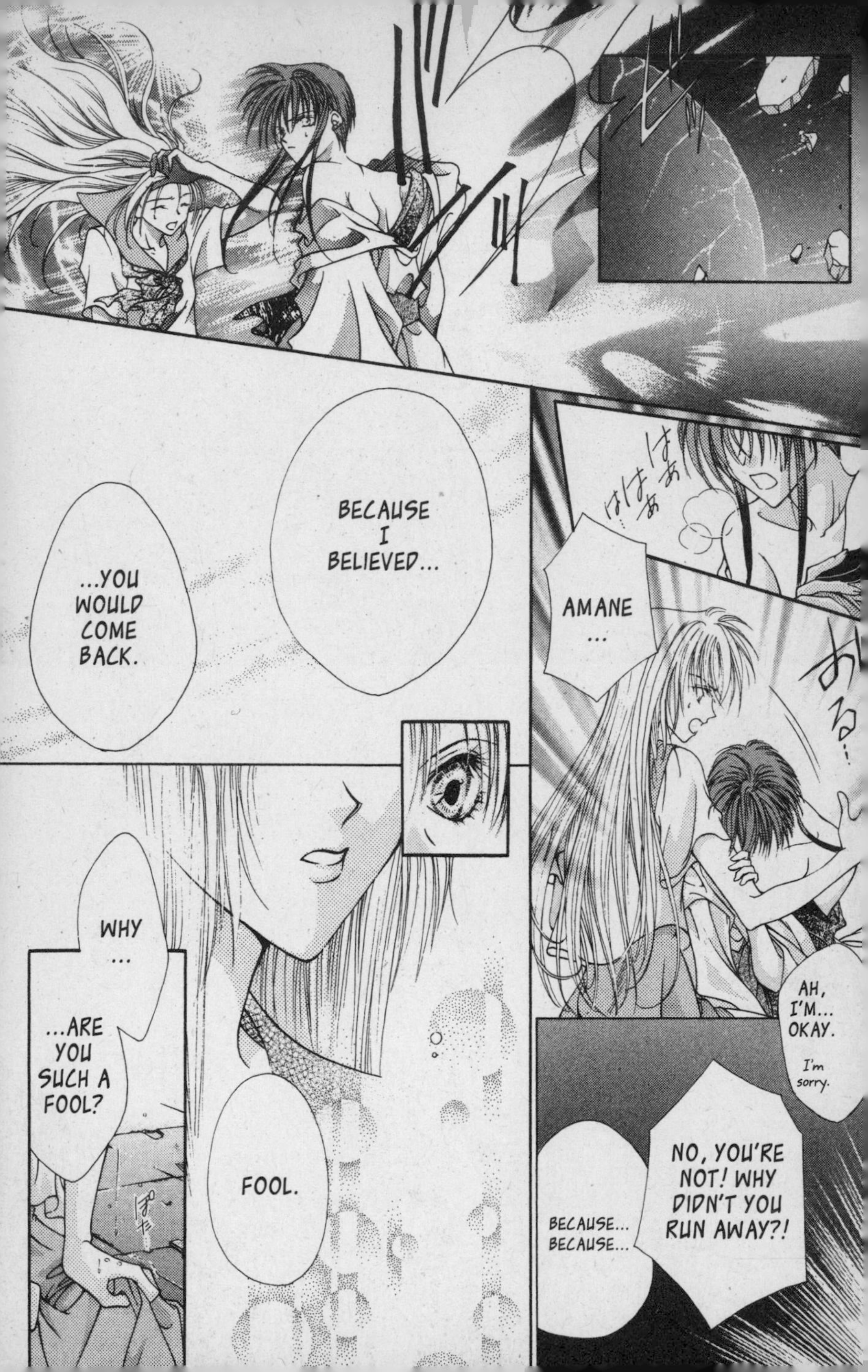
AMANE ...
AH, I'M... OKAY.
I'm sorry.
NO, YOU'RE NOT! WHY DIDN'T YOU RUN AWAY?!
BECAUSE... BECAUSE...
BECAUSE I BELIEVED...
...YOU WOULD COME BACK.
WHY ...
...ARE YOU SUCH A FOOL?
FOOL.

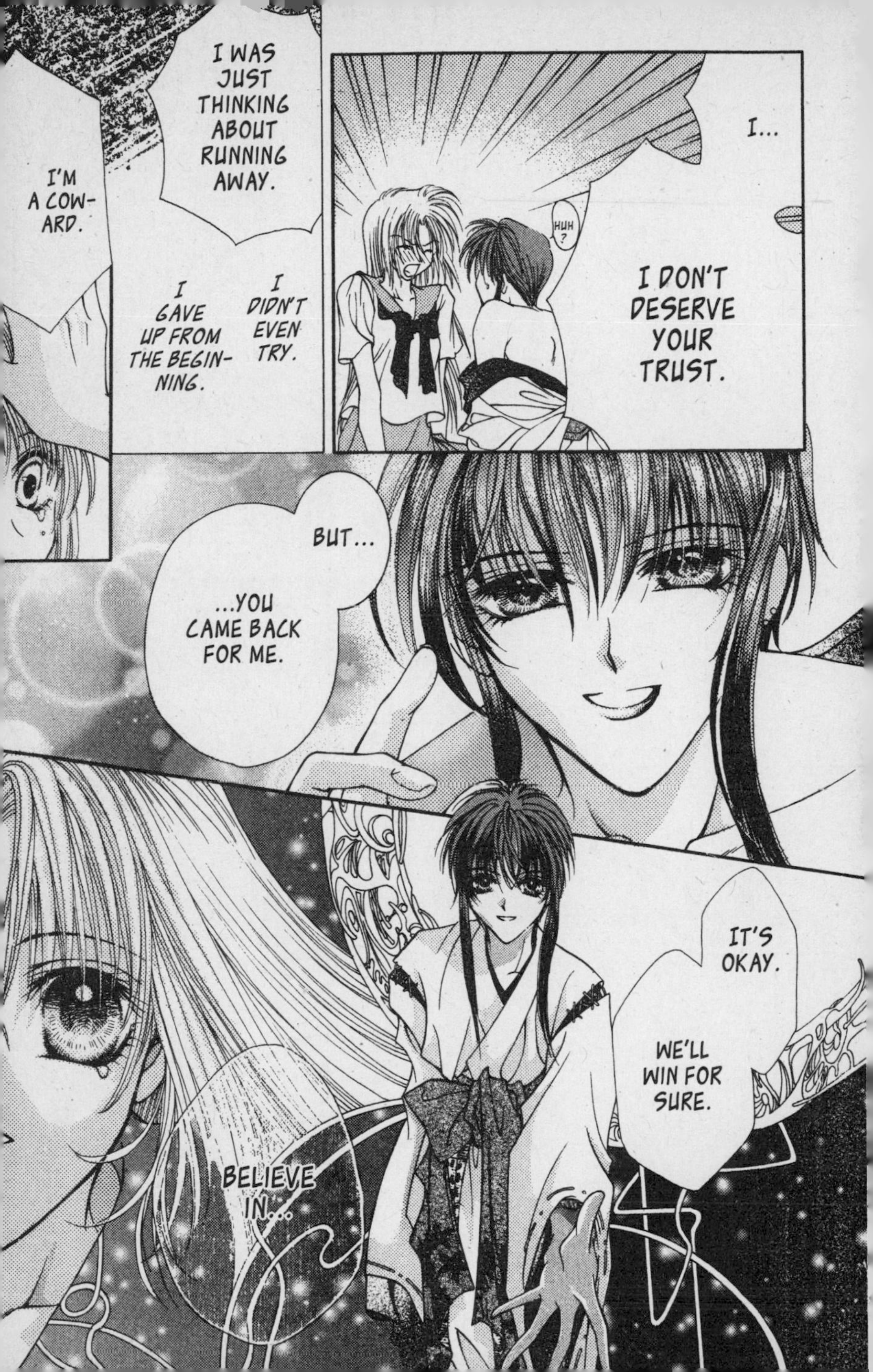
I...
HUH?
I DON'T DESERVE YOUR TRUST.
I WAS JUST THINKING ABOUT RUNNING AWAY.
I DIDN'T EVEN TRY.
I GAVE UP FROM THE BEGIN-NING.
I'M A COW-ARD.
BUT...
...YOU CAME BACK FOR ME.
IT'S OKAY.
WE'LL WIN FOR SURE.
BELIEVE IN...

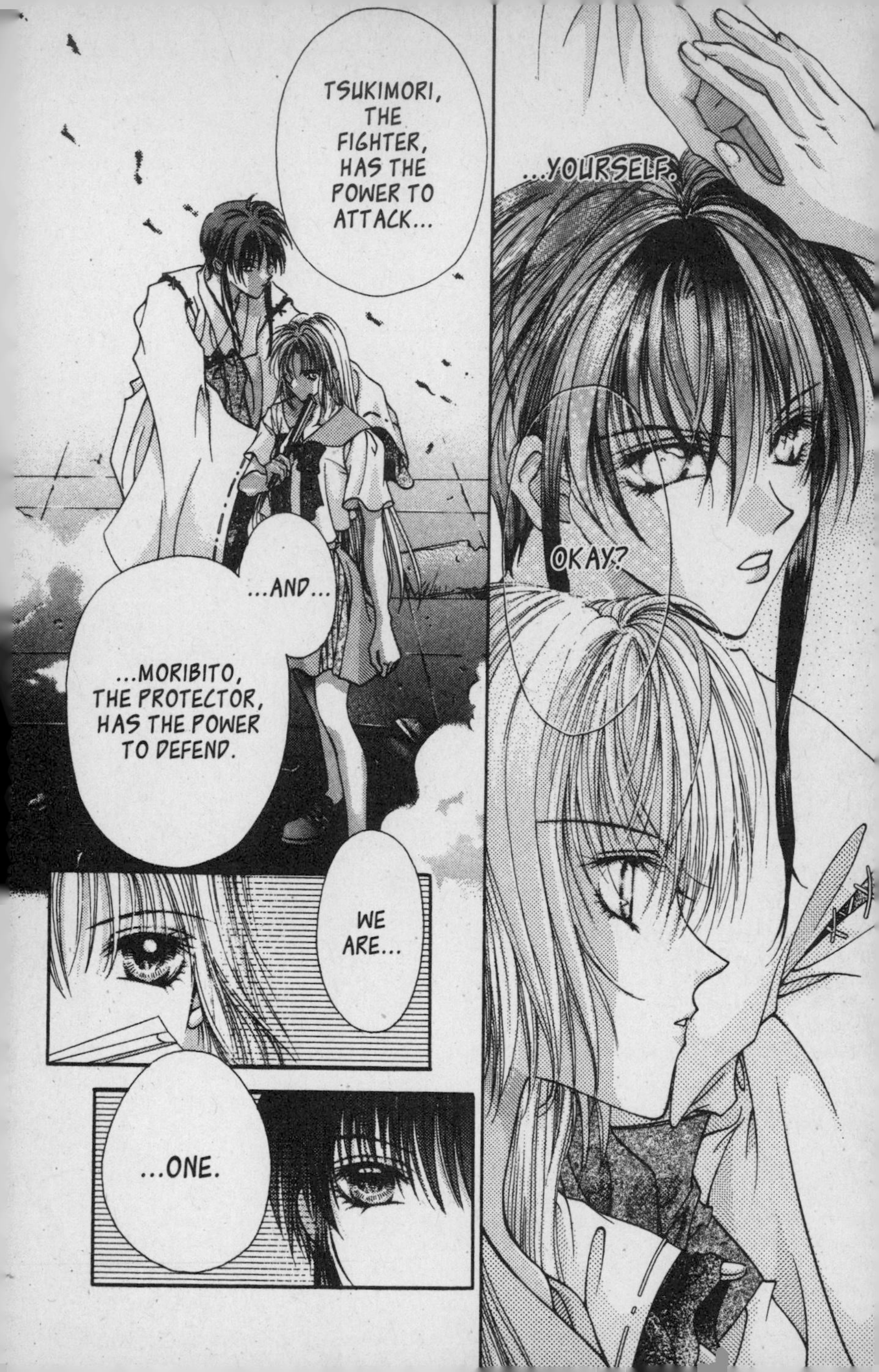
...YOURSELF.
OKAY?
TSUKIMORI, THE FIGHTER, HAS THE POWER TO ATTACK...
...AND...
...MORIBITO, THE PROTECTOR, HAS THE POWER TO DEFEND.
WE ARE...
...ONE.

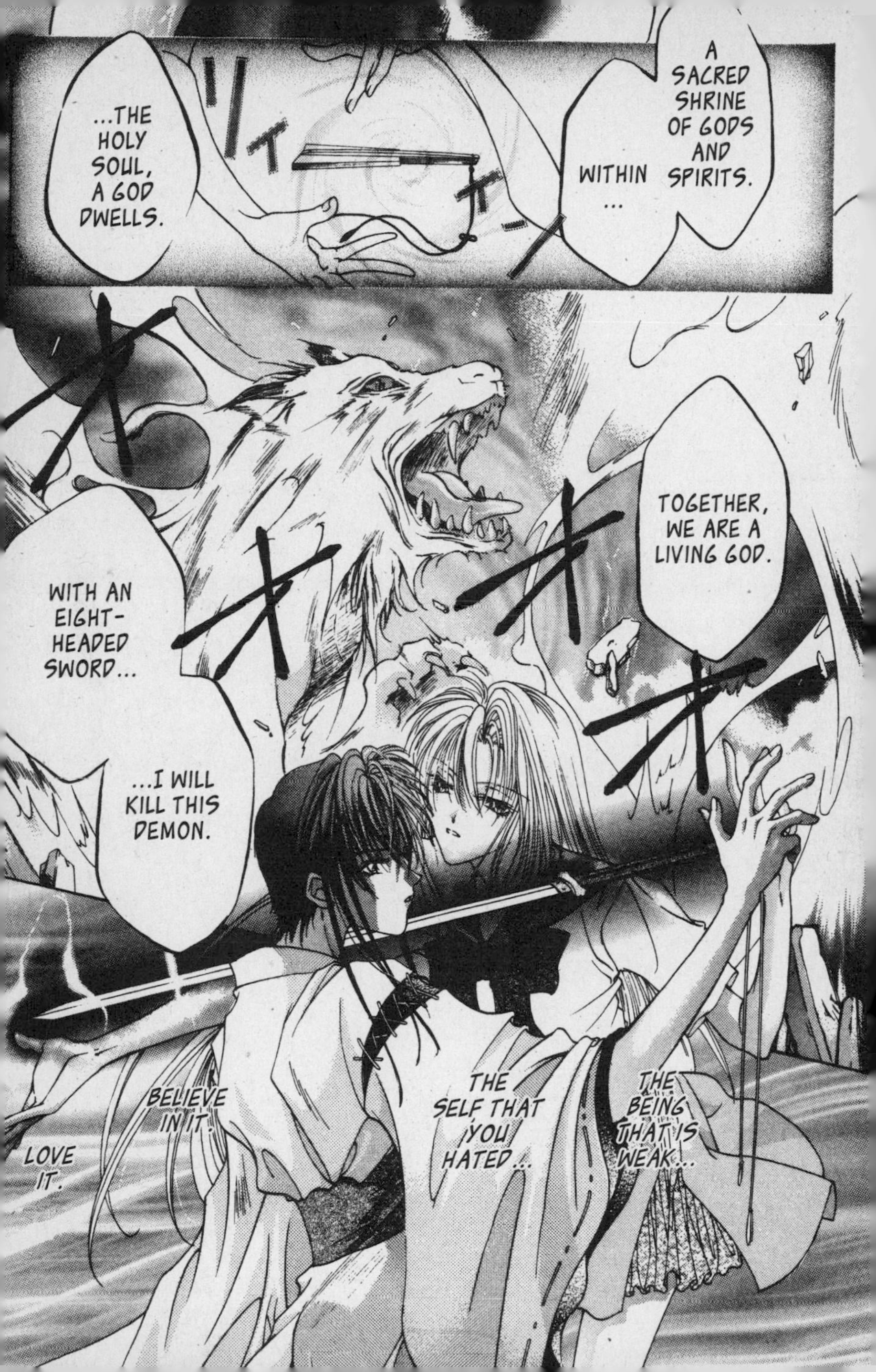
A SACRED SHRINE OF GODS AND SPIRITS.
WITHIN ...
...THE HOLY SOUL, A GOD DWELLS.
TOGETHER, WE ARE A LIVING GOD.
WITH AN EIGHT-HEADED SWORD...
...I WILL KILL THIS DEMON.
THE BEING THAT IS WEAK...
THE SELF THAT YOU HATED...
BELIEVE IN IT.
LOVE IT.

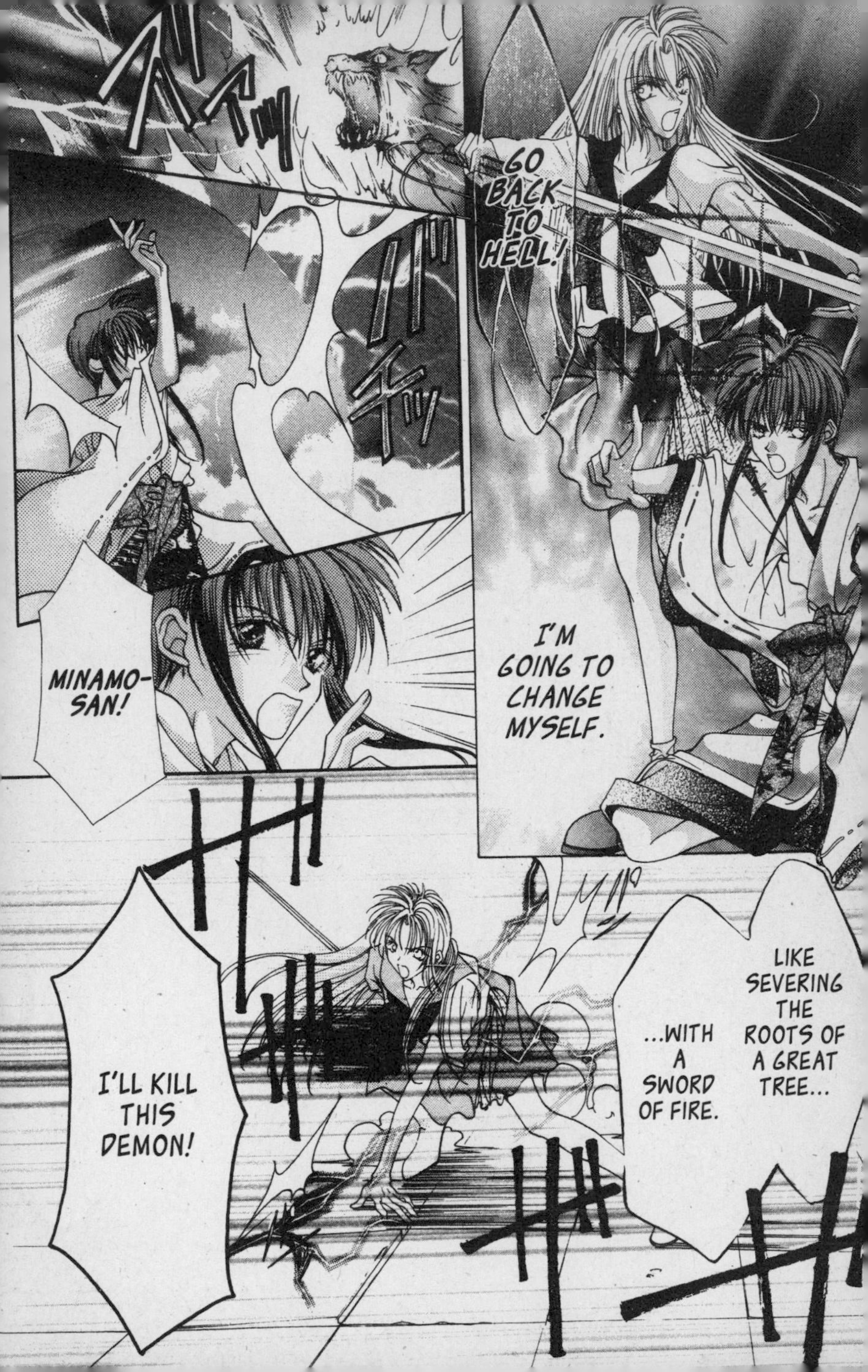
GO BACK TO HELL!
I'M GOING TO CHANGE MYSELF.
MINAMO-SAN!
LIKE SEVERING THE ROOTS OF A GREAT TREE...
...WITH A SWORD OF FIRE.
I'LL KILL THIS DEMON!

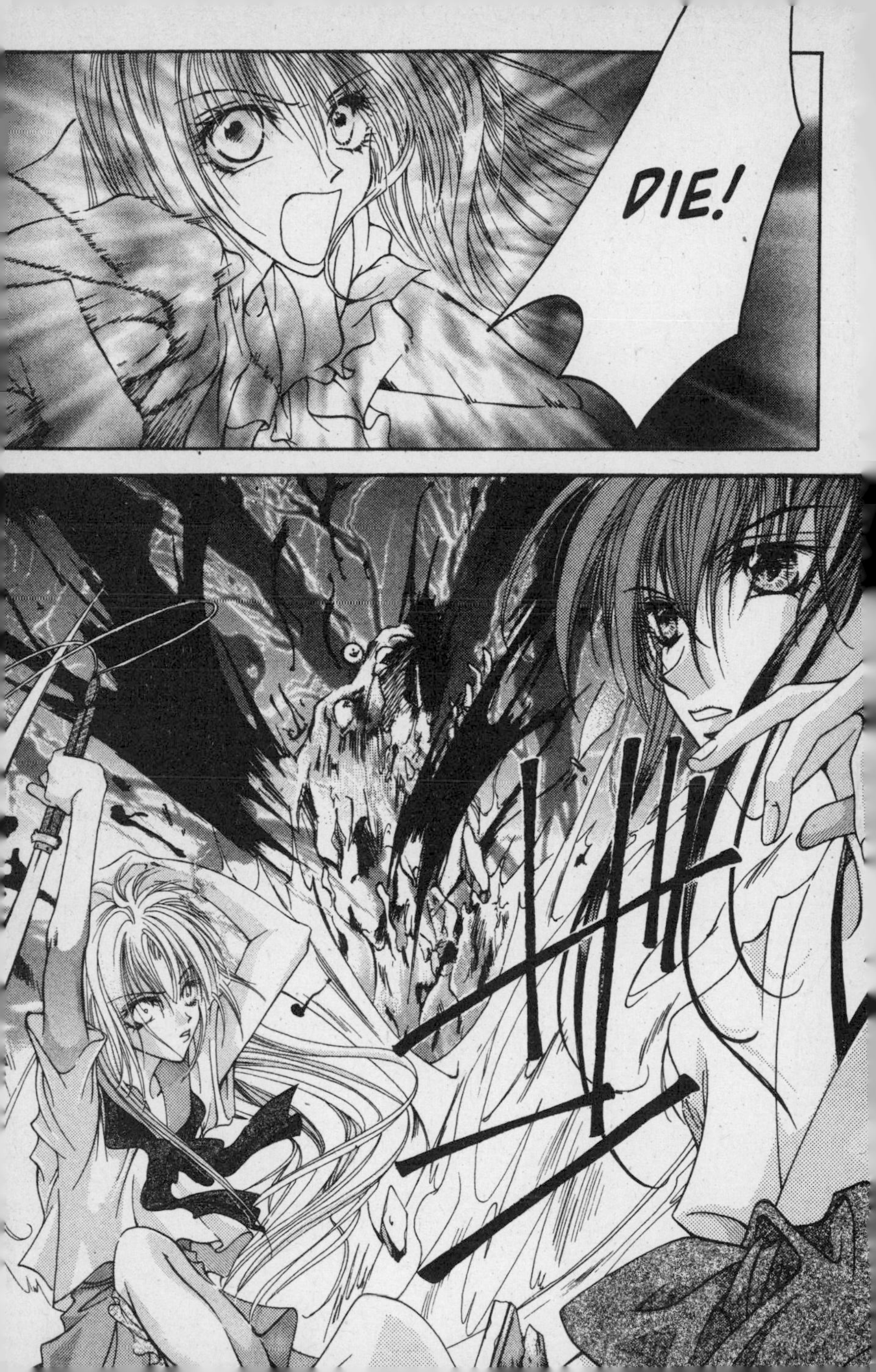
DIE!

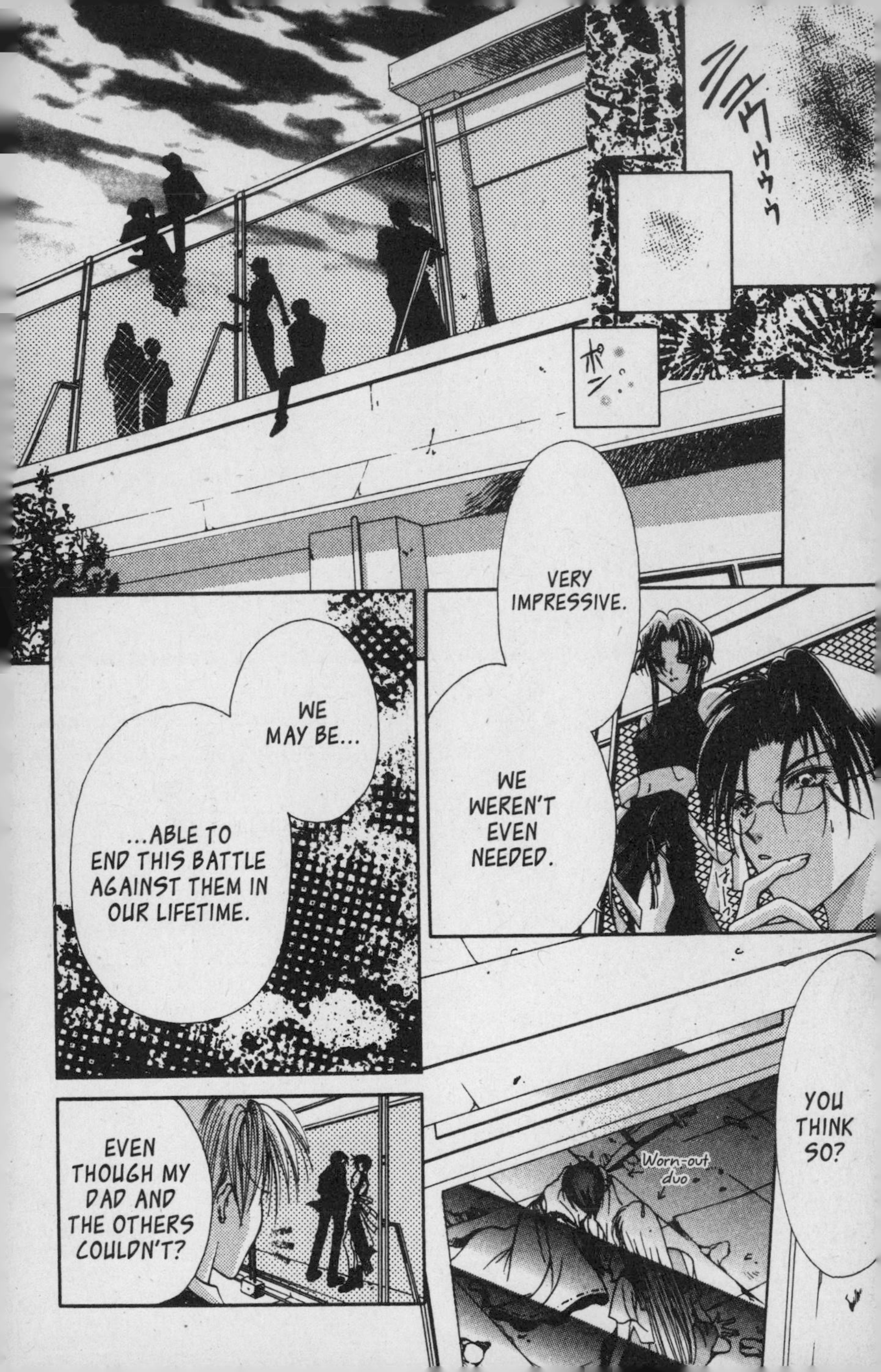
ポン
VERY IMPRESSIVE.
WE WEREN'T EVEN NEEDED.
WE MAY BE...
...ABLE TO END THIS BATTLE AGAINST THEM IN OUR LIFETIME.
YOU THINK SO?
Worn-out duo
EVEN THOUGH MY DAD AND THE OTHERS COULDN'T?

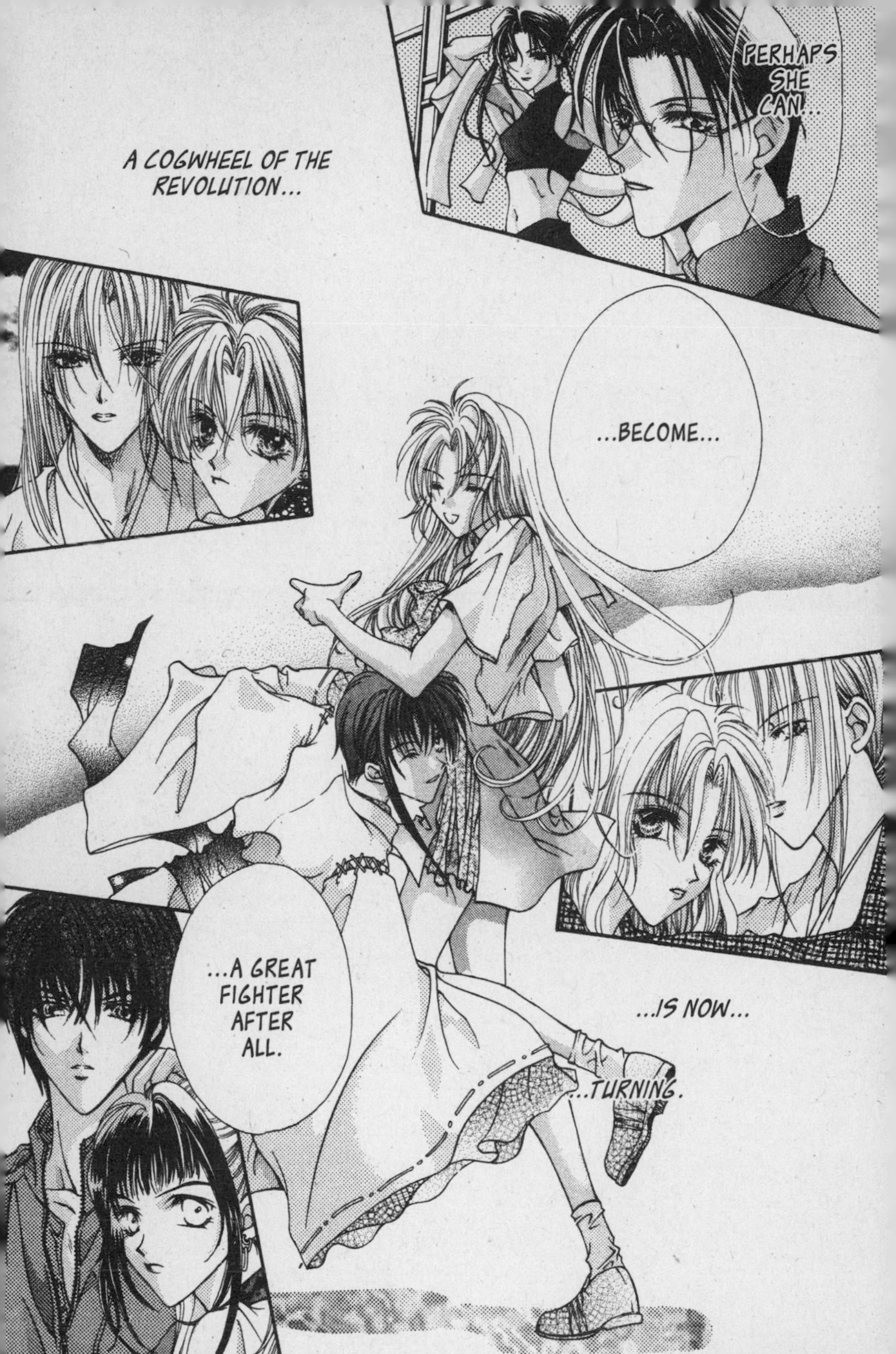
PERHAPS SHE CAN...
A COGWHEEL OF THE REVOLUTION...
...BECOME...
...A GREAT FIGHTER AFTER ALL.
...IS NOW...
...TURNING.

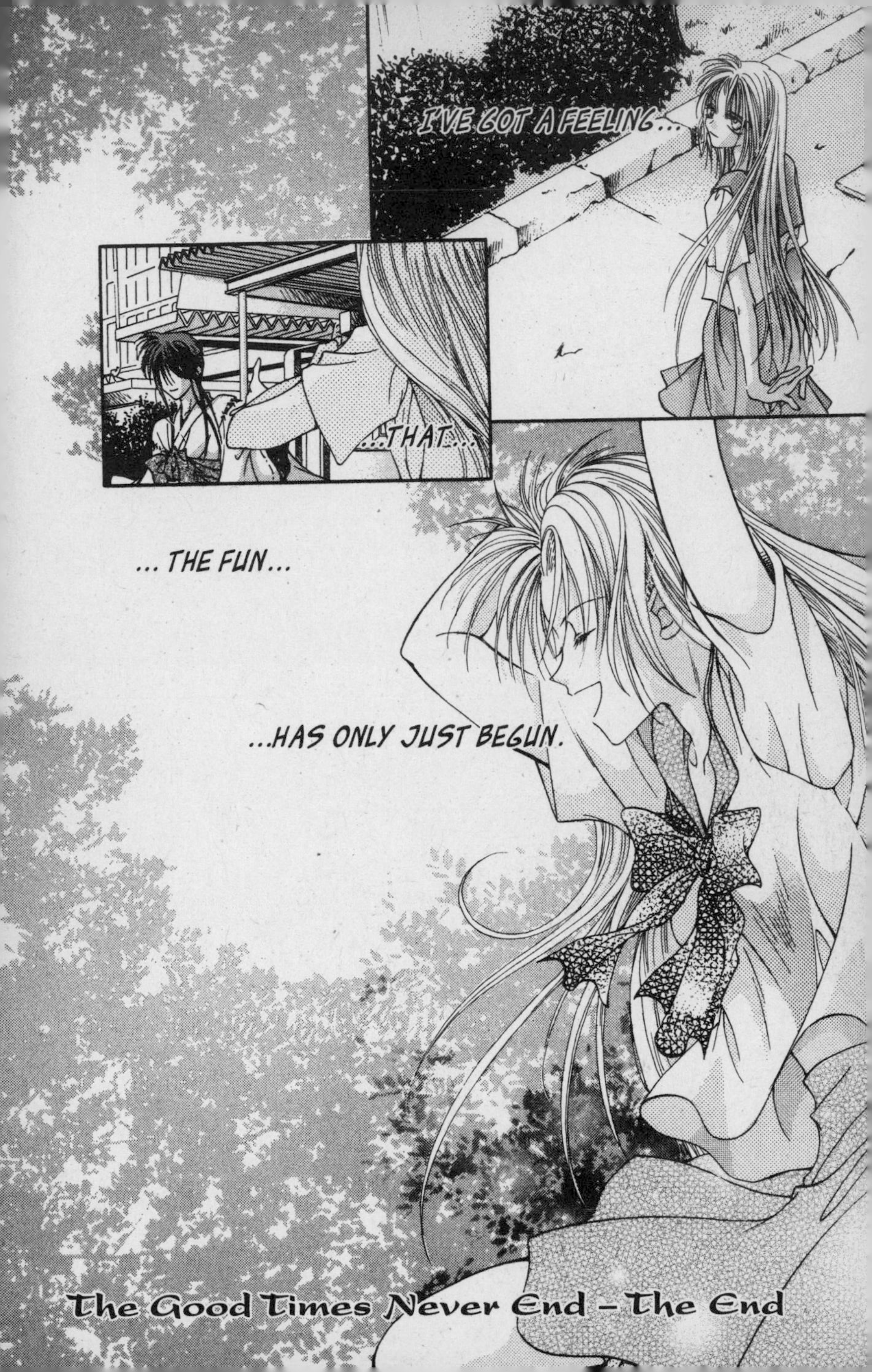
I'VE GOT A FEELING...
...THAT...
... THE FUN...
...HAS ONLY JUST BEGUN.
The Good Times Never End - The End

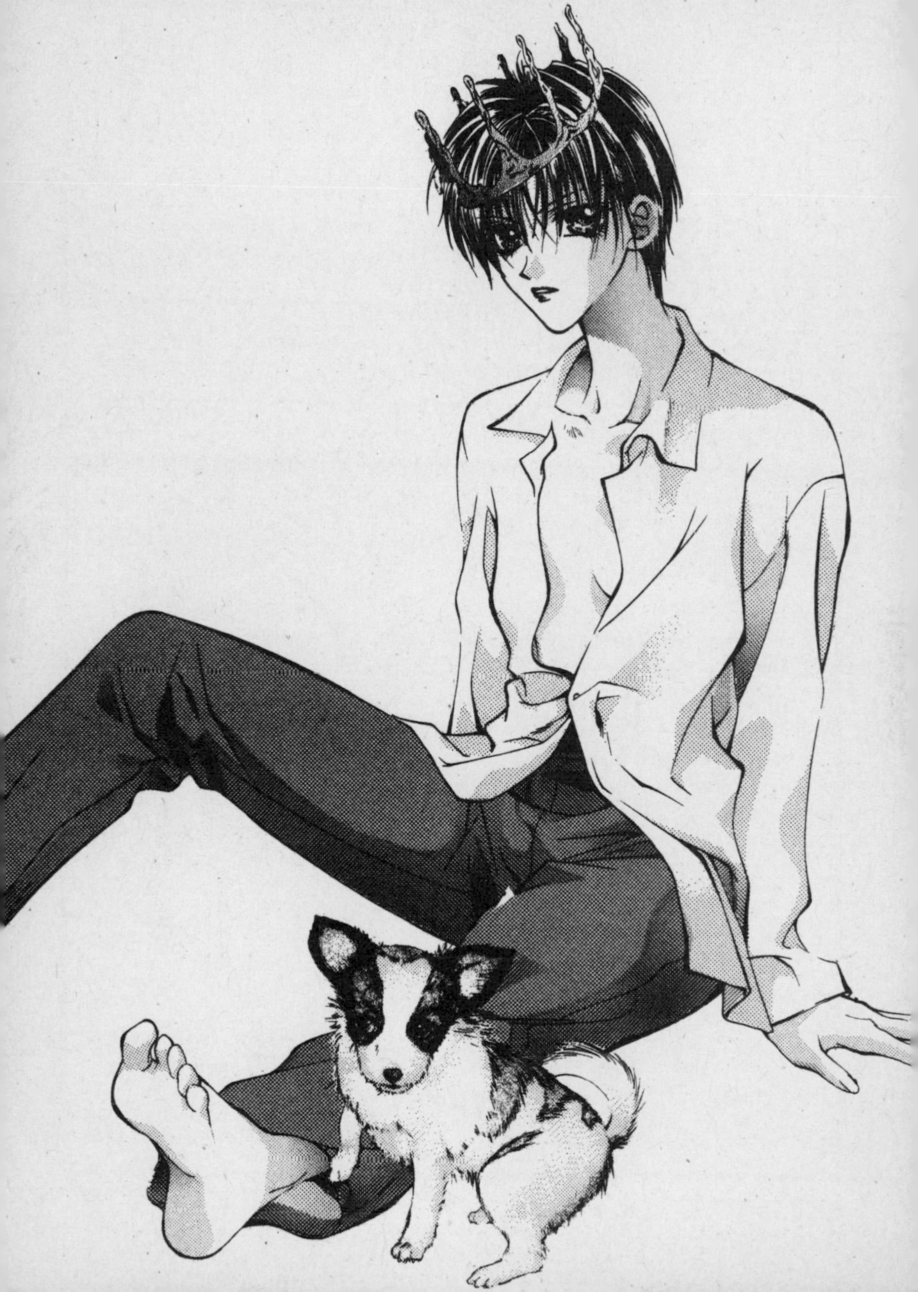

Emotions are twisted and feelings are warped in Volume 3 of Broken Angels.

Cousins Saya and Takahiro have always been close, but deeper feelings lie just beneath the surface. When Saya asks Sunao out, what was meant as an innocent show of affection ignites a destructive chain of cruelty and lies. In the end, will Saya and Takahiro come through for each other, or will this be a case of love turning to hate?

Later, Sunao and Kureha take a winter vacation, where they meet Cheko, Sakuto and Keisuke, three sword dancers with an eye for being the best. While Cheko has feelings for Sakuto, it's Keisuke that's the better dancer. So what's a jealous lover to do? Needless to say, it will fall on Sunao to sort this mess out before the backstabbing turns literal.

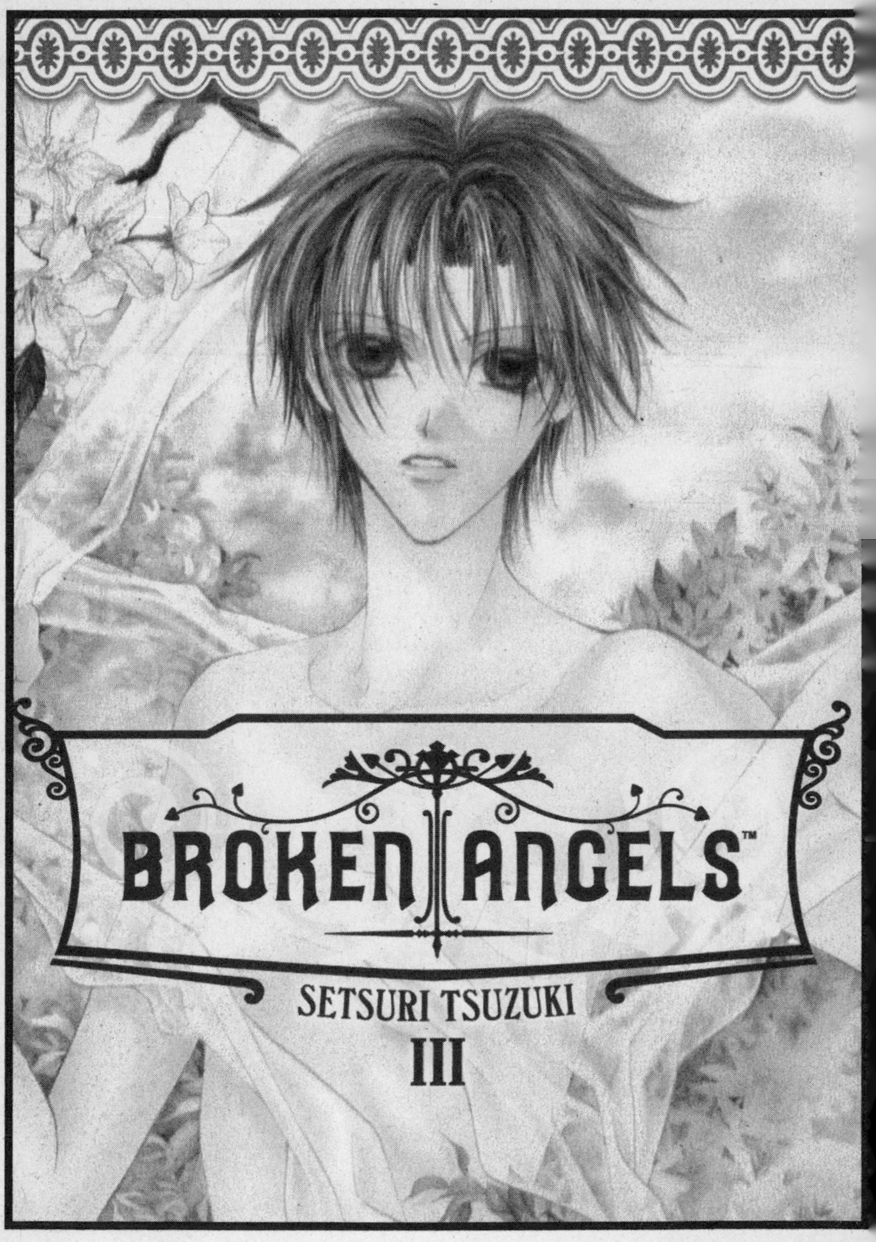
BROKEN ANGELS™
SETSURI TSUZUKI
III

TOKYOPOP SHOP

WWW.TOKYOPOP.COM/SHOP

HOT NEWS!
Check out the
TOKYOPOP SHOP!
The world's best
collection of manga in
English is now available
online in one place!

DOGBY WALKS ALONE

ANGEL CUP

WWW.TOKYOPOP.COM/SHOP

BIZENGHAST VOL. 2

- LOOK FOR SPECIAL OFFERS
- PRE-ORDER UPCOMING RELEASES
- COMPLETE YOUR COLLECTIONS

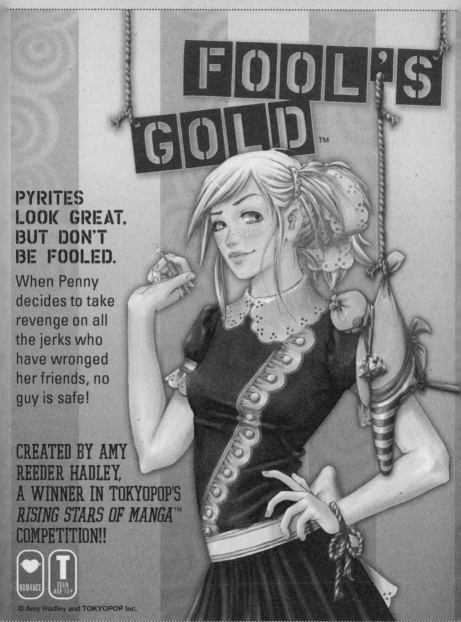

TOKYOPOP MANGA SUPPLEMENT

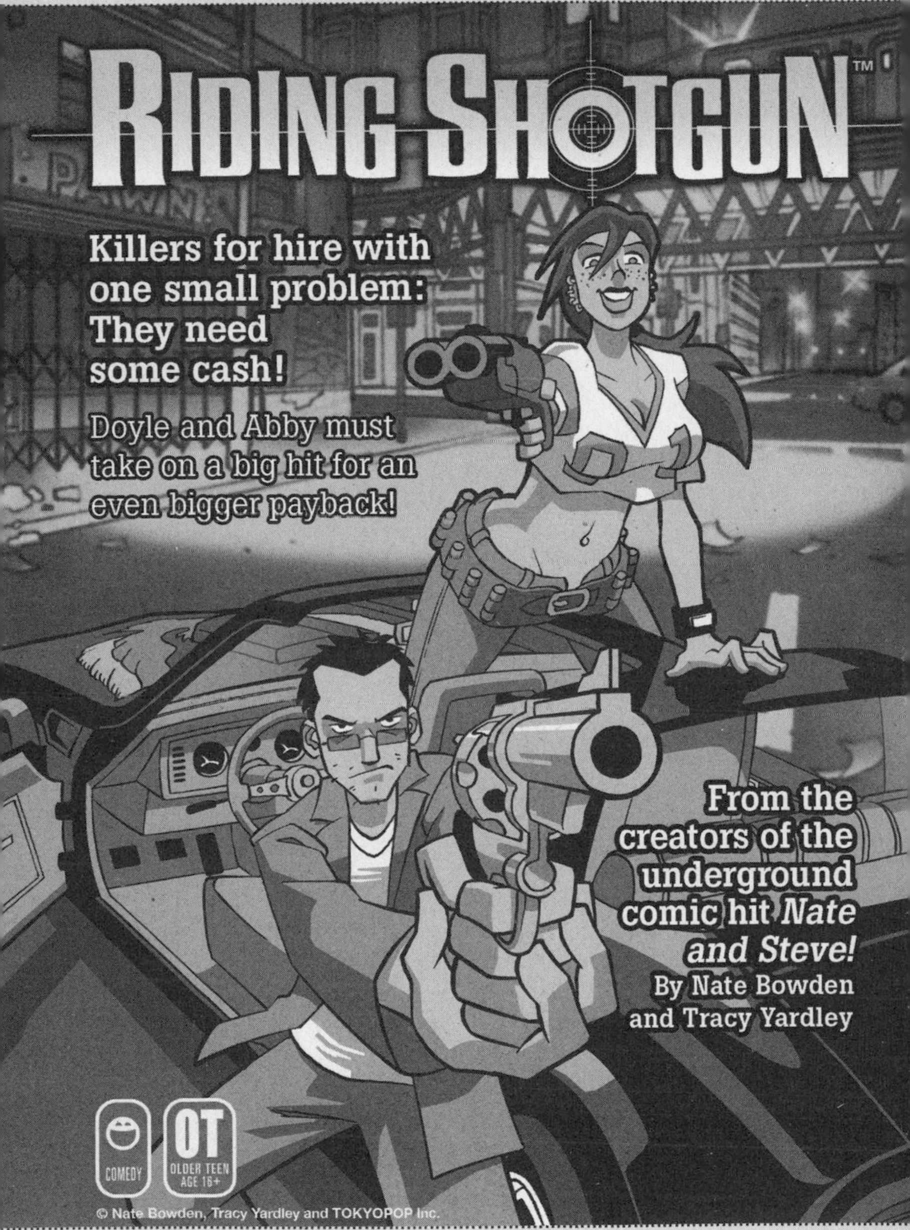
RIDING SHOTGUN™
Killers for hire with one small problem: They need some cash!
Doyle and Abby must take on a big hit for an even bigger payback!
From the creators of the underground comic hit *Nate and Steve!*
By Nate Bowden and Tracy Yardley
COMEDY
OT OLDER TEEN AGE 16+
© Nate Bowden, Tracy Yardley and TOKYOPOP Inc.

READ A CHAPTER ONLINE FOR FREE: WWW.TOKYOPOP.COM/MANGAONLINE

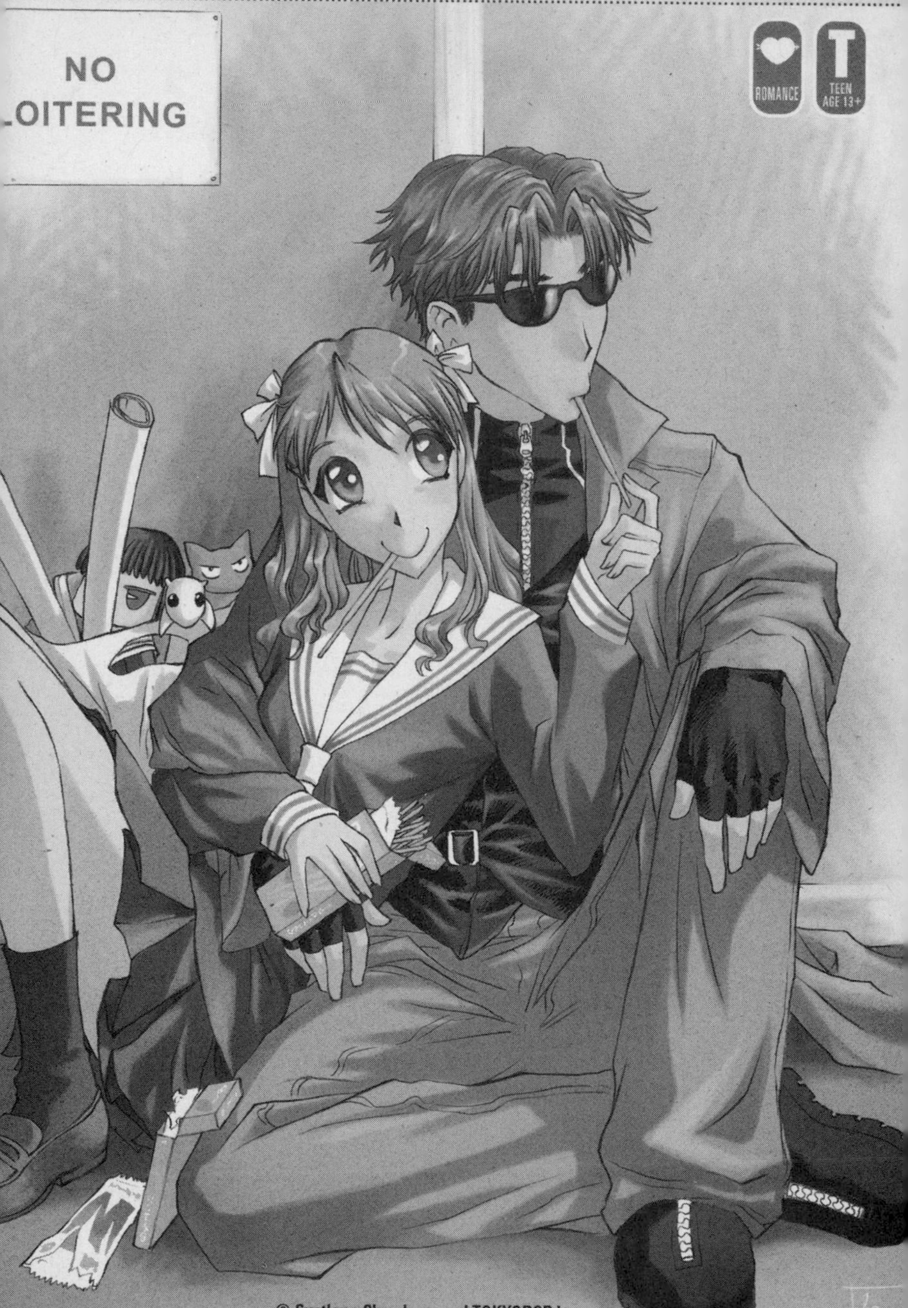
NO
OITERING
ROMANCE
T
TEEN
AGE 13+

O'TOGI ZOSHI
BY NARUMI SETO

An all-out samurai battle to retrieve the Magatama, the legendary gem that is said to hold the power to save the world!

Hot new prequel to the hit anime!

© NARUMI SETO. © IG/VAP/NTV.

STRAWBERRY MARSHMALLOW
BY BARASUI

Cute girls do cute things...in *very* cute ways.

A sweet slice of delight that launched the delicious anime series!

© Barasui.

TRASH
BY SANAMI MATOH

When your uncle is the biggest mob boss in New York, it's hard to stay out of the family business!

From the creator of the fan-favorite *Fake!*

© SANAMI MATOH.

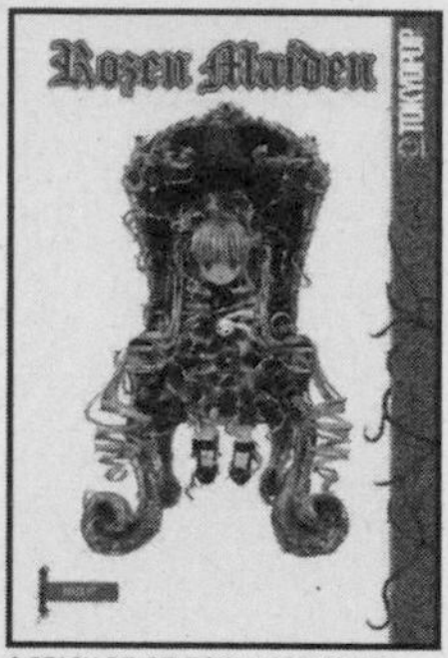
Rozen Maiden
TOKYOPOP

© PEACH-PIT, GENTOSHA COMICS INC.

ROZEN MAIDEN

BY PEACH-PIT

Welcome to the world of *Rozen Maiden* where a boy must enter an all-new reality to protect and serve a living doll!

FANTASY | T TEEN AGE 13+

From the creators of *DearS*!

BOYS OF SUMMER

BY CHUCK AUSTEN AND HIROKI OTSUKA

Just because you strike out on your first attempt at scoring with a girl doesn't mean you won't end up hitting a home run!

COMEDY | OT OLDER TEEN AGE 16+

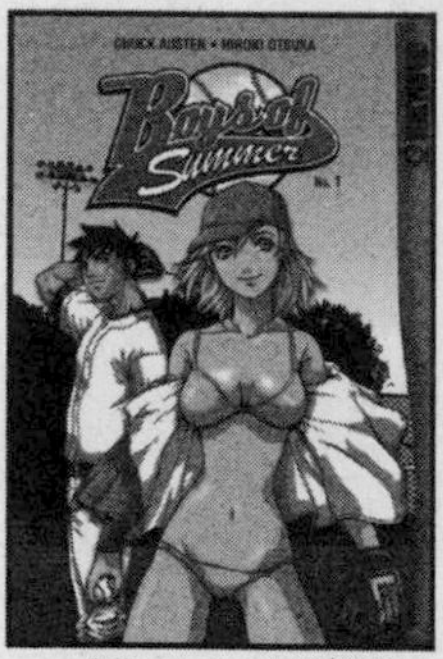
CHUCK AUSTEN • HIROKI OTSUKA
Boys of Summer

© Chuck Austen and TOKYOPOP Inc.

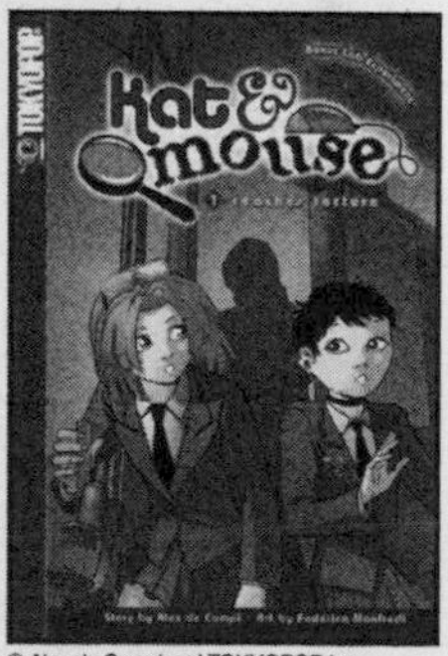
TOKYOPOP
Kat & Mouse

© Alex de Campi and TOKYOPOP Inc.

KAT & MOUSE

BY ALEX DE CAMPI AND FEDERICA MANFREDI

When science whiz Kat teams up with computer nerd Mouse, bullies and blackmailers don't stand a chance!

MYSTERY | A ALL AGES

SHRINE OF THE MORNING MIST

BY HIROKI UGAWA

When the spirit world suddenly shifts out of balance, it's up to sisters Kurako, Yuzu and Tama to save us—but first they must get through their family drama.

FANTASY T TEEN AGE 13+

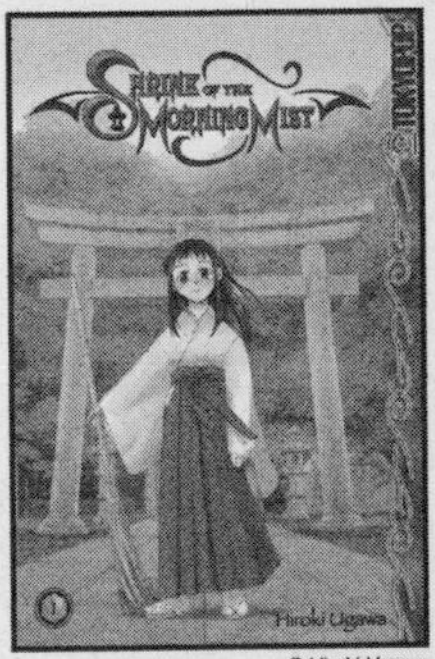
Shrine of the Morning Mist
TOKYOPOP
1
Hiroki Ugawa

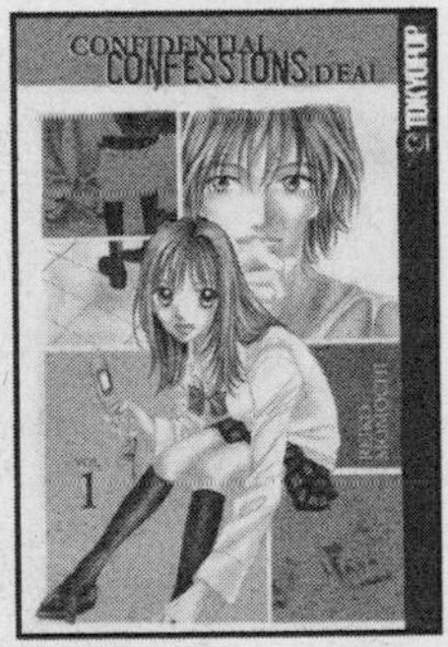
CONFIDENTIAL CONFESSIONS DEAI
TOKYOPOP
REIKO MOMOCHI
1

CONFIDENTIAL CONFESSIONS -DEAI-

BY REIKO MOMOCHI

In this unflinching portrayal of teens in crisis, silence isn't always golden...

DRAMA OT OLDER TEEN AGE 16+

DEATH JAM

BY JEON SANG YOUNG

Muchaca Smooth is an assassin with just one shot to make it big!

ACTION OT OLDER TEEN AGE 16+

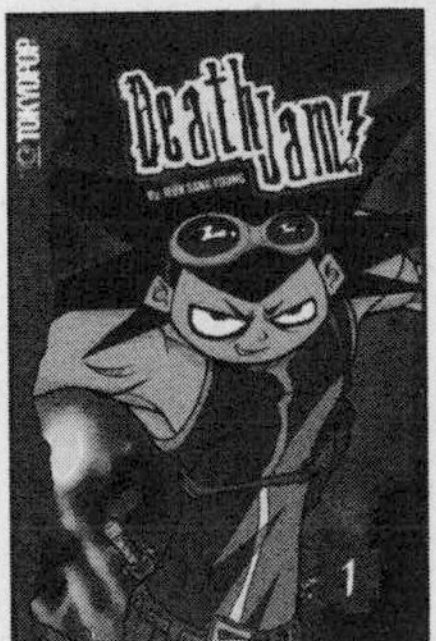
TOKYOPOP
Death Jam!
1

STOP!

This is the back of the book.
You wouldn't want to spoil a great ending!

This book is printed "manga-style," in the authentic Japanese right-to-left format. Since none of the artwork has been flipped or altered, readers get to experience the story just as the creator intended. You've been asking for it, so TOKYOPOP® delivered: authentic, hot-off-the-press, and far more fun!

DIRECTIONS

If this is your first time reading manga-style, here's a quick guide to help you understand how it works.

It's easy... just start in the top right panel and follow the numbers. Have fun, and look for more 100% authentic manga from TOKYOPOP®!